Negotiating Environmental Change

Negotiating Environmental Change

New Perspectives from Social Science

Edited by

Frans Berkhout

Director, ESRC Sustainable Technologies Programme and Senior Fellow, SPRU – Science and Technology Policy Research, University of Sussex, UK

Melissa Leach

Professorial Fellow, Environment Group, Institute of Development Studies, University of Sussex, UK

Ian Scoones

Professorial Fellow, Environment Group, Institute of Development Studies, University of Sussex, UK

Edward Elgar

Cheltenham, UK • Northampton, MA, USA

Published by
Edward Elgar Publishing Limited
Glensanda House
Montpellier Parade
Cheltenham
Glos GL50 1UA
UK

Edward Elgar Publishing, Inc.
136 West Street
Suite 202
Northampton
Massachusetts 01060
USA

A catalogue record for this book
is available from the British Library

Library of Congress Cataloguing in Publication Data
Negotiating environmental change : new perspectives from social science / edited by Frans Berkhout, Melissa Leach, Ian Scoones.
    p. cm.
   Includes index.
   1. Environmental policy. 2. Environmental policy—Research—Great Britain. I. Berkhout, F. (Frans) II. Leach, Melissa. III. Scoones, Ian.

GE170 N436 2003
333.7'2—dc21

                                           2002075240

ISBN 1 84064 673 X (cased)
ISBN 1 84376 153 X (paperback)
Printed and bound in Great Britain by MPG Books Ltd, Bodmin, Cornwall

Contents

Figures

Tables

Boxes

Contributors

W. Neil Adger is a Lecturer in Environmental Economics in the School of Environmental Sciences, University of East Anglia and a Senior Research Fellow in the Centre for Social and Economic Research on the Global Environment (CSERGE), UK.

Giles Atkinson is a Lecturer in Environmental Policy in the Department of Geography and Environment at the London School of Economics, UK.

Tracey Bedford is a Research Fellow in the Environment and Society Research Unit (ESRU) in the Department of Geography at University College London, UK.

Frans Berkhout is Director of the ESRC Sustainable Technologies Programme and a Senior Fellow in the Environment and Energy Programme at SPRU – Science and Technology Policy Research, University of Sussex, UK.

Jacquelin Burgess is Professor of Geography at University College London, UK.

Andrea Coulson is a Lecturer in Accounting in the Department of Accounting and Finance at the University of Strathclyde, UK.

Gail Davies is a Lecturer in the Department of Geography at University College London, UK.

Paul Ekins is Professor and Head of the Environment Group at the Policy Studies Institute and Professor of Sustainable Development at Keele University, UK.

Andy Gouldson is a Lecturer in Environmental Policy and Management in the Department of Geography and Environment at the London School of Economics, UK.

Ken Green is Professor in the Manchester School of Management at the University of Manchester Institute of Science and Technology (UMIST) and Director of the Centre for Research on Organisations, Management and Technical Change (CROMTEC), UK.

Nick Hanley is Professor of Economics at the University of Glasgow, UK.

Carolyn Harrison is Professor of Geography at University College London, UK.

Kersty Hobson completed her PhD in the Department of Geography at University College London, UK.

Andrew Jordan is a Lecturer in Environmental Politics in the School of Environmental Sciences at the UEA and a Research Fellow in the Centre for Social and Economic Research on the Global Environment (CSERGE), UK.

Melissa Leach is Professor and Fellow in the Environment Group at the Institute of Development Studies, University of Sussex, UK.

Richard Munton is Professor of Geography, University College London, UK.

Steve New is University Lecturer in Management Studies (Operations Management) in the Saïd Business School, University of Oxford, UK.

Anja Schaefer is a Lecturer in Management in the School of Physical Sciences and Engineering at King's College London, UK.

Ian Scoones is Professor and Fellow in the Environment Group at the Institute of Development Studies, University of Sussex, UK.

Jim Skea is Professor and Director of the Policy Studies Institute in London UK.

Andy Stirling is a Senior Lecturer in the Environment and Energy Programme at SPRU – Science and Technology Policy Research at the University of Sussex, UK.

John Vogler is Professor in the School of Politics, International Relations and the Environment (SPIRE) at Keele University, UK.

Preface

Frans Berkhout, Ian Scoones and Melissa Leach

This book is one of the final outputs of the Global Environmental Change (GEC) Programme, funded by the UK Economic and Social Research Council (ESRC) between 1991 and 2000. The ESRC is the main funder of social science research in UK universities and colleges, and the GEC Programme was, at that time, the largest single investment the council had ever made. As suggested by Michael Redclift, the Programme's first Director, the aim was ambitious: 'to put the environment into social science and to put social science into the environment'. The outcome was a broad programme of research marked out by a diversity of disciplinary, theoretical and methodological perspectives. In total, some 150 projects were funded involving over 350 researchers and producing over 1000 academic publications (for more details see: www.gecko.ac.uk). Beyond this, the Programme was linked to two UK research centres also funded by the ESRC, the Centre for Social and Economic Research on the Global Environment (CSERGE) at the University of East Anglia, and the Centre for the Study of Environmental Change (CSEC) at Lancaster University. While UK-based, much of the research carried out was international and global in scope, involving partnerships with institutions in Europe, Africa, Asia and elsewhere.

In conceiving this book, we decided that a summary of the many achievements of the programme was neither feasible, nor terribly useful. The breadth of the research was too broad to do it justice in one volume, and issues and perspectives had changed over time. Instead, drawing inspiration from an earlier review of GEC research,[1] we sought to identify a number of critical themes in the GEC's work, to review major developments in scholarship during the 1990s and to suggest how perspectives had shifted and evolved over that period. As editors, we have tried to encourage authors to think critically about what has been learnt in their fields, how debates have been reframed and reoriented, and what this can tell us about future research agendas. In the first chapter we have tried to bring together some of the main currents of thinking in environmental social science, as reflected in the other chapters in the volume, and to place these in a broader historical context. We add the caveat that we make no claims for being comprehensive or definitive. Ours is not the only interpretation that could have been placed on an historical review of recent developments in the social science of the environment.

Besides the work of the authors, this book rests on the endeavours of many others. As co-directors in the final phase of the Programme we are indebted to the work of the three Advisory Committees, chaired by Judith Petts, Jacquie Burgess and Tim O'Riordan, each dealing with one of the core themes that served as an organizing framework for this book. These themes were: uncertainty and environmental decision-making (Chapters 2–4); governance of the environment (Chapters 5–7); and sustainable production and consumption (Chapters 8-10). We also pay tribute to the work of Alister Scott for being the inspiration behind our greatest adventures, to Julia Hertin, Hilary Ougham, Michelle Harris and Kath Bowden for providing diligent and cheerful support, and to Jim Skea who preceded us as Director.

Finally, some words on the title of the book. By 'negotiating' we want to capture three meanings: in the sense of the dialogue and deliberation now viewed as central to the framing and handling of environmental problems; in the sense of travelling through an uncertain landscape towards the objective of greater sustainability; and in the sense of formal processes of governance that lead to new norms, expectations, agreements and commitments.

NOTES

1. Redclift, M. and E. Benton (1994), *Social Theory and the Environment*, Routledge: London.

1. Shifting perspectives in environmental social science

Frans Berkhout, Melissa Leach and Ian Scoones

INTRODUCTION

Any contemporary discussion of science, technology, governance and processes of modernization must take account of the ways in which conceptions of the environment are shaping them. Whereas, for much of the modern period, the environment has been considered distinct and separate: an object of inquiry and control, we are now becoming more aware of how ideas about the environment – and of environmental change – reflect deeper social and political preoccupations, while also influencing change in social institutions and social attitudes. We see increasingly that our knowledge of the environment is socially framed and embedded, including knowledge achieved through scientific methods. But we are also aware that responses to environmental change and people's perceptions of it are becoming more deep-seated and significant. The environment can no longer be disentangled so easily from social reality.

Nowhere has this complex, mutual link between environmental and technological and social change been more starkly illustrated than in the controversy over genetically modified (GM) crops and food. From the outset it seemed that GM crops were consistent with the demand for more environmentally-friendly forms of agriculture. Early innovators of GM crops made explicit use of environmental rhetorics in promoting the technology – arguing, for instance, that lower usage of pesticides and fertilisers lead to lower pollution and resource savings – while the introduction of new crop varieties was controlled by regulatory frameworks that included bio-safety and other environmental considerations. The international controversy and conflict that has emerged around GM, much of it based on concerns about environmental and social impacts, revealed a new set of problems about environmental knowledge and the management of environmental resources and risks (GECP, 1999). The GM controversy in Europe and elsewhere reflected a broadly-based understanding of the uncertainties surrounding assessments of impacts and risks, as well as public scepticism about government responses. Publics were unwilling to accept uncritically government claims that 'sound science' suggested GM foods are safe; they were critical of the biases and commercial interests which support such expert claims; and they questioned wider issues – such as the future of agriculture – implied by the turn to GM crops (Grove-White et al., 2000). In developing countries, the spectacle of farmers burning fields demonstrated vividly concerns about the ecological effects of GM crops and about the perceived creeping domination of agriculture by large western companies, symbolizing a new privatization of environmental resources. These emergent public attitudes to GM crops – and an increasing array of environmental issues – have had, in turn, ramifications for the governance of environmental change, creating the conditions for new alliances and affinities which cross-cut conventional boundaries and relations between the state and civil society.

Important elements in the controversies over GM foods are echoed not only in specific, visible environmental debates around climate change, ozone depletion and biodiversity loss, but also in the reshaping of society–environment relations more generally. Evident are changing relationships between people and experts; a more tentative relationship between knowledge, innovation and policy; and new roles for governments, corporations, international organizations and citizen action in 'governing' the environment. Above all, such debates and controversies imply an appreciation of the social basis of environmental knowledges and the governance of environmental resources, and a sharp departure from the assumption that, once identified, the solution to environmental problems is essentially a technical matter (Benton and Redclift, 1994). These conditions now define the contours for both academic debates and practical actions around the environment.

The pervasiveness of these social ruptures and controversies could hardly have been imagined twenty years ago. As we outline below, the models for addressing issues of environment and sustainable development defined in the 1980s envisaged a world that operated very differently. The assumptions of these mainstream sustainable development agendas and their unravelling forms the focal story of the first half of this chapter. As we indicate, this unravelling has been partly caused by processes and events taking place in the world, and partly by the manifest failure of conventional models and associated policy options to deal with these. At the same time, analysts have observed these failures from the vantage point of a growing environmental social science, leading to fundamental critiques of the assumptions informing the broader programme of 'sustainable development'.

As we go on to suggest, the social science analysis which has helped to expose the shortcomings of the conventional sustainable development agenda has also begun to suggest new ways forward. It is these advances, coming from different disciplinary angles and different foci – from issues of rural livelihoods in Africa or Asia, to debates over innovation policy in Europe and international responses to global climate change – which form the focus of this volume. We document in the second part of this chapter how a new synthesis is emerging, across three core themes: the negotiation of environmental knowledges; the application of notions of vulnerability, resilience and precaution in responding to environmental change; and the tension between local and global governance of the environment. Together these chart developments in an environmental social science while offering a highly illuminating lens for reflection on science, society and modernity.

ENVIRONMENT AND SUSTAINABLE DEVELOPMENT: THE MAINSTREAM AGENDA

A strong analytical and normative 'programme' emerged during the 1970s and 1980s concerning the nature of environmental problems and how to respond to them. Put briefly, science came to play a central role in revealing environmental problems, explaining their causes and providing the basis for defining solutions to them. These solutions would be carried out by government, normally national governments, but increasingly national governments co-operating through international regimes. State action was warranted because the environment was a public good which would be degraded without politically co-ordinated norms, rules and procedures to protect it. As an ever denser texture of formal controls was imposed on the use of the environment as both a resource and a sink, so the role of science grew in informing and justifying managerial and technocratic interventions by governments.

Other features of political and economic change supported this way of seeing and acting upon environmental problems. For instance, the internationalization of environmental governance, explained by the increasing recognition of the global nature of environmental problems, coincided with growing cooperation in other economic and political domains such as security, trade and investment, and at a time when roles were being defined for regional organizations such as the European Community. This in turn coincided with the rise of liberalization and market deregulation, leading to attempts to define environmental resources and services as goods that could be valued monetarily, and traded through markets.

In this context, a variety of analytical programmes – and modes of analysis to pursue them – emerged. One influential stream of work came from the sub-discipline of environmental economics. Hanley and Atkinson (Chapter 3) describe how this addressed the problem that the broad social and environmental costs of economic activities were consistently undervalued, by developing ways to assign artificial prices to environmental goods and services, so enabling environmental externalities to be taken into account in economic decision-making. Economic valuation became central to a programme to reveal the hidden costs and benefits of policy decisions, to make environmental policy more rational, transparent and democractic, to include the value of natural resources in national accounting systems, and to ensure that inter-generational effects were highlighted (Pearce and Turner, 1990; Markandya and Richardson, 1992; Hanley and Spash, 1993; Hockenstein et al., 1997; Bateman and Willis, 1999). Economists also contributed policy options to help manage the market failures that were frequently seen to cause environmental problems, such as the Polluter Pays Principle.

A related analytical and policy programme saw environmental problems as resulting more from policy failures such as inappropriate legal frameworks, or tenure systems which gave producers incentives to pollute or to degrade resources (Repetto and Gillis, 1988; Jänicke, 1990; Weale, 1992). In order to put things right, it was argued, a planned set of policy interventions was required to bring economic and environmental goals into harmony. Sustainable development plans (and their many variants) were born, premised on the assumption that a co-ordinated approach to policy planning and implementation by national governments would achieve the sustainable development vision.

Attention also focused on the roles of both business and consumers in relation to the environment, and on the changes needed to 'green' their behaviour (Schaefer et al., Chapter 8; Burgess et al., Chapter 10). This agenda focused attention on the attitudes of managers and consumers to their environmental impacts, and on the right balance between regulatory and incentive-based policy instruments for influencing them towards more environmentally-friendly behaviour (Roome, 1992; Skea, 1995; Welford, 1998). Voluntarism and the role of incentives rather than penalties were emphasized as precipitating processes of learning and change by organizations and individuals.

Finally, global concerns such as climate change, loss of biological diversity, acid rain and desertification were seen to be beyond the scope of any national government to address alone. Instead, international co-operation between states was seen to be required, rooted in a common commitment to sustainable development (Levy et al., 1992; Vogler and Imber, 1996; Vogler, 2001). International treaties, conventions and protocols were developed, culminating in the 1998 Kyoto Protocol of the UN Framework Convention on Climate Change. In these conventions national governments were seen as acting in the role of 'global citizens' protecting international public goods, rather than pursuing their own unique national interests, as had been the case in international trade and security regimes. In this sense, environmental problems extended the role and identity of the nation state.

Despite the wide variety of disciplines, concepts and analyses involved during this period, and the consequent array of definitions, indicators and methods, it is possible to identify a number of general features which united them, and characterized a dominant model of sustainable development to which they contributed. Environmental problems were analysed as being discrete, bounded and 'out there'. Their resolution relied heavily on technical expertise, whether of natural scientists, engineers or economists. Problems were portrayed as amenable to managerial solutions, whether by business, through national policy, or in the co-ordinated actions of the international community. As commentators on the notion of ecological modernization have observed, the programme was essentially for 'business as usual' only greener; and rested on fundamental assumptions that modernization and environmental sustainability could be rendered compatible through the exercise of reasoned action (Hajer, 1995; Mol and Spaargaren, 2000; Spaargaren et al., 2000). The language of zero-sum games and trade-offs was replaced by a language of 'win-win' and positive gains from environmentally-oriented change. The high point of all this debate was the UN Conference on Environment and Development held in Rio in 1992, when governments from around the world signed up to this vision with great fanfare.

But this was not the only vision. Other traditions of social science analysis picked up on different aspects of reality to construct different agendas, some of which became influential in defining alternatives to the mainstream. One important alternative had its roots in political economy and particularly in structural-Marxist analyses of economic systems, nationally and internationally. The work of Redclift (1984, 1987) and others pointed out that social and economic inequalities lay at the root of many environmental problems, especially in poorer and more resource-dependent societies (for example, Blaikie and Brookfield, 1987; Bryant, 1992; Peet and Watts, 1996). Such work showed that imbalances in exposure to environmental risks between the global north and south and within countries were to a large extent socially and politically determined. Other critics showed that many environmental issues (such as the destruction of fisheries, or the problem of waste) were the outcome of 'over-consumption'. This was frequently contrasted with resource use by 'indigenous' people who were seen as managing resources sustainably, while being marginalized by inequitable processes of economic growth. Without tackling systems and cultures of consumption in the developed world, there could be no mitigation of global environmental problems (Warde, 1990).

Still other critics argued that environmental problems at the heart of policy processes was virtual rather than real, and, in those cases where political commitment had been engaged, this was explained by opportunities that existed to secure greater institutional power and legitimacy, rather than a new attachment to environmental objectives (Boehmer-Christiansen, 1994). One line of critique suggested that solutions to environmental problems required a more fundamental reordering of political economy, evidence of which they saw in the emergence of new global civil society organizations which came to challenge national governments as the sole representatives of the public good (Princen and Finger, 1994; Wapner, 1996; Jamison, 1996). New spaces for political alignment and activity on environmental questions were being opened up at different levels of governance, from the local to the global, sometimes contesting the positions of government, and at other times enabling them to act. Versions of this vision chimed with the agendas of certain NGOs (for example, those starting to advocate indigenous people's rights) and with 'southern' responses to the mainstream sustainable development agenda (for example, in the Indian Centre for Science and Environment's portrayal of responses to climate change advocated in the West as 'northern imperialism') (Agarwal and Narain, 1991; see also Gupta, 1995). Yet, despite these differences, some common assumptions were shared between the mainstream sustainable development model and these critics: environmental systems were viewed as relatively stable and knowable; environmental problems were seen as being defined in technical terms with solutions informed by conventional technical expertise; and economic growth, albeit with its fruits more fairly distributed, could be reconciled with the mainten-ance of environmental services. These assumptions were all to come into question. This new questioning would bring other dimensions of social science work into prominence.

THE 'UNRAVELLING' OF THE MAINSTREAM AGENDA

During the decade following the 1992 Rio conference highpoint, the weaknesses of the analytical and policy 'programme' that it expressed have become increasingly apparent. Even if much has changed for the better, the formula that science reveals, states coordinate and incentives push private actors to enact solutions to environmental problems has proved incapable of achieving its goals. The vision of using economic and legal instruments to manage technically-defined environmental problems in the interests of a common good has been challenged. What we have termed 'mainstream' sustainable development encountered many difficulties both in analysing environmental problems and in implementing preferred courses of action. From a long potential catalogue of such difficulties, we choose just a few to illustrate how the mainstream agenda unravelled.

Science–Policy Relationships Questioned

While environmental problems were typically 'objectified' as stable and observable, it has become increasingly clear that definitions of environmental issues are not stable across different social groups, and vary even between groups of experts (Stirling, 1998). The long-standing critique of sociologists that controversies about the environment characterized as debates about risk really reflected conflict between different social and institutional commitments and values has become increasingly evident. Related to this, the capacity of scientific advice to provide unambiguous analysis and recommend effective action has been challenged by evidence of the uncertainties and indeterminacies that pervade both analysis and action (Wynne, 1992, 1996).

Failures of International Environmental Regimes

In many respects, the high hopes of a decade ago for a new form of global environmental governance have not been met. New international regimes have been difficult to put in place, while many of the new institutions and mechanisms have proved cumbersome, ineffective at ensuring compliance, and vulnerable to charges of unaccountability and non-representativeness. Accusations of unfairness have also been made, particularly by those in developing countries who see much of the international environmental agenda as being driven by northern interests. Thus a major threat to new forms of international environmental governance has been one of marginalization – especially from agreements about trade and economic co-ordination. At the same time, it has become evident that, for all the normative appeal of co-operative solutions to global problems, they are doomed to failure where these solutions do not also correspond with the broader economic and political interests of more powerful states.

Political Costs of Incentive-based Solutions

The idea that the costs of using environmental services should be fully expressed and borne by the user of those services is long established. Much effort has been focused on defining the environmental value of economic and social activities (Costanza et al., 1993), and to redefining environmental property rights (Jacobs, 1994). However, these have been hampered by methodological disputes about how to establish monetary values for the environment and by political difficulties in distributing the rights and costs (from carbon taxes to tradable permits). While there has been much experimentation with market-based instruments, they appear to be appropriate and effective only in rather specific circumstances (Gunningham and Gabrosky, 1998).

Paradoxes in 'Greening' Business

While many companies have begun to integrate sustainability considerations into their strategy, management systems and decisions, few regard them as central concerns (Fineman, 2000). Many companies, especially smaller ones, still do little more than comply reactively with minimum standards and regulations. The supposed link between innovation, resource productivity and competitiveness appears not to hold in many business contexts, so that predictions of a broad ecological modernization of business have not been borne out in practice (Schaefer et al., Chapter 8). The green consumer, while significant in some markets, has also proved to play a smaller role than expected. There is often a gap between a stated desire for a cleaner environment and the behaviour of consumers in buying, using and discarding products (Burgess, Chapter 10). Moreover, the consumer and the lifestyles supported through modes of consumption have themselves become a focus of analytical and policy interest as more has been understood about the spread of environmental impacts along product systems from 'cradle to grave'.

Challenges to National Governments

As the limits to policy action became clearer, as the distributional consequences of many environmental policies became more obvious (locally, nationally and internationally), and as the capacity of governments to define and exert control over environmental problems faltered, the role of government as the primary actor in environmental policy came to be questioned. More and more, governments have come to be seen, and to see themselves, as participants in more complex and multi-layered processes of deliberation and environmental action (Munton, Chapter 4; Vogler and Jordan, Chapter 5). This has called into question the notion of 'the public good', the way it should be defined, and how to achieve legitimacy and distribute the benefits of positive environmental change.

Resistance to Imposed Plans

Despite a growing rhetoric encouraging local participation and public consultation in the development of plans created in the name of sustainable development, very often such efforts have proved limited and perfunctory. Instead, as with previous attempts at planned intervention, a particular vision has been imposed. Whether involving the redesign of urban landscapes in Europe or environmental rehabilitation in Africa, such plans have carried with them certain assumptions about how people and the environment should live and interact (Leach and Mearns, 1996). Sometimes these were not shared by local inhabitants, and just as previous plans had been, sustainable development plans have not been immune from various forms of resistance, both covert and open, by people in their communities.

Social Difference and Environmental Justice

While the sustainable development agenda tended to map fairly uncritically a simple relationship between people and resources, in practice social differentiation and dynamics have proved critical to influencing who gets access to which resources. A clearer understanding of the multiple dimensions of social difference – by age, gender, wealth, class, race and so on – shows how environmental impacts are felt far from evenly. Issues of inequality of access and inequality of impact have highlighted the importance of environmental rights and justice (GECP, 2001b).

A CRISIS POINT? THE EMERGENCE OF AN ALTERNATIVE AGENDA

In a range of key areas, environmental social science work over the past decade has drawn attention to these and related difficulties. Taken together, it reveals how the mainstream sustainable development model of the 1980s is no longer well-matched with the contemporary dynamics of social, political and scientific processes in their engagement with dynamic natural systems. This explains why the model has struggled to deliver effective and legitimate policy solutions and to inform the processes of learning necessary to address the complex and interconnected problems.

The unravelling of the model suggests something of a crisis point for mainstream environment and sustainable development agendas: a crisis both in the analysis that informs them, and their policy prescriptions. Such a crisis is far from unique to the environmental field. Many authors (Beck, 1992, 1995; Giddens, 1991; Adam et al., 2000) have argued that the crisis besetting conceptions of the environment is symptomatic of a broader crisis of positivist, technocratic and managerial approaches in the face of the conditions of 'late modernity'. But while such a crisis is more general, there are also important ways in which sustainability as a political and rhetorical arena brings it particularly clearly into focus, and amplifies some of its dimensions. Put another way, there are a number of reasons why environmental issues invite the kind of social science which has proved particularly revealing of these contemporary issues.

A focus on the environment invites a problem-focus, in which multiple disciplines are brought to bear on a given issue, encouraging a potentially fruitful blending of perspectives. It also requires an engagement with natural, biophysical processes – therefore bringing social science into engagement with natural science debates which have been re-characterizing systems as uncertain, dynamic, and scale and path-dependent (Scoones, 1999). In addition, environmental issues confront head-on conflicts between public and individual goods – and hence questions about who defines public goods and the public good, about the social differentiation of access to resources, and the power relations that define them. Issues of environmental change increasingly must address global and cross-border effects, across a diversity of localities, identities and capabilities. This means that environmental issues challenge governance across different scales in a globalizing world. Finally, 'the environment' has become a label, a signifier of public consciousness, and of individual and collective reflexivity, leading to a variety of forms of political action, which disturb conventional boundaries and ways of thinking (Dobson, 1990; Grove-White, 1993; Yearley, 1995; Szerszynski, 1996).

Over the last decade environmental social science has made a significant contribution to developing our understanding not only of environmental issues per se, but a range of broader questions. Environmental problems have recently provided – and will continue to provide – a revealing lens through which to view and reflect on these emerging and fast changing contemporary conditions. In the following sections we highlight three areas where important advances have been made. The first area focuses on the challenges of dealing with complex and uncertain environmental problems, and the implications this has for expert institutions, decision-making and policy processes. The second area focuses on the particular challenges of global environmental governance, and the challenges which have emerged around new international environmental regimes and between environmental and trade regimes. The third area traces debates about sustainable production and consumption and the challenges this presents for business and regulation, as well as lifestyles and livelihoods. Together, this work questions the mainstream sustainable development agenda in quite fundamental ways, and begins to forge a new set of agendas, ones that resonate with wider analytical and policy concerns.

SCIENCE, KNOWLEDGE AND UNCERTAINTY

During the last ten years, uncertainty has been identified as a distinguishing characteristic of environmental change and policy. Environmental effects are usually complex, long term and uncertain; trade-offs between choices may be unclear; perceptions of both problems and solutions are value-laden and differ greatly amongst different social groups. The emergence of new technologies, such as genetic engineering, and large-scale environmental problems such as climate change, have deepened these uncertainties. Many environmental systems involve inherently unpredictable changes, or are too complex to be fully understood, at least in the foreseeable future. Time and space gaps between causes and effects are typical for environmental problems and increase these difficulties. Yet, despite this, as environmental social science research has illustrated, processes in the production of scientific knowledge and its relationship to policy have tended to preclude full representation of such uncertainties (Taylor and Buttel, 1992).

Global climate change can illustrate these difficulties. Understanding of the interaction between the factors influencing our climate remains incomplete and is permeated with uncertainties. It is difficult to project how greenhouse gas emissions would affect future atmospheric conditions. There will be as yet unknown feedback effects and unexpected regional effects. How future climate change will affect human life in twenty or forty years is to a large extent unknowable – social and economic forecasting is hampered by the combination of reflexivity, adaptation and surprise (Berkhout, Hertin and Jordan, 2002). However, policy-makers demand answers to these questions to guide their decisions and typically they turn to science. Scientists have attempted to satisfy these demands and to project future climate change as well as its possible effects. Within the politically influential Intergovernmental Panel on Climate Change a substantial consensus has built up, not only with respect to scientific findings but also to research approaches (IPCC, 2001). Climate change models combined with economic cost-benefit analysis have become the dominant methods. These in turn have a strong influence on national and global climate policies about how and when to respond to the possible causes and impacts of climate change (Shackley and Wynne, 1995).

Over the last decade, however, there has been an intense and controversial debate over the limits of standard valuation and risk assessment techniques. While methodological refinements to such approaches have developed rapidly, partly in response to critiques by economists themselves of the first generation of studies (Hanley and Atkinson, Chapter 3), such technically-driven decision approaches confront more fundamental, conceptual challenges. First, valuation requires firm, high quality data on environmental processes. Where conditions and outcomes are uncertain (where we don't know the probabilities of possible outcomes) or, perhaps more troublesome, where ignorance is prevalent (we don't know what we don't know), then many conventional approaches founder. As Stirling (Chapter 2) discusses, standard environmental decision-making tools may be misplaced under circumstances where uncertainties dominate. Indeed, it is precisely when such 'hard tools' are applied to uncertain environmental issues that 'soft disasters' such as BSE, radioactive waste management and GM foods regulation have arisen; political crises due to the erosion of public confidence and legitimacy (GECP, 2000a).

Second, other challenges relate to moral and ethical concerns with justice and equity: for example, is it legitimate to measure the value of, say, a lake, only in relation to its economic benefit for local swimmers, sailors and fishermen? Does nature not have values independent from human use? Is 'willingness to pay' an appropriate concept where consumers are actually unable to pay? In short, the question has been raised: are valuation techniques as objective, neutral and democratic as they are sometimes claimed to be?

Third, an acknowledgement that scientific research approaches and findings are not independent of political and institutional contexts has been an important theme of social science research. The traditional, linear model of policy drew a clear line between science and policy. In this view, research supplied objective and secure knowledge on the basis of which policy made value- and interest-based decisions. However, in reality, the line between science and policy is inevitably blurred, and scientific and policy processes are frequently co-constructed (for example, Jasanoff and Wynne, 1997; Keeley and Scoones, 1999).

These debates have, in turn, fed into questions about expertise in environmental decision-making. Policy decisions are usually strongly influenced by the advice of experts. However, the authority of scientific expert knowledge has been contested over the last decade, particularly in the area of the environment (Irwin, 1995). The perception of expert knowledge as being value neutral has been questioned because scientific approaches and results reflect in some way value judgements and underlying assumptions about society, and because these in turn are related to the particular positions, locations and interests of expert institutions. Value judgements play a major role in many questions relevant in environmental science: which health risk can be regarded as tolerable? How should local and global pollution effects be weighed against each other? To what extent should future ecological damage be considered in today's decisions? Scientists are not necessarily experts on personal, ethical and moral matters – so why should they have a privileged say in the weighing of these factors? Social scientists have, at the same time, emphasized the existence and value of many alternative forms of expertise, be they 'indigenous knowledges', 'lay expertise' or 'citizen science' (compare Richards, 1985; Warren et al., 1995; Scoones and Thompson, 1994; Fischer, 2000). Such knowledges are embedded in cultural assumptions and socio-political values which may contrast strongly with those of experts. Moreover, the failure of expert-based environmental policies and the social resistance they have encountered has thrown into question the role of mainstream scientific advice and lent greater force to arguments to take alternative knowledges (including social science) more seriously. Neither scientific expertise nor local knowledge can, of course, claim to be uniquely true or objective. Rather, different people and institutions start from different assumptions, perceptions, values, interests and knowledges (Agrawal, 1995; Murdoch and Clark, 1994). There are many ways of framing environmental problems: as problems of technocratic control; as problems of moral significance; as problems of entitlement for different groups in society. The challenge is to bring these orthogonal and competing framings together in a constructive way, while taking account of the power relations between those who hold different types of knowledge.

When major uncertainties over environmental outcomes prevail, and when public perceptions diverge significantly from expert opinion, trust becomes a key issue in policy-making. While decision-makers are usually aware that public confidence is the basis of successful policy, they have often failed to gain or preserve such confidence because they did not invest in building up trustful relationships. The issue of trust applies to many environmental areas, but is highlighted particularly vividly by the case of GM foods. On this issue, the gulf between the perceptions of policy-makers and the public grew to such an extent that profound misunderstandings have taken place. Politicians apparently failed to understand hostile public reactions to genetically modified foods, considering them misinformed and emotional. Among the public, however, mistrust of governments, companies and experts involved in environmental decision-making has continued to grow. Instead of relying on claims of safety, many people prefer to hold on to the right of choice. Another recent example in the UK has been the controversy over child immunization.

The main reason for this distancing between publics and policy-makers can be found in the nature of decision-making and communication processes. Policy choices are increasingly made on the basis of formal appraisal techniques. These focus on technical issues and often fail to reflect adequately the variety of social contexts in which choices are played out, wider public concerns and fundamental ethical questions. But who is the public? The public is in fact deeply fragmented, formed by people and groups with diverse, and possibly mobile, social backgrounds, interests, knowledges, attitudes, values and perceptions. Public trust therefore has many dimensions and cannot be achieved with a uniform strategy of communication seeking only to build a requisite level of consent for government policy. Trust depends, to some extent, on truth claims and on the capacity to validate them. In the absence of a means of validation, the authority of policy-makers and industry falls into sharp decline. Instead, re-building consent and trust in public institutions is recognized to require a public–policy dialogue addressing different concerns and diverse publics. While the decline of public trust has been reinforced through political and policy failures, it is primarily driven by deeper trends within society. Even as social reality for many people in the industrialized north has become more secure, the desire to control the risks that remain has apparently grown. Many people have become more cautious and critical concerning social institutions generally. For many groups in the developing south an opposite problem has arisen in respect of the deeply disruptive effects of processes of modernization which introduce new social risks and cleavages. In both these contexts, trust in public institutions and in their expertise cannot be restored in an absolute and unconditional fashion. Instead, it has to be continually built and re-built in an ongoing process. Regaining trust requires not only better institutions and new scientific knowledge, but also greater openness about risks, uncertainties and ignorance. There is therefore a role for new forms of policy process, which encourage greater transparency and inclusion, thereby creating conditions for greater trust in outcomes.

In response to these challenges, environmental social science has begun to investigate and innovate a range of approaches that encourage integration and inclusivity in decision-making. This includes integration of knowledge and expertise through interdisciplinary styles of research which acknowledges a range of different 'scientific' and 'lay' expertises. It also involves approaches which facilitate direct citizen involvement in environmental decision-making, such as the range of 'deliberative and inclusionary processes' (DIPs) reviewed here by Munton (Chapter 4).

So where has a decade of research on uncertainty and environmental decision-making got us? The journey has begun towards approaches which deal better with uncertainties that face social scientists, other specialists, decision-makers and the public. As the pace of environmental change and of scientific inquiry speeds up, so it becomes more urgent to develop approaches which can prevent contentious policy issues from degenerating into crises of public confidence. This will apply as much to environmental issues as to other areas of public policy. Amongst the many challenges ahead are how to combine quantitative and qualitative knowledge in ways appropriate to a broader range of social settings. Attempts to build trust amongst expert institutions and publics must deal with multiple audiences who may have quite different perspectives and opportunities to stake their opinions and claims. And co-existing with these social differences are relations of power between expert and citizen institutions. Alongside innovations in the toolbox for environmental decision-making, then, issues of power, equity and social context remain among the key challenges to be addressed.

WHO GOVERNS THE GLOBAL ENVIRONMENT?

Challenged by the slow progress and failures of international regimes, environmental social science researchers since the mid-1990s have been rethinking the question of how the global environment is – or should be – governed, from the perspectives both of effectiveness and fairness (GECP, 2000b). The proliferation of international agreements has led many researchers, as discussed by Vogler and Jordan (Chapter 5), to examine the functioning of agreements and the informal rules and procedures which surround them. Empirical studies have shown that the success of international regimes, although difficult to measure, varies greatly. For example, the regime on tropical timber is widely seen as a failure, while the agreement on stratospheric ozone is usually presented as a case of successful international policy-making. Some cases seem to confirm a pessimistic viewpoint: negotiations are arduous, states do not comply with agreed measures, monitoring is poor and effective sanctions are rarely put in place. In other cases, regimes have a number of indirect positive effects. They draw attention to a problem, contribute to a shared understanding about causes and effects, and lead to the improvement of institutional structures in a specific area. In the last decade environmental social science researchers have studied and compared different regimes to find out how success and failure can be explained, and how future agreements should be designed.

The success of international environmental regimes cannot be attributed to a single factor and the appropriate structure depends on the situation and the specific issue. However, a number of elements can be identified which improve the efficiency of environmental regimes. These include: (1) rules that ensure a fair distribution of costs and benefits, for example, through differentiated obligations for developed and developing countries, financial aid and technology transfer for poorer countries; (2) strong but acceptable non-compliance mechanisms which should embody 'carrots' (for example, advice and financial aid) as well as 'sticks' (for example, suspension of voting rights, denial of benefits, eventually trade sanctions); and (3) a strong institutional structure, including a secretariat well articulated with the science-base, holding regular scheduled meetings of the parties, mechanisms for monitoring compliance and harmonized reporting and data collection.

However, the direct effects of these formal procedures are only one aspect of regime effectiveness and other factors play an important role. Regimes cannot only give material incentives for co-operation but also shape the ways in which actors define their interests. For example, actors can choose to gain long-term political credibility by committing themselves to ambitious environmental policies, rather than trying to maximize short-term financial benefits. Regimes have also contributed to building trust between the parties and to improving their capacities to carry out effective policies. Although these outcomes are indirect, they can be encouraged by careful design of rules and procedures. Suggestions to enhance social learning include: procedures for revising regime procedures and commitments; implementation review processes which identify and help countries with difficulties to fulfil their obligations; transparent monitoring rules and conflict mediation processes aiming to build trust; and independent bodies providing scientific, technical and economic advice.

Given that countries invest different interests in environmental problems, only those agreements that confront the problem of fairness will gain wide support. General acceptance of the legitimate social priorities of poor countries, however, does not define a 'fair' international agreement. Negotiations on a climate change convention offered a remarkable example of how fundamental questions of justice translate into practical political questions: how should levels of carbon emission levels be established? Should the aim be to have similar levels of emissions per head of population or should all countries be obliged to make a similar effort? Should industrialized countries be accountable for their 'historic' emissions over the last hundred years? Several environmental regimes have sought to address issues of fairness. For example, the Montreal Protocol on ozone depleting substances imposed stricter obligations on developed than on developing countries. It also established a multilateral fund, which compensates developing countries for complying with the protocol because those who joined the agreement should not be worse off than those who remain outside. On the other hand, there are many barriers to these mechanisms, and their effects so far are mixed.

In the last decade, extensive research has shown how international trade systems have considerable effects on the potentials and limits of environmental protection (Ekins, Chapter 6). Those concerned with the environment have two main concerns: will an increasingly free flow of goods and services undermine national environmental policies? Could a dominant global trading system undermine the effectiveness of international environmental agreements?

The first concern assumes that global trade liberalization allows companies to gain competitive advantage by re-locating their production sites to 'pollution havens' and selling their products to countries with stricter environmental policies. This could prevent governments from taking environmental measures and encourage an ecological 'race to the bottom'. If countries were not allowed to impede the import of 'dirty' goods, national environmental policies would displace polluting activities internationally instead of reducing them. Considerable research effort has been devoted to finding out whether theory is borne out in practice (Vogler and Jordan, Chapter 5). The overall conclusion is that the potential for 'ecological dumping' depends on the specific conditions in countries, sectors and companies. The environmental impact of international trade should not be over-estimated but it is a matter of serious concern. Trade agreements that remove obstacles to the exchange of goods and services between countries, for example, those overseen by the World Trade Organisation (WTO), still operate largely independently of environmental and social considerations. This separation leads to inefficiencies by lowering the effectiveness of national and international environmental policies. An increasing number of actors, not only environmental groups, but also governments and international organizations such as the United Nations Environment Programme, call for further integration of environmental and social concerns in world trade regimes. A number of suggestions have been made to achieve this, such as drawing a clearer distinction between legitimate environmental requirements and unfair trade barriers.

The second concern refers to environmental regulations on the international level: who makes international environmental rules and do they take precedence over other principles and rules? In some cases, there are potential conflicts between international environmental agreements and WTO rules, as in, for example, the Cartagena Protocol on Biosafety. This highlights the need to clarify the relationship between environmental agreements and trade regimes. Free trade should not prevent the establishment of legitimate environmental regulations on the international level. If international mechanisms are often not up to the task, and national governments have few incentives to 'go it alone', then how should global environmental problems be dealt with? These questions reflect a changing reality in which, as discussed by Vogler and Jordan (Chapter 5), governance structures have gradually become more dispersed. Nation states have lost some of their capacity to exercise power directly and autonomously. Local, regional and international institutions have gained prominence, as have non-state actors such as semi-autonomous government agencies and NGOs (Newell, 2000). This tendency is partly due to an acknowledgement that increasingly complex and inter-dependent political, economic and social systems cannot be governed from a single level.

One important realization – highlighted by research from across the world – has been that many global environmental issues are best dealt with at a local level. This is true for activities aiming to prevent pollution, but particularly important for local-level adaptation to global environmental change (Adger, Chapter 7; Adger et al., 2001). For example, the effects of climate change are felt at the local level – more flooding, more frequent droughts, warmer winters and so on – but floods, droughts and winters have always occurred, perhaps not with such frequency or severity, and mechanisms for coping exist. A recent focus on local conditions comes from the study of the impacts of and responses to environmental change on natural and social systems. This builds on earlier findings that environmental crises are often not so much caused by natural events as by political or socio-economic circumstances, including inappropriate government policies, distorted economic structures and poor resource management. These institutional factors appear to be the main causes of human vulnerability to environmental change. Nurturing the local capacity to build institutionally-grounded resilience is often a more effective policy response than providing for international crisis relief. Local adaptive capacity will be central to the multiple responses necessary to the impacts of long-run environmental problems such as climate change. The challenge, then, is not to see global environmental change as somehow different, but as presenting another reason to support institutions which help people cope and adapt, reducing their vulnerability and increasing resilience (Berkes and Folke, 1998).

In today's interconnected, globalizing world, a wide range of different players influence local action from beyond local arenas. The answer to the question: 'who governs the global environment?' must look at interactions between multiple actors and multiple levels (Mehta et al., 2001). Much of the early debate about international environmental agreements was predicated on the assumption that states and governments were the sole parties to global governance arrangements. While NGOs, business interests, and public interest groups were involved in elements of global convention processes, it was governments who signed up and were expected to implement the agreements. But, as Vogler and Jordan (Chapter 5) discuss, without the backing of others, governments are increasingly unable to frame and to see through such commitments. Governments will therefore come to share decision-making and implementation with many partners. This will also force environmental governance to become more dispersed to both international and sub-national levels. Experience at the Johannesburg Summit bears out this trend.

Thus research over the last decade has shown both the potentials, but also the severe limitations of an international approach to global environmental issues. Reflections on this experience have pointed to important new directions for global environmental governance. The debate has moved from a focus on the state to a multitude of partners, including a wide range of civil society and business organizations; from the international level to governance on different levels; from a predominantly environmental focus to a more integrated approach; and from a largely formal, legalistic process to a more open and participatory response. Many challenges remain: identifying the appropriate level(s) of problem solving will become increasingly important, and attention will need to be paid to the interaction between multiple levels of policy-making, for example, between global environmental regimes, national governments and local communities. Knowledge and other resources will need to flow between these levels as a way of building capabilities and commitment. The new pluralism also raises questions about the legitimacy of the political influence of NGOs, corporations and other groups. Processes will need to be developed that ensure that new processes of multi-level environmental governance also become more transparent and accountable.

PRODUCTION AND CONSUMPTION, LIFESTYLES AND LIVELIHOODS

Environmental social science research has played an important part in debates about the role of business in environmental management and the ways in which policy can influence systems of production. More recently, the role of consumers and their lifestyles has been recognized as critical, with debates focused on northern industrial contexts showing certain parallels with, but also important differences from, those on 'sustainable livelihoods' in the south. Across the board, there has been an emphasis on more systemic approaches, and on innovation and learning as a way of reconciling economic development and sustainability (see Berkhout and Gouldson, Chapter 9; GECP, 2000c).

Debate about the effects of economic growth on the environment has long been polarized. On the one hand, there are those who argue that growth brings prosperity, changes in the structure of industry (the shift from manufacturing to service-based economies), new technology and social expectations that enable societies to invest in improving their natural environment. Environmental problems, they argue, can only be handled within dynamic, innovative, prosperous and trading economies. This perspective has been supported by empirical studies that have found a link between indicators of environmental quality and the average wealth of countries (Grossman and Kreuger, 1995; Jänicke et al., 1989). Wealthier countries tend to have cleaner local environments, and this seems to suggest that growth and environmental protection can be achieved together.

On the other hand, critics argue that wealthier economies consume more natural resources and contribute disproportionately to larger-scale environmental impacts such as climate change and the destruction of biodiversity. They argue that there are limits to the consumption of environmental services beyond which they will be threatened and the overall welfare of people will be at risk (de Groot, 1992; Daly, 1994). Merely encouraging growth is not enough. What matters more is the rate and direction of economic change, with technology playing a critical role. Today, most critics do not argue for 'limits to growth', the debate has rather been about the nature of growth. Economic growth may be reconciled with environmental protection, but only under special conditions.

Because research suggested that there was great potential for economic measures benefiting the environment, there was much expectation that business, once it was aware of these opportunities, would take a lead in the transformation to a sustainable economy. There has indeed been considerable change over the last ten years. Many progressive companies have adopted a more pro-active attitude towards the environment and sustainability, and developed new organizational capacity and routines (Berkhout and Howes, 1997). Environmental management systems are widespread in larger companies, environmental reporting is improving and levels of pollution in some industrial sectors fall considerably below the levels mandated by regulation. Leadership companies are now seeking to develop business strategies that combine social, economic and environmental goals (de Simone and Popoff, 1997; Hawken et al., 1999). This can partly be explained by economic rationality, including savings from more efficient use of resources and indirect gains from better risk management. Businesses are increasingly expected to share broader social responsibilities that go well beyond their role in producing and selling goods. Social pressures (from customers, lenders, regulators and NGOs), as well as new market conditions, are radically changing the conditions under which business operates. For reasons of internal cohesion (through a statement of corporate 'values'); survival in a more global market in which signals to investors and customers are attenuated (hence the growing importance of 'brands'), and in order to take opportunities in a new 'regulatory space' opening up as governments look for partners in the practice of governance, companies are being both pushed and pulled towards a broadly-defined corporate social responsibility (Berkhout and Hertin, 2002). These changed conditions and imperatives have implications for the ways in which the behaviour and boundaries of firms are thought about.

Yet, as Schaefer et al. (Chapter 8) show, the greening of industry is not universal and is a much more problematic process than many had expected. Technical potentials for environmental innovation are rarely exploited fully and a considerable number of companies do not even comply with existing standards and regulations. The majority of firms still have a reactive attitude towards regulatory and other pressures. Environmental initiatives, be they national or international, often face strong opposition from business lobby groups. Where alignment of business and environmental strategy has occurred, there are often rather specific reasons connected to the market and regulatory context, that are hard to generalize about (Howes et al., 1997). In addition, the search for more sustainable technologies and ways of doing things is fraught with uncertainty: (1) about the resource and environmental performance of technological alternatives (including the potential for undesirable impacts); (2) about trade-offs between varying impacts of the alternatives; and (3) about the dynamics of relative costs and benefits of alternatives over long periods (including learning effects and the impacts of changing regulation) (GECP, 2001a). These conditions mean that the 'optimality principle' invoked in much economic literature is being replaced by a greater concern with adaptation and learning along open-ended innovation pathways, invoking more qualitative principles such as diversity, reversibility, flexibility, resilience and precaution. Much effort is being devoted to the clearer definition of what these principles may mean in practice (Stirling, Chapter 2).

Because levels of environmental awareness are high in northern societies, buying and consumption habits were also expected to change. This has been demonstrated for some products such as organic food, which have found their place on the shelves of large supermarkets. Generally speaking however, 'green consumerism' remains a niche in most markets, even if it can be a significant one. There are examples (detergents, white goods) of whole families of products whose environmental performance has been positively influenced by the process of competition from new 'green' entrants on the margins. On the other hand, it is widely known that there is a dissonance between the environmental awareness of consumers and their behaviour (Burgess et al., Chapter 10). One explanation of this is that the analysis of consumption behaviour cannot begin from the presumption of an unbounded consumer rationality and sovereignty. Instead, much consumption behaviour has to be seen as 'constructed' out of the conventions, knowledges and opportunities that are open to consumers (Warde, 1999). Decisions about what to buy and how to use products are dominated by criteria such as functionality, price and quality. Policies for sustainable consumption have to acknowledge the limited success of past initiatives based on information and voluntary action. Instead, priority should be given to strategies that loosen the bonds of constructed behaviours, of broadening the range of alternatives that are made available, of shaping these to the consumer's expressed needs and desires (given that consumption is also a symbolic act; Miller, 1995), and of reducing the 'switching costs' that may act as barriers to a desired alternative behaviour.

Environmental social science research has identified other barriers to environmentally-aware consumer behaviour. Because shopping, driving and housekeeping are made up of innumerable small and isolated activities, people often feel that their individual decisions do not make a difference. Typically these activities also have a social value to consumers. Citizen-consumers are often sceptical as to whether government and business can be trusted to promote the sustainability of their way of life and expectations. Government attempts to encourage individual behaviour change will suffer unless supported by clear economic and other incentives. To overcome the public sense of powerlessness, strategies for more sustainable consumption need to focus on areas where consumer behaviour makes a noticeable difference and where production-oriented policies are less effective (Burgess et al., Chapter 10).

A parallel, but quite different, set of environmental social science debates has addressed people's behaviour and its impacts in rural settings in the south. In contexts where people (as farmers, pastoralists, forest and water users, and so on) are both producers and consumers, in ways only partially mediated by market relations, research has addressed the relationships between people's well-being (material and otherwise) and their use of environmental goods and services. It was initially supposed that population levels and technology accounted for environmental impacts (for example, UNFPA, 1991). Direct links were also drawn between poverty and environmental degradation, the assumption being that poor rural people would have no choice but to 'mine' environmental resources to survive (for example, Durning, 1989). However, numerous cases exist where local people effectively conserved and enriched the environment despite demonstrable material poverty and population growth (for example, Fairhead and Leach, 1996, 1998; Tiffen et al., 1994, Sillitoe, 1998; Scoones, 2001). Moreover, people's behaviour and its environmental impacts were shown to be influenced by a wider range of mediating factors, from knowledge and values, social difference and dynamics, and institutional and policy arrangements governing both access to and control over resources, to the terms on which technologies are employed (Adger, Chapter 7; Leach et al., 1999). In these respects, contemporary perspectives on 'sustainable livelihoods' in the south (Scoones, 1998) converge with northern work on sustainable lifestyles and consumption in emphasizing the broader institutional and policy processes that shape individuals' and groups' behaviour, and the need to address strategies for change towards these.

The greening of consumption, production, lifestyles and livelihoods has proved to be more arduous and challenging than was hoped for a decade ago. Despite the efforts of many organizations and a long tradition of environmental regulation, many environmental problems (biodiversity loss, the spread of toxic substances and climate change) continue to be of serious concern to many, and new ones are likely to emerge (endocrine disruptors, gene transfer between GM and non-GMOs). This points up two fundamental problems in the debate about the two-way links between business, technology and the environment. The first concerns the embeddedness and path dependency of many technological regimes, and the extent to which these regimes can be modified to be more sustainable. A better course may be to abandon an incumbent regime and manage a transition to a radically new way of meeting expressed social and economic preferences. Can a regime be changed from within, or should policy be directed at achieving a regime shift? The second, and linked, question concerns the nature of the technology, market and institutions which should replace prevailing 'unsustainable' models. The assumption, often held by advocates and critics alike, is that the costs and benefits of new regimes can be known, and that the problem, once a desired alternative has been identified, is one of implementation. However, this faith in foresight often turns out to have been illusory (Anderson and Cavendish, 1999). The history of technology tells us that the costs and benefits are often only very incompletely known at the outset. A putatively more sustainable technological path may, with hindsight, reveal new social and environmental costs, and display the same characteristics of economic and social 'lock in' as the system it replaced. How then can this be avoided, and what principles can we define that may make future technological developments more adaptive and resilient?

Even if it were possible to define a preferred development path to take, another important question concerns the means of achieving it. Beyond the pressures and imperatives that are reshaping business responses to sustainability, the role of public policy clearly remains critical. Over the last decade there has been an intense debate about the correct choice of policy instruments that may induce changes in production and consumption towards more sustainable paths. One striking development has been the marked broadening of the instruments considered, experimented with and introduced (Smith and Sorrell, 2001). A focus of research on policy processes has pointed up the limits of traditional 'command and control' regulation that sets standards or imposes bans. Economists have long argued that direct regulation is inefficient because it is uniformly applied, 'freezes' standards, and is usually based on the regulator's imperfect knowledge of the potential for and costs of improved environmental performance. This critique has been broadly accepted, and has underpinned the justification for a shift towards a wider portfolio of policy instruments, including market-based and information instruments and voluntary approaches. By creating economic incentives for businesses and consumers to change their behaviour these instruments should promote innovation and efficiently distribute effort among the regulated. Voluntary or negotiated agreements – commitments between government and industry to achieve defined environmental performance targets – are another way of trying to create incentives and new norms. In practical political terms, however, they are often hard to implement. More recently, there has emerged a greater interest in the broader link between environmental and innovation policies (GECPa, 2001). In this analysis, the generation and take-up of new technical knowledge and technological systems is intrinsically long-term and uncertain, represents a public good and therefore needs to be supported by public policy.

Over the past decade, then, the debate about business, technology, policy and the environment has been transformed, and produced new paradoxes. Even as the inflexibility of many technologies, business practices and consumption behaviours has been revealed, so has the need for more profound and systemic shifts in technologies, infrastructures and lifestyles (Kemp et al., 1998). Rather than relying on the rational pursuit of self-interest by single actors, a new geometry of environmental governance has emerged, including business (perhaps with a broader definition of its social responsibilities), policy-makers, consumers and civil society. In order to encourage movement towards more sustainable systems of production and consumption, policy instruments need increasingly to emphasize incentives, innovation and learning between actors.

A REVITALIZED SOCIAL SCIENCE OF THE ENVIRONMENT?

Looking across the bodies of work reviewed above, it is worth asking to what extent it is possible to identify a reconfiguration in the social science of the environment? We want to suggest that there are a number of important themes which cut across these different domains, and which studies across different domains, issues and locations pick out. These are not coherent enough to constitute a new 'programme' or 'model' in the sense of the 1980s sustainable development agenda we described earlier. Indeed it would go against the grain of recent social science analysis – and its characterization of contemporary societal conditions – to suggest that such singularity is possible or appropriate. Equally, these themes currently take the form more of common questions than of well-defined avenues of research interest and activity. Nevertheless they reflect framings of issues through which emergent strands of social science are confronting, reflecting on and engaging with the contemporary world and carrying implications forward practically.

Negotiating Knowledges: Science, Risk and Expertise

New risks generated by rapid economic and technological change are a pervasive feature of public and policy discourses. As discussed above, there is growing evidence of public mistrust in 'expert' institutions as these are variously seen to generate risk, to be guided by politically and economically-embedded science, and to lack legitimacy to address problems in ways meaningful to people's everyday lives. Lay knowledges frequently offer very different, though equally partial and socio-politically embedded, perspectives on the questions at issue.

Mistrust is also directed towards new forms of governance and private initiative, with citizen perspectives deployed to register protest and boycott, both locally and globally. Yet such reflexive, mobile citizenship is by no means universal, and a major challenge is to understand the diversity of responses for different people in different settings. Key questions include how, when and among whom reflexivity and protest about globalized economic and technological processes does or does not emerge; the roles of international media and communications in articulating debates across settings, including some and excluding others; and the ways that common social experiences and practices of citizenship may now link groups in the old global north and south.

A range of challenges is suggested. Across different settings, issues and technologies, how do social, cultural and political-economic positions influence the perception and experience of risk? How do certain ideas become embedded as authoritative in governance, while others are marginalized? And how does mistrust develop and become socially-distributed? Such insights will be important to inform thinking about how new, more effective and legitimate partnerships between lay knowledges and expertise, and knowledge production and governance processes might be forged.

Responding to Environmental Change: Flexibility, Resilience and Adaptation

Both technical/natural and social systems are increasingly seen, as discussed above, not in terms of stable, balanced equilibria, but as more dynamic and variable across overlapping temporal and spatial scales. Such a characterization gives rise to issues of path dependency, the potential for rapid transitions between states, and the significance of chaotic elements. This is true both of work on industrial technology in the north, as it is of pastoral, forest or flood ecology in the south.

If uncertainty, variety, surprise and, sometimes, chaos characterize the evolution of complex natural and social systems more often than equilibrium and stability, then conventional planning and policy frameworks become increasingly problematic. A focus on learning, flexibility and adaptation seems more appropriate, and suggests an important way of recasting our thinking about policy and planning approaches, both for local and global issues. This has major implications for the organization and training of professional expertise, and for bureaucratic and administrative procedures and regulatory frameworks, to name but a few.

For social science there are also important new challenges. In particular, there is a need for more integrative approaches to analysis, spanning the social and natural sciences; more exploratory and interactive methods of foresight; a deeper understanding of the attributes and conditions of adaptive capacity and resilience at different levels of social and economic systems; and questions of how principles like equity, precaution, reversibility and regime shifts can be infused into the normative appeal of sustainability.

Reconfigured Boundaries, New Patterns of Authority: Emerging Perspectives on Environmental Governance

As discussed above, the old categories and boundaries between the state, civil society and international organizations are being reshaped in the face of growing global political and economic complexity. New forms of permeability and interconnection are evident. In many places, the authority of nation states themselves is being reconfigured. Powerful alliances are emerging between certain state organizations, transnational corporations, and other international business and political players, with power and profit sometimes sustained through corruption and war. As already discussed, new forms of global governance and institution are emerging, yet are frequently dominated by powerful countries and their agendas. Locally, multiple initiatives and forms of decentralization – connected to different donor, government, private and globally-led initiatives – frequently overlap and conflict, generating further uncertainties. A better understanding of these shifting patterns and their effects is urgently needed to inform the generation of effective forms of multi-level governance.

Political, economic and cultural globalization is generating both new notions of 'global citizenship', and resurgences of particularistic identity claims, whether based on culture, ethnicity or religion. Old notions of community based on locality and of citizenship based on nationality have been challenged as individuals acquire multiple allegiances based on, for example, cultural claims, occupation, class, gender or experience of marginalization which extend transnationally. We need to ask what these new patterns of identity and authority mean for people's access and rights to environmental and other resources and their overall sense of well-being. Such understandings will be critical to serious thinking about new forms of social contract which may now be appropriate in 'negotiating' environmental change: between global regimes, states and citizens; between public and private; between (newly-defined) 'community' members and so on. Expectations about who delivers what to whom, who is accountable to whom and who represents whom are being reshaped. A key challenge for environmental social science is to reconcile the emergent politics of difference and diversity with older questions around social justice and redistribution.

CONCLUSION

In today's dynamic, more expectant world, old boundaries and distinctions are being compressed and stretched in new directions. The reconfigurations and complex, unpredictable processes that emerge pose fundamental challenges to conventional policy models espoused under the banner of sustainable development. The question is what an alternative to the mainstream sustainable development agenda might look like. While there are hints and possibilities in the three themes we have outlined – in notions of knowledge partnership, multi-level governance, local adaptation and flexibility, transnational community, reflexive citizenship and new forms of social contract, for instance – we need a far better understanding of these problems as they play out in different contexts. Such an understanding will require forms of analysis which continue the tradition of cross-disciplinarity and policy engagement that has characterized environmental social science in the last decade. If this often highly productive work can be sustained, environmental social science will continue to provide theoretical and practical policy insights of wide relevance, way beyond the territory conventionally demarcated as environmental.

REFERENCES

Adam, B., U. Beck and J. Van Loon (2000), *The Risk Society and Beyond: Critical Issues for Social Theory*, London, Thousand Oaks and New Delhi: Sage Publications.

Adger, N., M. Kelly, and Huu Ninh Nguyen (eds) (2001), *Living with Environmental Change: Social Vulnerability, Adaptation and Resilience in Vietnam*, London: Routledge.

Agarwal, A. and S. Narain (1991), *Global Warming in an Unequal World: a Case of Environmental Colonialism*, New Delhi: Centre for Science and Environment.

Agrawal, A. (1995), 'Dismantling the divide between indigenous and scientific knowledge', *Development and Change*, 26, 413–39.

Anderson, D. and W. Cavendish (1999), *Dynamic Simulation and Environmental Policy Analysis: Beyond Comparative Statics and the Environmental Kuznets Curve*, London: T.H. Huxley School, Imperial College, p. 35.

Bateman, I.J. and K.G. Willis (eds) (1999), *Valuing Environmental Preferences: Theory and Practice of the Contingent Valuation Method in the US, EU and Developing Countries*, Oxford: Oxford University Press.

Beck, U. (1992), *Risk Society: Towards a New Modernity*, London: Sage.

Beck, U. (1995), *Ecological Politics in an Age of Risk*, Cambridge: Polity.

Benton, T. and M. Redclift (eds) (1994), *Social Theory and Global Environmental Change*, London: Routledge.

Berkes, F. and C. Folke (eds) (1998), *Linking Social and Ecological Systems. Management Practices and Social Mechanisms for Building Resilience*, Cambridge: Cambridge University Press.

Berkhout, F. and J. Hertin (2002), *Towards a Political Economy of Corporate Social Responsibility*, June, Goteborg, Greening of Industry Conference.

Berkhout, F. and R. Howes (1997), 'The adoption of life-cycle approaches by industry: patterns and impacts', *Resources, Recycling and Conservation*, 20, 71–94.

Blaikie, P. and H. Brookfield (1987), *Land Degradation and Society*, London: Routledge.

Boehmer-Christiansen, S. (1994), 'Global climate protection policy: the limits of scientific advice', *Global Environmental Change*, 4 (2), 140–159.

Bryant, R. (1992), 'Political ecology', *Political Geography*, 11, 12–36.

Costanza R., L. Wainger, C. Folker and K.-G. Mäler (1993), 'Modelling complex ecological economic systems', *BioScience*, 43, 545–55.

Daly, H. (1994), 'Operationalising sustainable development by investing in natural capital', in A.-M. Jansson, M. Hammer, C. Folke and R. Costanza, *Investing in Natural Capital: The Ecological Economics Approach to Sustainability*, Washington, DC: Island Press, pp. 22–37.

de Groot, R.S. (1992), *Functions of Nature*, Amsterdam: Wolters-Noordhoff.

de Simone, L.B. and F. Popoff (1997), *Eco-efficiency: the Business Link to Sustainable Development*, Cambridge, MA: MIT Press.

Dobson, A. (1990), *Green Political Thought*, London: Routledge.

Durning, A. (1989), 'Poverty and the environment: reversing the downward spiral', *Worldwatch Paper 92*, Washington, DC: Worldwatch Institute.

Fairhead, J. and M. Leach (1996), *Misreading the African Landscape: Society and Ecology in a Forest-Savanna Mosaic*, Cambridge: Cambridge University Press.

Fairhead, J. and M. Leach (1998), *Reframing Deforestation. Global Analysis and Local Realities: Studies in West Africa*, London: Routledge.

Fineman, S. (ed.) (2000), *The Business of Greening*, London: Routledge.

GECP (1999), *The Politics of GM Food: Risk, Science and Public Trust*, ESRC Global Environmental Change Programme Special Briefing No. 5.

GECP (2000a), *Risky Choices, Soft Disasters. Environmental Decision-Making Under Uncertainty*, University of Sussex: ESRC Global Environmental Change Programme.

GECP (2000b), *Who Governs the Global Environment?*, University of Sussex: ESRC Global Environmental Change Programme.

GECP (2000c), *Producing Greener, Consuming Smarter*, University of Sussex: ESRC Global Environmental Change Programme.

GECP (2001a), *Innovation and the Environment: Challenges and Policy Options for the UK*, London: ESRC Global Environmental Change Programme, Imperial College and Fabian Society, p. 25.

GECP (2001b), 'Environmental justice. Rights and means to a healthy environment for all', in C. Stephens, S. Bullock and A. Scott (eds), *ESRC Global Environmental Change Programme, Special Briefing*, 7.

Giddens, A. (1991), *Modernity and Self-identity: Self and Society in the Late Modern Age*, London: Polity.

Grossman, G.M. and A.B. Kreuger (1995), 'Economic Growth and the Environment', *Quarterly Journal of Economics*, 110, 353–78.

Grove-White R. (1993), 'Environmentalism: a new moral discourse for technological society?', in K. Milton (ed.), *Environmentalism: A New Moral Discourse for Technological Society?*, London/New York: Routledge.

Grove-White, R., P. Macnaghten and B. Wynne (2000), *Wising Up: The Public and New Technologies*, Lancaster: Lancaster University.

Gunningham, N. and P. Gabrosky (1998), *Smart Regulation: Designing Environmental Policy*, Oxford: Clarendon Press.

Gupta, J. (1995), 'The GEF in North–South context', *Environmental Politics*, 4 (1), 19–43.

Hajer, M.A. (1995), *The Politics of Environmental Discourse: Ecological Modernization and the Policy Process*, Oxford/New York: Oxford University Press.

Hanley, N. and C.L. Spash (1993), *Cost Benefit Analysis and the Environment*, Aldershot: Edward Elgar.

Hawken, P., A. and H.L. Lovins (1999), *Natural Capitalism: Creating the New Industrial Revolution*, London: Earthscan.

Hockenstein, J.B., R.N. Stavins and B.W. Whitehead (1997), 'Crafting the next generation of market-based environmental tools', *Environment*, 39 (4), 12-18.

Howes, R., J.S. Skea and R. Whelan (1997), *Clean and Competitive: Motivating Environmental Performance in Industry*, London: Earthscan.

Intergovernmental Panel on Climate Change (2001), IPCC Third Assessment Report WG II: Climate change 2001: Impacts, adaptation and vulnerability, Geneva: IPCC.

Irwin, A. (1995), *Citizen Science: A Study of People, Expertise and Sustainable Development*, London: Routledge.

Jacobs, M. (1994), 'The limits of neo-classicism: towards an institutional environmental economics', in M. Redclift and E. Benton (eds), *Social Theory and the Global Environment*, London: Routledge, pp. 67-91.

Jamison, A. (1996), 'The shaping of the global environmental agenda: the role of NGOs', in S. Lash, B. Szerszynski and B. Wynne (eds), *Risk, Environment and Modernity: Towards a New Ecology*, London: Sage, pp. 224-45.

Jänicke, M. (1990), *State Failure: The Impotence of Politics in Industrial Society*, Cambridge: Polity Press.

Jänicke, M., H. Mönch, T. Ranneberg and U.E. Simonis (1989), 'Structural change and environmental impact: empirical evidence on thirty-one countries in East and West', *Environmental Monitoring and Assessment*, 12 (2), 99-114.

Jasanoff, S. and B. Wynne (1997), 'Science and decision-making', in S. Rayner and E. Malone (eds), 'Human choice and climate change: an international assessment', *The Societal Framework of Climate Change*, 1, Columbus, Ohio: Battelle Press.

Keeley, J. and I. Scoones (1999), 'Understanding environmental policy processes: a review', *IDS Working Paper*, 89, June, Brighton: IDS.

Kemp, R., J. Schot and R. Hoogma (1998), 'Regime shifts to sustainability through processes of niche formation: the approach of strategic niche management', *Technology Analysis and Strategic Management*, 10 (2), 175-95.

Leach, M. and R. Mearns (eds) (1996), *The Lie of the Land: Challenging Received Wisdom on the African Environment*, London: James Currey.

Leach, M., R. Mearns and I. Scoones (1999), 'Environmental entitlements: dynamics and institutions in community-based natural resource management', *World Development*, 27 (2), 225-47.

Levy, M.A., P.M. Haas and R.O. Keohane (1992), 'Institutions for the Earth - Promoting International Environmental Protection', *Environment*, 34 (4), 12.

Markandya, A. and J. Richardson (1992), *The Earthscan Reader in Environmental Economics*, London: Earthscan.

Mehta, L., M. Leach and I. Scoones (eds) (2001), 'Environmental governance in an uncertain world', *IDS Bulletin*, 32 (4), Brighton: IDS.

Miller, D. (1995), 'Consumption and commodities', *Annual Review of Anthropology*, 24, 141-61.

Mol, A.P.J. and G. Spaargaren (2000), 'Ecological modernisation theory in debate: a review', *Environmental Politics*, 9 (1), 17-49.

Murdoch, J. and J. Clark (1994), 'Sustainable knowledge', *Geoforum*, 25, 115-32.

Newell, P. (2000), *Climate for Change: Non-State Actors and the Global Politics of the Greenhouse*, Cambridge: Cambridge University Press.

Pearce, D., W. and R.K. Turner (1990), *Economics of Natural Resources and the Environment*, Baltimore: Johns Hopkins University Press.

Peet, R. and M. Watts (eds) (1996), *Liberation Ecologies: Environment, Development, Social Movements*, London: Routledge.

Princen, T. and M. Finger (1994), *Environmental NGOs in World Politics*, Routledge: London.

Redclift, M. (1984), *Development and the Environmental Crisis: Red or Green Alternatives?*, London: Methuen.

Redclift, M. (1987), *Sustainable Development: Exploring the Contradictions*, London: Methuen.

Repetto, R. and M. Gillis (eds) (1988), *Public Policies and the Misuse of Forest Resources*, New York: Cambridge University Press.

Richards, P. (1985), *Indigenous Agricultural Revolution: Ecology and Food Production in West Africa*, London: Hutchinson.

Roome, N. (1992), 'Developing environmental management strategies', *Business Strategy and the Environment*, 1 (1), 11-24.

Scoones, I. (1998), 'Sustainable rural livelihoods: a framework for analysis', *IDS Working Paper*, No. 72, Brighton: IDS.

Scoones, I. (1999), 'New ecology and the social science: what prospects for a fruitful engagement', *Annual Review of Anthropology*, 28, 479-507.

Scoones, I. (ed.) (2001), *Dynamics and Diversity: Soil Fertility and Farming Livelihoods in Africa*, London: Earthscan.

Scoones, I. and J. Thompson (ed.) (1994), *Beyond Farmer First: Rural People's Knowledge, Agricultural Research and Extension Practice*, London: Intermediate Technology Publications.

Shackley, S. and B. Wynne (1995), 'Global climate change: the mutual construction of an emergent science–policy domain', *Science and Public Policy*, 22.

Sillitoe, P. (1998), 'It's all in the mound: fertility management under stationary shifting cultivation in the Papua New Guinea Highlands', *Mountain Research and Development*, 18 (2), 123-34.

Skea, J. (1995), 'Environmental technology', in H. Folmer, H.L. Gabel and H. Opschoor, *Principles of Environmental and Resource Economics*, Aldershot: Edward Elgar.

Smith, A. and S. Sorrell (2001), 'Interaction between environmental policy instruments: carbon emissions trading and Integrated Pollution Prevention and Control', *International Journal of Environment and Pollution*, 15 (1), 22-41.

Spaargaren, G., A. Mol and F. Buttel (eds) (2000), 'Environment and Global Modernity', London: Sage.

Stirling, A. (1998), 'Risk at a turning point?', *Journal of Risk Research*, 2 (1), 97-109.

Szerszynski, B. (1996), 'On knowing what to do: environmentalism and the modern problematic', in S. Lash, B. Szerszynski and B. Wynne (eds), *Risk, Environment and Modernity. Towards a New Ecology*, London: Sage, pp. 104-38.

Taylor, P. and F. Buttell (1992), 'How do we know we have global environmental problems? Science and the globalization of environmental discourse', *Geoforum*, 23, 405-16.

Tiffen, M., M. Mortimore and F. Gichuki (1994), *More People, Less Erosion: Environmental Recovery in Kenya*, Chichester: John Wiley and Sons.

UNFPA (1991), *Population and Environment: The Challenges Ahead*, New York: United Nations Population Fund.

Vogler, J. (2001), 'Climate change and American foreign policy', *International Affairs*, 77 (3), 759-60.

Vogler, J. and M. Imber (eds) (1996), *The Environment and International Relations*, London: Routledge.

Wapner, P. (1996), *Environmental Activism and World Civic Politics,* Albany NY: State University of NY Press.

Warde, A. (1990), 'Introduction to the sociology of consumption', *Sociology*, 24, 1-4.

Warde, A. (1999), 'Consumption and the problem of variety: cultural omniverousness, social distinction and dining out', *Sociology*, 33 (1), 105-27.

Warren, D.M., L.J. Slikkerveer and D. Brokensha (eds) (1995), *The Cultural Dimension of Development: Indigenous Knowledge Systems*, London: IT Publications.

Weale, A. (1992), *The New Politics of Pollution*, Manchester and New York: Manchester University Press.

Welford, R. (1998), *Corporate Environmental Management 1,* Sterling VA: Stylus Publishing LLC.

Wynne, B. (1992), 'Uncertainty and environmental learning: reconceiving science and policy in the preventive paradigm', *Global. Environmental. Change*, June, 111-27.

Wynne, B. (1996), 'May the sheep safely graze? A reflexive view of the expert-lay knowledge divide', in S. Lash, B. Szerszynski and B. Wynne (eds), *Risk, Environment and Modernity: Towards a New Ecology*, London: Sage, pp. 44-83.

Yearley, S. (1995), 'Sociology, Environmentalism, Globalisation', London: Sage.

2. Risk, uncertainty and precaution: some instrumental implications from the social sciences

Andy Stirling[1]

RISK AND THE INSTRUMENTALITY OF SOCIAL SCIENCE

Social Sciences of Risk

Risk is a central theme in environmental social science. Modern notions of risk arose in the Enlightenment as ostensibly instrumental concepts in the service of gambling, investment and insurance (Hacking, 1975; Weatherford, 1982). Since then, these ideas have played a formative role in the unfolding of key elements of modernity: faith in progress, enterprise capitalism, the institutional management of liabilities and the administrative infrastructure of the industrial state (Bernstein, 1996). Derived concepts of risk and uncertainty are now widespread throughout the natural sciences (von Winterfeldt and Edwards, 1986; Morgan et al., 1990; Betts and Turner, 1992; Suter, 1993). Continuing the original instrumental trajectory, they also enjoy a central role in several of the normative social sciences of choice, including welfare economics (Arrow, 1970; McKenna, 1986), game theory (von Neuman and Morgenstern, 1947), decision analysis (Keeney et al., 1976) and cognitive social psychology (Tversky and Kahneman, 1974). All these perspectives prescribe an incisive and compelling instrumental approach to decision-making under uncertainty. They hold in common a basic reductive, quantitative architecture, conceiving risk as a function of the magnitudes and likelihoods of a determinate range of outcomes.

In recent times, broader-based, qualitative, descriptive social scientific ideas about risk have come to the fore. Indeed, the term 'risk' has been elevated to a somewhat iconic status in the grand integrated tradition of interpretive social theory. It assumes a central role in current understandings of late modernity, addressing what are sometimes held to be newly emerging themes such as alienation, insecurity and pollution (Giddens, 1990; Luhmann,

1993; Beck, 1992; Lash et al., 1996; Adam et al., 2000). Accordingly, social scientific perspectives on risk have begun to proliferate and diversify. Perhaps not surprisingly, activity has been especially productive in social studies of science and technology (Wynne, 1987; Porter, 1995; Irwin, 1995; Irwin and Wynne, 1996). However, complementary social scientific research on risk-related themes spans a variety of fields. These are as disparate as personal identity (Giddens, 1991), interpersonal relationships (Beck, 1996), institutional behaviour (Perrow, 1984), social movements (Yearley, 1994), the information revolution (Castells, 1996) and media studies (Allan et al., 2000). Analytic perspectives range from critical theory and hermeneutics to cultural theory (Douglas, 1985) and ethnographic accounts (Caplan, 2000).

Of course, this academic attention raises as many questions as it answers. For instance, the historic and cross-cultural pervasiveness of experiences like war, plague and famine may raise doubts about whether the supposedly formative conditions of the emerging risk society are as novel or as specific to late modernity as is sometimes claimed (Leach et al., 2001; Fairhead and Leach, forthcoming). Yet, taken together, contemporary social science does yield kaleidoscopic insights concerning the multivalent meanings of risk (Glickman and Gough, 1990; Krimsky and Golding, 1992; Lofstedt and Frewer, 1998; Lupton, 1999; Jaeger et al., 2001). Few themes in current social research are as rich, pervasive or exciting.

Amidst the complexity and diversity of social scientific discourses on risk, an interesting pattern emerges. Risk, as encountered in everyday life, can carry either negative or positive connotations. In gambling or finance, for instance, as well as in many personal lifestyle choices and leisure activities, risk is as much about opportunity, agency and incentive, as about constraints, exploitation or harm. Like the term 'hazard', historical derivations of risk display positive attributes such as daring, enterprise and reward alongside contemporary negative associations (OED, 1989). Yet, in much recent social science, otherwise disparate notions of risk display the common property that they are exclusively negative in their connotations. Risk is addressed in a loaded fashion, tacitly evaluated as unfavourable, at least under the perspective of the subjects in question. Under the reductive, quantitative tradition, on the other hand, risk is viewed in a wider and less overtly evaluative fashion. The scope and moral bivalence of enlightenment notions of risk are retained, for instance, in economics, which addresses risk as a positive as well as a negative phenomenon. The same is true in areas of environmental sociology, such as the ecological modernization literature (Hajer, 1997). It is paradoxical then, that in this respect at least, the narrow reductive approach to risk should better reflect the full range of social meanings, than does the ostensibly broader integrative tradition of social theory.

INSTRUMENTALITIES OF RISK

One possible significance of this paradox will be returned to in the final section of this chapter. For the moment, however, the picture is obscure. The sheer dynamism, intensity and scale of social scientific scrutiny on the subject of risk defy generalization. This presents some serious problems for any review of the social science of risk, uncertainty and precaution. First, the full epistemological implications of recent academic attention to risk have yet to coalesce. Second, the issues raised extend far beyond the scope of any one essay or the competence of any single author. Third, there may be a tendency for the breadth and thematic variety of social scientific insights loosely associated under the term 'risk', to obscure an appreciation of the particularities of the contribution made in any one area. Nowhere is this latter observation truer than in the original domain within which modern notions of risk emerged: the instrumental business of decision making under uncertainty. Despite much recent work, the importance of social scientific insights in this area seems under-appreciated outside the field.

Of course, current policy discourses on decision making under uncertainty do concede an important role for social science in addressing ethical, cultural, social or cognitive aspects of risk and prescribing appropriate managerial responses (NRC, 1996; EPA, 1997; RCEP, 1998; House of Lords, 2000). Yet this acknowledgement of the instrumental value of social science is largely confined to describing divergent social perspectives on risk (Fischoff et al., 1980), explicating their origins (Pidgeon et al., 1992; Adams, 1995), delivering social intelligence in risk governance processes (Grove-White et al., 1997; 2000) or prescribing appropriate institutional, procedural or communicative responses (Covello, 1998; Petts, 1995; Renn et al., 1995). There is a tendency to identify social science with problems framed in terms of credibility (Margolis, 1996), legitimacy (Otway and Wynne, 1989; Slovic, 1997) and trust (Misztal, 1996; Seligman, 1997). There are exceptions, of course, where practitioners have pointed out the direct pertinence of social scientific insights to the technical business of risk assessment itself (Shrader-Frechette, 1990; Wynne, 1992, 1996). For the most part, however, the proper application of social science is (to use the vocabulary of contemporary risk policy) conventionally seen to lie in the activities of risk management and risk communication rather than risk assessment.

This is curious, because it is arguably social science that has played the leading role in revealing a series of inherent limits and contradictions in otherwise potent reductive quantitative formulations of risk. Over the course of its ten-year progress, the ESRC's Global Environmental Change Programme played a significant role in fostering UK social science research in this area (GEC, 1999, 2000). In particular, work conducted at the GEC-funded

Centre for the Study of Environmental Change at Lancaster University can be singled out as having played a leadership role. Together with underlying and parallel work, some penetrating light has been cast on normative under-standings of decision making under uncertainty with a formative influence on the emerging style of UK risk policy in particular.

Without discounting the importance of broader issues, the present chapter will therefore focus on the particular contribution of social science to the instrumental business of decision making under uncertainty. Taking its cue from established processes of reasoning using reductive, quantitative concepts of risk, the discussion will take as a framework the key elements of magnitudes and likelihoods. It will look first at the way subjectivity and contingency bear on the idea of magnitude. Attention will then turn to the role of uncertainty, ambiguity and ignorance in relation to likelihood. Building on this, the final sections will explore some practical implications, as they are unfolding in current policy discourses over precaution, foresight and pluralism.

SUBJECTIVITY AND CONTINGENCY IN SCIENCE-BASED APPROACHES

Reduction and Quantification in Risk Science

It has already been noted that established instrumental approaches to decision making under uncertainty are typically reductive and quantitative in character. This is true almost irrespective of the extent to which they are informed by natural or social sciences. Indeed, quantification and reduction may be identified as key distinguishing characteristics of all enlightenment notions of risk in terms of a determinate set of outcomes, each with its associated magnitude and likelihood. Drawing on preceding traditions in economics, utility theory and operations research, these elegant abstractions offer a com-pelling pedagogical resource and present potentially powerful instrumental tools under the right circumstances. The resulting risk assessment style, epitomized in the seminal work of the engineer Chauncey Starr (1969), has been highly influential and currently occupies a dominant position in policy analysis on risk issues. However, although well established in the academic literature, the central properties of reduction and quantification raise a number of difficult challenges that remain neglected in policy discourses.

Although often based on qualitative specialist judgements, the idiom of this risk assessment approach is overwhelmingly quantitative. Both magnitudes and likelihoods are held to be readily characterized on a cardinal numerical scale. Any residual ambiguities are also held to be quantifiable. The intrinsically reductive character of this process is manifest in a variety of ways. First, the quantitative idiom requires simplification of a complex, contested and inchoate reality into a discrete set of ordered categories. Examples might be costs as distinct from benefits, or taxonomies of various environmental, social and economic impacts. Second, individual scalar indices (such as monetary, mortality, morbidity, toxicity or mass balance indices) are often aggregated, involving further, more ambitiously reductive, processes. Third, probabilities and magnitudes are articulated into a compound notion of risk, classically the simple product of probability and magnitude.

So deeply ingrained are these reductive quantitative procedures that they are typically viewed as necessary – and even sufficient – indications of rationality in the appraisal of risk. Indeed, such procedures are often upheld as being virtually synonymous with the application of science in risk assessment (Berlinski, 1976; Byrd and Cothern, 2000; USDA, 2000). Different varieties of this risk assessment style emerge to address different issues and policy contexts. Decision and policy analysis, for instance, highlight the sequential nature of decision processes (Hogwood and Gunn, 1984). Life cycle assessment focuses on defining analytical boundaries for the institutional and technological systems in question (van den Berg et al., 1995). Technology assessment concentrates on the dynamics of technological innovation processes (Loveridge, 1996). Probabilistic and comparative risk assessment concentrates on the quantification of likelihood (von Winterfeldt and Edwards, 1986; Suter, 1990). Multi-criteria approaches seek to make commensurate different risk magnitudes (Janssen, 1994; Clemen, 1996; Dodgson et al., 2001). And, of course, environmental cost-benefit analysis attempts to derive monetary values as a comprehensive index of risk (Pearce and Turner, 1990; Hanley and Spash, 1993).

Despite their differences, and the many distinct negotiated niches for application, there is a sense in which these apparently disparate approaches are competing in a single market of methods. All hold in common a tendency to treat the concept of risk, at least in principle, as an objectively determinate quantity. They tend to reify the process of decision-making such that the task of appraisal is conceived simply as one of identifying the acceptability of a particular product, technology or policy, the provenance and characterization of which is treated as a given. They tend to assume the acceptability of quantitative utilitarian trade-offs, rather than lexical orderings on grounds of qualitative principle (Holland, 1997; Spash, 2000). They tend to assume that decision making is discrete and unitary in form. They conceive appraisal as the determination of the best among a limited array of prior technology, policy or investment options. To this extent, they share the aim of convert-ing the ambiguous and controversial socio-political problems of risk into precisely defined and relatively tractable 'decisionistic' puzzles (Kuhn, 1970;

Funtowicz and Ravetz, 1989; 1990; Wynne, 1997). Those charged with the unenviable task of being held accountable for decisions or policies on risk have a strong interest in encouraging these ambitions. The imperatives of policy justification provide a powerful incentive to the sustaining of the resulting claims (Collingridge, 1983; Porter, 1995; Power, 1997).

One crucial problem that affects all risk assessment approaches is the multiplicity of different ways of conceiving of magnitude. Normally, the characterization of risks associated with any individual object of social choice (such as a technology, policy or investment option) invokes consideration of a wide variety of issues. In the energy sector for instance (where much of the pioneering and some of the most elaborate later work has been done), risks can take forms including global atmospheric effects, accident risks, the long term management of wastes, aesthetic appreciations of the landscape and issues of centralization and the social control of technology (Holdren, 1982). In the field of chemical risk analysis, appraisal encompasses different mechanisms of acute and chronic toxicity, including carcinogenicity, neurotoxicity, endocrine disruption along with ecological properties such as synergism, persistence and bioaccumulation (EEA, 2000). Likewise, in the field of biotechnology, the principal risks of concern span ecological and human health effects, economic issues, corporate power, world trade, global equity and deeply held sensibilities about the relationships between the body, nature and culture (Grove-White et al., 1997; Levidow et al., 1998; Stirling and Mayer, 1999). In all these areas, as in many others, we face the classic problem of comparing apples and pears.

Incommensurability and Impossibility in Rational Choice

Such difficulties are well known in fields such as measurement theory (Roberts, 1979; Ghiselli, 1981). Over the past four decades, however, it is social science that has taken a lead in establishing progressively more explicit and robust frameworks for conceiving of the instrumental implications of these multidimensional qualities. Although not necessarily motivated by this aim, nor always interpreted in this way, the effect has been to construct a strong challenge to the validity, legitimacy and efficacy of reductive quantitative approaches to risk assessment. The earliest work in this vein was conducted in the early post-war period in the field of social choice theory – a discipline sharing much of the language and precepts of what has become the hegemonic sound science paradigm. In short, it became an early matter of common ground in this field that there can in principle – in axiomatic logical terms – be no effective analytic means definitively to compare the intensities of subjective preference displayed by different social agents (Bezembinder, 1989). Indeed, even where social choices are addressed simply in ordinal terms – as a matter of relative option rankings – the economist Arrow went a long way toward earning his Nobel Prize by demonstrating formally that it is impossible under the rational choice paradigm to guarantee any definitive aggregation of preference orderings in a plural society (Arrow, 1963).

Although variously qualified by reference to frameworks outside this reductive rational choice programme (Sen, 1970; Jaeger et al., 2001), and forming the subject of a wide subsequent literature (Kelly, 1978; MacKay, 1980; Collingridge, 1982; Bonner, 1986), the central elegant tenets of this work have not been refuted within this paradigm. What is especially important about this result is that it is based on principles of rationality which themselves underpin reductive quantitative approaches to risk assessment. The irony, then, is that this 'impossibility' finding is itself (in these terms) a 'sound scientific' result. Aspirations (still more, claims) to 'science based' prescriptions on risk are not just unrealistic. In a plural society, they are a fundamental contradiction in terms.

In some ways, these findings in rational choice theory constitute a paradox within a paradox. The broader conundrum surrounding the Arrow Impossibility and associated findings is that they are so profound in their practical implications, and yet so under-appreciated in practice. Individual authorities in various branches of social science routinely refer to these insights as being well-known (Rayner and Cantor, 1987; Vatn and Bromley, 1994; Bohmann, 1996; Lele and Norgaard, 1996). The implications of the resulting incommensurabilities in risk and environment policy are well explored by researchers such as Collingridge (1982) and O'Neill (1993) and in technical philosophical and economic literature on environmental risk and technology choice (Foster, 1997). Yet these insights are typically seriously neglected in the presentation of risk assessment results, and overlooked in much general policy discussion of sound scientific approaches (Stirling, 1997a).

This is all the more curious, given the wealth of evidence over the practical manifestations of multidimensionality and incommensurability. Beginning in the energy sector – arguably one of the most mature fields for the application of sound scientific approaches to comparative risk assessment – early work by Holdren (1982) and Keepin and Wynne (1982) systematically documented the scale of the sensitivities displayed by ostensibly definitive technology assessment results. Similar results have been obtained by Shackley and Wynne with regard to climate change models (1996). Stirling's (1997a) analysis of contemporary high profile studies of energy risks shows how results for individual technologies are typically expressed with great precision, and yet vary by many orders of magnitude. Indeed, the variability displayed by these results is so great that, by judicious choice of framing assumptions, it is possible to justify virtually any ranking order across options like renewable energy, nuclear power and fossil fuels. Similar issues arise in other sectors, and with regard to the evaluation of policies and investments as well as products and technologies (Amendola et al., 1992; Levidow et al., 1998; von Schomberg, 1996, Stirling and Mayer, 1999; Saltelli, 2001). The intrinsic subjectivity and diversity of framing assumptions in appraisal typically render risk assessment results highly contestable.

Social science research has not been restricted simply to the definition of this problem and the documentation of its effects. Since the 1970s, much research has sought to provide an explanatory framework for interpreting the aetiology and implications of this intrinsic subjectivity in risk assessment. One influential early strand of work resulted in the basic finding that individual attitudes to, and understandings of, risk and uncertainty are framed by heuristics, guided by rules of thumb and subject to various unintentional forms of bias (Tversky and Kahneman, 1974). Crucially, this finding is true of specialist and lay perspectives alike (Slovic, 1997). Research in the psycho-metric tradition has documented the importance of contextual factors such as the degree to which different aspects of risk are voluntary, controllable, concentrated, immediate, familiar or reversible in nature (Fischoff et al., 1981). Economic and social psychological approaches have highlighted the role played by distributional issues, in terms of geography, society and time (Rayner and Cantor, 1987; Pidgeon and Beattie, 1998). Following seminal work by Douglas during the 1980s, the social grounding of these insights was reinforced by the fourfold plural rationalities of cultural theory (Douglas and Wildavsky, 1982; Douglas, 1985). Although criticized on a variety of grounds (Sjoberg, 1997; Boholm, 1998; Stirling, 1998), this work displayed a potent pedagogical appeal. It opened an important door, even in the most positivistic of policy circles, to an appreciation of the validity of different ways of reasoning about risk. In parallel, work in the fields of risk amplification (Kasperson et al., 1993) and social construction (Wynne, 1987) began, in different ways, to unravel the broader, more dynamic and complex, social and institutional determinants and consequences of subjectivity and diversity in reasoning about risk.

In addition to the wider social insights, the cumulative effect of this body of work has been to mount a formidable challenge to scientistic sound science rhetoric in risk assessment (Wynne, 1975; Barnes and Edge, 1982). Of course, there is no doubting the essential role played by scientific knowledge itself in the appraisal of risk. The question is rather whether science offers a sufficient, or just a necessary, input to decision making? Perhaps reflecting implicit patterns of disciplinary status and institutional power, the social science community is sometimes a little diffident in highlighting the full intellectual and policy implications of this question. With important exceptions (Shrader-Frechette, 1990; Irwin, 1995; Wynne, 1996; Stirling, 1998), the repercussions are more often discussed in relation to social perceptions of risk than the technical business of risk assessment itself. There is a tendency to acquiesce to fearful dismissals of relativism in risk policy. The real point, however, is not that anything goes in the interpretation of risk (Feyerabend, 1975, 1978), but that a number of perspectives may constitute equally valid interpretations of the available evidence. Distinct both from the naïve realism of reductive quantitative approaches and the caricature chaos of epistemological relativism, social science insights are pointing towards what might be termed a pluralistic realism. Just because more than one view of risk can be true, does not mean that anything is true (Rosa, 1998). Even where the truth is plural, it is still possible to be just plain wrong.

SOCIAL SCIENTIFIC INSIGHTS ON KNOWLEDGE AND INCERTITUDE

Beyond Probability: From Risk to Uncertainty

Over the two millennia since the time of Pliny the Elder, it has been well recognized that the only certainty is the absence of certainty (Morgan et al., 1990:i). The question is, what should we do about this? The discussion so far has addressed only one aspect of the reductive quantitative response to this question: the concept of magnitude. A parallel body of broadly social scientific work has gone some way in similarly exploring complementary notions of likelihood.

The development of probabilistic thinking over the past three hundred years has long been a focus for historical and philosophical work (Hacking, 1975; Weatherford, 1982). In recent times, just as with magnitude, the epistemological basis for definitive realist interpretations of probability has come under increasingly strong assault (Szekely, 1986; Klir, 1989; Watson, 1994; Porter, 1995). Early economic work (Knight, 1921; Keynes, 1921) developed a classic distinction between concepts of risk and uncertainty. Building on this, economists (Shackle, 1968; Arrow, 1974; Loasby, 1976; Faber and Proops, 1994; Rosenberg, 1996), decision and policy analysts (Luce and Raiffa, 1957; Collingridge, 1983; Brooks, 1986; Morgan et al., 1990; Rowe, 1994), psychologists (Smithson, 1989) and science studies researchers (Funtowicz and Ravetz, 1990; Hacking, 1986; Wynne, 1992) added a rich variety of further insights, including the introduction of new notions of ignorance.

One straightforward way to think about the issues raised in this complex multidisciplinary discourse is by means of the twofold distinction that underlies the conventional reductive quantitative approach itself. Recognizing the potential for greater or lesser knowledge about both likelihoods and magnitudes (or outcomes) yields four logical categories, as displayed in Figure 2.1. As well as providing a heuristic for thinking about concepts of risk, uncertainty and ignorance, this includes symmetrically a fourth category of ambiguity (Stirling, 1998). As will be seen, this underscores a deep-rooted epistemological link between the absence of certainty and the subjectivity and contingency that have already been discussed. The discussion that follows will therefore take this category scheme as a framework for reviewing this further contribution by social science to the instrumental business of decision making under uncertainty.

The first general point to make about the category scheme in Figure 2.1 is that it represents concepts as Weberian 'ideal types' (Weber, 1949): purely in terms of definitions. This avoids unnecessary digressions over secondary issues, such as the nature of any gradients based on these concepts or their relative priorities as nested cognitive domains. Of course, any real situation is likely to present elements of risk, uncertainty, ambiguity and ignorance. Although ignorance may be the most encompassing and indeterminate in its importance, the status of the definitions themselves is entirely symmetrical. A second point concerns nomenclature. Use of terms like risk, uncertainty,

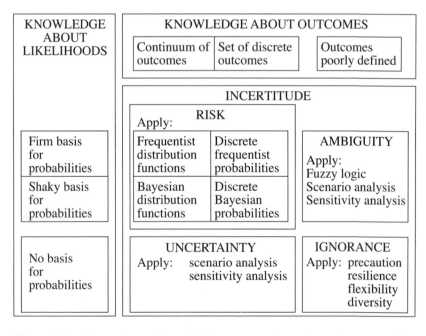

Figure 2.1   Dimensions of incertitude: an emerging scheme due to social science

ambiguity and ignorance in these strictly defined senses raises the question of what we should call the overarching condition. To avoid neologisms and retain the colloquial meanings as far as possible, it has been proposed that the term 'incertitude' be used in a sense which subsumes the four more specific meanings (Stirling, 1998).

To start in the top left quadrant of Figure 2.1 then, we begin with the concept of risk itself, in the strict classical sense of the term. This applies to where there exist credible grounds for the assignment of a discrete probability to each of a well-defined set of possible outcomes. Such probabilities may be taken to reflect established frequencies of occurrence of similar past events under comparable circumstances (or in a hypothetical series of trials). Where outcomes can be fully characterized under a single metric (such as mortality frequency), then probabilities may alternatively be expressed as a continuous density function over the chosen scale. These are the bases for the application of a variety of puzzle-solving techniques derived from probability theory.

Such frequentist, probabilistic, risk-based understandings of incertitude are useful conceptual tools in dealing with well-understood self-contained formal rule-based systems, such as games of chance (von Neumann and Morgenstern, 1949). They are also effective in addressing highly repetitive events involving a multitude of subjects in long term stable systems, as with life insurance in the absence of war, plague or famine (Bernstein, 1996). However, the validity of the underlying assumptions breaks down in the regulation of investments, policies or technological systems in the real world. Here, conditions are far less circumscribed and tractable. The social and physical systems impinging on the development of energy technologies, chemicals and genetically modified organisms, for instance, are imperfectly understood, open-ended, complex and dynamic. Serious doubts emerge over the crucial assumption of comparability between past and future circumstances and outcomes. Together, these features undermine the concept of a hypothetical series of trials which is so central to classical frequentist notions of probability.

Of course, the usual response to this familiar predicament is to adopt some more openly subjective Bayesian perspective and conceive probabilities as an expression of the relative likelihoods of different eventualities, given the best available information and the prevailing opinions of specialists (Jaynes, 1986; Wallsten, 1986). Yet, even this more modest approach requires heroic aspirations to complete information and exhaustive analysis concerning all possible options, outcomes and prior circumstances (Collingridge, 1982:22). Such assumptions are still difficult to justify in the face of issues like global warming, novel chemicals or genetically modified organisms. Yet, even if the basis for specialist understandings were acknowledged to be complete and robust, there remain a host of more technical practical problems. The random variability assumed by standard error determinations is often overwhelmed by non-random influences and systematic errors (Bailar, 1988; Evans, 1986). The form of a probability distribution is often as important as its mean value or its variance (Bailar, 1988). Where differing irregular or asymmetric probability density functions overlap, there exists no definitive means to order the performance of different options (Goodman, 1986; Beck, 1987). In short, a Bayesian extension of the probabilistic paradigm exchanges the positivistic hubris and restrictive applicability of the frequentist approach for enormous sensitivity to further subjective framing assumptions. Under a Bayesian approach to risk assessment, narrowly divergent (but equally reasonable) inputs may yield radically different results.

Where these difficulties are recognized, we confront the condition of uncertainty in the strict sense introduced originally nearly eighty years ago by the economist Knight (1921) and elaborated usefully many times since (Luce and Raiffa, 1957; Keynes, 1921). Here, we are in the lower left-hand quadrant of Figure 2.1. This is a situation where it is possible to define a finite set of discrete outcomes (or a single continuous scale), but where it is acknowledged that there simply exists no credible basis for the assignment of probability distributions. Although advocates of probabilistic approaches sometimes reject this distinction between situations where probabilities are knowable and those where they are unknowable (Keynes, 1921; Luce and Raiffa, 1957), such opposition often seems motivated more by a sentimental attachment to the facility and elegance of probability calculus than by any refutation of the practical depth and scope of incertitude in the real world (Lumby, 1984:108; Morgan et al., 1990:49; Andrews, 1995). Under this condition of strict uncertainty, certain quantitative methods such as scenario (Berkhout et al., 2001) and sensitivity (Saltelli, 2001) analysis have their uses. But techniques involving definitive assignments of probability are, in principle, inapplicable. In such contexts, we must accept the insights of the celebrated probability theorist, de Finetti that 'probability does not exist' (de Finetti, 1974 quoted in Morgan et al., 1990:49).

Whatever the intent, continued advocacy of probabilistic risk-based techniques under conditions of strict uncertainty can be highly misleading. For instance, even within the discipline of economics, the terms 'risk' and 'uncertainty' are sometimes used interchangeably (Lumby, 1984:108) simply to mean the general absence of certainty (McKenna, 1986:9). This sort of conflation can help foster quite fundamental misconceptions amongst non-specialists over the applicability and robustness of probabilistic approaches. Indeed, in fields like financial investment appraisal (Lumby, 1984; Brealey and Myers, 1988), it is often the case that probabilistic approaches are more prominent in teaching and research than they are in actual fund management (Myers, 1984; Malkiel, 1989). The same is true in pollution regulation (Smith,

2000). Taken together, the general treatment of uncertainty as if it were mere risk offers a prime example of what the Nobel economist von Hayek once lamented as the 'pretence at knowledge' (von Hayek, 1978:23).

Beyond Uncertainty: Ambiguity and Ignorance

Serious as they are, these difficulties are unfortunately only a part of the problem faced in operationalizing probabilistic notions of risk. For the accepted formal definition of risk implies two further complementary conceptual ideal types (represented in the right-hand column of Figure 2.1). The first relates back to the discussion of subjectivity and contingency in the last section. In a seminal paper, Wynne describes key elements of these issues as 'indeterminacy' (Wynne, 1992). However, for some, this term connotes a physical property of quantum and nonlinear systems (Faber and Proops, 1994; Ruelle, 1991), separable from subjective social processes (Harremoes, 2000). For such reasons, the term 'ambiguity' might be preferable. Either way, this is a condition under which the risks in question are acknowledged to be multidimensional in nature and where there are a number of different perspectives concerning the scope, characterization and prioritization of the various magnitudes involved.

Ambiguity describes a situation where a variety of divergent – but equally reasonable – framing assumptions precludes imposition of any single definitive scheme of outcomes (Rosenberg, 1996:340). An example might be the case of climate change. Here, some degree of consensus may be achievable concerning the relative likelihood of different global outcomes, characterized in highly aggregated terms on a temperature index (IPCC, 2001). Yet, though they may be felt well modeled probabilistically at one level, such outcomes may be highly ambiguous at another level. Should different global temperature increments be interpreted in ecological, epidemiological, economic or social terms? How should these be conceived and prioritized? Even in terms of temperature alone, there are large ambiguities over implications for particular locales. Indeed, such questions arise even where outcomes are already manifest and so, in a formal sense, entirely certain. In such cases, the answers are contingent on social and value commitments and so highly ambiguous. Instead of uncertainty, decision processes may thus involve contradictory certainties (Thompson and Warburton, 1985).

Many current contexts for decision making on risk are of this kind, where incommensurability and impossibility militate against the reduction of ambiguity. Of course, there may be specific disciplinary or institutional contexts where the reduction of risk problems under a single unified structure may not be a problem. This may be the case, for instance, where all possible outcomes are held a priori to be reducible under a single metric, such as the monetary bottom line in financial appraisal. Even here, however, complex, non-monetary strategic factors are often likely to introduce some element of ambiguity, even in private and corporate decision making (Collingridge, 1992; Genus, 1995). Likewise, ambiguity may also be minimized where institutional disciplines or contextual constraints are such that only one operational scheme exists for defining possible outcomes. One example of this might be where all pertinent features of the outcomes in question are held to be captured in a series of dichotomous categories: such as high or low values on some predetermined decision parameter like emissions, impacts or growth. Here, techniques such as fuzzy logic offer ways to capture certain ambiguities in terms of dualistic category schemes (Klir and Folger, 1988; Dubois et al., 1988; Zadeh and Kacprzyk, 1992). Similarly, sensitivity and scenario analysis can be applied to address aspects of ambiguity as well as uncertainty. In the end, the perceived utility of such approaches will largely be a function of institutional culture (Funtowicz and Ravetz, 1990). Indeed here, as elsewhere, recourse to unduly reductive quantification may be more a reflection of institutional insecurity than of ontological confidence (Porter, 1995).

Beyond ambiguity, however, lies a final major contribution of social science to the instrumental understanding of incertitude: the condition of ignorance (Keynes, 1921; Shackle, 1968; Loasby, 1976; Collingridge, 1980, 1982; Ford, 1983; Ravetz, 1986; Smithson, 1989; Wynne, 1992; Faber and Proops, 1994; Stirling, 1998). This is a state of knowledge under which we are able neither fully to quantify likelihoods nor definitively to characterize or make commensurate all the possible outcome parameters. Described variously as epistemological or ontological in character (Winkler, 1986; von Winterfeldt and Edwards, 1986; Rosa, 1998), or substantive or procedural in form (Dosi and Egidi, 1987), there exists a range of alternative typologies addressing the origins and forms of this condition of ignorance (Funtowicz and Ravetz, 1990; Faber and Proops, 1994). The waters are somewhat muddied by the pejorative overtones, and use of the term in different contexts with divergent implications (Shackle, 1968; Ford, 1983; Yager, 1992).

However it is labelled though, ignorance arises from many familiar sources, including incomplete knowledge, contradictory information, conceptual imprecision, divergent frames of reference and the intrinsic complexity and systemic indeterminacy of many natural and social processes (Medd, 2001; Wynne, 1992b). Put at its simplest, ignorance is a reflection of the degree to which 'we don't know what we don't know'. It represents our uncertainty about our uncertainty (Cyranski, 1986). It is an acknowledgement of the importance of the element of surprise (Brooks, 1986; Schneider et al., 1998). This emerges not just from the actuality of unexpected events, but from their very possibility (Dosi and Egidi, 1987). It is a predicament that intensifies directly in relation to the social and political stakes (Funtowicz and Ravetz,

1990) bearing on a particular decision. It emerges especially in complex and dynamic environments where social agents and their cognitive and institutional commitments may themselves influence supposedly exogenous 'events' (Dosi and Egidi, 1987; Wynne, 1992, 2000).

Although discussions of the condition of ignorance can become quite abstract, there are important practical implications. Many of the imponderables associated with global climate models, the number and functional unpredictability of chemicals and the unprecedented nature of genetic modification technology all present elements of ignorance alongside risk, uncertainty and ambiguity. Crucially, ignorance does not necessarily imply the complete absence of knowledge, but simply the possibility that certain relevant parameters may be unknown or unknowable. This raises important questions over the precise operational locus of ignorance. Sometimes, as in the examples cited above, this may best be seen at a societal level. Key elements of knowledge may quite simply be unavailable to society more broadly. This was the case, for instance, with endocrine disrupting chemicals (Thornton, 2000) and BSE prior to identification of the associated hazardous properties and agents (Millstone and van Zwanenberg, 2000).

Alternatively, the operational locus of ignorance may sometimes best be understood at a more specific institutional level. Key elements of pertinent knowledge may be available somewhere in society – among affected workers or consumers, for instance, or within particular marginalized professional disciplines – but nevertheless remain effectively excluded from the governance process itself. Historically, this has arguably been the case in the early stages of recognition of many occupational and public health hazards such as asbestos, benzene, and various organochlorine chemicals (EEA, 2001). Likewise, with stratospheric ozone depletion, pertinent knowledge was extant at an early stage in some areas of science, but was rather slow to influence policy processes (Farman, 2001).

All the above examples are real cases where problems lay not so much in determining likelihoods as in anticipating the very possibilities themselves. In different ways, all were surprises born of a state of ignorance. The ancient Chinese philosopher Lao-Tzu is reputed to have said that 'knowing one's ignorance is the best part of knowledge' (Morgan et al., 1990:1). Ironically, this essentially positivistic aspiration is frequently absent in science based risk assessment, where a distinguishing feature can be a reluctance to concede even the existence of ignorance (Lindsay, 1995). A major contribution of the social science of risk has been to show that the concepts of ambiguity and ignorance arise not just from external criticism of reductive quantification, but from the same framework of positive rationality on which risk assessment itself is based. They are of compelling theoretical as well as practical instrumental importance.

THE ADVENT OF PRECAUTION

Cumulative Policy Impacts

Since the late 1980s, these broad-based social scientific understandings concerning ambiguity and ignorance have posed a growing challenge to the policy status of reductive, quantitative approaches. Until this point, the canonical exposition of risk policy remained the major 1983 report of the US National Research Council (NRC, 1983). In the UK, a similar role was played by the 1983 study of the Royal Society (1983). Both documents displayed the hegemony of reductive, quantitative understandings, treating risk as an objectively determinate quantity. Issues of ambiguity and ignorance, where discussed at all, were implicit or confined to the narrow domain of risk communication and represented as spurious and recalcitrant features of public understandings of risk. The rationale for their study was to facilitate educational measures aimed at improved management of ill-founded anxieties (Covello, 1998). Gradually, however – as began to be reflected in later National Research Council reports (NRC, 1989) – the field of risk communication became increasingly ambivalent (Fischoff, 1995; Slovic, 1997). The diversity and robustness of public understandings of risk began to be acknowledged. Growing restraint was exercised in voicing judgements over the relative cognitive status of different perspectives. For the first time, the need for two-way communication between specialist and non-specialist communities began to be highlighted and acted upon.

In the UK, this trend reached a watershed with the 1992 report of the Royal Society, where an interdisciplinary study group – now including social science representation – was unable to reach a consensus (Royal Society, 1992). The result was a curious juxtaposition of incommensurable perspectives on risk. On the one hand, Chapters One to Four articulated a fairly traditional scientistic notion. On the other hand, Chapters Five and Six introduced a broader qualitative concept, including an authoritative treatment of many of the issues discussed here (Pidgeon et al., 1992). After this, the trend towards greater social scientific sophistication in official understandings of risk began to accelerate. A 1996 study of the National Research Council and subsequent report of a US Presidential Commission (EPA, 1997), for instance, achieved an admirably coherent synthesis of the position, emphasizing the necessity that the characterization of risk be undertaken as a deliberative process addressing at the outset the divergent value judgements of different groups of interested and affected parties (NRC, 1996). Likewise, buried in the 1995 UK Department of Environment Guidance on Risk Assessment, was an unprecedented acknowledgement that not only risk evaluation (the determination of significance) but also risk estimation (the analysis of probabilities and magnitudes) are both inherently subjective undertakings (DoE, 1995). The implications were not explored there, but have gradually unfolded since. Subsequent statements from bodies such as the UK Treasury (1996) and Health and Safety Executive (HSE) (1999) take successive steps towards highlighting the intrinsically subjective nature of judgements over risk.

For reasons that have themselves been under-researched (Jasanoff, 1990; Fisher, 2001), the subsequent trend has in some ways been more pronounced in the UK than in the US. Recent reports by the Royal Commission on Environmental Pollution (RCEP) (1998), the Office of Science and Technology (OST) (May, 2000) and the House of Lords Select Committee on Science and Technology (2000) illustrate the accelerating general influence of social scientific – and especially constructivist – insights. The same trend is evident on more specific issues, as with the Phillips Inquiry into BSE (Phillips, 2000) and the Stewart Report on mobile phones (IEGMP, 2000). All reveal an inexorable trend towards assimilation of the key themes reviewed here. They herald the demise of purely reductive and exclusively specialist-led understandings of risk in official policy making circles. Parallel trends are evident in other European countries (WBGU, 2000; OST, 2000), although typically lacking the overt constructivist influences discernible in UK policy. In particular, increasing interest in deliberative and inclusionary processes documented by Munton elsewhere in this volume indicate one institutional and policy response throughout industrialized countries (POST, 2001).

Plaintive appeals are still heard in various quarters (especially in popular discourse) for decision making on risk to proceed purely on the basis of sound science and rational economics (Byrd and Cothern, 2000; Morris, 2000; Lloyd, 2000). These issues are returned to in the final section of this chapter. However, though still undoubtedly at the early stages, it does seem that social scientific insights concerning the intrinsic subjectivity and diversity of risk understandings have had a profound if contested impact on policy making.

The Precautionary Principle

Nowhere is this cumulative effect better exemplified than in burgeoning international regulatory activity around the Precautionary Principle. Arising repeatedly in different guises since the 1972 Stockholm Environment Conference (O'Riordan and Cameron, 1994), the Precautionary Principle found its first coherent formal shape in the Vorsorgeprinzip in German environmental policy (Boehmer-Christiansen, 1994). Since then, largely through the campaigning and lobbying efforts of international environmental organizations, precaution has moved from the field of marine pollution (Hey, 1992) into diverse areas such as climate change, biodiversity, genetic modification, chemicals regulation, food safety, public health and trade policy

(Sand, 2000). As a result, the Precautionary Principle has become a potent and pervasive element in contemporary risk and environment policy (O'Riordan and Cameron, 1994; Fisher and Harding, 1999; Raffensberger and Tickner, 1999; O'Riordan et al., 2001). The classic and most globally influential exposition is found in Principle 15 of the 1992 Rio Declaration on Environment and Development, which holds that: 'Where there are threats of serious or irreversible damage, lack of full scientific certainty shall not be used as a reason for postponing cost-effective measures to prevent environmental degradation' (UNCED, 1992).

This language provides an elegant synthesis of a highly complex set of ideas. It raises many practical issues. Indeed, for some there follow a number of quite direct implications. In chemicals policy, for instance, the consequence might be that – where the Precautionary Principle is held to be triggered – regulation should take place on the basis of hazard rather than risk (MacGarvin, 1995; Johnson et al., 1998; EC, 2001b). This means basing decision making on criteria of seriousness and irreversibility (using properties like carcinogenicity, bio-accumulativity or persistence), rather than on an attempt to determine precise probability distributions under these various properties (Jackson and Taylor, 1992).

However, such interpretations remain hotly contested (Morris, 2000). And in other ways, too, formulaic statements of the Precautionary Principle are often found to be somewhat vague and underdetermining. Under the statement of precaution cited above, for instance, what threshold of likelihood is embodied in the notion of a threat? What are to be the criteria of seriousness or irreversibility? By what means and under what authority can the degree of scientific certainty be judged? What is the most appropriate metric of cost, and to whom? What is to be the yardstick of effectiveness? These kinds of question reproduce many of the issues that have already been discussed in relation to conventional reductive quantitative approaches to risk assessment.

Despite its undoubted appeal, formulaic versions of the Precautionary Principle therefore do not escape the kind of fundamental intractabilities in appraisal that have been identified in social scientific critiques of risk assessment. Of course, similar difficulties beset any other simple statement of principle, including many with which precaution is related and sometimes confused, such as prevention is better than cure (Tickner, 1998), the polluter pays (Costanza and Cornwell, 1992), the bio-centric ethic (Jordan and O'Riordan, 1998) or the substitution principle (Dovers and Handmer, 1995). Together with precaution, such general principles serve to define a new form of risk governance discourse (EC, 2001a). They hold considerable heuristic and pedagogical value. However, what all such principles – including precaution – tend to hold in common with narrow risk assessment, is that they take the form of putative decision rules. They deal in reified substantive characteristics of the problem in hand. In many ways, then, the concepts of seriousness and scientific certainty invoked in the Precautionary Principle present essentially similar difficulties to those posed by magnitude and likelihood in conventional risk assessment.

Precaution as Process

It is with recognition of this dilemma that the influence of social scientific understandings, though often tacit, is beginning to be positively felt in policy making on risk. This becomes most evident in considering the question of the precautionary approach, the means by which the Precautionary Principle can be implemented in environmental, health and technology policy (Stirling, 1999; Stirling and van Zwanenberg, 2001). Here attention turns away from attempts definitively to characterize the substance of an intrinsically intractable problem. Instead, the focus lies in the process of responding to this problem (Hunt, 1994; Fisher and Harding, 1999). When precaution is understood as a social process, rather than as a formulaic decision rule, a number of analytic, institutional, juridical, commercial and regulatory implications begin to grow clear (O'Riordan and Cameron, 1994; Raffensberger and Tickner, 1999; Fisher and Harding, 1999; Stirling, 1999; O'Riordan et al., 2001).

First, there is a requirement for reflectiveness concerning the constructed and partly contingent nature of scientific knowledge in the process of social appraisal (Wynne, 1992; Fisher and Harding, 1999). This entails a greater degree of humility on the part of the scientific disciplines and institutions involved (Dovers and Handmer, 1995; Mayer, 1994; Stirling, 1999). Associated with this, there is the implication that the social appraisal process be as open to the perspectives of those who stand to be affected by a course of action, as those proposing it (O'Riordan and Cameron, 1994). Taken together, these lead to a process in which the onus of persuasion (sometimes expressed more narrowly as proof) is placed more with the beneficiaries of a risk-inducing activity than with the institutions of civil society (Wynne, 1996). Beyond this, precaution holds a number of quite specific implications for the social appraisal process. It requires scrutiny of claims to benefits and justifications as well as the adverse effects (Jackson and Taylor, 1992; MacGarvin, 1995). Likewise, consideration extends to the production system as a whole, including resource chains and life cycles, rather than a single product or technology viewed in isolation (Jackson and Taylor, 1992; MacGarvin, 1995; Tickner, 1998). Full account is given to the comparative merits of alternative options, rather than restricting attention to the acceptability of a single option (Johnston et al., 1998; O'Brien, 2000). In addition to comparing options on an individual basis, attention should be given to general systemic properties displayed by different portfolios of options, including diversity, resilience, flexibility and adaptability (Collingridge, 1983; Holling, 1994; Killick, 1995; Faber, 1995, Stirling, 1994, 1999). Beyond this, attention is devoted to the entire innovation process, addressing consequences at the earliest stages of technological or infrastructural developments rather than simply through ex post regulation (Rip et al., 1996; Rip, 1999; Grove-White et al., 2000). Finally, emphasis is placed on the need for knowledge claims to be exposed to constant challenge by continual deliberate research and monitoring (Jackson and Taylor, 1992; Tickner, 1998; EEA, 2001). In short, a precautionary approach involves the adoption of more long-term, holistic, integrated and inclusive social processes for the governance of risk than are typically embodied in conventional risk assessment (Stirling, 1999; EEA, 2001).

Of course, these particular understandings of what constitutes the precautionary approach are not universal. The implementation of precaution as a social process continues to encounter considerable institutional inertia. As with the vocabulary of sustainability before it, the language of precaution offers a potent rhetoric (O'Riordan and Cameron, 1994). It is hotly contested and, as a consequence, in danger of debasement to the level of a banal common denominator (Sand, 2000). There are persistent tensions with established reductive quantitative approaches to regulatory appraisal and many residual confusions (ILGRA, 2001; EC, 2000). These disjunctures between precautionary and established approaches to risk are reproduced in different ways in different national contexts. However, the gulf looms particularly wide in currently high-profile policy debates over the terms of world trade and the harmonization of regulatory systems (Majone, 2001). For instance, there have been a series of recent, quite intense, disputes between the US and the European Union under the broad auspices of the World Trade Organisation (Millstone et al., 1994, 1999; Millstone and van Zwanenberg, 2000). These have focused on issues such as beef hormones and bovine somatotropin, with similar disputes emerging over genetically modified crops. In each case, the US Government has argued that the invoking of the Precautionary Principle, in itself, implies a retreat from the disciplines of sound science in risk assessment (USDA, 2000).

The prominence and intensity of these trade disputes, and the scale of the associated political and economic stakes, serve to highlight the crucial instrumentality of the social science findings reviewed in this paper. The key point is, of course, that the representation of reductive quantitative risk assessment as being synonymous with sound science is at best misleading. It fails to recognize the intrinsic limitations and contradictions in the rational choice foundations that underlie risk assessment. In particular, the conditions of ambiguity and ignorance militate against any general aspiration to derive uniquely definitive results in the social appraisal of risk. In this sense, then, a sound science of reductive quantitative risk assessment is a fundamental contradiction in terms.

Seen in this way, the adoption of a precautionary approach to the social appraisal process represents an eminently rational and instrumental response to the problems of ambiguity and ignorance. One way to understand this is to see the different elements of precaution-as-process, discussed above, as representing a multidimensional broadening out of regulatory appraisal. Conventional processes of risk assessment take place in circumscribed institutional settings, involving a narrow range of specialist perspectives, oriented towards discrete definitive conclusions and engaged in largely one-way communication with external sociopolitical discourses. By including consideration of a wider range of options, uncertainties, disciplinary contributions and socio-cultural perspectives, on the other hand, a precautionary process extends the knowledge base for appraisal. By addressing justifications and benefits as well adverse effects, by shifting the burden of persuasion, intensifying research and monitoring and directing attention at system level properties and earlier formative stages in the development of risk-inducing technologies or activities, the appraisal process becomes deeper, more diverse and more complete in its scope (Stirling, 1999). Only in this way can ambiguity be effectively accommodated and ignorance rigorously addressed.

LOOKING FORWARD

Precaution, Foresight and Deliberate Momentum

The precaution debate is not the only domain within which the influence of broadly constructivist understandings of science and technology can be documented in mainstream risk policy debates. All the more interesting for being culturally and ideologically detached from the precaution discourse, essentially parallel developments have been gaining ground in Europe and Japan under the rubric of technology foresight. Hitherto, these initiatives have tended to adopt rather closed expert-centred notions of relevant knowledge. They have tended to focus on the competitiveness of national innovation systems, construed according to rather narrow corporate-oriented perspectives (Irvine and Martin, 1984; Martin and Irvine, 1989; Martin, 1995). However, these activities have, over the past decade, been subject to a variety of broad influences from the social science of technology and risk (Martin and Johnston, 1999; Grupp and Linstone, 1999; Hansen and Clausen, 2000).

One such influence has come from emerging understandings of the way technologies can be socially shaped (MacKenzie and Wajcman, 1999; Bijker et al., 1986; Bijker and Law, 1992). Much like the relationship between framing assumptions and risk science already discussed, there is recognition that the form taken by evolving technologies is not entirely determined by physical imperatives, but is open, within bounds, to formative influences from contingent (or directed) social and institutional forces (Bijker, 1995; MacKenzie, 1996; Williams and Edge, 1996). In this way, innovation typically proceeds along a sub-set of possible viable developmental trajectories (Dosi, 1982; Saviotti, 1986). The resulting technological systems acquire a self-reinforcing momentum (Hughes 1983), displaying a certain autonomy from wider social or environmental imperatives (Winner, 1977). These processes can be compounded by deliberate organizational strategies of entrapment (Walker, 2000). They can be further reinforced by powerful positive feedback effects in normal market processes which lock in particular technological configurations that are manifestly sub-optimal from the point of view of society at large (David, 1985; Arthur, 1989).

As a reflection of these kinds of insights, there have followed a series of concrete instrumental implications from social science for the business of technology foresight. First, at the level of society as whole, there has been the advent of new understandings of interdisciplinary and cross-sectoral processes for social learning and the generation of knowledge, which move away from exclusively expert-led understandings (Nowotny et al., 1995). Second, there are emerging insights in institutional economics concerning the origins and development of technological trajectories, with diverse cultural and institutional contexts seen as providing both a stimulus and selection environment for positive innovations in the widest sense (Grabher and Stark, 1997). Third, and at a still lower level of social aggregation, there is the cumulative thrust of technology studies, revealing the importance of interdisciplinary alignments and institutional heterogeneity in fostering innovation (Callon et al., 1986).

These converging themes have exerted a strong influence on technology foresight, rendering it more broad-based, pluralistic and open-ended. This is occurring between disciplines (with greater engagement with social sciences), along supply chains (with greater involvement by purchasers and consumers), across sectors (with greater attention to synergies and cross-cutting system-level innovations) and among interest groups (with increasing participation from public interest groups and other stakeholders) (Rip, 1999). The point is not that properties like technological momentum can – or indeed should – be eliminated. Even where the effects of a particular technological system are deemed to be benign, the acquisition of momentum and the harnessing of lock in processes are important – and sometimes essential – features of any successful strategy (Berkhout, 2001). The point is rather that institutional provision for influencing the direction of technological innovation can become more explicit, reflexive and accessible. In other words, the social process of acquiring technological momentum can become more deliberate. Such an aspiration towards more deliberate momentum implies conditions both of deliberate social intentionality and deliberative social processes.

Of course, there are obvious contrasts between precaution and foresight discourses. Whereas precaution reflects pessimistic and critical perspectives on technological innovation, foresight embodies more up-beat sentiments. Precaution addresses the restrictive aspects of social ambiguity and the dangers of ignorance. Foresight highlights the creative propensities of social diversity and the positive potentialities of incertitude. For all these differences, however, both precaution and foresight are concerned with intrinsic indeterminacy, social contingency and path dependency in processes of technological innovation. Both display similar trends towards the broadening of methodological, institutional, and socio-cultural engagement. Together, they offer the prospect of more socially responsive technologies.

In some ways, this dual relationship between precaution and foresight might be seen to reflect the ironic contrast observed at the beginning of this chapter. Reductive, quantitative approaches (like economics) tend to view risk in its full enlightenment scope, incorporating both positive and negative connotations. Interpretive, qualitative social science, on the other hand (as in the risk society tradition) tends to see risk as narrow and exclusively negative. Perhaps a convergence in the cultures of foresight and precaution might be seen as a process of reintegration. In this light, it is interesting that the German word *Vorsorge*, which gives the English term 'precaution', might equally reasonably be translated as 'foresight' (Boehmer-Christiansen, 1994). Either way, the multiple conceptual and practical interlinkages between foresight and precaution do seem compelling. Perhaps the time has come explicitly to institutionalize this convergence and so move away from artificial and balkanized debates over individual risks into more effective general discourses on technology choice and alternative futures (Bohmann, 1996; Sclove, 1995; Grove-White et al., 2000).

Reflective and Reflexive Instrumentalities of Risk

Whatever substantive or rhetorical appeal they may hold, these kinds of processual prescriptions have a certain apple pie quality about them. They fall short of more hard-nosed notions of instrumentality. The question remains as to how these general characteristics of a broad-based precautionary process for the governance of risk can be implemented in practice. It is at this point that we encounter some deep-rooted sensitivities concerning the meaning and role of instrumentality in social science (Gellner, 1974). On the one hand, disciplines such as economics or decision analysis may identify instrumentality simply with reduction, quantification and aggregation of the kind performed in conventional risk assessment. Here, problems such as ambiguity and ignorance are seen as philosophical abstractions to be reasonably overlooked under the practical imperatives of decision making. On the other hand, the broader tradition of qualitative interpretive social science sometimes portrays instrumental aspiration as a problem in itself, militating against reflexivity and threatening a serious loss of subtlety in relation to the social meanings of risk (Wynne, 1997). Here, problems such as ambiguity and ignorance may seem prohibitive of anything but the most qualified of policy prescriptions.

Neither of these caricature positions addresses the key point that – given their inescapable positive reality – recognition of the problems of ambiguity and ignorance is itself highly instrumental. Beyond this, though, there is the point that instrumental simplification may sometimes offer the best expression of reflective self-awareness in relation to these kinds of problems in real social and institutional settings. One example of an approach that attempts to embody this latter kind of reflective instrumentality, is constructive technology assessment – CTA (Schwarz and Thompson, 1990; Rip, 1995; Rip et al., 1996; Schot and Rip, 1997; Grin et al., 1997; Schot, 2001). Developed largely in the Netherlands over the past two decades, CTA is an approach that potentially spans the gap between precaution and foresight. It is doubly interesting in that it is informed by social constructivist ideas and designed to address issues here termed ambiguity and ignorance. Despite this constructivist background, CTA remains an essentially positive modernist endeavour – seeking to improve the quality of the technological choices made by society. Indeed, it sets out to achieve this in much the same way that an engineer seeks to optimize the robustness of a design in terms of physical forces.

Although at an early stage of development, and still restricted in its dissemination, CTA has been employed in policy making initiatives addressing a variety of technological risk issues (Rip et al., 1996). It displays a number of concrete characteristics of interest (Rip, 1999). First, it has the objective of transcending the institutional separation between the promotion and control of technology. A central theme is that the anticipation of future effects, as well as subsequent learning, should be integrated into the essentially promotional processes of technology development and dissemination. Accordingly, it focuses on the innovation and demonstration stages in technological development, rather than the final market dissemination. A second major characteristic of CTA is the aim of opening up the social and institutional networks typically associated with innovation and technology development to include a far wider range of actors and perspectives, including those who stand to be affected. Third, CTA has inspired the development of a number of specific strategic approaches. A technology forcing strategy, for instance, is concerned with the rapid development of new technologies in circumstances where this is held to be required by some wider sociopolitical imperative (Rip and Kemp, 1998). A strategic niche management approach involves the deliberate nurturing of options in different experimental settings (Rip, 1992). This environment of contained, provisional and conditional license helps to overcome the polarization of risk debates and so foster effective social learning about the operational characteristics of the risks in question (Kemp et al., 1998).

CTA provides an example of how instrumentality on risk can be reflective in the broadest and most deliberate of fashions. However, it is also possible to be reflexive in a more subtle and recursive sense (Adam et al., 2000). Beyond the aim of reflecting broad social concerns, an instrumental approach might also be reflexive in aiming to transform the notion of instrumentality itself. One micro-methodological example of an attempt at a kind of instrumentality that is both reflective and reflexive in these senses is a technique called multi-criteria mapping – MCM (Stirling, 1997b; Stirling and Mayer, 1999, 2000; Burgess et al., 2001; Yearley, 2001). This is all the more relevant here, because – unlike CTA – it resonates strongly with the reductive quantitative rational choice paradigm.

Multi-criteria mapping employs techniques adapted from decision analysis. It involves iterative open-ended appraisal of an open-ended set of policy or technology options under an unconstrained array of evaluative criteria. Performance is characterized under each perspective on a cardinal rating scale, with explicit attention to a wide range of pessimistic and optimistic assumptions. Criteria priorities are represented by scalar weightings. Specialized computer software generates graphic representations of option performance and permits comprehensive sensitivity testing, addressing key aspects of social contingency and potential surprise. Institutional ignorance is addressed by including different bodies of knowledge, societal ignorance by allowing explicit attention to properties like flexibility and portfolio diversity (Stirling, 1994, 1998; Stirling and Mayer, 2000). By allowing for explicit exclusion of options displaying certain characteristics, the method accommodates lexical as well as utilitarian perspectives. Multi-criteria mapping can be employed in individual interview or small group settings to characterize different stakeholder viewpoints. As shown in Figure 2.2, different perspectives are expressed as sets of option rankings, each showing ranges between pessimistic and optimistic assumptions. The individual perspectives are not aggregated.

Such an approach harnesses reductive, quantitative methods, but in a qualified conditional fashion. The result is a heuristic, rather than prescriptive, tool. It is instrumental in the sense that different viewpoints are systematically explored and compared, with their embodied reasoning rendered transparent to third parties. Attention is focused pragmatically on clear orderings of

Academic scientists

Government safety advisers

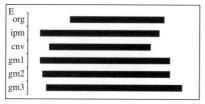 

Public interest

 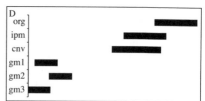

Industry

 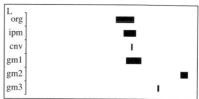

Notes:
Each chart shows one perspective on the relative performance of six agricultural options for producing oilseed rape.
Individual perspectives are grouped according to their affiliation with four different constituencies.
In descending sequence on the vertical axis, the options are organic farming, integrated pest management, conventional intensive agriculture and three different strategies for the implementation of genetically modified crops.
The horizontal axis shows option performance and uncertainties on a subjective linear scale (low to left, high to right).

Source: After Stirling and Mayer, 1999, 2000.

Figure 2.2   Example of results obtained in a multi-criteria mapping exercise

options generated under each perspective. Common ground can readily be identified, yielding conclusions that are all the more robust for being founded on detailed consideration of dissenting views. Yet this is achieved without sacrificing a high degree of reflectiveness concerning the problems of ambiguity and ignorance. The instrumentality is also reflexive, in the sense that the open-ended nature of the results themselves embodies a distinct notion of what instrumentality can mean under conditions of ambiguity and ignorance. The freedom permitted in choosing and defining options, criteria, weightings, framing assumptions and pessimistic and optimistic scenarios, serve to address the intrinsic complexity, contingency and open-endedness in the social appraisal of risk. Indeed, these kinds of approach can be claimed to address – at least in principle – all the key features of a broad-based integrated precautionary foresight approach identified here.

The point here is not to extol the claimed virtues of any one approach. A host of other ostensibly reductive quantitative techniques can be used in a similarly reflective and reflexive way. Examples might include some uses of decision (Gregory and Slovic, 1997), sensitivity (Saltelli, 2001) and scenario (Berkhout et al., 2001) analysis and Q-method (Addams and Proops, 2000). The same is true of some forms of qualitative participatory deliberation (Holmes and Scoones, 2000; Cornwall and Gaventa, 2001). The point is rather that there is no reason either in principle or in practice why the potentially paralysing challenges of ambiguity and ignorance may not be responded to in an instrumental fashion. Indeed, the truly reflexive instrumentality of heuristic tools like MCM lies in the relative ease with which the quantitative idiom can convey the otherwise unpalatable implications of ambiguity and ignorance into the technocratic and power-laden institutional settings in which social appraisal typically takes place. Of course, no one approach can ever be considered to address the full implications of ambiguity and ignorance. However, recognition of the mutual construction and co-evolution of methods and institutional contexts means that it may often be through the apparently reductive medium of method, that some of the most effective anti-reductive influences may be brought to bear on institutions.

Pluralism, Diversity and Dissent

The different instrumental implications of social science for decision making under uncertainty converge in several different ways on the theme of pluralism. First, there is interdisciplinarity and wider participation as a means positively to engage the different bodies of substantive knowledge and experience relevant to the appraisal of risk. Second, there is systematic consideration of a variety of framing assumptions associated with different sociopolitical values and interests to address the intrinsic subjectivity and contingency of risk science. Third, there is the maintaining of institutional, technological and policy diversity as a means of conferring resilience in the face of ignorance and ambiguity. Finally, there is the role of contestability and dissent as quality control in the articulation of contending perspectives. Each raises a number of issues.

The implications of pluralistic engagement are an important area of enquiry in their own right (Norgaard, 1989; Rescher, 1993). Many of the issues raised extend well beyond the scope of the present account. Several are tackled in the accompanying chapter by Munton. Perhaps the main point that needs to be emphasized here is that instrumental rationales for pluralism arising in the risk field are somewhat distinct from other ways of approaching the issue of inclusive deliberation. For instance, participatory forms of governance are conventionally justified by reference either to normative democratic principles, or to an evaluative position concerning the substantive outcomes that arise or (in some cases) to expediency in the securing of consent, compliance and control (Fiorino, 1989; Joss and Durant, 1995; Renn et al., 1995; Covello, 1998; Holmes and Scoones, 2000). Each of these themes applies as strongly to the governance of risk as it does in any other area. However, the issues around the gathering of knowledge to address ignorance, and the systematic exploration of framing assumptions to accommodate ambiguity, introduce a different instrumental reason for an interest in wider engagement. Effectively this amounts to a quite separate argument for participatory pluralism based on positive notions of robustness in social appraisal: being as rigorous about the framing assumptions as about the data.

This said, it is far from clear that – whatever their other merits – particular deliberative and inclusionary processes will necessarily offer the best means to address this positivistic imperative for pluralism. Following early insights by Habermas (1968), much social science work has sought to address apparent tensions between the properties of fairness and competence in citizen engagement (Renn et al., 1995). The positivistic qualities of pluralism in broad-based appraisal raise a rather different issue. There is no guarantee that any given participatory process will display the full breadth and depth of a precautionary approach, giving attention to uncertainties, options, justifications and benefits, system boundaries, systematic monitoring, innovation processes or strategic properties such as diversity, resilience and flexibility. More particularly, deliberative and inclusionary processes can be just as subject to contingent framing conditions as conventional reductive quantitative risk assessment (Levidow, 1998; Wakeford, 2001). Indeed, the relatively uncritical normative basis for some participatory exercises and the emphasis placed on consensus may make them especially vulnerable to the concealed volatility of outcomes in the face of subjectivity and contextual contingencies (BBSRC, 1994; UKCEED, 1999). Just as in risk assessment, the combination of variability, opacity and normative hubris can provide a favourable environment for deliberate manipulation.

A further implication flows from this point concerning the necessarily plural and conditional nature of appraisal results. Moves are currently being made in a number of countries – and at international level in the EU – to complement existing scientific advisory committees with similar bodies for eliciting stakeholder viewpoints or ethical expertise. Examples in the UK are provided by the new strategic commissions developed during the late 1990s, such as the Food Standards Agency, the Agriculture and Environment Biotechnology Commission, and the Human Genome Commission. Like traditional expert committees, these are essentially deliberative institutions. Although not participatory, they are more inclusive in relation to different disciplines and stakeholder interests. The very existence of such bodies is testament to the policy influence of the social science critique of risk assessment. Indeed, some key protagonists are members (Grove-White, 1996; Mayer, 2000) and this literature features prominently in documentation (AEBC, 2001). However, though there are signs that such bodies may have helped stimulate interest in more extensive pluralistic engagement, there is also the possibility that they will serve to contain this momentum and direct it towards a more closed model, based on patronage and consensus. It is early days yet, and a range of possibilities remains open (Grove-White, 2001).

However there is already one feature of these new institutional forms that is becoming evident. Whatever the consequences may be, it is clear that a large part of the Government rationale for such institutional innovations in the UK arose from a motivation to contain increasingly embarrassing and unmanageable public alienation on risk issues such as genetically modified crops. Far from recognizing the importance of exploring articulations between risk science and associated sociopolitical framing assumptions, senior officials cite as justification the need for fire walls between science and politics (Fisk, 1999). Indeed, although often displaying an excellent intellectual grasp of the insights (Fisk, 1999; May, 1999; Blundell, 1999), senior scientific advisors routinely express private concern about what are held to be the associated perils of relativism. The difference between pluralist and relativist epistemologies of risk, discussed earlier, seemingly remains under-appreciated.

The substantive point seems to be the relative priority attached to science and pluralism in the risk appraisal process. On the one hand, there is the formal intention that strategic bodies simply debate value-based concerns and accept uncritically the scientific facts as generated by the more traditional elements in the advisory system on the other side of the fire wall. On the other hand, there is an emerging propensity for such bodies immediately to address the intimate inter-relationship between values and science. A particularly interesting example of this latter tendency can be seen in the attention given by the AEBC to the UK field trials programme for genetically modified crops (Grove-White, 2001; Grant, 2001; AEBC, 2001).

Either way, the instrumental message from social science seems clear. Divergent public interests and values, and their role as alternate framing conditions for risk science, cannot adequately be addressed by bolting on inclusive deliberation exclusively at the end of a conventional, reductive, specialist-led process. Nor can this be achieved by ad hoc inclusion of individual theological, ethical or social scientific experts, or a few lay members. To address the challenges of ambiguity and ignorance, the engagement between specialist expertise and divergent socio-political interests and perspectives needs to be more broad based, directly articulated and symmetrical. In particular, both expert and participatory deliberation should avoid single prescriptive recommendations. The plural and conditional nature of appraisal results can then be systematically addressed by exploring relationships between recommendations and associated conditioning assumptions. Indeed, this distinction between prescription and mapping is in many ways as important as those between qualitative and quantitative or expert and participatory.

At its simplest, this instrumental conclusion can be incorporated relatively easily even within existing expert institutions of risk appraisal. Indeed, incipient aspirations in this direction can already be discerned in the UK, though they have yet to be implemented (May et al., 2000). Instead of making single prescriptive recommendations, scientific advisory committees on risk might be required always to recommend a number of alternatives, each justified by reference to a different set of framing assumptions. This highlights the intrinsically political nature of arbitration between such assumptions, rendering the final decision more clearly subject to the appropriate procedures of political accountability. A discursive space is constructed for scrutiny and challenge of different socially contingent assumptions. The implications may be radical, but the initial reform itself is ostensibly relatively trivial.

This leads to one final aspect of pluralism that arises in considering the instrumentality of the social science of risk. This concerns the relationships between an appraisal process and the wider governance discourse of which it is part – and, in particular, the role of dissent. There are tendencies (certainly with reductive specialist-based processes, but also with some participatory approaches) to see appraisal as a black box for resolving complex and intractable issues. Unitary, determinate prescriptive recommendations are constructed, and then (depending on the approach) variously justified by appeals to the authority of analytic, communicative or procedural rationality, or to some transcendent normative principle of trust, legitimacy or democracy. Indeed, some of the more instrumental perspectives on participation sometimes imply that such processes may be seen as substitutes for the messiness and inconvenience of political conflict. This can lead, for instance, to tortuous claims and counter-claims over notions of statistical representativeness. The real implication of the literature reviewed here, however, is that we might build a more humble role for the risk appraisal process in wider socio-political discourses. The key objective is not the engineering of trust or consent. Rather, the aim is to achieve as much transparency as possible in the elucidation of dissenting views, such that third parties may systematically audit the practical implications of different perspectives for the available science. This is the reflexive instrumentality discussed above in relation to approaches like MCM. Just as organized scepticism is often seen as a fundamental element within positivistic conceptions of science, so might the upholding of dissenting views be seen as crucial to the wider social quality control of risk science. Rather than fighting distrust, we should be valuing dissent.

In the end then, the real instrumental value of the social science of risk arises from pluralistic understandings of precaution as process. Associated approaches (like CTA, MCM, scenario techniques or open-ended participatory deliberation) can offer benefits in their own right. Properly conducted, they address more fully than risk assessment the breadth, depth and diversity of social meanings of risk. More importantly, however, these new processes offer means to other ends. By encouraging greater humility, they may help restore the integrity and credibility of risk science. By militating against scientism, they reveal the importance of divergent interests and values and so uphold the central role of spontaneous political discourse, democratic accountability and public consent. Taken together, they may even offer a chance to realise more deliberate, diverse and socially robust technological futures.

NOTES

1. Thanks are due to SPRU colleagues, especially Frans Berkhout, Erik Millstone and Paddy van Zwanenberg. Obvious debts are also owed to Robin Grove-White, Sue Mayer and Brian Wynne. Liz Fisher, Melissa Leach, Ben Martin, Adrian Smith and Ed Steinmueller gave additional valuable comments on the manuscript. Remaining embarrassing flaws are the author's own.

REFERENCES

Adam, B., U. Beck and J. van Loon (2000), *The Risk Society and Beyond: Critical Issues for Social Theory*, London: Sage.

Adams, J. (1995), *Risk*, London: University College Press.

Addams, H. and J. Proops (2000), *Social Discourse and Environmental Policy: An Application of Q Methodology*, Cheltenham: Elgar.

AEBC (2001), UK Agriculture and Environment Biotechnology Commission, *Crops on Trial*, Department of Environment, Food and Rural Affairs, London, September.

Allan, S., B. Adam and C. Carter (2000), *Environmental Risks and the Media*, London: Routledge.

Amendola, A., S. Contini and I. Ziomas (1992), 'Uncertainties in chemical risk assessment: results of a European benchmark exercise', *Journal of Hazardous Materials*, 29, 347–63.

Andrews, C. (1995), 'Evaluating Risk Management Strategies in Resource Planning', *IEEE PES Transactions*, 10 (1), 420–26.

Arrow, K. (1963), *Social Choice and Individual Values*, New Haven: Yale University Press.

Arrow, K. (1970), *Essays in the Theory of Risk Bearing*, Amsterdam: North-Holland.

Arrow, K. (1974), *The Limits of Organisation*, New York: W.W. Norton.

Arthur, W. (1989), 'Competing technologies, increasing returns, and lock-in by historical events', *Economic Journal*, 99.

Bailar, J. (1988), *Scientific Inferences and Environmental Problems: The Uses of Statistical Thinking*', North Carolina: Institute for Environmental Studies, University of North Carolina.

Barnes, B. and D. Edge (1982), *Science in Context: Readings in the Sociology of Science*, Milton Keynes: Open University Press.

BBSRC Science Museum (1994), *UK National Consensus Conference on Plant Biotechnology, Final Report*, London: Science Museum.

Beck, M. (1987), 'Water quality modeling: a review of the analysis of uncertainty', *Water Resources Research*, 23 (8).

Beck, U. (1992), *Risk Society: Towards a New Modernity*, London: Sage.

Beck, U. (1996), 'World risk society as cosmopolitan society: ecological questions in a framework of manufactured uncertainties', *Theory, Culture and Society*, 13, 4, 1.

Berkhout, F. (2001), 'Technological regimes, environmental performance and innovation systems: tracing the links', paper for conference on *Environmental Innovation Systems*, Gaermisch-Partenkirchen, September.

Berkhout, F., J. Hertin and A. Jordan (2001), *Socio-economic Futures in Climate Change Impact Assessment: Using Scenarios as 'Learning Machines'*, Tyndall Centre Working Paper No. 3. Tyndall Centre for Climate Change Research, Norwich.

Berlinski, D. (1976), *On Systems Analysis: An Essay Concerning the Limitations of Some Mathematical Models in the Social, Political Biological Sciences*, Cambridge MA: MIT Press.

Bernstein, P. (1996), *Against the Gods: The Remarkable Story of Risk*, London: Wiley.

Betts, D. and R. Turner (1992), *Introductory Statistical Mechanics*, Reading: Addison-Wesley.

Bezembinder, T. (1989), 'Social Choice Theory and Practice', in Vlek and Cvetkovitch, *Social Decision Methodology for Technological Projects*, Dordrecht: Kluwer.

Bijker, W. (1995), *Of Bicycles, Bakelite and Bulbs: Toward a Theory of Socio-technical Change*, Cambridge, MA: MIT Press.

Bijker, W. and J. Law (1992), *Shaping Technology/Building Society: Studies in Socio-technical Change*, Cambridge MA: MIT Press.

Bijker, W., T. Hughes and T. Pinch (1986), *The Social Construction of Technological Systems: New Directions in the Sociology and History of Technology*, Cambridge, MA: MIT Press.

Blundell, T. (1999), 'Risk assessment, uncertainty and the need to involve the public', in V. Ellis (ed.), *Oracles or Scapegoats: Scientists and Scientific Advice in Government Policy Making*, London: Institute of Managers, Professionals and Civil Servants.

Boehmer-Christiansen, S. (1994), 'The precautionary principle in Germany: enabling government', in T. O'Riordan and J. Cameron (eds), *Interpreting the Precautionary Principle*, London: Cameron May.

Bohmann, J. (1996), *Public Deliberation: Pluralism, Complexity and Democracy*, Cambridge, MA: MIT Press.

Boholm, A. (1998), 'Risk perception and social anthropology: critique of cultural theory', *Ethnos*, 61 (1–2), 64–84.

Bonner, J. (1986), *Politics, Economics and Welfare: An Elementary Introduction to Social Choice*, Brighton: Harvester Press.

Brealey, R. and S. Myers (1988), *Principles of Corporate Finance*, 3rd edn, New York: McGraw-Hill.

Brooks, H. (1986), 'The Typology of Surprises in Technology, Institutions and Development', in W. Clarke and R. Munn, *Sustainable Development of the Biosphere*, Cambridge: Cambridge University Press.

Burgess, J., J. Clark, A. Stirling, K. Studd, J. Chilvers and S. Lewis (2001), *Local Outreach*, R&D Technical Report SWCON 204, Bristol: Environment Agency.

Byrd, D. and C. Cothern (2000), *Introduction to Risk Analysis: a Systematic Approach to Science-based Decision Making*, Rockville: Government Institutes.

Callon, M., J. Law and A. Rip (1986), *Mapping the Dynamics of Science and Technology: Sociology of Science in the Real World*, Basingstoke: Macmillan.

Caplan, P. (ed.) (2000), *Risk Revisited*, London: Pluto.

Castells, M. (1996), *The Information Age: Economy, Society, and Culture*, three volumes, Oxford: Blackwell.

Clemen, R. (1996), *Making Hard Decisions*, 2nd edn, Duxbury: Belmont.

Collingridge, D. (1980), *The Social Control of Technology*, Milton Keynes: Open University Press.

Collingridge, D. (1982), *Critical Decision Making: A New Theory of Social Choice*, London: Pinter.

Collingridge, D. (1983), *Technology in the Policy Process: Controlling Nuclear Power*, London: Pinter.

Collingridge, D. (1992), *The Management of Scale: Big Organisations, Big Decisions, Big Mistakes*, London: Routledge.

Cornwall, A. and J. Gaventa (2001), *From Users and Choosers to Makers and Shapers: Repositioning Participation in Social Policy*, IDS working paper 127, Brighton: Institute for Development Studies.

Costanza, R. and L. Cornwell (1992), 'The 4P approach to dealing with scientific uncertainty', *Environment*, 34 (9), 12–42.

Covello, V. (1998), 'Risk communication', in P. Calow (ed.), *'Handbook of Environmental Risk Assessment and Management*, Oxford: Blackwell.

Cyranski, J. (1986), 'The Probability of a Probability', in *Justice*.

David, P. (1985), 'Clio and the Economics of QWERTY', *American Economic Review*, 75, 332–7.

de Finetti, N. (1974), *Theory of Probability*, New York: Wiley.

Dodgson, J., M. Spackman, A. Pearman and L. Phillips (2001), *Multi-criteria Analysis: a Manual*, Department for Transport, Local Government and the Regions, London: HMSO.

Department of Environment UK (DoE) (1995), *A Guide to Risk Assessment and Risk Management for Environmental Protection*, London: HMSO.

Dosi, G. (1982), 'Technological paradigms and technological trajectories', *Research Policy*, 11.

Dosi, G. and M. Egidi (1987), 'Substantive and procedural uncertainty, an exploration of economic behaviours in complex and changing environments', *SPRU DRC Discussion Paper* No. 46, 1987, Sussex: SPRU.

Douglas, M. (1985), *Risk Acceptability According to the Social Sciences*, New York: Russell Sage Foundation.

Douglas, M. and A. Wildavsky (1982), *Risk and Culture: The Selection of Technological and Environmental Dangers*, Berkeley, CA: University of California Press.

Dovers, S. and J. Handmer (1995), 'Ignorance, the precautionary principle and sustainability', *Ambio*, 24 (2), 92–7.

Dubois, D., H. Prade and H. Farreny (1988), *Possibility Theory: an Approach to Computerised Processing of Uncertainty*, New York: Plenum.

EPA (1997), G.S. Omen, A.C. Kessler, N. and T. Anderson, *Framework for Environmental Health Risk Management*, US Presidential/Congressional Commission on Risk Assessment and Risk Management, final report Volume 1, Washington: EPA.

Evans, N. (1986), 'Assessing the risks of nuclear energy', in G. Harrison and D. Gretton (eds), *Energy UK 1986*, Newbury: Policy Journals.

European Commission (EC) (2000), *Communication from the Commission on the Precautionary Principle*, COM(2000)1, Brussels, February.

European Commission (EC) (2001a), *European Governance: A White Paper*, COM(2001)428 final, Brussels, July.

European Commission (EC) (2001b), *White Paper: Strategy for a Future Chemicals Policy*, COM(2001)88 final, Brussels, February.

European Environment Agency (EEA) (2000), United Nations Environment Programme, *Chemicals in the European Environment: Low Doses, High Stakes?*, Copenhagen: European Environment Agency.

European Environment Agency (EEA) (2001), D. Gee, P. Harremoes, J. Keys, M. MacGarvin, A. Stirling, S. Vaz and B. Wynne, *Late Lesson from Early Warnings: The Precautionary Principle 1898-2000*, Copenhagen: European Environment Agency.

Faber, M. and J. Proops (1994), *Evolution, Time, Production and the Environment*, Berlin: Springer.

Faber, S. (1995), 'Economic resilience and economic policy', *Ecological Economics*, 15, 105-7.

Fairhead, J. and M. Leach (2003), *Science, Society and Power: Environmental Knowledge and Policy in West Africa and the Caribbean*, Cambridge: Cambridge University Press (forthcoming).

Farman, J. (2001), 'Halocarbons, the ozone layer and the precautionary principle', in EEA, D. Gee, P. Harremoes, J. Keys, M. MacGarvin, A. Stirling, S. Vaz and B. Wynne, *Late Lessons from Early Warnings: The Precautionary Principle 1898-2000*, Copenhagen: European Environment Agency.

Feyerabend, P. (1975), *Against Method*, London: Verso.

Feyerabend, P. (1978), *Science in a Free Society*, London: Verso.

Fiorino, D. (1989), 'Environmental risk and democratic process: a critical review', *Columbia Journal of Environmental Law*, 14, 501.

Fischoff, B., S. Lichtenstein, P. Slovic, S. Derby and R. Keeney (1981), *Acceptable Risk*, Cambridge: Cambridge University Press.

Fischoff, B. (1995), 'Risk perception and communication unplugged: twenty years of progress', *Risk Analysis,* 15 (2), 137-45.

Fischoff, B., P. Slovic and S. Lichtenstein (1980), *Labile Values: A Challenge for Risk Assessment*, London: Academic Press.

Fisher, E. and R. Harding (eds) (1999), *Perspectives on the Precautionary Principle*, Sydney: Federation Press.

Fisher, E. (2001), 'From deliberating risk to rationalising risk: administrative constitutionalism and risk regulation in the US, UK and EC', paper to Oxford-University of Texas Faculty Exchange Seminar, University of Texas, Austin, April.

Fisk, D. (1999), 'The nature of scientific evidence', in V. Ellis (ed.), *Oracles or Scapegoats: Scientists and Scientific Advice in Government Policy Making*, London: Institute of Managers, Professionals and Civil Servants.

Ford, J. (1983), *Choice, Expectation and Uncertainty: an Appraisal of G.L.S. Shackle's Theory*, Totowa: Barnes and Noble.

Foster, J. (1997), *Valuing Nature: Economics, Ethics and Environment*, London: Routledge.

Funtowicz, S. and J. Ravetz (1989), 'Managing the Uncertainties of Statistical Information', in P. Brown (1989), *Environmental Threats*, London: Belhaven.

Funtowicz, S. and J. Ravetz (1990), *Uncertainty and Quality in Science for Policy*, Amsterdam: Kluwer.

GEC (1999), B. Adam, F. Berkhout, T. Dyson, R. Grove-White, T. Marsden, T. O'Riordon, I. Scoones, A. Scott, A. Stirling, C. Williams and B. Wynne, *The Politics of GM Food: Risk, Science and Public Trust*, ESRC Global Environmental Change Programme, Special Briefing No. 5, Sussex, October 1999 (available at: <http://www.sussex.ac.uk/Units/gec/gecko/gec-gm-f.pdf> October 2001).

GEC (2000), <http://www.gecko.ac.uk/doc-a/index.html>, downloaded October 2001.

Gellner, E. (1974), 'The new idealism - cause and meaning in the social sciences', in A. Giddens, *Positivism and Sociology*, London: Heinemann.

Genus, A. (1995), *Flexible Strategic Management*, London: Chapman and Hall.

Ghiselli, E. (1981), *Measurement Theory for the Behavioral Sciences*, San Francisco: Freeman.

Giddens, A. (1990), *The Consequences of Modernity*, Stanford, CA: Stanford University Press.

Giddens, A. (1991), *Modernity and Self-Identity. Self and Society in the Late Modern Age*, Cambridge: Polity Press.

Glickman, T. and M. Gough (1990), *Readings in Risk*, Washington, DC: Resources for the Future.

Goodman, J. (1986), 'On criteria of insignificant difference between two risks', *Risk Analysis*, 6 (2), 1986, Soc. Risk Anal., USA.

Grabher, G. and D. Stark (1997), 'Organizing diversity: evolutionary theory, network analysis and post-socialism', *Regional Studies*, 31 (5), 533–44.

Grant, M. (2001), *Background on GMOs and Biotechnology: Science and Ethics; Benefits and Risks*, paper presented at conference of the International Bar Association on 'The law and politics of GMOs, biotechnology and food safety: a delicate balance', Paris, 7–8 June.

Gregory, R. and P. Slovic (1997), 'A constructive approach to environmental valuation', *Ecological Economics*, 21, 175–81.

Grin, J., H. van de Graaf and R. Hoppe (1997), *Technology Assessment through Interaction: A Guide*, The Hague: Rathenau Institute.

Grove-White, R. (1996), *Environmental Knowledge and Public Policy Needs: On Humanising the Research Agenda*, in S. Lash, B. Swerszynski and B. Wynne (eds), *Risk, Environment and Modernity: Towards a New Ecology*, London: Sage.

Grove-White, R. (2001), *New Wine, Old Bottles? Personal Reflections on the New Biotechnology Commissions*, paper to conference on 'Assessing the new science and society commissions' organized by the Science and Governance Group and Gresham College, held at Gresham College, London, June.

Grove-White, R., P. Macnaghten, S. Mayer and B. Wynne (1997), *Uncertain World. Genetically Modified Organisms, Food and Public Attitudes in Britain*, Centre for the Study of Environmental Change, Lancaster: Lancaster University.

Grove-White, R., P. Macnaghten, S. Mayer and B. Wynne (2000), *Wising Up: The Public and New Technologies*, Centre for the Study of Environmental Change, Lancaster: Lancaster University.

Grupp, H. and H. Linstone (1999), 'National technology foresight activities around the globe: resurrection and new paradigms', *Technological Forecasting and Social Change*, 60, 85–94.

Habermas, J. (1968), *Toward a Rational Society: Student Protest, Science and Politics*, London: Heinemann.

Hacking, I. (1975), *The Emergence of Probability: A Philosophical Study of Early Ideas About Probability Induction and Statistical Inference*, Cambridge: Cambridge University Press.

Hacking, I. (1986), 'Culpable ignorance of interference effects', in A. MacLean, *Values at Risk*, New Jersey: Rowman and Allanheld.

Hajer, M. (1997), *The Politics of Environmental Discourse: Ecological Modernization and the Policy Process*, Oxford/New York: Oxford University Press.

Hanley, N. and C. Spash (1993), *Cost-benefit Analysis and the Environment*, Cheltenham: Edward Elgar.

Hansen, A. and C. Clausen (2000), 'From participative TA to TA as participant in the social shaping of technology', TA *Datanebank Nachrichten*, 3 (9), October.

Harremoes, P. (2000), *Methods for Integrated Assessment*, paper to International Workshop on Information for Sustainable Water Management, Nunspeet, The Netherlands, 25–28 September.

Hey, E. (1992), *The Precautionary Principle and the LDC*, Rotterdam: Erasmus University.

Hogwood, B. and L. Gunn (1984), *Policy Analysis for the Real World*, Oxford: Oxford University Press.

Holdren, J. (1982), 'Energy hazards: what to measure, what to compare', *Technology Review*, Boston: MIT.

Holland, A. (1997), 'The foundations of environmental decision-making', *International Journal of Environment and Pollution*, 7 (4), 483–96.

Holling, C. (1994), 'Simplifying the complex: the paradigms of ecological function and structure', *Futures*, 26 (6), 598–609.

Holmes, T. and I. Scoones (2000), *Participatory Environmental Policy Processes: Experiences from North and South*, IDS working paper 113, Brighton: Institute for Development Studies.

House of Lords Select Committee on Science and Technology, UK (2000), 3rd Report, *Science and Society*, HL 38, March, London: HMSO.

HSE (1999), UK Health and Safety Executive, *Reducing Risks, Protecting People*, December, London: Health and Safety Executive (UK).

Hughes, T. (1983), *Networks of Power: Electrification in Western Society 1880–1930*, Baltimore: Johns Hopkins University Press.

Hunt, J. (1994), *The Social Construction of Precaution*, in T. O'Riordan and J. Cameron, *Interpreting the Precautionary Principle*, London: Earthscan.

IEGMP (2000), Independent Expert Group on Mobile Phones (chair: W. Stewart), *Mobile Phones and Health*, London: HMSO.

ILGRA (2001), UK Interdepartmental Liaison Group on Risk Assessment, *The Precautionary Principle: Policy and Application*, Health and Safety Executive, November 2001.

IPCC (2001), Intergovernmental Panel on Climate Change (J. McCarthy), *Climate Change 2001: Impacts, Adaptation, and Vulnerability: Contribution of Working Group II to the Third Assessment Report*, Cambridge: Cambridge University Press.

Irvine, J. and B. Martin (1984), *Foresight in Science: Picking the Winners*, London: Pinter.

Irwin A. (1995), *Citizen Science: A Study of People, Expertise and Sustainable Development*, London: Routledge.

Irwin, A. and B. Wynne (1996), *Misunderstanding Science?: The Public Reconstruction of Science and Technology*, Cambridge: Cambridge University Press.

Jackson, T. and P. Taylor (1992), 'The Precautionary Principle and the Prevention of Marine Pollution', *Chemistry and Ecology*, 7, 123–34.

Jaeger, C., O. Renn, E. Rosa and T. Webler (2001), *Risk: Uncertainty and Rational Action*, London: Earthscan.

Janssen, R. (1994), *Multi-objective Decision Support for Environmental Management*, Dordrecht: Kluwer.

Jasanoff, S. (1990), *The Fifth Branch: Science Advisers as Policymakers*, Cambridge, MA: Harvard University Press.

Jaynes, E. (1986), 'Bayesian methods: general background', in *Justice*.

Johnston, P., D. Santillo and R. Stringer (1998), *Risk Assessment and Reality: Recognizing the Limitations*, Exeter University.

Jordan, A. and T. O'Riordan (1998), *The Precautionary Principle in Contemporary Environmental Policy and Politics*, paper delivered to conference on 'Putting the precautionary principle into practice: how to make "good" environmental decisions under uncertainty', London Resource Centre, April.

Joss, S. and J. Durant (1995), *Public Participation in Science: The Role of Consensus Conferences in Europe*, London: Science Museum.

Kasperson, R., O. Renn, P. Slovic, H. Brown, J. Emel, R. Goble, J. Kasperson and S. Ratick (1993), 'The social amplification of risk: a conceptual framework', *Risk Analysis*, 8 (2), 177–87.

Keeney, R., H. Raiffa and R. Meyer (1976), *Decisions with Multiple Objectives: Preferences and Value Trade-offs*, New York: Wiley.

Keepin, B. and B. Wynne (1982), 'Technical analysis of IIASA energy scenarios', *Nature*, 312.

Kelly, J. (1978), *Arrow Impossibility Theorems*, New York: Academic Press.

Kemp, R., J. Schot and R. Hoogma (1998), 'Regime shifts to sustainability through processes of niche formation: the approach of strategic niche management', *Technology Analysis and Strategic Management*, 10 (2), 175–95.

Keynes, J. (1921), *A Treatise on Probability*, London: Macmillan.

Killick, T. (1995), 'Flexibility and Economic Progress', *World Development*, 23 (5), 721–34.

Klir, G. (1989), 'Is there more to uncertainty than some probability theorists might have us believe?', *International Journal of General Systems*, 15, 347–78.

Klir, G. and T. Folger (1988), *Fuzzy Sets, Uncertainty and Information*, New Jersey: Prentice Hall.

Knight, F. (1921), *Risk, Uncertainty and Profit*, Boston: Houghton Mifflin.

Krimsky, S. and L. Golding (1992), *Social Theories of Risk*, Westport: Praeger.

Kuhn, T. (1970), *The Structure of Scientific Revolutions*, Chicago: Chicago University Press.

Lash, S., B. Swerszynski and B. Wynne (eds) (1996), *Risk, Environment and Modernity: Towards a New Ecology*, London: Sage.

Leach, M., I. Scoones and L. Thompson (2001), 'Citizenship, science and risk: conceptualising relationships across issues and settings', *IDS Bulletin*, 32 (2), 40–48.

Lele, S. and R. Norgaard (1996), Sustainability and the Scientist's Burden, *Conservation Biology*, 10 (2), 354–65.

Levidow, L. (1998), 'Democratising technology or technologising democracy', *Technology in Society*, 20 (2), 211–26

Levidow, L., S. Carr, R. Schomberg and D. Wield (1998), 'European biotechnology regulation: framing the risk assessment of a herbicide-tolerant crop', *Science, Technology and Human Values*, 22 (4), 472–505.

Lindsay, R. (1995), 'Galloping Gertie and the Precautionary Principle: how is environmental impact assessment assessed?', in T. Wakeford and N. Walters, *Science for the Earth*, London: Wiley.

Lloyd, L. (2000), 'The Tyranny of the L-shape Curve', *Science and Public Affairs*, February.

Loasby, B. (1976), *Choice, Complexity and Ignorance: An Inquiry into Economic Theory and the Practice of Decision Making*, Cambridge: Cambridge University Press.

Lofstedt, R. and L. Frewer (eds) (1998), *Risk & Modern Society*, London: Earthscan.

Loveridge, D. (ed.) (1996), 'Special issue on technology assessment', *International Journal of Technology Management*, 11 (5/6).

Luce, R. and H. Raiffa (1957), 'An axiomatic treatment of utility', in R. Luce and H. Raiffa, *Games and Decisions*, New York: John Wiley.

Luhmann, N. (1993), *Risk: A Sociological Theory*, New York: Aldine de Gruter.

Lumby, S. (1984), *Investment Appraisal*, 2nd edn, London: Van Nostrand.

Lupton, D. (1999), *Risk*, London: Routledge.

MacGarvin, M. (1995), 'The implications of the precautionary principle for biological monitoring', *Helgolander Meeresuntersuchunge*, 49, 647-62.

MacKay, A. (1980), *Arrow's Theorem: The Paradox of Social Choice - A Case Study in the Philosophy of Economics*, New Haven: Yale University Press.

Mackenzie, D. (1996), *Knowing Machines: Essays on Technical Change*, Cambridge: MIT Press.

MacKenzie, D. and J. Wajcman (eds) (1999) *The Social Shaping of Technology*, Buckingham: Open University Press.

Majone, G. (2001), *The Precautionary Principle and Regulatory Impact Analysis*, paper to International Seminar on Regulatory Impact Analysis organized by Progetto AIR, Rome, June.

Malkiel, B. (1989), 'Is the stock market efficient?', *Science*, 243, 1313-18.

Margolis, H. (1996), *Dealing with Risk*, Chicago: Chicago University Press.

Martin, B. (1995), 'A review of recent overseas programmes', *Technology Foresight 6*, London: Office of Science and Technology.

Martin, B. and J. Irvine (1989), *Research Foresight: Priority-setting in Science*, London: Pinter.

Martin, B. and R. Johnston (1999), 'Technology foresight for wiring up the national innovation system', *Technological Forecasting and Social Change*, 60 (1), 37-54.

May, R. (1999), 'The use of scientific evidence in policy making', in V. Ellis (ed.), *Oracles or Scapegoats: Scientists and Scientific Advice in Government Policy Making*, London: Institute of Managers, Professionals and Civil Servants.

May, R. (2000), *Guidelines 2000: Scientific Advice and Policy Making*, London: Office of Science and Technology, Department of Trade and Industry, July.

May, R., L. Donaldson and J. Krebs (2000), *Review of Risk Procedures used by the Government's Advisory Committees Dealing with Food Safety*, Department of Trade and Industry, July.

Mayer, S. (1994), *An Environmentalist's Perspective*, in R. Earll, *The Precautionary Principle: Making it Work in Practice*, workshop report, London: Environment Council.

Mayer, S. (2000), 'How safe is safe? Biotechnology and risk assessment', in R. Blatt (ed.), 'Biotechnology: the science and the impact', *Journal of Biolaw and Business*, Special Supplement, pp. 34-7.

McKenna, C. (1986), *The Economics of Uncertainty*, Brighton: Wheatsheaf-Harvester.

Medd, W. (2001), 'Complexity science and social policy', *Social Issues*, special issue, 1 (2).

Millstone, E., E. Brunner and I. White (1994), 'Plagiarism or protecting public health?', *Nature*, 371 (6499), 647-8.

Millstone, E., E. Brunner and S. Mayer (1999), 'Beyond substantial equivalence', *Nature*, 401, 525-6.

Millstone, E. and P. van Zwanenberg (2000), 'Food safety and consumer protection in a globalised economy', *Swiss Political Science Review*, 6 (3), 109-18.

Misztal, B. (1996), *Trust in Modern Societies*, Cambridge: Polity Press.

Morgan, M., M. Henrion and M. Small (1990), *Uncertainty: A Guide to Dealing with Uncertainty in Quantitative Risk and Policy Analysis*, Cambridge: Cambridge University Press.

Morris, J. (ed.) (2000), *Rethinking Risk and the Precautionary Principle*, London: Butterworth Heinemann.

Myers, S. (1984), 'Finance theory and financial strategy', *Interfaces*, 14.

Norgaard, R. (1989), 'The case for methodological pluralism', *Ecological Economics*, 1.

Nowotny, H., P. Scott and M. Gibbons (1995), *Re-thinking Science: Knowledge and the Public in an Age of Uncertainty*, London: Polity Press.

NRC (1983), National Research Council Committee on the Institutional Means for Assessment of Risks to Public Health, *Risk Assessment in the Federal Government: Managing the Process*, Washington: National Academies Press.

NRC (1989), National Research Council Committee on Risk Perception and Communication, *Improving Risk Communication*, Washington: National Academies Press.

NRC (1996), H. Fineberg, *Understanding Risk: Informing Decisions in a Democratic Society*, National Research Council Committee on Risk Characterisation, Washington: National Academies Press.

O'Brien, M. (2000), *Making Better Environmental Decisions: An Alternative to Risk Assessment*, Cambridge, MA: MIT Press.

O'Neill, J. (1993), *Ecology, Policy and Politics: Human Well-being and the Natural World*, London: Routledge.

O'Riordan, T. and J. Cameron (1994), *Interpreting the Precautionary Principle*, London: Earthscan.

O'Riordan, T., J. Cameron and A. Jordan (2001), *Reinterpreting the Precautionary Principle*, London: Cameron May.

OED (1989), J. Simpson and E. Weiner, *The Oxford English Dictionary*, 2nd edn, Oxford: Oxford University Press.

OST/Office of Science and Technology (2000), R. Barre, L. Esterle and V. Charlet, 'Science and Governance: The case of France', Observatoire des Sciences et des Techniques, Paris in S. Glynn, K. Flanagan, M. Keenan (eds), *Science and Governance: Describing and Typifying the Scientific Advice Structure in the Policy Making Process – a Multinational Study*, Seville: European Science and Technology Observatory.

Otway, H. and B. Wynne (1989), 'Risk communication: paradigm and paradox', *Risk Analysis*, 9 (2).

Pearce, D. and K. Turner (eds) (1990), *Economics of Natural Resources and the Environment*, New York: Harvester Wheatsheaf.

Perrow, C. (1984), *Normal Accidents: Living with High-risk Technologies*, New York: Basic Books.

Petts, J. (1995), 'Waste management strategy development: a case study of community involvement and consensus-building in Hampshire', in *Journal of Environmental Planning and Management*, 38, 519–36.

Phillips, 2000, The BSE Inquiry, *The Inquiry into BSE and Variant CJD in the United Kingdom*, London: HMSO.

Pidgeon, N., and J. Beattie (1998), 'The psychology of risk and uncertainty', in P. Calow (ed.), *Handbook of Environmental Risk Assessment and Management*, Oxford: Blackwell.

Pidgeon, N., C. Hook, D. Jones, B. Turner and R. Gibson (1992), 'Risk perception', in Royal Society Study Group, *Risk: Analysis, Perception, Management*, London: Royal Society.

Porter, T. (1995), *Trust in Numbers*, Princeton: Princeton University Press.

POST (2001), G. Kass, *Open Channels: Public Dialogue in Science and Technology*, Report No. 153, London: Parliamentary Office of Science and Technology.

Power, M. (1997), *The Audit Society: Rituals of Verification*, Oxford: Oxford University Press.

Raffensberger, C. and J. Tickner (eds) (1999), *Protecting Public Health and the Environment: Implementing the Precautionary Principle*, Washington: Island Press.

Ravetz, J. (1986), 'Usable knowledge, usable ignorance: incomplete science with policy implications', in W. Clarke and R. Munn, *Sustainable Development of the Biosphere*, Cambridge: Cambridge University Press.

Rayner, S. and R. Cantor (1987), 'How fair is safe enough? The cultural approach to societal technology choice', *Risk Analysis*, 7 (1), 3.

RCEP (1998), Royal Commission on Environmental Pollution, *Setting Environmental Standards*, Twenty-first Report, London: HMSO.

Renn, O., T. Webler and P. Wiedemann (1995), *Fairness and Competence in Citizen Participation: Evaluating Models for Environmental Discourse*, Dordrecht: Kluwer.

Rescher, N. (1993), *Pluralism: Against the Demand for Consensus*, Oxford: Clarendon Press.

Rip, A. (1992), 'Expert advice and pragmatic rationality', in N. Stehr and R. Ericson (eds), *The Culture and Power of Knowledge*, Berlin: De Gruyter, pp. 357-73.

Rip, A. (1995), 'Introduction of new technology: making use of recent insights from sociology and economics of technology,' *Technology Analysis & Strategic Management*, 7 (4), 417-31.

Rip A. (1999), 'Contributions from the social studies of science and constructive technology assessment', in A. Klinke, O. Renn, A. Rip, A. Salo and A. Stirling (eds), *On Science and Precaution in the Management of Technological Risk*, Volume II: Case studies, Seville: European Science and Technology Observatory, July 2000.

Rip, A. and R. Kemp (1998), 'Technological Change', in S. Rayner and E. Malone (eds), *Human Choice and Climate Change*, Columbus, Ohio: Battelle Press, Volume 2, Ch. 6, pp. 327-99.

Rip, A., T. Misa and J. Schot (1996), *Managing Technology in Society*, London: Pinter.

Roberts, F. (1979), *Measurement Theory: With Applications to Decision-making, Utility and the Social Sciences*, Boca Raton: Addison-Wesley.

Rosa, E. (1998), 'Meta-theoretical foundations for post-normal risk', *Journal of Risk Research*, 1 (1), 15-44.

Rosenberg, N. (1996), 'Uncertainty and technological change', in R. Landau, T. Taylor and G. Wright, *The Mosaic of Economic Growth*, Stanford: Stanford University Press.

Rowe, W. (1994), 'Understanding Uncertainty', *Risk Analysis*, 14 (5), 743-50.

Royal Society (1983), *Report of the Study Group on Risk Assessment*, London: Royal Society.

Royal Society (1992), *Risk: Analysis, Perception and Management*, report of a Royal Society study group, London: Royal Society.

Ruelle, D. (1991), *Chance and Chaos*, London: Penguin.

Saltelli, A. (2001), *Sensitivity Analysis for Importance Assessment*, EC Joint Research Centre, Ispra, available at: <http://www.ce.ncsu.edu/risk/pdf/saltelli.pdf>, December.

Sand, P. (2000), 'The precautionary principle: a European perspective', *Human and Ecological Risk Assessment*, 6 (3), 445-58.

Saviotti, P. (1986), 'Systems theory and technological change', *Futures*.

Schneider, S., B. Turner and H. Garriga (1998), 'Imaginable surprise in global change science', *Journal of Risk Research*, 1 (2), 165-86.

Schot, J. (2001), 'Towards new forms of participatory technology development', *Technology Analysis and Strategic Management*, 13 (1), 39-52.

Schot, J. and A. Rip (1997), 'The past and future of constructive technology assessment,' *Technological Forecasting and Social Change*, 54, 251-68.

Schwarz, M. and M. Thompson (1990), *Divided We Stand: Redefining Politics, Technology and Social Choice*, New York: Harvester Wheatsheaf.

Sclove, R. (1995), *Democracy and Technology*, New York: Guilford Press.

Seligman, A. (1997), *The Problem of Trust*, Princeton: Princeton University Press.

Sen, A. (1970), *Collective Choice and Social Welfare*, Amsterdam: North-Holland.

Shackle, G. (1968), *Uncertainty in Economics and other Reflections*, Cambridge: Cambridge University Press.

Shackley, S. and B. Wynne (1996), 'Representing uncertainty in global climate change science and policy: boundary-ordering devices and authority,' *Science, Technology & Human Values*, 21, 275-302.

Shrader-Frechette, K. (1990), 'Scientific method, anti-foundationalism and public decision-making' in *Health, Safety and Environment*, 1, 23-41.

Sjoberg, L. (1997), 'Explaining risk perception: an empirical evaluation of cultural theory', *Risk Decision and Policy*, 2, 113-30.

Slovic, P. (1997), *Trust, Emotion, Sex, Politics and Science: Surveying the Risk Battlefield*, Chicago: University of Chicago Legal Forum.

Smith, A. (2000), 'Policy networks and advocacy coalitions: explaining policy change and stability in UK industrial pollution policy', *Environment and Planning C*, 18, 95-114.

Smithson, M. (1989), *Ignorance and Uncertainty: Emerging Paradigms*, New York: Springer.

Spash, C. (2000), 'Ecosystems, contingent valuation and ethics: the case of wetland re-creation', *Ecological Economics*, 34 (2), 195-215.

Starr, C. (1969), 'Social benefit versus technological risk: what is our society willing to pay for safety?', *Science*, 165, 1232-38.

Stirling, A. (1994), 'Diversity and ignorance in electricity supply investment: addressing the solution rather than the problem', *Energy Policy*, 22, 3.

Stirling, A. (1997a), 'Limits to the value of external costs', *Energy Policy*, 25 (5), 517-40.

Stirling, A. (1997b), 'Multi-criteria mapping: mitigating the problems of environmental valuation?', chapter in J. Foster (ed.), *Valuing Nature: Economics, Ethics and Environment*, London: Routledge.

Stirling, A. (1998), 'Risk at a turning point?', *Journal of Risk Research*, 1 (2), 97-110.

Stirling, A. (1999), *On 'Science' and 'Precaution' in the Management of Technological Risk*, report EUR19056 EN, IPTS, Sevilla: *EU Forward Studies Unit*.

Stirling, A. and S. Mayer (1999), *Rethinking Risk: a Pilot Multi-criteria Mapping of a Genetically Modified Crop in Agricultural Systems in the UK*, Sussex: SPRU, University of Sussex.

Stirling, A. and S. Mayer (2000), 'Precautionary approaches to the appraisal of risk: a case study of a GM crop', *International Journal of Occupational and Environmental Health*, 6 (3), October-December.

Stirling, A. and P. van Zwanenberg (2001), *Background Report on the Implementation of Precaution in the European Union*, interim report to PRECAUPRI project, Sussex: SPRU, Sussex University, December.

Suter, G. (1990), 'Uncertainty in environmental risk assessment', in G. von Furstenberg, *Acting under Uncertainty*, Dordrecht: Kluwer.

Suter, G. (1993), *Ecological Risk Assessment*, Boca Raton: Lewis.

Szekely, G. (1986), *Paradoxes in Probability Theory and Mathematical Statistics*, Dordrecht: Reidel.

Thompson, M. and M. Warburton (1985), 'Decision making under contradictory certainties: how to save the Himalayas when you can't find what's wrong with them', *Journal of Applied Systems Analysis*, 12.

Thornton, J. (2000), *Pandora's Poison: On Chlorine, Health and a New Environmental Strategy*, Cambridge: MIT.

Tickner, J. (1998), *A Commonsense Framework for Operationalizing the Precautionary Principle*, paper presented to Wingspread Conference on Strategies for Implementing the Precautionary Principle, Lowell: University of Massachusetts.

Treasury, UK (1996), Interdepartmental Liaison Group on Risk Assessment, *Report on DOE Methodology for Setting Safety Standards*, ILGRA, London: HM Treasury, available at: http://www.hse.gov.uk/dst/ilgra/stands1.htm.

Tversky, A. and D. Kahneman (1974), 'Judgment under uncertainty: heuristics and biases', *Science*, 185.

UKCEED (1999), *Final Report of Consensus Conference on Radioactive Waste Management*, Cambridge: United Kingdom Centre for Economic and Environmental Development.

UNCED (1992), *Final Declaration of the UN Conference on Environment and Development*, Rio de Janeiro: United Nations.

USDA (2000), C. Woteki, *The Role of Precaution in Food Safety Decisions*, remarks prepared for Under Secretary for Food Safety, Food Safety and Inspection Service, Washington: US Department of Agriculture, March.

van den Berg, N., C. Dutilh and G. Huppes (1995), *Beginning LCA: A Guide to Environmental Life Cycle Assessment*, Rotterdam: CML.

van Zwanenberg, P. and E. Millstone (2001), *Mad Cow Disease - 1980s-2000: How Reassurances Undermined Precaution*, in D. Gee, P. Harremoes, J. Keys, M. MacGarvin, A. Stirling and B. Wynne, *Late Lesson from Early Warnings: The Precautionary Principle 1898-2000*, Copenhagen: European Environment Agency.

Vatn, A. and D. Bromley (1994), 'Choices without prices without apologies', *Journal of Environment Economics and Management*, 26.

von Hayek, F. (1978), *New Studies in Philosophy, Politics, Economics and the History of Ideas*, Chicago: Chicago University Press.

von Neumann, J. and O. Morgenstern (1947), *Theory of Games and Economic Behaviour*, Princeton, NJ: Princeton University Press.

von Schomberg, R. (1996), 'The laborious transition to a discursive policy process on the release of genetically modified organisms', in A. van Dommelen, *Coping with Deliberate Release: The Limits of Risk Assessment*, Tilbury: International Centre for Human and Public Affairs.

von Winterfeldt, D. and W. Edwards (1986), *Decision Analysis and Behavioural Research*, Cambridge: Cambridge University Press.

Wakeford, T. (2001), 'A Comparison of Deliberative Processes', *PLA Notes*, 40, IIED, London.

Walker, W. (2000), 'Entrapment in large technical systems: institutional commitment and power relations', *Research Policy*, 29 (7-8), 833-46.

Wallsten, T. (1986), *Measuring Vague Uncertainties and Understanding Their Use in Decision Making*, in D. von Winterfeldt and W. Edwards (1986), *Decision Analysis and Behavioural Research*, Cambridge: Cambridge University Press.

Watson, S. (1994), 'The meaning of probability in probabilistic safety analysis', *Reliability Engineering and System Safety*, 45, 261-9.

WBGU (2000), German Advisory Council on Global Change, *World in Transition: Strategies for Managing Global Environmental Risks*, Berlin: Springer.

Weatherford, R. (1982), *Philosophical Foundations of Probability Theory*, London: Routledge and Kegan Paul.

Weber, M. (1949), *The Methodology of the Social Sciences*, translated and edited by E. Shils and H. Finch, New York: The Free Press.

Williams, R. and D. Edge (1996), 'The social shaping of technology', *Research Policy*, 25, 865-99.

Winkler, G. (1986), *Necessity, Chance and Freedom*, in D. von Winterfeldt and W. Edwards, *Decision Analysis and Behavioural Research*, Cambridge: Cambridge University Press.

Winner, L. (1977), *Autonomous Technology: Techniques Out of Control as a Theme in Political Thought*, Cambridge, MA: MIT Press.

Wynne, B. (1975), 'The rhetoric of consensus politics: a critical review of technology assessment', *Research Policy*, 4.

Wynne, B. (1987), 'Risk perception, decision analysis and the public acceptance problem', in B. Wynne (ed.), *Risk Management and Hazardous Waste: Implementation and the Dialectics of Credibility*, Berlin: Springer.

Wynne, B. (1992), 'Uncertainty and environmental learning: reconceiving science and policy in the preventive paradigm', *Global Environmental Change*, 111-27.

Wynne, B. (1996), 'May the sheep safely graze?', in S. Lash, B. Szerszynski and B. Wynne (eds), *Risk, Environment and Modernity: Toward a New Ecology*, London: Sage, pp. 44-83.

Wynne, B. (1997), 'Methodology and institutions: value as seen from the risk field', in J. Foster (1997), *Valuing Nature*, London: Routledge.

Wynne, B. (2000), *Science and Governance Within the EU - New Challenges and New Visions from the Field of Environment, Precaution and Risk*, paper to seminar on 'Science and governance in the European Union', Brussels: Directorate General of the Joint Research Centres, March.

Yager, R. (1992), 'Decision making under Dempster-Shafer uncertainties', *International Journal of General Systems*, 20, 233-45.

Yearley, S. (1994), 'Social movements and environmental change', in M. Redclift, and T. Benton (eds), *Social Theory and the Global Environment*, London: Routledge.

Yearley, S. (2001), 'Mapping and interpreting societal responses to genetically modified crops and food', *Social Studies of Science*, 31 (1), 151-60.

Zadeh, L. and J. Kacprzyk (1992), *Fuzzy Logic for the Management of Uncertainty*, New York: Wiley.

3. Economics and sustainable development: what have we learnt, and what do we still need to learn?

Nick Hanley and Giles Atkinson

INTRODUCTION

In this chapter, we summarize the most important insights arising from a large body of work that has applied economic thinking to the slippery concept of sustainable development. This leads us to look not only at how sustainability is defined but also at how it can be measured, at its implications for policy-making and at how sustainable paths (or otherwise) can be modelled. Much of this literature has emerged in the last ten years, but we can identify many earlier efforts of relevance to the sustainability debate. This includes work on resource scarcity in the 1970s (for example, Solow, 1974; Hartwick, 1977); and much earlier thought on the environmental limits of economic activity in the nineteenth century (for example by Mill, Jevons, Ricardo). We also highlight, in the last section, what we consider to be the main unresolved questions within the sustainability debate, and how future research might address these.

DEFINITIONS AND INTERPRETATIONS OF SUSTAINABLE DEVELOPMENT

'Sustainable Development' (SD) has become a political buzzword. But what exactly does it mean? That is a difficult question to answer since SD means different things to different people: people place differing emphases on different aspects of the rather vague notion that is SD. The best-known definition is that given by the Brundtland Commission in 1987: 'development that meets the needs of present generations without compromising the ability of future generations to meet their own needs' (WCED, 1987). Another definition was offered by Asheim (1994): 'A requirement to our generation to manage the resource base such that the average quality of life we ensure ourselves can potentially be shared by all future generations'.

It is important to note that many see sustainable development as serving several goals: economic development, a better environment, a particular concern for the poor, a requirement for community participation in decision-making, and so on (Pearce and Atkinson, 1998). However, two common features of many definitions of SD are fairness and equity across generations and fairness and equity within generations. Most of the economics literature has in fact emphasized the former, focusing on equity over time. Economists would say that SD is indeed principally an equity, rather than efficiency, issue. However, the bigger the economic pie (broadly defined as total 'quality of life'), the more of it is there is to go around, and economic growth raises the average level of well-being. There is thus a potential complementarity between promoting both efficiency and equity. This view, however, is controversial: some would argue (for example, Meadows et al., 1992) that economic growth is in itself the cause of declining sustainability, since simplistic economic analysis does not recognize environmental constraints on the operation of the joint economic–environmental system. It is also possible to distinguish between the idea of sustainability, namely the property of any system whose performance can be maintained over time, and sustainable development, namely the extent to which development can be sustained. However, in general, the terms sustainable development and sustainability are used interchangeably.

Equity in itself may be thought of in two ways. First, in terms of outcomes, such as quality of life, income or consumption levels. Here, an equitable distribution of resources could be one which gives everyone the same income or well-being, for example. This might be termed an 'outcome approach'. Second, in terms of allowing all people, present and future, access to equal amounts or values of resources: this might be termed an 'opportunity approach'. Here, an equitable distribution of resources is one where each person has access to the same opportunities. Other contributions urge a very different emphasis, most notably those definitions of equity that focus upon procedural concerns such as the requirement for greater public participation in decision making (Toman, 1998). Furthermore, others have stressed that sustainable development has a strong intra-generational equity component. For example, the WCED (WCED, 1987) definition makes it clear that the emphasis on future generations is only part of the story: concern with the poor now is also important, indeed for them the highest priority.

Economists' views of what defines a sustainable development path for an economy over time may be divided into two broad groups along the same lines. The first (the outcome approach) is concerned with how the economic process affects human well-being directly. 'Well-being' is synonymous with the standard economic concept of utility welfare of an individual. Hence, sustainability can be defined as non-declining utility per capita over time

(Pezzey, 1989). However, whilst very useful as a theoretical concept, utility cannot easily be measured empirically. Thus, an alternative outcome-based approach is to define SD in terms of the observable determinants of utility. In other words, if we know what factors affect utility – for example, the level of consumption – then by examining changes in these factors we can infer whether a sustainable path is being followed according to Pezzey's definition.

In Figure 3.1, we show three time paths of consumption per capita for three hypothetical economies. We assume all paths are feasible. Path A is clearly unsustainable since consumption per capita falls after time t_1. Path B is sustainable, in that after an initial rise, consumption levels off. Path D is also sustainable, in that consumption rises continuously. An interesting question concerns democracy: would people today vote for path A over B or D? Would they prefer B to D if A were unavailable? If path A gets the biggest vote, then how do we justify trying to steer the economy towards an alternative? The usual responses to this last question involve either an appeal to the rights of future generations (Page, 1977) or to a model with the preferences of future generations counting in the present generations' preferences (Howarth and Norgaard, 1995).

We can also use these three simple paths to point out some weaknesses of the consumption-based measure. First, suppose that utility depends on environmental quality levels E as well as consumption, C. Then path D might

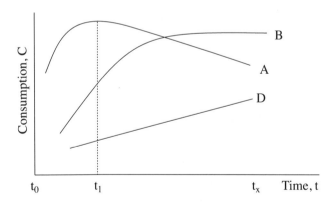

Note: In this simple economy, optimal consumption reaches a peak at t* and then starts to fall. Production starts to fall before this. Maximum sustainable consumption (the highest level of consumption that can be sustained in any period) is always less than optimal consumption. Having a sustainable level of consumption therefore requires us to reduce actual consumption to below its optimal level.

Source: For detailed explanation, see Pezzey, 1998.

Figure 3.1   Time paths of consumption per capita

involve falling utility after some time period if rising consumption implies falling environmental quality, the balance depending on the actual physical impacts of rising C on environmental quality, and the rate at which people are willing to trade off increases in C against reductions in E. Another criticism relates to the use of per-capita U or per-capita C as a measure of 'welfare'. Average consumption could be rising in the face of increasing income inequalities. If SD is about intra-generational equity as well as inter-generational equity, then neither B nor D may represent sustainable development. Finally, we may note that whilst development path A is sustained over the time period t_0 to t_1, it is not sustainable over the longer time scale to t_∞.

Despite the problems noted above, economists have found these outcome-based definitions to be very useful in theoretical work, allowing exploration of issues such as the implications of technological change, non-renewable resource scarcity and pollution (see, for example, Toman et al., 1995; Weitzman, 1997; and Aronsson et al., 1997). A further emergent, important issue concerns the possible conflicts between economic efficiency over time and sustainability. Economic efficiency over time is usually represented as an outcome which maximizes the present value (that is, discounted sum) of utility over an infinite time horizon, given technological constraints in the economy which 'produces' this utility. The basic results which emerge are (1) the economically efficient time path is probably not sustainable and (2) there are several alternative sustainable paths which we can choose between at different moments in time. However, it is worth remembering that many of the theoretical models these results are based on represent highly simplified economy–environment systems.

The second approach to an economic definition of SD is to consider the means that are available to society to generate well-being or consumption, namely its resources. Resources consist of physical stocks and the technology used to exploit them. Economists have considered SD from this viewpoint in terms of the concept of capital. Four forms of capital may be distinguished:

1. Produced capital, Km: this is the 'capital' that most economics students are familiar with. It comprises the results of past production, as the excess of output over consumption. Km includes factories, machinery, roads, bridges, telephone networks and satellites, and may be used up in the production of consumption goods and services. This depreciation needs to be offset with new investment or the stock of Km will decline over time.
2. Human capital, Kh: human capital is people, their skills and knowledge. The stock of Kh can also depreciate (for example, if unemployed people lose their skills), and can be added to through training and education.

3. Natural Capital, Kn: natural capital comprises all gifts of nature, and so includes renewable and non-renewable energy and material resources; clean air and water; nutrient and carbon cycles, and biodiversity. Natural capital can clearly be depreciated when, for example, a non-renewable resource such as oil is used up or when a species dies out. Investments in Kn would include forest re-planting and re-stocking of fisheries.

    An absolutely crucial aspect of the concept of Kn is how it is aggregated. Some authors have suggested an energy unit of account, but the most common *numeraire* is money. If money values could be given to all elements of Kn, then we could aggregate them into a total value. Several problems exist here, however: first, although market values exist for some elements of Kn, these may understate true social values; second, no market values exist for a vast range of types of Kn, so they would have to be estimated using environmental valuation, a colossal task; and third, a money value measure conflates how much of a physical stock exists with how valuable each unit is. Thus one blue whale which UK inhabitants were willing to pay £10 million to save has the same aggregate value as 10 000 blue whales worth £1000 each. If Kn cannot be aggregated in this way, then it would be necessary instead to aggregate groups of elements in physical terms: for example, all woodlands in a country; all stocks of a certain fish, or all rivers of a certain quality.

4. Social Capital, Ks: recent attention has been directed towards the link between 'social capital' and sustainability (see, for a discussion, World Bank, 1997). Putnam (1993) speaks of social capital as comprising certain features of social organization: norms of behaviour, networks of inter-actions between people and institutions, and trust between people. This could be important for sustainability in several ways. First, it is argued that there is an 'economic pay-off' from social capital whereby conditions favourable to economic growth are fostered by a climate of trust between agents (Knack and Keefer, 1997). Second, there could also be an 'environmental pay-off' whereby, for example, strong community ties help enforce ownership regimes and management systems for common property (Grafton, 2000). While the social capital debate is a valuable addition to understanding sustainable development, arguably its specific implications are less clear at present. We therefore omit social capital from further discussion in this chapter.

Weak and Strong Sustainability

Starting from these three types of capital, two different opportunity-based definitions of sustainability can be offered. The first, which has become known as 'weak sustainability', requires that the real value of the total capital stock K, where $\{K = Kn + Kh + Km\}$, be non-declining. This permits natural capital to be run down (through using up oil stocks, say) so long as human and produced capital is increased sufficiently. Maintaining constancy in the overall asset balance implies consuming merely the interest on this aggregate capital (Solow, 1986). This view clearly presumes that we can aggregate Kn, Kh and Km in the same units, and that they are substitutes for each other in terms of their capacity both to produce welfare and to maintain system functioning. The genuine savings and green net national product indicators of sustainability (discussed in the next section) both derive from this weak sustainability view of the world.

An alternative view has been to maintain that SD requires the stock of Kn itself to be prevented from declining. This view has been called 'strong sustainability', and derives primarily from the view that reductions in Kn cannot be substituted for by increases in Kh or Km (Norton and Toman, 1997). Support for the concept of strong sustainability is also based on a view that ecological systems are characterized by non-linearities and discontinuities, which mean that the welfare losses from declines in Kn, both present and future, are hard to predict (Pearce et al., 1996). In other words, environmental limits matter, and breaking these limits is not compatible with long-term system stability. Strong sustainability requires the physical protection of absolute levels of environmental goods. This position has also been characterized by a focus on 'critical' natural capital only. Critical natural capital is the sub-set of Kn which is either (1) essential for human survival and/or (2) not substitutable for by increases in either other elements of Kn, or in Kh or Km. An example might be the natural climate and atmospheric composition regulation functions of the earth. Sustainability, according to this view, is defined as no declines in this stock of critical natural capital.

Sustainable development thus has two economic meanings. In the outcome approach, it means that consumption or utilities do not decline over time. In the opportunity approach, it means we pass on to future generations at least as much capital as we have, so that they have no less a chance than us to be happy. Both meanings can be shown to relate, in fact, to the same underlying theoretical model of the economy–environment system, differing only in what aspect of the performance of that system is prioritized (Dasgupta, 1995). However, while maintenance of a constant K intact could be viewed as a necessary condition for sustainability, it is not a sufficient condition if it fails to guarantee some other aspect of what is understood by sustainable development (such as a more egalitarian income distribution). Something else has to happen.

Opposing Views

Not all economists, and certainly not all academics working in the field of sustainable development, would agree that the two interpretations of sustainability summarized in the previous section are useful. Criticism both within and beyond economics has centred on two issues. First, the substitutability between capital types which lies beneath the concept of weak sustainability is certainly a non-trivial assumption, which many have objected to (for example, Cabeza Gutés, 1996) on both theoretical grounds (Daly, 1990) and empirical ones. In theoretical terms, Pearce and Barbier have recently argued that for some elements of Kn, it is actually quite easy to think about such substitutions, for example, as technological innovation reduces resource requirements per capita, or emissions per unit output. Endogenous growth theory (Barbier, 1999) makes it more likely that such innovations will indeed reduce our 'draw down' on aspects of Kn, and make growth and sustainable development more compatible, assuming the development of appropriate policies and institutions. However, other aspects of Kn, such as biodiversity and ecological functioning, are less likely to be substituted for by changes in Kh or Km.

The second critique revolves around the aggregation of the natural capital stock. As noted above, an implicit assumption in the weak sustainability framework is that Kn can be aggregated somehow, ideally through monetary valuation. For example, Pearce and Barbier (2000) see valuation as very important to monitoring the extent to which depletion of natural capital is offset by investments in produced and human capital. Other economists, however, reject the practicality of aggregating in this way (for example, Bowers, 1997, p. 196), especially in the context of developing sustainability indicators (see next section). But there is also a much wider debate about the underlying philosophical basis to economic valuation, and about the way in which it proceeds in practice. We take this issue up again briefly on p. 102.

Finally, alternative views about what characterizes critical natural capital stock have been put forward. For example, Ekins (2000) argues that it is not possible to describe critical Kn in terms of different elements of this stock. The complexity of natural systems means that interactions are important in maintaining what we really need, which are ecosystem functions. These functions comprise source functions (for example, providing resources), sink functions, life support functions and 'human health and welfare' functions. Maintaining critical Kn implies maintaining this functioning at acceptable levels, according to three criteria: maintaining human health, avoiding threats and maintaining economic value. This translates in practice into rules such as keeping pollution emissions below damage thresholds (see below). Interestingly, Ekins makes the point that his approach to identifying critical Kn avoids the need to value it in monetary terms.

INDICATORS OF SUSTAINABLE DEVELOPMENT

The development of the economic understanding of what SD means has led to significant and parallel advances in its measurement. Indeed, such indicator work has often been at the forefront of the broader debate. Alerting decision makers to the underlying 'true' trends in the economy and to the ways in which their policies may affect those trends is a prerequisite to informing decision making that is not systematically biased towards environmental degradation and over-extraction of resources. Difficult challenges confront policy-makers who have publicly stated their commitment to sustainable development, and many governments have begun to respond to this responsibility by developing numerous indicators by which rhetoric can be judged against the reality of performance. However, because sustainable development is such an all-embracing concept, there has been a natural tendency for governments to define it to include all possible and desirable policy themes, making it more difficult to distinguish between relevant and irrelevant aspects of the debate. However, it is only by reference to a concept of sustainable development firmly grounded in theory that progress (or otherwise) can be properly evaluated. This mitigates against the use of ad hoc measures of sustainability, and in favour of those with an underlying theoretically consistent framework. Unfortunately, the ad hoc approach has characterized most 'official' responses to the measurement problem (for example, Department of Environment, 1996; DETR, 1999), whilst some academic writings on the subject also propose a multiplicity of indicators (Bell and Morse, 1999). Economics offers one basis for a theoretical grounding for SD indicators, and we focus on economic indicators here. However, as we indicate below, theoretical supports can also be drawn from other disciplinary perspectives.

We now discuss two measures put forward by economists: green national accounts, and genuine savings (see Atkinson et al., 1997). Both derive from one fundamental insight: that the asset boundary in conventional national accounts should be extended to include all forms of capital, including natural capital, in all its forms.

Green National Accounts

A large literature has recently emerged on whether the well-known macroeconomic measure Gross National Product (GNP) can be transformed to produce an indicator of SD (see Hanley, 2000, for a review). GNP has traditionally been thought of both as a welfare measure and as a measure of national income. By relating this to a particular concept of income put forward by Hicks in 1946, some authors have sought to transform GNP into an indicator of SD. Hicks's view was that income represented that portion of the value of output which could be consumed in any year without reducing one's wealth, defined as one's potential future consumption. This clearly has resonance with certain definitions of SD. In this sense, then, an adjusted or green national income aggregate would tell us the maximum level of consumption sustainable in any year, being one that leaves enough of a residual to be invested to preserve the national capital stock or national wealth. Since the standard definition of GNP can be thought of as the return on the nation's stock of produced (and human) capital, then green GNP could be thought of as the return on all forms of capital. If green net national income is rising, then an economy is, according to this literature, behaving sustainably.

Why is it necessary to adjust the conventional accounts? Because these accounts omit many of the inputs which the environment provides to the economy, since they are unpriced by the market. When a country depletes its natural capital, this is typically ignored in national accounts, even though depreciation of produced capital is allowed for (to convert from GNP to Net National Product, NNP: that is, NNP = GNP − δKm, where δKm is net depreciation of produced capital in the accounting period).

Calculating green NNP thus involves correcting for these omissions. Two approaches have been taken to calculate corrections. One, associated with Robert Repetto and the UN, involves a series of ad hoc deductions for depreciation in natural capital stocks, to allow for development impacts such as deforestation, ground water depletion and soil erosion (van Tongeren et al., 1993). The second includes the same effects, but tries to value them in a way consistent with economic theory. This latter approach draws heavily on a paper by Weitzman in 1976, and incorporates three distinct adjustments. First, for non-renewable resources, deduct from NNP an amount equal to the value of annual production multiplied by the difference between price and marginal costs. This difference is referred to as the Hotelling rent. Second, for renewable resources, annual production is first deducted from annual growth. This amount (the net change in the stock) is then valued using the same (price minus marginal cost) term. Lastly, for pollution, deduct an amount equal to the change in the stock of each pollutant multiplied by its marginal damage.[1]

We can say that this will give us a green NNP measure equal to:

$$\text{green NNP} = \text{NNP} - p(R-G) - v(E-A) \tag{1}$$

where: p = unit resource rental; R = resource extraction or harvest; G = growth rate of the resource (zero for non-renewables); v = marginal social damages from pollution; E = emissions; A = natural assimilation of pollutants. Hence, the terms $p(R-G)$ and $v(E-A)$ are respectively the value of depreciation of natural resources and the value of net pollution damage. In practice, one would have to aggregate over many different non-renewable and renewable resource types, and over many pollutants.

An example of the uses of green NNP is offered by the work of Hanley et al. (1999) on the sustainability of the Scottish economy during 1980–93. Estimates of environmental depreciation were made for oil and gas, minerals, forests, commercial fish stocks and some forms of pollution. These were then valued using prices minus average cost, and deducted from conventional NNP. The resulting estimate of green NNP was found to rise over the period in question, again indicating a sustainable path (Figure 3.2).[2] Oil price changes had relatively large impacts on the environmental adjustments made. Problems with the results include the use of average rather than marginal costs, and an incomplete set of environmental accounts.

How good a measure of sustainability is green NNP? Several weaknesses may be noted. First, economists disagree over how exactly adjustments to the conventional accounts should be made (for example, how to treat new discoveries; and how to value environmental liabilities). It is also true that, for the adjustments to be correct, the price and marginal cost values used should be those which result from a competitive, dynamically optimal use of resources. However, the well-known problem of the absence of clearly defined property rights means this is unlikely to be true. Second, economists dispute whether green NNP can be used, even in principle, as a sustainability

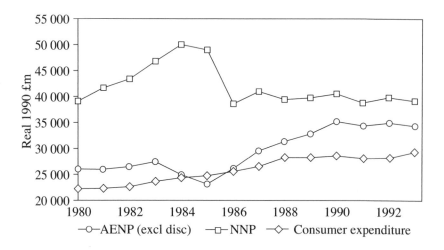

Source: Based on Hanley et al. (1999).

Figure 3.2 Green net national product (AENP, excluding discoveries), net national product and consumer expenditure for Scotland, 1980–1993

indicator. For example, for the original Weitzman (1976) result to hold, some very restrictive conditions must be met. Dasgupta, Kriström and Mäler (1996) suggest in a less restrictive model that if a correctly evaluated green NNP is rising, then the country's long-term welfare is also increasing. Asheim (1994), in contrast, shows that unless the adjustments to conventional GNP are made using the prices that would hold along a sustainable (as distinct from an efficient) path, then green NNP tells us nothing about sustainability. Third, green NNP measures only potential sustainable income: it does not address the question of whether actual savings will be high enough to maintain this income indefinitely.

Other problems exist with green NNP as a sustainability indicator. For instance, if we are unsure about future environmental impacts of current activities, then increasing green NNP does not ensure non-declining wealth. Finally, green NNP does not address the issue of intra-generational equity, which many would see as an important aspect of SD. For all these reasons, green NNP is now predominantly viewed as a better welfare measure than was available before, but not a particularly good indicator of SD. Attention has shifted instead to the related concept of genuine savings.

Genuine Savings

An alternative economic indicator of SD is the genuine savings concept, put forward originally by Pearce and Atkinson (1993) and Hamilton et al. (1994, 1996). Genuine savings (GS) compares saving in an economy with depreciation of both natural and produced capital. It is defined as:

$$GS = S - \delta K_m - p(R{-}G) - v(E{-}A) \qquad (2)$$

Gross investment could be used instead of gross savings, S. We could also include changes in the stock of human capital, Kh, in equation (2). The genuine savings measure tests for weak sustainability: that is, it assumes that natural capital and produced capital are perfect substitutes for each other. It is thus an empirical test for whether a country is, on average, following the Hartwick rule (see p. 93). If GS is negative, then this is a clear indication of unsustainable behaviour. Investments in the aggregate capital stock must be increased, and consumption reduced. This increased investment would include investments in pollution treatment, fisheries and forest stocks, and searching for new, economically viable non-renewable resource deposits. It could equally comprise increased investments in hospitals, schools and railways.

The GS indicator has recently been extended to allow for international trade effects (Vincent et al., 1997, Proops et al., 1999). Genuine savings and green

NNP are closely linked since they are both derived from the same underlying theory. It is possible to show formally that they are equivalent tests of sustainability: if GS is positive over time, then green NNP cannot be falling. Empirically, however, the two measures may well give different signals, due to measurement errors, international capital flows, and the economy behaving non-optimally over time.

Hamilton and Atkinson (1996) estimate genuine savings for the United Kingdom for the period 1980 to 1990. The UK genuine savings rate over this period is illustrated in Figure 3.3, plotted alongside estimates using other definitions of the UK savings ratios, beginning with gross savings. Shown as a proportion of GDP, these display the successive deductions from gross saving proposed above, with 'Res. net saving' indicating traditional net saving less the value of resource depletion. On this measure the UK appears persistently to have under-saved during much of the 1980s. In the period 1980 to 1986 genuine savings rates were between –1.6% and –3.1% of GDP. This is a striking result: by simply redefining a nation's savings rates to be net of the depletion of non-renewable resources and the value of air pollution, it is shown that inadequate provision to offset asset loss was made during the 1980s in the UK. The measure of genuine saving also indicates that the UK stopped dis-saving towards the end of the decade. Some of this increase is attributable to a reduction in the value of resource depletion, which in turn is largely due to the reduction in world oil prices after 1986. Paradoxically, this

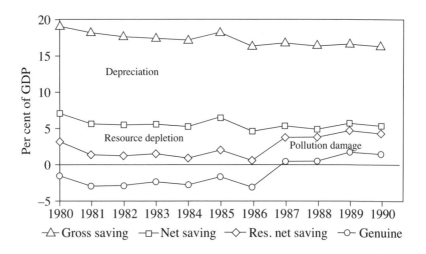

Source: Hamilton and Atkinson (1996).

Figure 3.3 Genuine savings in the United Kingdom, 1980–1990

conveys the impression that, other things being equal, a decrease in the price of oil raises genuine saving. Offsetting this is the fact that the remaining oil reserves are now a less valuable form of wealth, which could conceivably result in a lower level of future welfare. It can be shown that the capitalized value of these increased savings exactly equals the decrease in resource wealth associated with the fall in resource price.

Results from the Hanley et al. (1999) study for GS of Scotland are given in Figure 3.4. The Scottish economy can be seen to have been behaving unsustainably for much of the 1980s since GS was negative, mirroring the UK-wide findings. However, the discrepancy between depreciation of capital stocks and saving starts to decrease towards the end of the period.

Some examples of the application of the GS concept to sustainability in the developing world are illustrated in Table 3.1 (see World Bank, 1997). In these estimates, genuine savings are defined as gross savings net of the depreciation of produced capital and resource depletion (that is, no allowance has been made for environmental damage). Nevertheless, the results indicate that, on average over the period 1980–1994, GS was negative for all featured countries except Argentina, Brazil and Colombia. It is reasonable to speculate that this reflects failure adequately to re-invest the proceeds of resource depletion in alternative assets. Put another way, several Latin American and Caribbean countries appear, on balance, to have been liquidating their assets. Understanding the reasons for this persistent dis-saving, designing policy

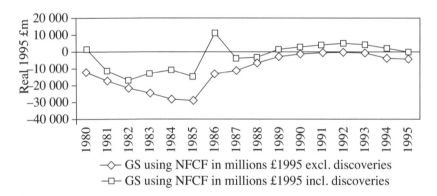

—◇— GS using NFCF in millions £1995 excl. discoveries
—□— GS using NFCF in millions £1995 incl. discoveries

Notes:
NFCF is 'Net Fixed Capital Formation', one measure of investment in man-made capital for an economy.
GS is 'Genuine Savings'.

Source: Based on Hanley et al. (1999).

Figure 3.4   Genuine savings in Scotland

Table 3.1　Genuine savings in selected Latin American and Caribbean economies, 1980-1994

Country	Average genuine savings rate (% of GDP)
Argentina	2
Bolivia	−30
Brazil	6
Chile	−3
Colombia	2
Ecuador	−14
Guatemala	−2
Haiti	−7
Jamaica	−12
Mexico	−3
Peru	−1
Trinidad and Tobago	−23
Venezuela	−24

Source:　World Bank (1997).

responses to manage an economy's portfolio of assets more carefully in the future, are integral to making good commitments to the goal of sustainable development.

How good is GS as a sustainability measure? Two criticisms may be noted. First, GS is a measure of weak sustainability only. If sufficient substitution possibilities do not exist between the different types of capital, then a positive GS will not guarantee non-declining welfare over time. Second, Asheim (1994) and Common and Perrings (1992) both argue that market prices cannot be used to calculate correctly the depreciation term for Kn, although for different reasons: for Asheim, the reason is that prices need to be sustainability prices. For Common and Perrings, the reason is that an additional condition must be imposed on the economy–environment system, which safeguards total system resilience. Taking all these views together, the best conclusion is that GS is a one-sided indicator of sustainability in that negative savings signal non-sustainability and must be corrected. However, a positive GS rate at a given point in time is not sufficient to guarantee that the economy is on a sustainable path and further evidence must be sought before any firm judgement can be made.

Whilst much debate exists on whether either of these economic indicators is a robust measure, recent theoretical progress is improving the prospects for versions of these indicators to provide more useful information, both in terms of levels of well-being, and in terms of sustainability (Pezzey and Toman, 2002).

Other Sustainability Indicators

Other notable contributions to the sustainability indicator debates include 'distance to goal' approaches in which, for example, deviations of ambient concentrations from sustainability 'targets' are aggregated to derive an overall performance indicator (Hammond et al., 1995). The green national accounting counterpart of this is offered by Hueting et al. (1992) and is couched in terms of the costs of reaching these goals. Ekins and Simon (1999) have recently built upon this approach in proposing an analogous indicator: the sustainability gap. The focus here is on the distance between the current level of impact on a natural asset and a sustainability standard, whether in physical or monetary terms.

As mentioned above, indicators of sustainable development have been developed by many other disciplines than economics. Insights from ecology have led to measures such as the net primary productivity–consumption ratio (sometimes referred to as appropriated carrying capacity), the Amoeba indicator system (Ten Brink et al., 1991), ecological footprints (Rees and Wackernagel, 1994), and measures of system resilience (Ives, 1995). Socio-political indicators also exist, notably the Index of Sustainable Economic Welfare and the Genuine Progress Indicator, whilst Bell and Morse (1999) outline community-based indicators. For details and examples of all of these, see Moffat et al. (2001). Focusing on a traditional indicator of economic development, Atkinson et al. (1997) and Neumayer (2001) have also proposed a way of turning the UNDP Human Development Index into a sustainability measure. Finally, we note that all the indicators described here are typically intended to be calculated at the national level. There is also a growing literature on sustainability indicators at the regional, industry and individual firm level (see, for example, Atkinson, 2000).

POLICY-MAKING AND SUSTAINABILITY

In thinking about policy-making for sustainable development, an important prior question is whether the free market, left to its own devices, will produce a sustainable outcome. There are three reasons why this is unlikely to be the case. First, and most importantly, there is a big difference between sustainable development and economic efficiency. As noted earlier, an economically optimal time path for an economy is almost certainly not sustainable, in the sense that consumption (or utility) eventually declines. This will be the case so long as the impact of discounting future welfare outweighs the rate of technological progress (Toman et al., 1995; Pezzey and Withagen, 1998). Yet a major claim for the operation of free markets is precisely that, under certain very restrictive conditions, an optimal growth path will result.

Second, we know that many environmental resources have economic values, which are very different to the market price (if any) which they command, due to market failure. This means that economies are likely to over-use environmental assets (run them down too fast) from the viewpoint of economic efficiency. If this is so, then it seems very unlikely that the resultant pattern of resource use will be environmentally sustainable (Common and Perrings, 1992). Third, sustainable development is also concerned with fairness in the allocation of resources between members of the current generation: very few economists have ever claimed that a free market outcome is a fair outcome.

It therefore seems likely from an economics viewpoint that governments will have to intervene to steer economies onto sustainable courses. But how can this be done? And what are the special characteristics of sustainable development policy? Extending insights from economics, it may be argued that policy towards SD has three main defining features:

1. Concern for future well-being. Sustainable development policy may force us either to think further into the future than we are used to thinking, or to review how we handle future costs and benefits. Relevant questions include how far into the future we need to count welfare impacts; the implications of technological change for future welfare, and the use of discounting as part of a number of policy appraisal techniques such as cost-benefit analysis. We also need to be clear what we are trying to achieve for future generations, whether it be in terms of future opportunities, future welfare levels, or safeguarded rights.
2. Concern with environment–economy linkages. This has long been a feature of environmental economic analysis: the new feature from an SD point of view is to include a wider grasp of the social impacts of policy in the analysis.
3. Focusing on the sound management of all assets in the system: social, economic and environmental. This raises questions concerning minimum acceptable levels of assets and substitutability between assets, which were discussed on p. 83.

Finally, what types of policy might help us achieve a more sustainable development path? Economists have thought about this question in terms of alternative 'sustainability rules'.

Four possibilities have been suggested:

1. Value all environmental goods and services at their correct prices
2. The 'Hartwick rule'
3. Rules set in terms of natural capital itself
4. Maintaining system resilience

We now consider each of these in turn.

1. Value all Environmental Goods and Services at their Correct Prices

As already noted, one reason why environmental resources are over-used is because correct prices are not attached to their use. For example, a factory pays no price to use the air as a waste disposal facility, and thus has an insufficient incentive to reduce pollution. A popular perception is that one of the main barriers to attaining SD is that too great a burden is placed on the world's ecosystems by economic activity (too much pollution, too much forest clearance and so on). Placing correct prices on the environment through eco-taxes, for example, might be thought to move us closer to SD, since the environment would then be less exploited. However, whilst such a policy might encourage more efficient use of and lesser burdens on the environment, and increase the size of the economic pie, it would not necessarily address the inter-temporal fairness aspects of SD (Howarth and Norgaard, 1995). As already noted, an economically efficient use of resources is not the same as a sustainable use of resources.

2. The Hartwick Rule

The Hartwick rule underpins the idea of weak sustainability and precedes it historically. Hartwick (1977, 1978) showed that an economy dependent on a non-renewable resource as one input to production could have constant (that is non-declining) consumption levels over time provided that it followed a simple rule: re-invest all rents from exploiting that resource in produced capital. If we adopt a broader notion of capital, then the rents could equally well be invested in human capital, or in other types of natural capital. This result has been extended to consider the role of renewable resources and changes in environmental liabilities (Hartwick, 1978; Mäler, 1991; Hamilton, 1996). It is by following an extended Hartwick rule that the basic requirement for weak sustainability, that the change in the (real) value of assets should be non-negative in aggregate, is fulfilled. This, in turn, ensures that under certain assumptions the definition of sustainability in terms of non-declining per capita utility or well-being is satisfied.

The primary problem with this rule is that it only works if the various forms of capital are adequate substitutes for each other. Some, however, have argued that there are critical natural assets, crucial for human welfare, that have no substitutes and therefore cannot be traded off for other forms of wealth (Pearce et al., 1990).

3. Rules Based on the Natural Capital Stock

The 'strong sustainability' view is that SD requires a non-declining stock of natural capital, however defined. It is clear that this could be a very restrictive rule. If, for example, no trade-offs are allowed between different components of Kn (wetlands, forestland and so on) then no economic action which depleted the stock of any component could be allowed, no matter how large the economic benefits. A way around these potentially high foregone benefits lies in the idea of shadow projects (Pearce et al., 1990; Hanley and Spash, 1993). This requires any action that reduces the stock of, say, wetlands, to be offset by a physical project which generates a replacement (by creating a new wetland). Costing in such a replacement would be an essential part of cost-benefit analysis. However, considerable practical and theoretical difficulties exist. For example, if a 1000-year-old oak forest is threatened with destruction, does a newly planted oak forest of equivalent size provide an acceptable offset? What if the new wood is planted on an area of heathland? Now the area of heathland has fallen, so an offset must be created for this. Finally, for many environmental effects, no physical substitute exists (for example, if a unique national park is threatened). Does this imply that no development should be allowed which threatens such unique assets?

One answer to this question is provided by the concept of the Safe Minimum Standard or SMS (Randall and Farmer, 1995). The SMS is a means of assessing a proposed change which threatens wildlife or habitats. It involves first identifying the minimum viable population or habitat size for a population, or minimum required stock of some other natural asset. Management alternatives for safeguarding this minimum are then identified, and cost estimates made of these actions. If a proposed development threatens the SMS, then decision-makers are presumed to rule against it, unless the social opportunity costs of so doing are judged to be 'too high'. For example, Berrens et al. (1998) describe the means by which an SMS for endangered fish populations in the Colorado River is identified, and estimate the costs of the management actions needed to defend these SMSs.

Imposing an SMS is considered by some to be an appropriate response when irreversibility, and uncertainty about environmental damages, are high. Farmer and Randall (1998) suggest that the SMS places certain areas of natural resource exploitation 'off-limits' to cost-benefit analysis calculations of how to manage them. In doing so, the SMS, they claim, 'structurally embeds respect for three moral heuristics' that most would agree to. These are: (1) the existence of future humans is valued; (2) the welfare of future humans is valued; and (3) moral agents have intra-generational obligations to each other.

However, the most obvious problem with the SMS principle is the difficulty of identifying how society should decide the 'tolerable level of sacrifice', or whether the cost of defending the SMS is 'too high', given that people's views of what constitutes an acceptable cost depends on their value systems. Argument can thus be expected. Other problems with the SMS include extending the concept to elements of Kn other than wildlife populations and their habitats and to natural resource stocks; and the difficulty in identifying safe minimum population/habitat sizes/resource stocks (which might well change over time).[3]

4. Maintaining System Resilience

Resilience is a concept taken from systems ecology, which has recently been promoted as a useful way of thinking about sustainability (Levin et al., 1998; Ludwig et al., 1997). As explained by Holling (1973), resilience refers to the ability of major ecosystem processes to remain functional in the presence of exogenous shocks. Ecosystem variables may well undergo large changes as a result of such shocks, but the overall functioning of the system is maintained within bounds. This view of ecosystem functioning contrasts with the view that systems are characterized by steady-state conditions. As economic growth increases our demands on ecosystems via resource depletion and rising emissions, so society becomes more sensitive to external shocks as the environmental system becomes more sensitive (Arrow et al., 1995). Boosting resilience is equivalent to reducing this sensitivity. This is important since the nature of the dynamics of the economy–environment system (non-linear, adaptive and far-from-equilibrium) means that the system can suddenly lurch from one state to another, radically different state (Holling et al., 1995). Whilst such changes do not have to be undesirable, in an environmental context they have often proved to be so (for example, the collapse of certain ocean fisheries).

Levin et al. (1998) argue that, in general, resilience is a desirable property. Maintaining resilience might be viewed as an SD strategy since it maintains system functioning over time. But how can this be done? Resilience is determined by flexibility and the ability to change adaptively. Flexibility can come from many sources. One important source is argued to be biodiversity, so that maintaining biodiversity helps maintain resilience, and diversity itself becomes a measure of resilience. However, maintenance of diversity is not sufficient according to Levin et al. Resilience also depends on 'the coupling of stimulus and response in terms of space, time and organizational scales'. Combined with the idea of flexibility, this means that promoting free market competition and effective government intervention when markets fail is vital. Effective intervention might include making more use of near-market mechanisms such as pollution taxes and tradable pollution permits to regulate pollution, or tradable catch quotas to regulate fisheries.

As Common and Perrings (1992) note, most economic models of sustainable development omit to include any concept of resilience within their structure: the concept still seems to lie mainly in the domain of systems ecologists, rather than environmental economists. However, work in this direction has been undertaken by some: for example, Perrings and Pearce (1994) look at optimal penalties for actions which damage ecosystems when these systems are subject to threshold effects, and where there is uncertainty over these thresholds. This very much relates to the recent thinking about the Safe Minimum Standards concept, as described above.[4]

MODELLING SUSTAINABLE DEVELOPMENT

In designing policies to improve the sustainability of the economy–environment system in a country, it would be useful to be able to predict their impacts on indicators of SD. This could assist governments or other organizations to judge the expected relative success of policy alternatives, as well as to predict the impact of other policies, or of exogenous shocks (such as rising energy prices) on sustainability. Predictions are made using models of varying degrees of sophistication. In this section, we review some alternative economic approaches to modelling impacts, and provide some recent examples of their use.

Much economic analysis is taken up with model construction and estimation. A model is a simplification of a real system, typically written in mathematical form, which allows the user to see the predicted impacts on a number of defined variables (such as pollution emissions) of a number of policy actions (such as a rise in energy taxes). Models operate at varying scales, both spatial (national, local, catchment-based, field-based) and temporal (static models, dynamic models, medium term versus long term). Models also vary in terms of their underlying theoretical framework. Economic models relevant to sustainable development policy include three approaches described here: econometric, computable general equilibrium, and input–output. In almost all cases, implications for sustainable development are implicit, and are in terms of predicted changes in pollution, output, and in some cases in the distribution of income.

Econometric Models

Econometric models rely on systems of equations, whose parameters have been estimated from observed data. For example, production of carbon emissions in an economy could be estimated as depending on fossil fuel consumption and level of technology. Fossil fuel consumption could in turn depend on energy prices and incomes in the economy. Econometric models are frequently used in a predictive sense, in that variables in any of the model equations can be changed, and the estimated impacts on variables of interest observed. For example, in the above case, the impact of a rise in energy prices on emissions could be studied. Econometric models have been very widely used to study the links between economic activity and the environment (for example, work by Barker et al., 1995 on carbon emissions in the UK), and between environmental conditions and the economy (for example, Barbier and Strand's 1998 model which relates wetland area to fisheries production). They suffer from two main problems: first, predictions depend on the estimation method adopted and choice of functional form. Second, predictions outside of the range of observed data are often viewed with some suspicion. For instance, the effect of changes in climate on agricultural productivity would be difficult to predict outside the range of observed variations in climate.

Computable General Equilibrium (CGE) Models

In one sense, CGE models are a sub-set of econometric models. A CGE model's structure represents the structure of the economy, in terms of production, consumption, savings and investment. The relationships between these sectors are specified in such a way that: (1) there is some vector of prices at which all markets clear; and (2) the behaviour of firms and households in the model is consistent with profit and utility maximization respectively. Computable General Equilibrium modelling begins with a general representation of the linkages within the economy consistent with (1) and (2). This yields a set of equations with parameters to be specified (such as demand elasticities). Values for these parameters may be taken from the literature or else estimated econometrically. Parameter values are varied until the model can be sufficiently well calibrated against observed outcomes (for output, consumption, incomes and so on). Links to the environment are often in the form of production functions for pollution emissions. Policy simulations can then be undertaken by changing any of the prices in the model (for example, through a carbon tax) or by changing technological relationships. If more than one income group is specified in the household sector of the model, then impacts on income distribution can be predicted.

Computable General Equilibrium models have been used fairly intensively

to study the economic implications of environmental policy. Two examples
are Beauséjour et al. (1995) and Conrad (1999) on the impacts of carbon taxes.
Nevertheless, three main problems may be noted. First, one may object to the
underlying theoretical assumption of perfect market clearing: in one sense,
CGE results may be best seen as very long run outcomes when all adjustments
in the system to some initial change in prices or technology have taken place.
Second, results are often very sensitive to the parameterization process. Third,
many CGE models present the economy in a highly aggregated way, which
reduces the detail in which predictions can be made. Finally, the environment
appears in a very limited way, most usually as an emissions sink.

Input–Output (I/O) Models

Input–output modelling has been around for a long time, ever since Wassily
Leontief published the first such model of the US economy in 1936. Since then
I/O models have been used in numerous instances to represent the complex
flow of goods, money, energy, water and pollution through an economic
system. Such studies are frequently capable of handling 100 or more sectors
or industries over numerous geographical regions (for example, Hafkamp,
1991).

Input–output models incorporating pollution generation and pollution
abatement sectors were widely used in the late 1970s and early 1980s (see, for
example, Førsund, 1985). On the whole, environmental I/O models have been
used to study changes in the level and composition of final demand,
requirements for emission reductions, technological changes, and energy
conservation. Other issues studied include changes in the spatial location
of discharges and regional impacts of non-uniformly mixed pollutants, while
Proops et al. (1999) use I/O to analyse trade in resources between countries.

Moffatt et al. (2001) use an environmental–economic I/O model to
investigate the effects on emissions of twelve pollutants of changes in
industrial structure and transport policy for Scotland. Their model uses a 28
sector representation of economic activity, which is linked to emissions and
abatement of CO_2, SO_2, NO_x, black smoke, VOCs, methane, CO, waste, lead,
and radioactive waste to air, land and water. An illustration of the model's
output is given in Table 3.2 below, for a policy initiative which produces a
switch from road to rail transport of the value of £100 million per annum. As
may be seen, the biggest impacts on emissions are for CO, lead and black
smoke. Some small 'knock-on' effects on other industrial sectors (such as
electricity production) are also produced; this will have indirect effects on
emissions, which are handled by the model.

A major limitation of I/O models is the assumption of linearity. Each
industrial sector must be able to expand or contract output to any level whilst

maintaining the same linear relationship between inputs and outputs. Furthermore, I/O models typically have zero elasticity of substitution in production, as input–output coefficients are fixed: substitution between inputs as relative price changes cannot thus be studied. Further, infinite factor supplies can be drawn on with no impact on these coefficients, unless a mathematical programming (constrained optimization) route is taken (again, see Moffatt et al. (2001) for an example). Finally, it is possible to make I/O models dynamic, but this raises the thorny problem of specifying changes in the technical coefficients. Despite these problems, I/O models provide a disaggregated, internally consistent representation of a complex economy seen as an interdependent productive system, which can be useful for modelling the impacts of changes in economic structure and activity on the environment.

In summary, economists have developed many ways of modelling the relationship between economic activity and the environment, which may be useful in looking at the implications for sustainability of different policy actions. Using certain forms of model (for example, CGE), impacts on the current distribution of income (that is, equity) can also be studied. One important aspect of these modelling efforts is their potential for aiding the design of a range of environmental and resource policies or the monitoring of the environmental impacts of economic policy (Atkinson et al., 1997). However, policy advice can be confused if different models give different results when applied to the same problem (see Weyant and Hill, 1999 for a very good illustration of this point). Finally, the linking of such models to indicators of SD is an exercise still in its infancy in economics, but one that seems important for the future.

VALUES AND SUSTAINABILITY: (WORLD) VIEWS APART?

In the late 1980s, a 'new' approach to environmental economics was launched on the world: this was ecological economics, which in the late 1980s acquired two of the necessary conditions for being a recognized school of thought, namely a learned society and a journal, *Ecological Economics*. Ecological economics is often held up as an alternative to what is referred to as Environmental and Natural Resource Economics (ENRE), which had developed out of the standard neo-classical school. Whether the two approaches are really so different is a matter of debate. *Ecological Economics* (EE) claimed that 'it is a new approach to economics and ecology that recognizes the need to make economics more cognisant of ecological impacts and dependencies ... and ecology more sensitive to economic forces, incentives and constraints' (Costanza, 1989). Hanley et al. (2001) doubt that

Table 3.2 Predicted changes in outputs and emissions due to a change in transport policy

	Sector	OUTPUT			
		Current demand £m	Change in demand £m	Change in output X £m	% change
1	Agriculture	292.3	0.00	-0.04	0.00
2	Forestry	53.4	0.00	0.01	0.01
3	Fishing	172.7	0.00	-0.01	0.00
4	Coal	38.3	0.00	0.17	0.09
5	Oil/gas	696.3	0.00	0.47	0.04
6	Oil refining	1486.0	0.00	3.01	0.13
7	Electric	746.2	0.00	5.19	0.37
8	Gas supply	383.2	0.00	0.06	0.01
9	Water supply	88.6	0.00	0.19	0.11
10	Metal manufacture	742.7	0.00	1.65	0.13
11	Mineral extraction & processing	405.6	0.00	0.63	0.07
12	Chemical & fibre manufacture	1454.5	0.00	0.18	0.01
13	Metal goods	415.1	0.00	0.74	0.10
14	Instrument engineering	6693.0	0.00	1.26	0.02
15	Transport equipment	1392.6	0.00	0.44	0.03
16	Food, drink and tobacco	5094.3	0.00	-0.07	0.00
17	Textiles	1498.3	0.00	0.38	0.02
18	Paper & publishing	1208.3	0.00	-0.48	-0.02
19	Other manufacturing	923.0	0.00	0.35	0.02
20	Construction	2767.3	0.00	-0.25	-0.01

21	Distribution	6630.3	0.00	-3.24	-0.04
22	Railways	160.3	100.00	99.82	37.51
23	Road	685.5	-100.00	-100.11	-7.48
24	Sea	378.4	0.00	0.03	0.01
25	Air	503.2	0.00	-0.09	-0.01
26	Finance & business	3134.7	0.00	-11.59	-0.18
27	Other services	910.5	0.00	-1.52	-0.11
28	Public & admin. services	9710.4	0.00	-0.02	0.00

IMPACTS ON POLLUTION

Pollutant	Change in pollution (000 tonnes)	Total pollution	% change
CO_2 (C weight)	-77.5	11 663.7	-0.66
SO_2	0.9	360.1	0.24
Black smoke	-0.8	18.3	-4.39
NO_x	-4.9	224.8	-2.17
VOC	-3.9	179.3	-2.19
CO	-25.8	368.3	-7.01
Methane	0.0	419.3	0.00
Waste	21.1	36 920.0	0.06
Lead	0.0	0.1	-7.48
RA (air)	0.0	5.1	0.37
RA (water)	0.0	0.3	0.37
RA (solid)	0.3	233.3	0.14

Source: Moffatt et al., 2001.

the methods are really so different, merely stressing different aspects of the same problems (with EE stressing environmental limits, and ENRE stressing human adaptation and response).

Ecological Economics claimed to be new in being truly interdisciplinary, but all good economics for the environment is interdisciplinary. We even find that the same people who were responsible for founding ENRE as a modern discipline were also highly influential in founding EE (see Crocker, 1999). One defining characteristic might be that ecological economists would be more likely to be sympathetic to the idea of strong sustainability, and more likely to object to the concept of weak sustainability and the economic indicators based on it. However, even this distinction is questionable in that by no means all proponents of ENRE would characterize the real world according to the weak sustainability view. Thus, it might be argued that a meticulous search for distinctions between EE and ENRE is not all that helpful or productive.

One area where the two schools have claimed to be different is in valuing the environment. Valuation is important to the sustainability debate in that it allows us to measure changes in natural capital in units that can be aggregated with other changes (typically, in money units). EE has stressed methods and approaches based on ecosystem function values, rather than relying on values stated or revealed by people, for instance, in the contingent valuation method. Even here, though, it is interesting to note a substantial cross-over, both in terms of who is doing the work (see, for instance, Barbier and Strand, 1998) and in that ecosystem function values are also typically related back to changes in utility, as are stated and revealed preference methods. However, EE has also given a stronger platform to qualitative valuation approaches, which stress the personal, in contrast to the optimizing/econometric route favoured by others who would be described as 'conventional economists'. Nevertheless, it is also worth noting that the most ambitious attempt to measure the economic value of ecosystems at the global level has come from proponents of the EE school (Costanza et al. 1997). Moreover, some of the most vociferous criticisms of this valuation of the totality of ecosystem functions came from those at the forefront of the environmental application of stated and revealed preference methods (see, for a discussion, Pearce, 1998).

The valuation literature has seen a wide apparent polarization of approaches: examples of two ends of the spectrum in the UK are Foster et al. (1997), on the qualitative/personal side and Bateman and Willis (1999) on the optimized/econometric side. Yet even in Bateman and Willis's work we find perspectives on alternative views. Recently there has also been a combining of participatory and deliberative techniques adapted from the qualitative approach with quantitative methods, for example, in 'workshop contingent valuation' (Kenyon et al., 2001), or 'market stall contingent valuation' (Macmillan et al., 2001). The way forward thus partly involves finding helpful insights in what appear to be opposing worldviews, and making use of them to improve economic approaches to valuation and decision-making. This adding of value to the discipline of environmental economics by using insights from other fields of valuation (participatory, qualitative) echoes the way in which insights from ecology (resilience, thresholds) are also strengthening economic methods and understanding.

CONCLUSIONS

More than one decade on from the Brundtland Report, there have been great advances in both the conceptual understanding of sustainable development and the ways in which that development might be indicated. While there also remains much to be done regarding the implementation of policy based on this understanding, what is not in doubt is the political relevance and importance of the current debate. Indeed, such is the appeal of the idea of SD that the term 'sustainable' is now prefixed to numerous and disparate objectives in various official policy statements. In this respect, it is clear that decision-makers face considerable challenges not only in understanding what they have committed themselves to but also in constructing credible policy responses and analytical frameworks to monitor progress.

The substantial economics literature on SD since the Brundtland Report is intended to address this challenge. For example, one well-established proposition is that past policy decisions have too often neglected, for example, the well-being of near- or far-off future generations. Thus, to correct this bias, policies need to be more forward looking, whether to encourage saving for the future in general or to conserve particular natural assets. In addition, this discussion is not divorced from the social side of policy-making as the recent focus on social capital indicates. Perhaps most notably, the green accounting literature has been particularly useful in focusing the attention of theoreticians, practitioners and policy-makers on the construction of frameworks whereby sustainability can be evaluated and measured. An interesting question is whether green accounts may, in the future, be used to construct indicators that could provide a synopsis of SD. Green national accounting aggregates, such as genuine saving, are obviously incomplete in terms of satisfying all criteria of the broader SD debate. However, the estimation of genuine savings rates has provided numerous insights into the sustainability of development across a wide range of countries.

A number of significant challenges still present themselves. First, there are costs and benefits to policies to attain SD, and hence there is likely to be a trade-off between SD and other socially desirable goals. On the whole, advocates of sustainability have not made a detailed examination of these trade-offs but it is clear that to enhance policy relevance, this shortcoming needs to be addressed. Second, it is notable that many governments that would see themselves at the forefront of the construction of SD strategies have largely failed to seek guidance from the sustainability literature. There is little evidence in most countries of official attempts at green accounting having markedly influenced the formulation of environmental policy. Lastly, arguably the most notable implication of the literature on measurement is its stress on the need to monitor changes in the real value of assets. Of course, policy-makers cannot focus exclusively on a single indicator to inform complex questions such as those surrounding the goal of sustainability. In this respect, there remains the challenge of strengthening the representation of ecological dimensions within existing operational frameworks and in particular the construction of a meaningful measure of strong sustainability. This would allow policy-makers to balance the conservation of certain natural assets within a broader goal of managing the portfolio of assets held by an economy over time, thereby capturing much of the essence of the sustainable development debate.

NOTES

1. At the optimum this will be equivalent to the marginal cost of abatement in these models.
2. Hanley et al. (1999) term this approximate environmentally-adjusted national product (AENP).
3. For another look at sustainability rules set in terms of natural capital, see Daly (1990).
4. More recent work on the idea of resilience may be found, for instance, in Brock, Mäler and Perrings (2000).

REFERENCES

Arrow, K., B. Bolin, R. Costanza, P. Dasgupta, C. Folke, C. Holling, B.-O. Jansson, S. Levin, K.-G. Mäler, C. Perrings and D. Pimentel (1995), 'Economic growth, carrying capacity and the environment', *Science*, 268, pp. 520–21.
Aronnson, T., P.-O. Johansson and K.-G Löfgren (1997), *Welfare Measurement, Sustainability and Green National Accounting*, Cheltenham: Edward Elgar.
Asheim, G.B. (1994), 'Net national product as an indicator of sustainability', *Scandinavian Journal of Economics*, 96 (2), 257–65.
Atkinson, G. (2000), 'Sustainable development and policy', in D. Helm (ed.), *Environmental Policy in the UK*, Oxford: Oxford University Press.
Atkinson, G., W.R. Dubourg, K. Hamilton, M. Munasinghe, D.W. Pearce, and C.E.F. Young (1997), *Measuring Sustainable Development: Macroeconomics and the Environment*, Cheltenham: Edward Elgar.
Barbier, E. (1999), 'Endogenous growth and natural resource scarcity', *Environmental and Resource Economics*, 14 (1), 51–74.

Barbier, E. and I. Strand (1998), 'Valuing mangrove-fishery linkages: a case study', *Environment and Resource Economics*, 12 (2), 151–66.

Barker, T., P. Ekins and N. Johnstone (eds) (1995), *Global Warming and Energy Demand*, London/New York: Routledge.

Bateman, I.J. and K.G. Willis (1999), *Valuing Environmental Preferences: Theory and Practice of the Contingent Valuation Method in the US, EU and Developing Countries*, Oxford: Oxford University Press.

Beauséjour, L., G. Lenjosek and M. Smart (1995), 'A GCE approach to modelling carbon dioxide emissions control in Canada and the United States', *The World Economy*, Vol. 18, pp. 457–89.

Bell, S. and S. Morse (1999), *Sustainability Indicators: Measuring the Immeasurable*, London: Earthscan.

Berrens, R., D. Bishop, M. McKee, and C. Schmidt (1998), 'Implementing the safe minimum standards approach: two case studies', *Land Economics*, 74 (2), 147–61.

Bowers, J. (1997), *Sustainability and Environmental Economics: An Alternative Text*, Harlow, Essex: Addison-Wesley Longman.

Brock, W.A., K.-G. Mäler and C. Perrings (2000), 'Resilience and sustainability: the economic analysis of non-linear dynamic systems', Discussion paper 133, Beijer Institute of Ecological Economics.

Cabeza Gutes, M. (1996), 'The concept of weak sustainability', *Ecological Economics*, 17, 147–56.

Common, M. and C. Perrings (1992), 'Towards an ecological economics of sustainability', *Ecological Economics*, 6 (1), 7–34.

Conrad, K. (1999), 'Computable General Equilibrium Models for Environmental Economics and Policy Analysis', in J.C.J.M. van den Bergh (ed.), *Handbook of Environmental and Resource Economics*, Cheltenham, UK and Northampton, MA: Edward Elgar.

Costanza, R. (1989), 'What is ecological economics?', *Ecological Economics*, 1 (1), 1–7.

Costanza, R., R. D'Arge, S. de Groot, S. Farber, M. Grasso, B. Hannon, K. Limburg, S. Naeem, R. O'Neill, J. Paruelo, R. Raskin, P. Sutton and M. van den Belt (1997), 'The value of the world's ecosystem services and natural capital', *Nature*, 387, May 15, 253–60.

Crocker T. (1999), 'A brief history of environmental and resource economics', in J van den Bergh (ed.), *Handbook of Environmental and Natural Resource Economics*, Cheltenham: Edward Elgar.

Daly, H.E. (1990) ,'Toward some operational principles of sustainable development', *Ecological Economics*, 2, 1–7.

Dasgupta, P. (1995), 'Optimal development and the idea of net national product', in I. Goldin and A. Winters (eds), *The Economics of Sustainable Development*, Cambridge: Cambridge University Press.

Dasgupta, P., B. Kriström and K.-G. Mäler (1996), *Net National Product as a Measure of Social Well-being*, Stockholm: The Beijer Institute.

Department of Environment (1996), *Indicators of Sustainable Development for the United Kingdom*, London: HMSO.

Department of Environment, Transport and the Regions (DETR) (1999), *Monitoring Progress*, London: DETR.

Ekins, P. (2000), 'Sustainability and critical natural capital: conclusions from the CRITINC project', *Working paper* 14, SPIRE, Keele University.

Ekins, P. and S. Simon (1999), 'The sustainability gap: a practical indicator of sustainability in the framework of the national accounts', *International Journal of Sustainable Development*, 2 (1), 32–58.

Farmer, M. and A. Randall (1998), 'The rationality of the safe minimum standard', *Land Economics*, 74 (3), 287–302.

Førsund, F.R. (1985), 'Input–output models, national economic models and the environment', in A.V. Kneese, and J.L. Sweeney (eds), *Handbook of Natural Resource and Energy Economics*, Amsterdam: North-Holland.

Foster, J. (ed.) (1997), *Valuing Nature: Economics, Ethics and Environment*, London: Routledge.

Grafton, R.Q. (2000), 'Governance of the commons', *Land Economics*, 76 (4), 504–17.

Hafkamp, V. (1991), 'Three decades of environmental modelling', in F. Dietz et al. (eds), *Environmental Policy and the Economy*, Amsterdam: Elsevier.

Hamilton, K. (1996), 'Pollution and pollution abatement in the national accounts', *Review of Income and Wealth*, 42 (1), 13–33.

Hamilton, K. and G. Atkinson (1996), 'Air pollution and green accounts', *Energy Policy*, 24, 675–84.

Hamilton, K., D.W. Pearce, G. Atkinson, A. Gomez-Lobo and C.E.F. Young (1994), 'The policy implications of environment and resource accounting', *CSERGE Working Paper*, GEC 94-18, Centre for Social and Economic Research on the Global Environment (CSERGE), University College London and University of East Anglia.

Hammond, A., A. Adriaanse, E. Rodenburg, D. Bryant and R. Woodward (1995), *Environmental Indicators*, Washington, DC: World Resources Institute.

Hanley, N. (2000), 'Macroeconomic measures of sustainability', *Journal of Economic Surveys*, 14, 1–30.

Hanley, N. and C. Spash (1993), *Cost-Benefit Analysis and the Environment*, Cheltenham: Edward Elgar.

Hanley, N., I. Moffatt, R. Faichney and M. Wilson (1999), 'Measuring sustainability: a time series of indicators for Scotland', *Ecological Economics*, 28, 55–73.

Hanley, N., J. Shogren and B. White (2001), *Introduction to Environmental Economics*, Oxford: Oxford University Press.

Hartwick, J.M. (1977), 'Intergenerational rents and the investing of rents from exhaustible resources', *American Economic Review*, 67 (5), 972–4.

Hartwick, J.M. (1978), 'Investing returns from depleting renewable resource stocks and intergenerational equity', *Economics Letters*, 1, 85–8.

Hicks, J.R. (1946), *Value and Capital*, 2nd edn, Oxford: Clarendon Press.

Holling, C.S. (1973), 'Resilience and stability in ecological systems', *Annual Review of Ecology and Systematics*, 4, 1–24.

Holling, C.S., D.W. Schindler, B.W. Walker and J. Roughgarden (1995), 'Biodiversity in the functioning of ecosystems', in C. Perrings et al. (eds), *Biodiversity Loss: Ecological and Economic Issues,* Cambridge: Cambridge University Press.

Howarth, R. and R. Norgaard (1995), 'Intergenerational choices under global environmental change', in D. Bromley (ed.), *The Handbook of Environmental Economics,* Oxford: Basil Blackwell.

Hueting, R., P. Bosch and B. de Boer (1992), 'Methodology for the calculation of sustainable national income', *Statistical Essays*, Central Statistics Bureau, the Netherlands.

Ives, A. (1995) 'Measuring resilience in stochastic systems', *Ecological Monographs*, 65, 217–33.

Kenyon, W., N. Hanley and C. Nevin (2001), 'Citizens' juries: an aid to environmental valuation?', *Environmental Planning C: Government and Policy*, 19 (4), 557–66.

Knack, S. and P. Keefer (1997), 'Does social capital have an economic payoff? A cross country investigation', *Quarterly Journal of Economics*, November (1997), 1251–88.

Levin, S., S. Barrett, S. Anikyar, W. Baumol, C. Bliss, B. Bolin, P. Dasgupta, P. Ehrlich, C. Folke, I.-M. Gren, C. Holling, A. Jansson, B.-O. Jansson, K-G. Mäler, D. Martin, C. Perrings and E. Sheshinski (1998), 'Resilience in natural and socio-economic systems', *Environment and Development Economics*, 3, 222–35.

Ludwig, D., B. Walker and C.S. Holling (1997), 'Sustainability, stability and resilience', *Conservation Ecology*, 1 (1), 7.

Macmillan, D., L. Philip, N. Hanley and B. Alvarez-Farizo (2001), 'Valuing the non-market benefits of wild goose conservation: a comparison of individual interview and group based approaches', Discussion paper, Department of Agriculture and Forestry, University of Aberdeen.

Mäler, K.G. (1991), 'National accounts and environmental resources', *Environmental and Resource Economics*, 1 (1), 1–16.

Meadows, D., D. Meadows and J. Randers (1992), *Beyond the Limits*, London: Earthscan.

Moffatt, I., N. Hanley and M.D. Wilson (2001), *Measuring and Modelling Sustainable Development*, Carnforth, Lancs: Parthenon Press.

Neumayer, E. (2001), 'The human development index and sustainability: a constructive proposal', *Ecological Economics*, 39, 101–14.

Norton, B.G. and M.A. Toman (1997), 'Sustainability: economic and ecological perspectives', *Land Economics*, 73 (4), 553–68.

Page, T. (1977), *Conservation and Economic Efficiency*, Baltimore: Johns Hopkins Press.

Pearce, D.W. (1998), 'Auditing the earth', *Environment*, 40 (2), 23–8.

Pearce D.W. and G. Atkinson (1993), 'Capital theory and the measurement of sustainable development: an indicator of weak sustainability', *Ecological Economics*, 8 (2), 103–8.

Pearce, D.W. and G. Atkinson (1998), 'The concept of sustainable development: an evaluation of its usefulness ten years after Brundtland', *Swiss Journal of Economics*, 134 (3), 251–69.

Pearce D.W. and E. Barbier (2000), *Blueprint for a Sustainable Economy*, London: Earthscan.

Pearce, D.W., E. Barbier and A. Markandya (1990), *Sustainable Development: Economics and Environment in the Third World*, Cheltenham: Edward Elgar.

Pearce, D.W., K. Hamilton and G. Atkinson (1996), 'Measuring sustainable development: progress on indicators', *Environment and Development Economics*, 1 (1), 85–101.

Perrings, C. and D.W. Pearce (1994), 'Threshold effects and incentives for the conservation of biological diversity', *Environmental and Resource Economics*, 4 (1), 13–28.

Pezzey, J. (1989), 'Economic analysis of sustainable growth and sustainable development', Environment Department Working Paper No. 15, Washington, DC: World Bank.

Pezzey, J. (1997), 'Sustainability constraints', *Land Economics*, 73 (4), 448–66.

Pezzey, J. and M. Toman (2002), 'Progress and problems in the economics of sustainability', in T. Tietenberg and H. Folmer (eds), *Yearbook of Environmental and Resource Economics, 2002–3*. Cheltenham: Edward Elgar.

Pezzey, J. and C. Withagen (1998), 'Single-peakedness and initial sustainability in capital-resource economies', *Scandinavian Journal of Economics*, 100.

Proops, J.L.R., G. Atkinson, B.F. von Schlotheim and S. Simon (1999), 'International trade and the sustainability footprint: a practical criterion for its assessment', *Ecological Economics*, 28, 75–97.

Putnam, R.D. (1993), *Making Democracy Work: Civic Traditions in Modern Italy*, Princeton: Princeton University Press.

Randall, A. and M. Farmer (1995), 'Benefits, costs and the safe minimum standard of conservation', in D. Bromley (ed.), *Handbook of Environmental Economics*, Oxford: Basil Blackwell.

Rees, W. and M. Wackernagel (1994), 'Ecological footprints and appropriated carrying capacity: measuring the natural capital requirements of the human economy', in A.M. Jansson, M. Hammer, C. Folke and R. Costanza (eds), *Investing in Natural Capital: the Ecological Economics Approach to Sustainability*, Washington, DC: Island Press.

Solow, R.M. (1974), 'Intergenerational equity and exhaustible resources', *Review of Economic Studies*, 41, 29–45.

Solow, R.M. (1986), 'On the intergenerational allocation of exhaustible resources', *Scandinavian Journal of Economics*, 88, 141–9.

Ten Brink, B., S. Hosper and F. Colijn (1991), 'A quantitative approach for description and assessment of marine ecosystems: the AMOEBA approach', *Marine Pollution Bulletin*, 23, 265–70.

Toman, M.A. (1998), 'Sustainable decision-making: the state of the art from an economics perspective', RFF Discussion Paper 98-39, Resources for the Future, Washington, DC.

Toman, M.A., J. Pezzey and J. Krautkraemer (1995), 'Neo-classical economic growth theory and "sustainability"', in D. Bromley (ed.), *Handbook of Environmental Economics*, Oxford: Basil Blackwell.

van Tongeren, J., G. Schweinfest, E. Lutz, M. Gomez Luna and G. Martin (1993), 'Integrated environmental and economic accounts: a case study for Mexico', in E. Lutz (ed.), *Toward Improved Accounting for the Environment*, Washington, DC: World Bank.

Vincent, J.R. (1997), 'Resource depletion and economic sustainability in Malaysia', *Environment and Development Economics*, 2, 19–37.

Vincent, J.R., T. Panayotou and M. Hartwick (1997), 'Resource depletion and sustainability in small open economies', *Journal of Environmental Economics and Management*, 33 (3), 274–86.

Weitzman, M.L. (1976), 'On the welfare significance of national product in a dynamic economy', *Quarterly Journal of Economics*, 90 (1), 156–62.

Weitzman, M.L. (1997), 'Sustainability and technical progress', *Scandinavian Journal of Economics*, 99 (1), 1–13.

Weyant, J.P. and J.N. Hill (1999), 'Introduction and overview', in J. Weyant (ed.), *The Costs of the Kyoto Protocol: A Multi-model Evaluation*, Special Issue of the *Energy Journal*, pp. vi–lxliv.

World Bank (1997), *Expanding the Measure of Wealth: Indicators of Environmentally Sustainable Development*, Environmentally Sustainable Development Studies and Monographs Series No. 17, Washington, DC: World Bank.

World Commission on Environment and Development (WCED) (1987), *Our Common Future*, Oxford: Oxford University Press.

4. Deliberative democracy and environmental decision-making

Richard Munton[1]

INTRODUCTION

Outside the corporate domain it is, today, quite difficult to find examples of environmental decision-making where there has been no public consultation or other form of public involvement in the process. Whether the nature of that involvement is deemed satisfactory is quite another matter. Nonetheless, its nature and extent are important indicators of the condition of late modernity and, in particular, the role of civil society. It highlights the range of different knowledges that decision-makers need to access, especially in circumstances of scientific uncertainty (see Stirling, Chapter 2), and challenges the assumption that environmental problems can be addressed primarily through market regulation. It also raises interesting questions for the contemporary functioning of representative democracy. On the one hand, public involvement challenges the established roles and authority of elected representatives and the experts and officials who support them, whilst on the other it asks of individual citizens what active contribution they are prepared to make to advance the public sphere. To what degree are they content to delegate that responsibility (and opportunity) to elected representatives, to their experts and officials, or even to interest groups who claim to speak for them? And assuming that they wish to make their voices heard, how have they gone about it and how easy is it for them to overcome the institutional obstacles that frequently constrain their full participation?

Empirical evidence suggests that answers to these questions are very variable. Some citizens engage extensively, either individually or through community or national organizations, but most do not; yet many are known to hold strong opinions. Instead, considerable political space is allocated by the state to powerful stakeholders, usually representing the interests of science, business and the other professions, in various forms of partnership with it. These arrangements may be only loosely spelled out in statute and are rarely more than tangentially accountable in democratic terms. Thus while the emergence of this kind of governance extends the range of participants beyond elected representatives and their officials in an effort to cope with the problems set by an increasingly complex and uncertain world, it also continues to privilege certain kinds of knowledge and established interest and to foster an administrative or market rationalism in the management of the public sphere. Moreover, there is some evidence (Renn et al., 1993) that it is these powerful interests that are least inclined to extend consultation to unorganized publics. They sometimes claim, for example, that citizens have no clear sense of the complexities of the issues confronting society, or the knowledge necessary to address them, and therefore such matters should be left to them. As organizations embedded legally, commercially or socially within society, they argue that they are required to accommodate, if not represent, the public interest in their decisions anyway. There are enormous and challengeable assumptions in this position, and whilst there can be no guarantee that broader public engagement will bring better management of the public sphere, this position is now regularly contested on both moral and democratic grounds. Whose world is it, anyway? Such questioning has been stimulated by a continuing decline in trust among the governed of those in authority; and when it comes to public consultation there is a real difference between 'involving those who "represent" different public interests...[and]...those who are "representative" of these interests' (Petts, 2000, p. 57).

These trends in governance have led to considerable debate around the notion of deliberative democracy and the value of participative practice in the development and delivery of public policy. These debates are by no means restricted to environmental issues but environmental decisions are often in the vanguard because of their complexity, the uncertainty surrounding their scientific understanding and the range of moral, ethical and political values that underpins them. Furthermore, green ideology is strongly linked to arguments for non-hierarchical decision-making, while the concepts of sustainable development and ecological modernization, which now dominate mainstream environmental discourse and practice, require environmental issues to be treated holistically and in conjunction with social and economic concerns. These integrating perspectives, when combined with the insistence that Agenda 21 programmes be built substantially from below, demand that considerable attention be paid to how lay publics and other local interests can be brought into policy making (see, for example, Burgess et al., 1998; Macnaghten and Jacobs, 1997). Indeed, in the absence of overwhelming scientific evidence, in a plural society there will be a plethora of 'right' answers. This suggests the need for inclusive processes that encourage debate, learning, adaptation and consent. But once recognized, how should this situation be addressed?

One response is to advocate a much greater use of deliberative and inclusionary processes in decision-making.[2] The reasoning is two-fold. One justification is directed towards improving the quality of environmental governance on the ground. It is argued that better decisions are reached by incorporating the views of a wide range of members of the public. They will bring breadth of experience and expertise and their involvement will increase the political legitimacy of the decisions. Second, and beyond these specific environmental objectives, lies the more general search for dialogic mechanisms of decision and accountability that emphasize inclusivity, reflexivity and social learning (Barnes, 1999), or the creation of a more engaged and informed society in terms of its collective interests. These two objectives pose a direct challenge to those arguments derived from a top-down 'deficit model' of communication where experts of all kinds are seen (or see themselves) as the means of informing lay publics so as to reduce their ignorance or even deliberately to align public opinion with their views (for an example, see Goodwin, 1998).

Alternative mechanisms have yet to be fully accepted (see Blaug, 2002) and the debates about them have to be viewed in part against the wider backcloth of the anticipated importance of environmental issues in the future. If the survival of the planet as we know it is to become a central issue in the conduct of public affairs then institutional (in terms of rights, obligations, processes) and organizational (in terms of structures) reform will be required, not least because the environment presents particular challenges. For example, environmental processes function over a wide range of spatial scales that rarely correspond with established patterns of jurisdictional responsibility and accountability. They are only occasionally bounded by the territories of nation states and often hold greater meaning and material significance for citizens at a local scale while presenting global threats to a weak set of global institutions. Multi-level systems of governance are clearly called for but their functioning will also have to be flexible and responsive if they are to cope with their own inbuilt redundancy arising from the constant re-creation of networks of interests across local, national and international spaces (for a local illustration, see Murdoch and Marsden, 1995; see also Selman, 2000; Davies, 2002).

The purpose of this chapter is to review what might be gained from a more deliberative and inclusionary approach to environmental governance. Most empirical evidence comes so far from local case studies simply because deliberative practice is easier to organize at this scale. The sheer range of empirical material makes its detailed description impractical and so the chapter focuses on the principles and the problems of developing generic assessments of the practices in use. Most advocates of deliberative approaches see them as a means of enriching rather than replacing representative democracy. But this is not to diminish the emancipatory message that lies behind their use, following from the writings of Habermas (1984; 1996; see also Dryzek, 1990; 1995; Mason, 1999). His arguments in favour of communicative action and its basis in rational argument, agreement and maximal inclusion are not neutral. As a critical theory of democracy, his demands for inclusion and deliberative practice are designed to redistribute power and have attracted opposition from established political interests as a consequence. Despite their objections, however, his detractors have not stilled the debate for more transparent, inclusive and reflexive decision-making. The practical issues involved in achieving this, from its framing to its conduct and evaluation, make up the second half of the chapter.

CONTEXT

Representative democracy is predominantly understood to function through the aggregation of independently formed preferences among citizens, normally revealed through voting, leading to particular administrations and their public policy programmes. These preferences are acted upon by institutional structures that determine who is enfranchised and, where preferences conflict, how decisions are to be reached within acceptable definitions of equality and efficiency. Deliberative democracy approaches the same issues by arguing that differences in preferences are better addressed through processes which require them to be exposed to public debate and where arguments have to be presented in terms of the public good rather than personal benefit (Dryzek, 1990; Miller, 1992; Bohman and Rehg, 1997; Jacobs, 1997; Elster, 1998; Button and Mattson, 1999). It is suggested that extensive participation in such debates more faithfully reflects the notion of popular sovereignty than voting because it allows citizens to have a fuller say in the decisions that affect them (Webler and Renn, 1995). Participation reduces free riding while encouraging respect and trust between those holding opposing views.

Deliberative processes are directed towards reaching agreement rather than encouraging competition between opposing positions. Consensus may act as the ideal, but the search for agreement does not assume ultimate unanimity of position. Nonetheless, advocates of deliberative processes presume that open discussion can reduce differences of position and outcomes will be reached that are more fruitful than mere compromise (Miller, 1992). As O'Neill argues '[T]his means that incommensurability [of positions] must not be taken as a given, or something to be elaborated. Nor should it be brushed aside as something that will inevitably be overcome' (2000, p. 505). All parties are assumed to learn from a process that encourages respect for alternative views and, at a minimum, one that enhances understanding of the consequences for different interests even if agreement cannot be reached. The key practical question is how to provide the most effective fora for such debates. This requirement has spawned a range of practices, such as focus groups, deliberative polling and citizens' juries. Their contribution lies as much in the legitimacy they bring to particular decisions as to the specific outcomes but in the long run they must be seen to make a difference to outcomes if they are to retain the confidence of those who take part. They are, therefore, sometimes viewed as ways of trying to 'democratize democracy', addressing some of the limitations of representative democracy in today's dynamic and diverse societies (Bloomfield et al., 2001).

In the context of environmental questions, the particular salience of deliberative processes is seen to lie in two kinds of situation. First, they are viewed as especially apposite to the management of what Rittel and Webber (1973) famously termed 'wicked problems', or problems that challenge established values, institutions and means of governing, have no ready solution based upon scientific knowledge or professional expertise, and where value judgements have to be made at each step in the decision process. Environmental issues frequently fit this description, being characterized as 'ill-defined, tightly coupled with other sectors and questions, and reliant upon elusive and transitory political agreement for their resolution' (Coenan et al., 1998, p. 2). These conditions suggest the need for a wide range of voices to be engaged, if only as a means of reducing the risk of mistakes arising from the exclusive use of a narrow set of expert knowledges, as well as ensuring sufficient political support across traditionally discrete sets of interests and unreflexive bureaucracies (for a case study, see Hunold and Young, 1998).

The need for reflexivity and adaptability in such dynamic environments builds naturally towards the idea of a learning society, a notion implicit in partnership governance. One way of improving the chances of success is to ask prospective partners what they would want from a close working relationship. Clark et al. (2001), for example, asked seventeen public and private stakeholders what they would seek from a partnership with the Environment Agency of England and Wales. Although no two respondents had exactly the same requirements, the most valued aspects of any relationship were said to be the opportunity to learn together in a transparent and supportive (trusting) manner, provided the discussions were 'action-oriented' and 'solutions focused'.

Second, the value of deliberative processes seems especially apparent where decisions are likely to be hotly contested but where members of the public, if not stakeholder groups, have yet to adopt fixed positions. A good example is provided by north American experience over the siting of waste dumps. Research reveals that neither state-directed, expert-led decision processes nor market-driven exercises have much chance of success. Only practices that involve extensive local consultation, despite the risk this brings of heightened self-interest, can provide the basis for an agreed outcome. Even then, agreement may depend on an acceptable compensation package and an open debate about the distribution of risks and benefits between communities and groups within communities (Huitema, 1998; see also Petts, 2001). But in all situations, the major benefit offered by a deliberative process is the building of trust between decision-makers and citizens. No process can guarantee this, but extensive personal contact usually helps to increase trust provided a positive view is held by the participants of the competence of the decision makers, their ability to empathize with the concerns of those who will be affected by the decision, and the perceived fairness and transparency of the process. More cynically, such processes may be used by decision makers to shift some of their responsibility onto others because any decision they take will upset some interests.

New skills are required of decision makers with little experience of engaging with lay publics, not least the ability to manage the publics' conflicting interests, in a world of increasing social and cultural 'difference'. Greater education and the confidence that this brings have encouraged social groups to assert their difference and to argue for it to be respected through more inclusive political engagement (see, for example, Young, 1990; 1996). Paradoxically, this raises the stakes for those groups who do not, or prefer not, to engage, as it creates new exclusivities; and recognizing difference does not necessarily lead to a more equitable re-distribution of power. In her assessment of ecological democracy, Plumwood (1998), for example, examines the significance of difference through a discussion of 'remoteness', or the explicit recognition of differential power. Remoteness is treated partly in a geographical sense in which decision makers may neither understand nor have to live with the consequences of their decisions, which arise 'elsewhere', in effect failing to acknowledge the interests of geographically marginalized others. It is also treated in a social sense where decisions are taken by an elite who, at best, fail to communicate their intentions to other interests, or more generally create systems of opportunity and governance which reinforce their preferential positions over the distribution of ecological outcomes. They retain the means to avoid or mediate the effects of ecological bads in ways not open to other sections of society.

Overall however, the political purpose of deliberative democracy is to suggest that meaningful and just action depends upon the continuing involvement of citizens in the making and delivery of policy and that representative democracy is potentially (and actually) an unresponsive system of governance because it focuses upon the act of voting. The normative expectations of deliberative democracy[3] thus go well beyond the 'truncated' politics of stakeholder engagement to advocate widespread citizen participation. The benefits of engagement, which include a greater sense of collective responsibility for and ownership of governance decisions (a sense of 'civicness'), assume an equal significance to the benefits of 'better' decisions, as measured in terms, say, of environmental outcomes, so prized by more managerial views of governance.

LOCAL ACTIONS

In democratically stable societies debates over public consultation, participation and even control over the decision-making process (see Arnstein, 1969) are largely indicative of a search for incremental change where representative and deliberative means can add value to each other. Effective complementarity depends largely upon the issue concerned (its degree of complexity, technicality, uncertainty), on the socio-political context and on local circumstance. The search for change may, therefore, be reduced to the pragmatic matter of agreeing upon 'fitness for purpose' of a particular practice in a context of broadly common purpose and values. This can suit established interests because they may then still feel in control of the process. However this assumption probably underestimates the long-term cumulative effect of deliberative practice if it becomes commonplace.

In less stable societies in parts of the 'south' and the former Socialist bloc, incremental change may be neither sought nor sufficient. In some situations, issues of sustainable development and environmental protection have become an acceptable form of protest politics allowing the defence of existing civil institutions or the righting of injustices that would have been prohibited under traditional class politics (Peet and Watts, 1996; Lemos, 1998; Haynes, 1999). As authoritarian regimes have retreated under a combination of their own contradictions, a neo-liberal climate for international trade, and the actions of major international agencies and donors seeking community involvement as part of aid packages, local responses have ranged from the enthusiastic and inclusive to ones of elite, stakeholder politics. The latter have thrived where democratic institutions have never held much authority, legal provision for civil rights is limited and class and ethnic distinctions are endemic (Coenan et al., 1998).

Comparisons between experience in the north and the south need to be handled with the utmost care. It is sometimes suggested, for example, that: (1) outsiders are more prominent in the planning of community development in the south, widening even further the economic and cultural interests and biases involved; (2) that solving environmental problems in the south is directed more towards achieving material outcomes than improving democratic processes; (3) that unlike the north individual citizens are rarely involved in setting policy options and are mainly called upon for their local knowledge (Holmes and Scoones, 2000); and (4) that modernization, in the form of mass education, has penetrated societies much less fully in the south. The latter reduces the opportunity for reaching common understandings while increasing the potential for conflict between local knowledges and a 'universal' science in the weighing of evidence and the evaluation of options. These differences may be true but the north has much to learn from the greater experience of the south in bottom-up community planning, not least because trust in its own institutions, including science, is declining (see for example, Irwin, 1995; Wynne, 1996). There are also many examples of considerable grassroots capacity in the south in the management and monitoring of local resources (Zazueta, 1995; Bucek and Smith, 2000), including, for example, community forestry development in India (Banerjee, 1999) and wetland management in India and Pakistan (Gujja et al., 1998).

An interesting illustration of contemporary participative practice in the south is provided by Warner (1997). Drawing upon the commitment of Agenda 21 to citizen consultation, capacity building and empowerment, he describes an approach to the management of protected areas in Zambia. His Framework for Consensus Participation in Protected Areas (FCPPA) is not based upon seeking complete agreement among stakeholders but upon the creation of conditions that all parties can live with. It seeks to combine the benefits of 'popular' participation, developed partly in relation to Participatory Rural Appraisal (Chambers, 1994a; 1994b), with the need to engage with powerful local and external stakeholders. The aim is an inclusive but realistic process, arguing that 'the *empowerment* objective behind "popular" participation escapes the reality that external stakeholders are integral to local social and environmental sustainability, and the *institutional sustainability* objective behind "selective" participation is inadequate in its accounting of social and environmental capital' (Warner, 1997, p.416, emphasis in the original).

The FCPPA requires both collaboration between stakeholders and capacity building to allow less powerful stakeholders the means to engage on level terms. Success depends significantly upon the recruitment and training of experienced facilitators able to ensure that a sense of consensus is achieved throughout the process from analysis and negotiation to implementation and evaluation, and this sometimes creates a cost barrier. Warner draws a careful distinction between the purpose of his framework, which is broad-based enough to apply to a wide range of situations, and management strategies developed for specific locations and projects that are sensitive to socio-cultural differences and local power structures. The ideal is that 'consensus-building, not empowerment or institutional sustainability, should be the driving force behind participation' (Warner, 1997, p. 430).

In almost all cases, north and south, participative politics has been most active at the local scale, for practical reasons, although the growing use of internet technologies may alter this. In the north, in the environmental field, among its most widespread expressions are Citizen Advisory Committees in the United States and the activities of Local Agenda 21 programmes in western Europe (Lafferty and Eckerberg, 1998). The latter have not always been successful in meeting their goals, often finding it difficult to achieve an appropriate balance between economic and environmental interests (Gibbs et al., 1996; Harrison et al., 1996), and between local wishes and national intent (Blake, 1999), as well as being able to establish an appropriate engagement with the local state. Regularly promoted and managed by local government, Local Agenda 21 has often been bound by the resources, powers and interests of the local state (Andringa, 1998; Smith et al., 1999). More interesting are the differing responses of local publics in different places to attempts by the local state to lead and direct the process, reflecting distinct national political cultures. For example, in the cities of Eindhoven in the Netherlands and Nottingham in England the immediate response of both local political elites to media criticism of their policies was to seek internal institutional reform rather than sharing the issue with local publics. In Eindhoven, this strong lead was welcomed by local publics but in Nottingham it only encouraged greater demands for the sharing of knowledge and power (Burgess et al., 1998; see also Burgess et al., Chapter 10).

This continuing sense among some civil interests of being merely the institutionalized and acceptable face of sustainable development practice has encouraged the emergence of more radical protest groups, such as Reclaim the Streets. They reject present political structures, are strongly committed to green ideologies, are highly sceptical of a search for consensus (accommodation) and are immensely critical of the capitalist system and its environmental lackey, the ecological modernization agenda. They believe their position is strengthened by the regular reporting of a lack of commitment among businesses to more than a shallow green agenda (Coenan, 1998; Gibbs et al., 1998; Eden, 1999; see also Schaefer et al., Chapter 8). Again, direct action has been most vigorous at the local scale and often associated with single issues such as road-building schemes or the location of waste dumps, but recent worldwide protests over the policies of the World Trade Organisation and global capitalism more generally may herald a change of emphasis. At the local level, protest groups are sometimes able to harness the sense of powerlessness that individual citizens feel in the face of global or even national forces for change, the local acting as the one arena where most individuals feel their actions may make a difference and where they can see the consequences of their protest. To the more sophisticated opponents of current institutions, however, local protest is not seen as essentially or even primarily that, but as the means by which local actions can be made to tap into wider senses of injustice, leading to more coordinated and more generalized forms of protest. Indeed, the electronic age provides the means for an active, networked form of 'post-modern politics' of resistance (Routledge, 1997) based upon the mobile phone and the internet, creating newsworthy media campaigns that lie beyond the control of the spin doctors of established interests (Burgess, 1990; Burgess et al., 1991; Hansen, 1993; Rawcliffe, 1998).

These remarks position deliberative practices largely as a set of 'insider' activities seeking to achieve significant but incremental shifts in governance within the basic structure of politically stable market democracies, even if they may play a more immediate and substantial role in effecting governance change in societies where representative democratic procedures are less well established. Their general acceptance may prove important to the greater recognition of environmental issues in government. With the notable exception of the German Green Party, green parties have not been especially successful within representative democracy at the nation state scale, especially where first past the post electoral systems are in operation. The environmental movement has had to function largely through the agendas of other parties and to be sustained by the actions of a wide range of pressure groups, some with substantial memberships. The latter groups are professional and well resourced, and combine 'insider' strategies designed to influence public policy through negotiations with government and other sectional interests with protest actions directed at private corporations or public agencies (Lowe and Goyder, 1983; Maloney et al., 1994; Jordan and Maloney, 1997). Thus while members of the environmental movement have acquired long experience and considerable skills in political lobbying and the promotion of media campaigns, and have regularly sought access to policy making by demanding more inclusive means, they have also acted competitively with each other in order to gain access to privileged sites of decision making. In so doing, some of the more influential have come to act as professional stakeholders as much as 'citizens' organizations'. They use their mass memberships to endorse the political legitimacy of their negotiating positions and to provide the financial means to take part in expert-driven debate, often within decision-making fora framed by the state (see Rawcliffe, 1998). This is not a criticism of their tactics but an acknowledgement that in terms of practical politics they are not always at the forefront of public inclusiveness even if they are heavily involved in stakeholder politics.

DELIBERATIVE AND INCLUSIONARY PRACTICES (DIPS)

The chapter now turns to discuss a set of practices that incorporate deliberative and inclusive elements as means of engaging citizens and stakeholders in environmental decision making. The same concept of public participation is used here as in Renn et al. (1995). They define public participation as: *forums for exchange that are organised for the purposes of facilitating communication between government, citizens, stakeholders and interest groups, and businesses regarding a specific decision or problem* (Renn et al., 1995, p. 2 (italics in the original)). This definition explicitly omits expert workshops (although some stakeholder discussions come close to this format); consultation via surveys of opinions and preferences, and protest actions.

In a recent survey covering both the north and the south, Holmes and Scoones (2000) describe a broad range of cases. Some involve considerable public consultation, some the engagement of stakeholders only. Some are based on extensive surveys of public opinion, others on in-depth, qualitative analyses of the consultative process. They select thirty-five separate uses of DIPs, each demonstrating novel methods or approaches. These include citizens' juries, citizens' panels, consensus conferences, facilitated workshops and focus groups, deliberative opinion polls, stakeholder decision analysis, visioning exercises and multi-criteria mapping (see also DETR, 1998), sometimes used in combination, reflecting varying degrees of deliberation and inclusion in each case. To such surveys may be added a growing literature that critically examines one or more of these techniques, often in specific settings (see, for example, Petts, 1995; Burgess et al., 1988a; b; Renn et al., 1997; Ward, 1999; Davies, 1999; Smith and Wales, 1999; Cowie and O'Toole, 1998). Most of these studies reveal several overlapping purposes that at the broadest level can be divided into those directed towards instrumental goals, usually linked to the achievement of a policy or environmental decision, or broader educative or democratic goals where the process is designed, *inter alia*, to reveal underlying conflicts, to help participants learn and take responsibility, or to build human and social capital more generally.

Participants tend to define goals, even collective goals, in ways advantageous to themselves and may prefer to be vague in stating what these are to other participants. Thus all participants may genuinely want extensive consultation but with different ends in mind. The issue is how closed, or non-negotiable, are their initial positions. For example, public bodies may place limits on their ability to negotiate, blaming their statutorily-defined responsibilities and their inability to debate matters that are the responsibility of other agencies. In contrast, public companies may argue that their positions are bounded by their legal obligations to shareholders, irrespective of the strengths of competing arguments (see, for example, Tewdwr-Jones and Thomas, 1998). In practice, quite different purposes and limits to negotiation may have to be held in tension at a particular moment or within a particular process, but very few purposes are beyond alteration in the longer term. The key is to share values and possible solutions rather than thinking about winners and losers, and because many processes involve participants with unbridgeable values and expectations, an efficient objective may be to seek workable outcomes rather than insist on meeting the ideal of consensus (for discussion, see Owens and Cowell, 2002, pp. 58–64).

These well-recognized difficulties should not act as arguments against attempts to hold more transparent debates. Differences of opinion and intractability of position are there to be explored as part of the process. How this is done is crucial. The role and interests of those who frame the process are very important to its conduct and outcome. It is inevitable that someone or some organization has to take the lead but, ideally, independent facilitators should be engaged to manage the process where serious differences of view are known to exist or where new ideas are genuinely sought. From a position of relative impartiality, facilitators can seek to identify in advance the relevant communities of interests, and establish how these interests are networked and who trusts whom. Effective preparation also allows the facilitator the opportunity to establish what each participant is looking for by way of fairness in any outcome, and how each would handle disagreement. As O'Riordan et al. say:

> the culture of accommodative participation does not always come quickly. There are hundreds of local views, and not all can be solicited and accommodated. So the trick is to spend ... time in preparation, ... in sensing ... how stakeholders [may] develop their positions, how they may be enabled to accommodate others' views, and in building confidence in the negotiating process (O'Riordan et al., 1999, p. 22).

Burgess (2000) describes such a case. Under the Environment Act 1995, the Environment Agency of England and Wales is charged with preparing a comprehensive set of non-statutory Local Environment Agency Plans (LEAPs). The plans are required to promote an integrated and sustainable approach to local environmental management incorporating a vision, a strategy and a plan of action. The costs and benefits of each set of proposals have to be assessed and all interested parties have to be involved in plan preparation. Using the New Forest in Hampshire as an example, Burgess was asked by the agency to develop a robust but efficient process that could become a model of best practice for LEAPs generally. In this case, the agency commendably agreed to abide by the outcomes of the process and to put these to wider public consultation.

Intellectually, Burgess situates the practical task of plan preparation within the connections to be made between post-normal science (Funtowicz and Ravetz, 1994) and the cultural turn in social science. Plan preparation consists of a Stakeholder Decision Analysis with 14 stakeholders from the public, private and voluntary sectors employing a rigorous process of criteria selection, weighting and evaluation (multi-criteria analysis), together with extensive debates between participants over the values underlying their different positions. The connections with post-normal science and culture structure the approach, actively engaging with the uncertainty and range of knowledges surrounding science, the significance of context, and the need for exchange, reflexivity and respect between stakeholders. In more practical terms, the power of the approach lies in its inclusiveness of values. Evaluation criteria are examined for their 'validity' rather than in order to seek consensus on which are 'right'. This allows all views to be considered, but in a non-confrontational way, while still requiring the participants to draft a plan within three months through a series of workshops. The approach not only encourages reflexivity and a broad consideration of the issues, but also assists the participants to reach clear priorities for decision-making through the use of semi-quantitative multi-criteria analysis.

(1) Deliberation

Habermas argues that the benefits of deliberation go far beyond their contribution to better quality decisions. Deliberation invigorates the public sphere by generating convictions and by obtaining the greater engagement of citizens in governance issues. The essence of his claim for an ideal communicative rationality lies in his assumption of the superiority of reasoned argument. He believes that reaching reasoned and critical judgements are facilitated by public debate in which language is oriented towards mutual understanding and, ideally, consensus in decision making (see also Innes, 1996; Healey, 1998). In more mundane terms, deliberative processes are characterized by face-to-face contact over an extended period with participants valuing and respecting the positions of others (Forester, 1999). Individual positions are realigned in the face of other, better-reasoned arguments; and strategic or self-interested ends among participants are flushed out by the collective and transparent nature of debate. The aim is to search for values and positions that can be respected, even if they cannot be agreed upon, and for participants to see the process as one of learning as well as decision making. The process should be treated as cyclical with feedback leading to individual and institutional realignment within a culture of reasonableness and tolerance.

Powerful criticisms can be levelled at these ideals of communicative rationality and consensus, not least the assumption of a single rationality to which all subscribe. These criticisms arise as much from empirical observations of how decision making occurs and how society is conceptualized as from objections to the ideals themselves. First, there are the difficulties raised by public choice theorists. Drawing upon a conceptualization that regards society as consisting of an aggregation of special interests or self-interested individuals, they question whether sufficient incentives exist for individuals to seek collective solutions to problems from which they may not immediately benefit. The costs in time, effort and resources of DIPs could easily be too high for participants if they believe their contribution to the outcomes is likely to be limited. These circumstances, it is argued, encourage sporadic engagement and where it does occur the stimulus will be for special interests to collude or even act independently to capture the process (Tewdwr-Jones and Allmendinger, 1998). The disincentives are greater in the case of public goods, such as environmental benefits, because they are often non-excludable and indivisible, increasing the incentive to free ride (Rydin and Pennington, 2000).

These observations notwithstanding, we still have to explain why many private interests seek to promote the public good where there is limited self-interest in doing so. Some explanations challenge the basic assumption of public choice theory of individual self-interest, preferring a socialized conception of behaviour rooted in exchange and moral commitment, and where the incentives to act are not just material or individualized. Ostrom, for example, describes many local institutions where the benefits of collective outcomes to individual welfare are especially evident, and perhaps more so than in larger, more open social systems. The costs and benefits of collective action may be evaluated differently in local settings simply because of the greater familiarity that exists between individuals (Ostrom, 1990; 1996). Disagreement may also be more easily handled.

A second criticism is that in his commitment to the ideal of consensus, Habermas paid insufficient attention to power relations, with the powerful being favoured in numerous ways, including within the process of deliberation itself. This particular accusation of Habermas' naivete is contested (Bloomfield et al., 2001) but it is unarguable that powerful participants invariably have the greater resources, and within 'partnership politics' there are insider and outsider interests with varying scope to determine options or to act in self-interested ways (Flyvbjerg, 1998; Hillier, 2000; Pløger, 2001). Moreover, the notion of reasoned consensus favours certain forms of argument, enhanced by articulacy and expert knowledge, further marginalizing voices more familiar with the telling of everyday stories (see Irwin, 1995; Young, 1996; Button and Mattson, 1999). Thus deliberation based upon reasoned argument, unless carefully facilitated, can create internal exclusion through its very practice and search for consensus. This may increase feelings of powerlessness, discouraging participation, while heavy demands on resources may encourage fatigue even among those individuals and organizations most committed to deliberative decision making.

(2) Inclusion and Representation

Inclusion is the act of including others in the processes of consideration, decision and implementation. It is, therefore, about more than who is allowed to take part. It is also about when participation is to be allowed in the decision process, what aspects of the agenda are open to determination by whom, who decides upon the rules and procedures of the deliberative process (Webler, 1995), and what arrangements are made for those who cannot be present. The latter is a well-recognized issue in environmental decision-making, invoking Plumwood's discussion (see above) on social and geographical remoteness. In particular, how are the interests of future generations and of nature to be articulated? At best, these can only be realized by proxy, such as through the representations of environmental agencies, while the immediacy of current economic and political concerns regularly overshadows the interests of children unborn (Laws, 1996; O'Neill, 2001). Moreover, almost all deliberative practices tend to hinder the participation of some sections of society including children, the elderly, ethnic minorities and the disabled. Meetings are never equally convenient; their agendas, for reasons of knowledge and experience, are not equally accessible, and the ways in which they function as round-table discussions tends to favour those comfortable with 'meeting practice' and verbal exchange.

Given the impracticality of totally inclusive participation, those framing the process have a difficult trade-off to manage between extensive involvement and the conduct of an effective process in which those present feel able to make a positive contribution. When it comes to selecting those who might participate, a range of considerations apply. For example, allowing self-selection favours participants with time, resources and education, and a strong reason for being involved. The selection of participants by the organizer of the process, or even the facilitator, is likely to favour those known to have an interest in the outcome. It is not that those most affected should not be involved, but that the process tends to marginalize groups who might bring less pre-formed positions to the table. These methods of selection will always be open to charges of bias, undermining the perceived legitimacy of the process, but a better process is not ensured if a random or systematic selection of citizens is attempted. Furthermore in a democracy there can be no requirement to participate even if all citizens with an interest should have an equal opportunity to do so. But again it can be argued that this opportunity must be supported by a set of capabilities (personal and otherwise) that permit the participants to engage effectively, or what O'Neill terms 'an equality of effectiveness in the exercise of communicative freedom among all citizens' (O'Neill, 2000, p. 512). This situation may never be realized but it should represent the ideal against which to assess what is done.

These practical matters draw attention to the issue of representation, what it means and how it should work. For example, in many communities there are 'self-appointed advocates of a community's interests' (Selman, 1998, p. 538; see also Pratchett, 1999) who may, genuinely, not be able to discern between their personal interests and those of the community they claim to represent. This raises issues of accountability and legitimacy, especially as deliberative processes, by definition, cannot operate on a mandating principle. Participants must have the scope and responsibility to amend their positions. If they do not have the authority to reach negotiated decisions then deliberative arenas cannot progress beyond talking shops, reducing the incentive for participants to take part (Stirling and Maher, 1999). Moreover, the raising of subsequently unfulfilled expectations would be a serious indictment of any particular process, and may require some agreement in advance – on the part of those with the capacity to act – to do so on the conclusions reached.

Two kinds of objection can be raised to the representation present in most DIPs where the numbers involved are small and the problem has wide-ranging social consequences. First, limited representation may provide an inadequate basis for generalizing the findings given the complexity and diversity of modern societies. Even attempts to select participants according to their social and economic characteristics so as to ensure a broadly representative sample of the population can be queried, because of a frequent lack of theorization of the relationships between these characteristics and environmental issues. But the strength of this objection is also open to challenge. Only some practices, such as citizens' juries, are conducted with the aim of making wide-ranging generalizations. For the most part, their value lies as much in gathering intelligence relevant to the making of decisions, including outlining ways in which differing positions may be harmonized.

Second, as previously noted, there is concern over the legitimacy of those doing the representing. Those arguing for a politics of presence for example (Young, 1990), would insist that only those with particular life experiences or characteristics, such as gender, race, age, wealth, can represent those groups in the community. This claim immediately challenges the ideal requirement of both inclusion and deliberation. If 'all' interests have to be directly represented then the practicality of conducting DIPs, never mind attempts to seek a convergence of views, seems remote indeed. The problem is further aggravated if the need to recognize difference through a politics of presence is argued defensively as constituting a threat to identity. The demands of identity may well encourage the promotion of sectional interests rather than their immersion in a politics of collaboration.

Throughout, a distinction has been drawn between those seeking to represent themselves (individual citizens) and stakeholders who claim to represent particular and pre-determined interests. This distinction can be over-emphasized, as all citizens have interests in the environment, legal or merely claimed, and as individuals may have some of the 'expert' qualities normally attributed to stakeholders and their representatives. Nonetheless, both for practical reasons such as access to resources, and also for reasons of power politics, stakeholders with known initial positions are often identified as the major players in the process. This begs the question of how different sections of society should be involved in the process in ways that would maximize the value of their contribution.

Renn et al. (1993) suggest a three-step model designed to integrate three forms of knowledge and experience to best advantage. These are the social interests and advocacy of stakeholders, the knowledge of technical experts, and the common sense and personal experience of citizens, which, they suggest, should be exploited sequentially. In the first stage, stakeholders reveal their values and concerns and develop criteria for judging different options. The second involves experts assessing the impact of each option against indicators derived from the stakeholder criteria. The third seeks to establish lay publics' preferences through their evaluation of the different options as the basis of policy decisions. This approach has the benefit of giving each of the three groups the opportunity to reject, amend or accept the recommendations of the other two. Its weaknesses lie in the assumption that these are discrete groups of interest and that the sequence of engagement creates equal access to the final outcome. For example, concentrating the role of citizens in the final stage of the process might be said to restrict their contribution because the initial framing could have created critical boundaries to the choice of alternatives. Likewise, stakeholders might question the competence of citizens, especially as they are primarily involved in the crucial last phase of the process. Despite its analytical and practical advantages, too much systemization of the process between the roles of groups and between the steps may undermine the larger integrating objective (see also the experience of Hajer and Kesselring, 1999).

(3) Evaluation

As emancipatory practices, the relevance and legitimacy of DIPs are frequently questioned in the political arena. A practical means of defending their value would be to point to rigorous, independent and transparent evaluations of their contribution to environmental governance. The assessment of particular cases would be a start even if more generic analyses might have broader purchase. But the need for generic assessment is easier to assert than to deliver for five main reasons:

1. the wide range of deliberative practices in use
2. the importance of context to outcomes
3. the wide range of procedural and outcome goals that DIPs claim to address, and the varying importance that different actors attach to each
4. agreeing which evaluative criteria to use and who should do the evaluation
5. deciding how to establish whether the process has made a 'difference' and on what basis that conclusion is reached

The present situation is characterized by limited evidence. Despite the many examples of DIPs, there are few rigorous evaluations of either procedures or outcomes, and even fewer of the relations between them. Evaluation is the poor relation of the process. Goodin's observation reveals one fundamental difficulty: 'to advocate democracy is to advocate procedures, to advocate environmentalism is to advocate outcomes: what guarantee can we have that the former procedures will yield the latter sort of outcomes?' (Goodin, 1992, p. 68). There can, by definition, be no guarantee. Even if agreement were reached on the priority to be given to different kinds of outcome, how they are sought would depend on context as much as the means employed. Learning through simple comparison risks privileging particular means rather than seeing them within the broader political and managerial strategies of which they are a part. A failure to understand the roles of local cultures, practices and organizations would undermine any attempt to evaluate specific cases, never mind provide the basis for an exchange of best practice.

It is also necessary to recognize the dynamic and contested nature of DIPs and the need for evaluation to be built into the process from the outset. It may even be that evaluation becomes a key vehicle through which 'participants clarify what they mean by the action in which they are engaged' (Barnes, 1999, p. 66). Such an approach could ensure that baselines are established early on against which achievements are evaluated, provided the baselines themselves do not then become fixed positions that set boundaries for subsequent deliberation. This suggests the need for the evaluation process to build in its own reflexivity rather than to act in a purely judgemental way on whether the original objectives are achieved. It might also encourage the use of complementary methods of evaluation to allow the full range of considerations (procedural and outcomes) to be assessed. Such a broad-based approach is also more likely to establish whether particular outcomes are a direct result of the practice used or the conjunction of a set of events of which the practice was but one.

More generally, debates over outcomes can drift into negativity through blame allocation over perceived failure or unrealistic expectations of 'success'. A much more positive approach is to assess gains in institutional and personal resources, not only amongst participants but also in the mobilization of social and intellectual capacity more generally. All participants will doubtless make private evaluations of their experiences and these may well differ as each will have had different objectives underlying their engagement. For example, those who will have to act on the positions reached usually seek unambiguous outcomes based upon maximum agreement in the hope that this will reduce uncertainty, or even conflict, over what they then decide to do. Those framing the process may be more concerned to raise levels of trust in local decision makers, while established interests will rarely want outcomes that undermine their positions.

There have been several attempts to develop generic criteria for evaluating the effectiveness of DIPs. Many concentrate on aspects of process, notably Webler (1995) who selected the notions of fairness and competence. Fairness concerns the equitable distribution of opportunities among participants to initiate discussion, to challenge and defend claims, and to decide. Competence refers to the procedures employed and whether participants appreciate and understand them. Renn et al. (1995) go on to use these criteria to make a comparative evaluation of eight 'models' of deliberative decision making. These 'models' (or practices) range from established methods such as citizen advisory committees and citizens' juries to more specific techniques such as mediation, compensation and benefit sharing, assessing them in terms of the constraints they impose on who is allowed to participate, access to knowledge, and the scope of the discussion. Rowe and Frewer (2000) attempt to make these criteria more operational by listing a number of indicators of public acceptance and effectiveness of process (see Box 4.1). They also evaluate different kinds of methods (public hearings, consensus conferences, focus groups and so on) against their criteria. Like Renn et al. (1995), they conclude that each has its own strengths and weaknesses. This suggests that methods might be usefully used in combination and that their selection must suit the problem in hand and its particular social and political context. These are matters that must be addressed at the outset.

The nature of the process and who is to be consulted are not independent of the environmental issue under investigation. For example, Renn et al. (1995) suggest that where the debate concerns the interpretation of factual information and the outcome affects a small, undifferentiated constituency, it may well be best addressed through formal schemes of negotiated rule-making and compensation driven by experts. Issues concerning the public's confidence in the competence of decision makers require transparent debates designed to increase mutual understanding and a commitment to joint action to restore confidence, as may be realized through citizens' juries. Different again are conflicts over competing values and worldviews, which extend

BOX 4.1   EVALUATIVE CRITERIA FOR PUBLIC ACCEPTANCE AND EFFECTIVENESS OF A PROCESS

Criteria for acceptance – potential public acceptance of a procedure

- representativeness: representative sample of the affected population
- independence: process conducted in an independent, unbiased way
- early involvement: increases sense of ownership and role at the stage when value judgements are important
- influence: visible impact on policy
- transparency: the public should be able to see progress and that decisions are being made

Criteria for effective process – effective construction and implementation of a process

- resource accessibility: access to appropriate resources (information, time, experts, materials) to enable participants to fulfil their brief successfully
- task definition: the scope of the exercise, its procedural mechanisms and the expected outputs should be defined at the outset
- structured decision-making: to enable debate over the underlying assumptions, how the decision was made, the extent to which it was supported
- cost-effectiveness: process suitable to the scale and importance of the decision in terms of the investment in time and money

Source: Based upon Rowe and Frewer (2000)

beyond the realm of public confidence in local managers and technical expertise. Such conflicts require lengthy, inclusive and open debate if any form of consensus is to be reached.

Other studies draw attention to the importance of the quality of the outcomes in environmental terms if confidence in deliberative practice is to be retained (for example, Petts, 2000). Pestman (1998), for example, describes the history of public involvement in infrastructure investment decisions in the Netherlands. He concludes that public participation has achieved better decisions environmentally through the encouragement of technological innovation and the increased attention paid to the social and environmental costs of infrastructure programmes. However public authorities have been cautious in accepting recommendations as they are sensitive to the possibility of making mistakes which would in turn undermine public confidence in them and in the public's role. The expectations for public involvement must not be set too high, not least among members of the public.

This conclusion reminds us of the importance of the governance setting in which DIPs are used. First, there are the ways in which their outcomes are likely to engage with public decision-making processes, especially the receptiveness of what Healey (1997) defines as the 'hard' infrastructure, or the formal institutions of society (such as the constitution, the law, property rights) and their mutually reinforcing processes (see also Hanf and Jansen, 1998). More broadly, how responsive are institutionalized sources of power to the claims-making processes (including DIPs) of civil society? Second, in the light of the previous point, what general status is accorded to deliberative processes? Are they seen as 'insider' or 'outsider' practices, as constructive or threatening forces for change? The challenge for those designing DIPs is to find an appropriate accommodation between the need for independence and integrity whilst retaining sufficient authority within the relevant governance structure for their recommendations to have an impact on policy or decision making.

CONCLUSION

This last point returns us to the question posed at the outset concerning the manner in which the outcomes of deliberative processes should engage with established bureaucratic regimes and the functioning of representative democracy and what we, as citizens, should make of this. Even if we take a more critical stance than Selman, who argues that for all its failings representative democracy is a 'well understood and constitutional method which bestows a genuine legitimacy on elected representatives to speak on behalf of constituents' (Selman, 1998, p. 538), the majority of citizens still respond to the failings of the present with inactivity, including non-voting, except in very specific circumstances in which their interests are directly affected. Here, they may turn to protest. It could even be argued that the polity itself is more concerned to make incremental adjustments to its practices in order to increase trust in itself, perhaps for self-serving reasons, than citizens are prepared to push for change. However, real change, including a sense of ownership over it, must come from below, and its failure to do so risks unsatisfied expectations, inertia and resort by the committed to protest.

Where does this leave environmental issues, a quintessential area of public policy in which all citizens have a stake? Environmental politics is in the vanguard of calls for deliberative democracy, associated with debates over bottom-up policy making and the use of DIPs, but that position may also be contributing to its continuing marginalization within the politics of capitalism in the absence of environmental catastrophe. This is not to argue that environmental values and objectives are completely absent, or that notable events, such as those surrounding the disposal of the Brent Spar, have not from time to time mildly ruffled capitalist waters. But for those seeking genuine but incremental change within current economic and political arrangements, there is a long row to hoe if civil society at large is to be persuaded to respond actively to several important arguments: (1) that the incertitude associated with many environmental issues demands that the widest possible range of knowledges be brought to bear on their management; (2) that the complexity and breadth of consequence of environmental problems requires integrated approaches to their solution, cutting across the narrow confines of compartmentalized expert knowledge and the responsibilities of established institutions and organizations; and (3) that the concerns of environmental justice speak loudly to the under-represented and even silent voices of current environmental discourses, including nature and future generations.

More specifically, as experimentation with DIPs as means of securing that active civil engagement becomes more extensive, so their potential contribution will be more critically examined. At present, it could be argued, there is still insufficient empirical evidence to demonstrate their value to justify the effort, especially in the face of public and political demands for evidence of immediate benefits, preferably at limited cost. Thus it could be concluded that their greatest long-term value may lie not so much in their contribution to particular environmental issues as they arise, such as the siting of waste sites, but with providing better anticipatory mechanisms for emergent technologies or whole areas of policy. It is, for example, an intellectual, administrative and political indictment that the BSE crisis in Britain could have proceeded for so long in the absence of inclusive, deliberative and open debate. Partnership governance between public and private interests may be a reality but, as revealed in this case, if conducted in closed, expert-led fora it can fail to deliver the critical reflexivity that open and inclusive practices are more likely to do. But significant, transformative changes will not be realized from DIPs until their findings are accepted by powerful stakeholders as making legitimate and necessary contributions to environmental decision-making in democratic societies.

To be able to aspire to such a prize, much more detailed inquiry into the functioning and outcomes of DIPs is required. Three of the more important areas are as follows. First, the development of more rigorous, independent evaluations of their benefits is urgently needed, especially of the tension that can exist between meeting process and outcome goals, if only to allow those charged with framing future practices a better sense of what constitutes 'fitness for purpose' in defined circumstances. Second, not only do we need to know more about the direct links between the specific uses of DIPs and ensuing environmental decisions, but we also need a better understanding of the more general relations between their conduct and the functioning of the 'hard' infrastructures of democratic societies within different political cultures. Third, are DIPs an effective means of building social capital? Do they have the capacity to create a virtuous circle of civic learning, capacity building and engagement? And under what circumstances can they stimulate a permanent sense of public commitment to the environment as an increasingly important part of the public sphere?

NOTES

1. I would like to thank Kate Studd and Sam Gardner for their constructive comments on a draft of this chapter.
2. There is no singular definition of deliberative and inclusionary processes or practices appropriate to all contexts although their general purpose is clear. They are committed to engaging as broad a representation of society as practically possible in public decision making and in ways that require debate and reflexivity. Here, the term process refers to the general principles surrounding this purpose and the institutional settings that prompt them, whilst practices refer to the specific methods or techniques (e.g. focus groups, consensus conferences) used to achieve the purpose.
3. See, for example, Fishkin, 1991; Miller, 1992; Philips, 1995; Benhabib, 1996; for links with environmental justice, see Harvey, 1996; Low and Gleeson, 1998; Dobson, 1999.

REFERENCES

Andringa, J. (1998), 'The influence of Local Agenda 21 on local policy and the quality of decision-making: the pioneer city of The Hague', in F. Coenan, D. Huitema and L. O'Toole (eds), *Participation and Quality of Environmental Decision-Making*, London: Kluwer, pp. 107–24.

Arnstein, S. (1969), 'A ladder of citizen participation', *Journal of the American Institute of Planners*, 35 (4), 216–24.

Banerjee, A. (1999), 'Community forestry development in India', in M. Palo and J. Kusivuori (eds), *World Forests, Society and Environment*, London: Kluwer, pp. 196–203.

Barnes, M. (1999), 'Researching public participation', *Local Government Studies*, 25 (4), 60–75.

Benhabib, S. (1996), 'Toward a deliberative model of democratic legitimacy', in S. Benhabib (ed.), *Democracy and Difference*, Princeton, NJ: Princeton University Press.

Blake, J. (1999), 'Overcoming the value-action gap in environmental policy: tensions between national policy and local experience', *Local Environment*, 4, 257–78.

Blaug, R. (2002), 'Engineering democracy', *Political Studies*, 50, 102–16.

Bloomfield, D., K. Collins, C. Fry and R. Munton (2001), 'Deliberation and inclusion: vehicles for increasing trust in UK public governance?', *Environment and Planning C*, 19, 501–13.

Bohman, J. and W. Rehg (eds) (1997), *Deliberative Democracy: Essays on Reason and Politics*, Cambridge, MA: MIT Press.

Bucek, J. and B. Smith (2000), 'New approaches to local democracy: direct democracy, participation and the "third sector"', *Environment and Planning C*, 18, 3–16.

Burgess, J. (1990), 'The production and consumption of environmental meanings in the mass media: a research agenda for the 1990s', *Transactions of the Institute of British Geographers*, 15, 139–61.

Burgess, J. (2000), 'Situating knowledges, sharing values and reaching collective decisions: the cultural turn in environmental decision-making', in I. Cook, D. Crouch, S. Naylor and J. Ryan (eds), *Cultural Turns/Geographical Turns: Perspectives on Cultural Geography*, Harlow, UK: Pearson Education, pp. 273–87.

Burgess, J., C. Harrison and P. Filius (1998), 'Environmental communication and the cultural politics of environmental citizenship', *Environment and Planning A*, 30, 1445–60.

Burgess, J., C. Harrison and P. Maiteny (1991), 'Contested meanings: the consumption of news about nature conservation', *Media, Culture and Society*, 13, 499–516.

Burgess, J., M. Limb and C. Harrison (1988a), 'Exploring environmental values through the medium of focus groups, I: Theory and practice', *Environment and Planning A*, 20, 309–26.

Burgess, J., M. Limb and C. Harrison (1988b), 'Exploring environmental values through the medium of focus groups, II: Illustrations of a group at work', *Environment and Planning A*, 20, 457–76.

Button, M. and K. Mattson (1999), 'Deliberative democracy in practice: challenges and prospects for civil deliberation', *Polity*, 31 (4), 609–37.

Chambers, R. (1994a), 'The origins and practice of participatory rural appraisal (PRA)', *World Development*, 22 (7), 953–69.

Chambers, R. (1994b), 'Participatory rural appraisal (PRA): Analysis of experience', *World Development*, 22 (9), 1253–68.

Clark, J., A. Stirling, K. Studd and J. Burgess (2001), *Local Outreach*, Research and Development Technical Report, SWCON 204, Bristol, UK: Environment Agency.

Coenan, F. (1998), 'Participation in strategic planning in the Netherlands', in F. Coenan, D. Huitema and L. O'Toole (eds), *Participation and the Quality of Environmental Decision-Making*, London: Kluwer, pp. 129–48.

Coenan, F., D. Huitema and L. O'Toole (eds) (1998), *Participation and the Quality of Environmental Decision-Making*, London: Kluwer.

Cowie, G. and L. O'Toole (1998), 'Linking stakeholder participation and environmental decision-making: assessing decision quality for interstate river basin management', in F. Coenan, D. Huitema and L. O'Toole (eds), *Participation and the Quality of Environmental Decision-Making*, London: Kluwer, pp. 61-72.

Davies, A. (1999), 'Where do we go from here? Environmental focus groups and planning policy formation', *Local Environment*, 4, 295-316.

Davies, A. (2002), 'Power, politics and networks: shaping partnerships for sustainable communities', *Area*, 34 (2), 190-203.

DETR (Department of the Environment, Transport and the Regions) (1998), *Guidance on Enhancing Public Participation in Local Government*, London: DETR.

Dobson, A. (ed.) (1999), *Fairness and Futurity: Essays on Environmental Justice and Social Justice*, Oxford: Oxford University Press.

Dryzek, J. (1990), *Discursive Democracy: Politics, Policy and Political Science*, Cambridge, UK: Cambridge University Press.

Dryzek, J. (1995), 'Political and ecological communication', *Environmental Politics*, 4 (4), 13-30.

Eden, S. (1999), '"We have the facts" – how business claims legitimacy in the environmental debate', *Environment and Planning A*, 31, 1295-310.

Elster, J. (ed.) (1998), *Deliberative Democracy*, Cambridge, UK: Cambridge University Press.

Fishkin, J. (1991), *Democracy and Deliberation: New Directions for Democratic Reform*, London: Yale University Press.

Flyvbjerg, B. (1998), *Rationality and Power*, Chicago, IL: Chicago University Press.

Forester, J. (1999), *The Deliberative Practitioner: Encouraging Participatory Planning Processes*, Cambridge, MA: MIT Press.

Funtowitz, S. and J. Ravetz (1994), 'The worth of a songbird: ecological economics as post-normal science', *Ecological Economics*, 10, 197-207.

Gibbs, D., J. Longhurst and C. Braithwaite (1996), 'Moving towards sustainable development? Integrating economic development and the environment in local authorities', *Journal of Environmental Planning and Management*, 39, 317-32.

Gibbs, D., J. Longhurst and C. Braithwaite (1998), '"Struggling with sustainability": weak and strong interpretations of sustainable development within local authority policy', *Environment and Planning A*, 30, 1351-65.

Goodin, R. (1992), *Green Political Theory*, Oxford, UK: Polity.

Goodwin, P. (1998), '"Hired hands" or "local voice": understandings and experience of local participation in conservation', *Transactions of the Institute of British Geographers*, 23, 481-99.

Gujja, B., M. Pimbert and M. Shah (1998), 'Village voices challenging wetland-management policies: PRA experiences from Pakistan and India', in J. Holland (ed.), *Whose Voice? Participatory Research and Policy Change*, London: Intermediate Technology Publications, pp. 57-66.

Habermas, J. (1984), *The Theory of Communicative Action. Volume I: Reason and the Rationalisation of Society* (translated by T. McCarthy), London: Heinemann.

Habermas, J. (1996), 'Popular sovereignty as procedure', in J. Habermas (ed.), *Between Facts and Norms: Contributions to a Discourse Theory of Law and Democracy*, Cambridge, MA: MIT Press, pp. 463-90.

Hajer, M. and S. Kesselring (1999), 'Democracy in risk society? Learning from the new politics of mobility in Munich', *Environmental Politics*, 8 (3), 1-23.

Hanf, K. and A.-I. Jansen (eds) (1998), *Governance and Environment in Western Europe: Politics, Policy and Administration*, Harlow, UK: Longman.

Hansen, A. (eds) (1993), *The Mass Media and Environmental Issues*, Leicester, UK: Leicester University Press.

Harrison, C., J. Burgess and P. Filius (1996), 'Rationalising environmental responsibilities: a comparison of lay publics in the UK and the Netherlands', *Global Environmental Change*, 6 (3), 215–35.

Harvey, D. (1996), *Justice, Nature and the Geography of Difference*, London: Blackwell.

Haynes, J. (1999), 'Power, politics and environmental movements in the Third World', *Environmental Politics*, 8 (1), 222–42.

Healey, P. (1997), *Collaborative Planning: Shaping Plans in Fragmented Societies*, Basingstoke, UK: Macmillan.

Healey, P. (1998), 'Collaborative planning in a stakeholder society', *Town Planning Review*, 69, 1–21.

Hillier, J. (2000), 'Going round the back? Complex networks and informal action in local planning processes', *Environment and Planning A*, 32, 33–54.

Holmes, T. and I. Scoones (2000), *Participatory Environmental Policy Processes: Experiences from North and South*, Brighton, UK: Institute of Development Studies.

Huitema, D. (1998), 'Hazardous decisions: the siting of hazardous waste facilities in Canada and the United States', in F. Coenan, D. Huitema and L. O'Toole (eds), *Participation and the Quality of Environmental Decision Making*, London: Kluwer, pp. 223–46.

Hunold, C. and I. Young (1998), 'Justice, democracy and hazardous siting', *Political Studies*, 46, 82–95.

Innes, J. (1996), 'Planning through consensus-building: a new view of the comprehensive planning ideal', *Journal of the American Planning Association*, 62, 460–72.

Irwin, A. (1995), *Citizen Science*, London: Routledge.

Jacobs, M. (ed.) (1997), *Greening the Millennium: The New Politics of the Environment*, Oxford: Blackwell.

Jordan, G. and W. Maloney (1997), *The Protest Business*, Manchester, UK: University of Manchester Press.

Lafferty, W. and K. Eckerberg (eds) (1998), *From Earth Summit to Local Agenda 21*, London: Earthscan.

Laws, D. (1996), 'The practice of fairness', *Environmental Impact Assessment Review*, 16, 65–70.

Lemos, M. (1998), 'Popular participation and pollution control', in F. Coenan, D. Huitema and L. O'Toole (eds), *Participation and the Quality of Environmental Decision Making*, London: Kluwer, pp. 267–86.

Low, N. and B. Gleeson (1998), *Justice, Society and Nature: An Exploration of Political Ecology*, London: Routledge.

Lowe, P. and J. Goyder (1983), *Environmental Groups in Politics*, London: Allen and Unwin.

Macnaghten, P. and M. Jacobs (1997), 'Public identification with sustainable development: investigating cultural barriers to participation', *Global Environmental Change*, 7, 5–24.

Maloney, W., G. Jordan and A. McLoughlin (1994), 'Interest groups and public policy: the insider/outsider model revisited', *Journal of Public Policy*, 14, 17–38.

Mason, M. (1999), *Environmental Democracy*, London: Earthscan.

Miller, D. (1992), 'Deliberative democracy and social choice', *Political Studies*, 40 (special issue), 54–67.

Murdoch, J. and T. Marsden (1995), 'The spatialization of politics: local and national actor-spaces in environmental conflict', *Transactions of the Institute of British Geographers*, 20, 368–80.

O'Neill, J. (2001), 'Representing people, representing nature, representing the world', *Environment and Planning C*, 19, 483–500.

O'Neill, S. (2000), 'The politics of inclusive agreements: towards a critical discourse theory of democracy', *Political Studies*, 48, 503–21.

O'Riordan, T., J. Burgess and B. Szerszynski (eds) (1999), *Inclusive and Deliberative Processes: A Report from Two Seminars*, Working Paper PA 99–06, Norwich, UK: Centre for Social and Economic Research on the Global Environment (CSERGE), University of East Anglia.

Ostrom, E. (1990), *Governing the Commons: The Evolution of Institutions for Collective Action*, Cambridge, UK: Cambridge University Press.

Ostrom, E. (1996), 'Crossing the great divide: co-production, synergy and development, *World Development*, 24, 1073–87.

Owens, S. and R. Cowell (2002), *Land and Limits: Interpreting Sustainability in the Planning Process*, London: Routledge.

Peet, R. and M. Watts (eds) (1996), *Liberation Ecologies: Environment, Development, Social Movements*, London: Routledge.

Pestman, P. (1998), 'Dutch infrastructure policies, public participation and the environment in the 1990s: the politics of interfering logics', in F. Coenan, D. Huitema and L. O'Toole (eds), *Participation and the Quality of Environmental Decision Making*, London: Kluwer, pp. 185–202.

Petts, J. (1995), 'Waste management strategy development: a case study of community involvement and consensus-building in Hampshire', *Journal of Environmental Planning and Management*, 38, 519–36.

Petts, J. (2000), *Evaluating Methods for Public Participation: Literature Review*, Research and Development Technical Report E 135, Bristol, UK: Environment Agency.

Petts, J. (2001), 'Evaluating the effectiveness of deliberative processes: waste management case studies', *Journal of Environmental Planning and Management*, 44 (2), 207–26.

Phillips, A. (1995), *The Politics of Presence*, Oxford, UK: Oxford University Press.

Pløger, J. (2001), 'Public participation and the art of governance', *Environment and Planning B*, 28, 219–41.

Plumwood, V. (1998), 'Inequality, eco-justice and ecological rationality', reprinted in J. Dryzek and D. Schlosberg (eds) (1999), *Debating the Earth: The Environmental Politics Reader*, Oxford, UK: Oxford University Press.

Pratchett, L. (1999), 'New fashions in public participation: Towards greater democracy?', *Parliamentary Affairs*, 52 (4), 616–33.

Rawcliffe, P. (1998), *Environmental Pressure Groups in Transition*, Manchester, UK: Manchester University Press.

Renn, O., B. Blatten-Mink and H. Kastenholz (1997), 'Discursive methods in environmental decision-making', *Business Strategy and the Environment*, 6, 218–31.

Renn, O., T. Webler, H. Rakel, P. Dienel and B. Johnson (1993), 'Public participation in decision making: a three step procedure', *Policy Sciences*, 26, 189–214.

Renn, O., T. Webler and P. Weidemann (eds) (1995), *Fairness and Competence in Citizen Participation*, London: Kluwer.

Rittel, H. and M. Webber (1973), 'Dilemmas in a general theory of planning', *Policy Sciences*, 4.3, 155–69.

Routledge, P. (1997), 'The imagineering of resistance: Pollock Free State and the practice of post-modern politics', *Transactions of the Institute of British Geographers*, 22 (3), 359–76.

Rowe, G. and L. Frewer (2000), 'Public participation methods: a framework for evaluation', *Science, Technology and Human Values*, 25, 3–29.

Rydin, Y. and M. Pennington (2000), 'Public participation and local environmental planning: the collective action problem and the potential of social capital', *Local Environment*, 5 (2), 153–69.

Selman, P. (1998), 'Local Agenda 21: substance or spin?', *Journal of Environmental Planning and Management*, 41 (5), 533–53.

Selman, P. (2000), 'Networks of knowledge and influence: connecting planners and the planned', *Town Planning Review*, 71, 109–21.

Smith, G. and C. Wales (1999), 'The theory and practice of citizens' juries', *Policy and Politics*, 27 (3), 295–308.

Smith, J., J. Blake, R. Grove-White, E. Kashefi, S. Madden and S. Percy (1999), 'Social learning and sustainable communities: an interim assessment of research into sustainable communities projects in the UK', *Local Environment*, 4 (2), 195–207.

Stirling, A. and S. Maher (1999), *Rethinking Risk: a Pilot Multi-criteria Mapping of Genetically Modified Crops in Agricultural Systems in the UK*, Brighton, UK: Science and Policy Research Unit, University of Sussex.

Tewdwr-Jones, M. and P. Allmendinger (1998), 'Deconstructing communicative rationality: a critique of Habermasian collaborative planning', *Environment and Planning A*, 30, 1975–89.

Tewdwr-Jones, M. and H. Thomas (1998), 'Collaborative action in local plan-making: planners' perceptions of "planning through debate"', *Environment and Planning B*, 25, 127–44.

Ward, H. (1999), 'Citizens' juries and valuing the environment: a proposal', *Environmental Politics*, 8 (2), 75–96.

Warner, M. (1997), '"Consensus" participation: an example for protected areas planning', *Public Administration and Development*, 17, 413–32.

Webler, T. (1995), '"Right" discourse in citizen participation: an evaluative yardstick', in O. Renn, T. Webler and P. Wiedemann (eds), *Fairness and Competence in Citizen Participation*, London: Kluwer, pp. 35–86.

Webler, T. and O. Renn (1995), 'A brief primer on public participation: philosophy and practice', in O. Renn, T. Webler and P. Wiedemann (eds), *Fairness and Competence in Citizen Participation*, London: Kluwer, pp. 17–34.

Wynne, B. (1996), 'May the sheep safely graze? A reflexive view of the expert–lay knowledge divide', in S. Lash, B. Szerszysnki and B. Wynne (eds), *Risk, Environment and Modernity: Towards a New Ecology*, London: Sage, pp. 44–83.

Young, Iris (1990), *Justice and the Politics of Difference*, Princeton, NJ: Princeton University Press.

Young, Iris, (1996), 'Communication and the other: beyond deliberative democracy', in S. Benhabib (ed.), *Democracy and Difference*, Princeton, NJ: Princeton University Press.

Zazueta, A. (1995), *Policy Hits the Ground: Participation and Equity in Environmental Policy Making*, Washington, DC: World Resources Institute.

5. Governance and the environment

John Vogler and Andrew Jordan

THE ENVIRONMENTAL IMPORTANCE OF GOVERNANCE

In the 1980s it was increasingly apparent that the existing network of global institutions centred on the United Nations (UN) was inadequate for the urgent task of taking remedial action to counter global processes of environmental change. The much-quoted UN Brundtland Report on human development and the environment identified the challenge succinctly:

> The integrated and interdependent nature of the new challenges and issues contrasts sharply with the nature of institutions that exist today. These institutions tend to be independent, fragmented and working to relatively narrow mandates with closed decision processes ... The real world of interlocked economic and ecological systems will not change; the policies and institutions concerned must (WCED, 1987, p. 310).

The moment appeared to be propitious. The ending of the Cold War, which was confirmed by the collapse of the Berlin Wall in 1989 and the dissolution of the Soviet Union in 1991, appeared to open up a space for a new kind of politics predicated upon shared perceptions of social, economic and, above all, environmental interdependence. It was quickly accepted that pollution control, habitat loss and waste, all of which arise from otherwise socially legitimate activities such as consumption, travel and trade, require the state (or states when problems spill across borders) to set the parameters of human activity in order to place society on a more environmentally, socially and economically sustainable path. This recognition places the study of government – or, more broadly governance – at the very centre of environmental social science, now and for the immediate future.

ENVIRONMENTAL SOCIAL SCIENCE IN AN ERA OF SUSTAINABILITY AND GOVERNANCE

Since the first UN Conference on the Human Environment, held at Stockholm in 1972, many states had defined the environment as a new area of governmental activity and dedicated ministries were duly created. However, their status was generally never very high and the environment was left to function as a somewhat marginal and unconnected issue at the margins of mainstream policy and politics. During the 1990s, however, there was a discernible trend in the UK and other industrialized countries away from a narrow treatment of the environment per se (Lafferty and Meadowcroft, 2000) to one embracing sustainable development. Politically speaking, sustainability is a much more diffuse and interconnected political notion than either environmental policy or global environmental change (Jordan, 2000a; O'Riordan, 2001). Among other things, it raises new and difficult challenges for the way we govern the environment; challenges which environmental social science must find new ways of addressing. The first aim of this chapter is, therefore, to examine how environmental policy has been gradually superseded in political and policy terms by sustainable development.

However, just as these new demands were being made upon governments, the continued effectiveness of the state itself was becoming increasingly problematic. There was not only real evidence of state failure and disintegration in many parts of the world, but also a dominant ideological disposition towards the reduction of state activities and responsibilities and the limitation of the extent and costs of international organization. Grounded in neo-liberal economic rather than environmental or sustainability orthodoxy, this shift too was clearly associated with the end of the Cold War and led to widespread privatization, agencification and new public management the world over. Direct public ownership and control over significant enterprises such as transport, energy production, waste-water and sewage treatment was frequently relinquished or, at the very least, significantly loosened. The corporate sector was evidently going to acquire much greater significance, but by the 1992 UN Earth Summit in Rio it was abundantly clear that something loosely termed global civil society had also to be taken into account (Jordan, 1994). The green NGOs can lay claim to have been the vanguard of this movement and pressed their involvement in policy-making related to sustainability at all levels. All this provides some indication of why the term 'governance', implying the exercise of government-like functions without or sometimes alongside formal government, is now a concept in wide currency.

Therefore, a second purpose of this chapter is to discuss the implications of the secular transformation of environmental government into governance. According to Stoker (1998, p. 17), the word 'government' refers to activities undertaken primarily or wholly by bodies, particularly those 'which operate at the level of the nation state to maintain public order and facilitate collective action'. Typically these latter functions were performed by the state within its own territory via different parts of the public sector. The term 'governance', on the other hand, refers to the emergence of new styles of governing in which the boundaries between the public and private sector, national and international, are more blurred. For Stoker, then, 'the essence of governance is its focus on governing mechanisms which do not rest on recourse to the authority and sanctions of government' (Stoker, 1998). Under a system of governance, services tend to be supplied by the market with the state retaining control over core functions such as law and order, regulation and civil defence. This therefore requires new ways of steering and controlling activities undertaken by a mixture of public and private sector bodies through more indirect mechanisms such as financial control and voluntary agreements. Though not taken for environmental reasons, the long term environmental implications of these changes could be potentially enormous, although they remain very poorly understood.

A third purpose of the chapter is to examine to what extent environmental concerns have been taken to the heart of the social sciences, especially with respect to the study of government and governance. Traditionally, political scientists, policy analysts and organizational theorists have shown very little interest in understanding environmental problems or framing policy solutions. To what extent is this still true today? Sustainability calls for environment to be an integral part of every policy area. But have environmental concerns been integrated into the heart of the political and policy sciences?

The fourth and final purpose of the chapter is to identify the new research agenda that is emerging around the interlinked concepts of governance and sustainability.

FROM ENVIRONMENT TO SUSTAINABILITY

Research in the early 1990s was inevitably shaped by the prevailing political climate of the time. It asked the question 'what is to be governed and for what purpose?' Initially the answer appeared to be relatively straightforward and solutions were framed in terms of improving environmental policy. Yet very quickly, researchers had to grapple with the gradual transformation of environmental policy into the much more socially and politically diffuse notion of sustainability, which cuts across the domains of the economy, society and the environment. Researchers initially concentrated upon problems that were regarded as uniquely global and environmental in character such as climate change and biodiversity. These foci reflected the policy concerns of the day. At the international level there was an emphasis on the institutionalization of environmental policy driven, in particular, by the need to construct an effective climate regime. This responded to a definition of solutions in terms of the requirement to align divergent national policies and to set standards of behaviour for governments (O'Riordan and Jäger, 1996). In one respect at least, striking successes were achieved. By comparison with the normally glacial progress of international institution building, the 1990s represented a period of unprecedented institutional innovation. Framework conventions on climate (1992) and biodiversity (1992) were negotiated, a steady strengthening of the ozone depletion regime followed the 1987 Montreal Protocol, and Agenda 21 provided a vast blueprint for implementing sustainable development. At the same time, international conventions on the transport of hazardous wastes (1989) and desertification (1994) were developed, along with a large network of regional environmental agreements. Following the Earth Summit an ongoing review process was instituted involving the newly created UN Commission on Sustainable Development.

Associated with these developments were research questions involving the possibility of international co-operation, the circumstances under which it might be achieved and the effectiveness of international institutions in restraining environmentally damaging behaviour and encouraging sustainability at a global level. Churchill et al. (1995), for example, compared three atmospheric regimes: the Montreal Protocol, the Long Range Transboundary Air Pollution Convention and the EC's Large Combustion Plant Directive. Their analysis revealed that high levels of compliance by parties to these regimes was relatively easy to achieve because the regimes – that is sets of norms, principles, rules and decision-making procedures – largely codified existing national policies. The research also confirmed something that was already an integral part of the nascent climate change regime; the significance of allowing differential obligations when there is a wide economic disparity between parties.

Much research in this period had direct policy relevance. As well as reflecting upon the building of international institutions, researchers sometimes influenced the process. For example Cameron and Sands, two international legal researchers from the Foundation for International Law and Development (FIELD) in London, were influential in the founding and development of the Alliance of Small Island States (AOSIS) (Leggett, 2000, p. 23). Other researchers, such as Greene and Salt (1993), and Jordan and Werksman (1994; 1995) also took an active part in shaping the construction of the climate change regime (Greene, 1996) and the operation of its financial mechanism, the Global Environment Facility of the World Bank (Jordan, 1995).

However, the easy assumption that the negotiation of an environmental treaty, duly signed and ratified by the state parties, represented a necessary and sufficient condition for global problem solving was well overdue for revision. Questions of compliance, monitoring and verification were evidently crucial to the negotiation process and in the longer term to the ultimate question of environmental effectiveness. Environmental regimes seek not just to establish formal commitments from governments, but also to reach down to the levels at which polluting activities occur and to alter the behaviour of organizations and individuals. Such issues have been informed by work on the legal dimensions of compliance systems (Cameron et al., 1995) and policy-related studies of implementation review and verification systems for the climate convention process (Greene, 1996), as well as wider studies of the implementation and effectiveness of regimes (for example O'Riordan and Jäger, 1996; Victor et al. 1998; Young, 1999a; Young, 1999b; Young, 2001).

The one overwhelming conclusion emerging from much of this work was that, even in the paradigm case of the Montreal Protocol, there were significant, and on occasion apparently insurmountable, problems in translating international agreements into sustainable solutions on the ground. O'Riordan and Jäger (1996), and Jordan (1998a) examined the implementation of the climate change and ozone regimes respectively, and concluded that the adoption of an international agreement was really just the beginning of a long and slow process which must involve actors at successively lower levels of governance – local authorities, national departments of state, small and medium sized enterprises – whose knowledge of the initial agreement is often extremely basic (Purvis et al., 1997; Shove, 1995).

By the mid-1990s the concept of sustainable development had become the dominant *leitmotif* of modern environmental policy (see Berkhout et al., Chapter 1). Its popularity reflected a greater awareness of the complexity of environmental problems and their intimate relationship with social and economic agendas (as exemplified by the problems of making international conventions truly effective in terms of changing human behaviour and remedying environmental damage). Meanwhile, perceptions of the scale at which problems had to be tackled were also changing. From the 1970s, natural scientists had developed an ever more sophisticated conception of global scale phenomena. In political discourse, the urge to think and act global post-Rio was irresistible. The global prefix was to become de rigueur in calls for global governance, in the naming of the Global Environment Facility (in reality an international environmental arm of the World Bank) and, of course, in the naming of the ESRC's research programme. On closer inspection, however, there was a growing sense that in terms of their causation and eventual solution, global problems were not really global at all (see Adger, Chapter 7). Instead they were a summation of the effects of problems at successively smaller scales. Nor were they purely environmental because their causes and consequences normally resided in societies and the economy (Paterson, 2000). Researchers reacted to this concern by initiating a range of social scientific investigations which adopted a more local perspective on global problems. A popular topic was the Agenda 21 process which spawned countless 'mini' Local Agenda 21s in towns and cities across the world (O'Riordan and Voisey, 1998; Selman, 1996; Young, 2000). In developing countries, other researchers were reaching similar conclusions about the need to reconcile local and global imperatives via the adoption of local coping and adaptation strategies (Adger, 2000; and Chapter 7).

So, what does all this mean for environmental social science? Nowadays, the central intellectual and policy problem is to establish the ways in which our fragmented knowledge of the various sectors and levels of the environmental change and sustainability problem can be fitted together. The diffuseness of sustainability as a political and policy issue raises two especially difficult challenges for contemporary systems of governance. First, it demands a more integrated approach to problem solving, whereby environmental policies are permanently fused with policies in policy areas such as welfare, social security, agriculture, energy production and transport. This is commonly termed environmental policy integration, or EPI, and it is centrally concerned with improving the horizontal coordination between different policy sectors (Jordan and Lenschow, 2000). Currently, there are large gaps between international institutions, between the various environmental regimes for example, but more significantly between environmental institutions and those that govern world trade and investment and facilitate the advance of economic globalization (see Ekins, Chapter 6). Traditionally, environmental policy has tried to ameliorate the damaging effects of social and economic activities. By contrast, a policy predicated upon sustainability has to go one step further and tackle the driving forces of environmental damage, and the social disruption and economic imbalance that may lie at its roots. Such a transition is fraught with difficulty given the powerful vested interests that thrive on current patterns of unsustainable development and the fragmented nature of institutions described by Brundtland (see above).

Second, sustainability means improving the vertical coordination between different levels of governance – international, regional, national and local. Achieving vertical integration requires forms of multi-level environmental governance (Jordan, 1999). A multi-level governance perspective concentrates upon the respective roles and responsibilities of institutions from the local to the global scale in responding to environmental change. Environmental social science research has begun the task of uncovering the myriad links between the governance arrangements established at different spatial scales and in different policy areas, but an emerging awareness of the limitations of our knowledge of such interconnections serves to set the agenda for the future (see Berkhout et al., Chapter 1).

In summary, as the research unfolded through the 1990s, the complexity of the global sustainability problem and the variety of levels at which governance might have to be practised became increasingly clear. The fact that an environmental problem might be identified as occurring at a global scale did not necessarily imply that the appropriate governance institutions would be international. Indeed, much significant work highlighted transnational phenomena and the regional and sub-national components of global environmental regimes.

If there is one issue which typifies these problems, it is climate change. The attempts to construct a global climate regime began confidently enough in the early 1990s, but soon ran into trouble as it became increasingly apparent that the sources of greenhouse gas emissions and spatial distribution of any impacts were going to be diverse, multiple and far removed from the formal inter-governmental machinery of the climate convention. This, and other insights from the Agenda 21 process, has opened up a set of intriguing questions about the legitimacy and effectiveness of governments, the identity of those who might alternatively provide governance as and when states take a less direct role, and the absence of any coordinated linkages between them. It is these issues that have, in turn, taken centre stage in the study of environmental governance across multi-type scales.

FROM GOVERNMENT TO GOVERNANCE

These alterations in the nature of the environmental problematic occurred at the same time as the mechanisms for making and implementing policy were also undergoing enormous changes. Rosenau (1992), for example, regards the modern world as one in which authority is simultaneously moving up towards supranational groups and down to sub-national actors. This chimes with Rhodes' (1997) point about the modern nation state becoming more differentiated and hollowed out by the centrifugal forces created by globalization (pushing power upwards away from the state) and the desire for greater local autonomy (which pushes power downwards to local service delivery agencies). Kooiman's (1993) fuller elaboration is particularly pertinent to the EU. Governance, he explains, is:

> a pattern or structure that emerges in socio-political systems as a 'common' result or outcome of the interacting intervention efforts of all the involved actors. This pattern cannot be reduced to one actor or group of actors in particular. No single actor, public or private, has all the knowledge and information required to solve complex, dynamic and diversified problems; no actor has sufficient overview to make the application of particular instruments effective; no single actor has sufficient action potential to dominate unilaterally in a particular governing model. (Kooiman, 1993, p. 4.)

The word 'government' usually refers to the authoritative exercise of power by the organs of a sovereign state. State institutions are by definition independent and in the context of the global system the corollary is a fragmentation of authority. The enduring problematic in the study of international politics has therefore been the possibility of order in an essentially anarchic state system. Pessimistic realist scholars have always argued that the only basis for such order lies in the maintenance of a balance of power or the exercise of hegemony by one dominant state. Their liberal institutionalist critics, while largely recognizing that world government remains a chimera, are heir to a long tradition of inter-governmental cooperation and law-making exemplified by the international public unions of the late nineteenth century and the contemporary UN system. Confronted with transnational and then global scale environmental problems, it was a logical step to apply this experience of international cooperation to the environmental problematic in the hope that it would provide the functional equivalent of world government.

As we have seen, in the years preceding the Earth Summit, the most evident lack of effective environmental governance appeared to be at the international level. The global commons, areas beyond national sovereignty such as the oceans, Antarctica, outer space and the global atmosphere, were subject to or threatened by potentially unrestrained human exploitation. Garret Hardin's (1968) much quoted analogy of the 'tragedy of the commons' was frequently applied at the global scale. The only solutions proposed, either control by a central authority or privatization through enclosure, were not available for the global commons. However, as critics of Hardin pointed out, it was possible at the local level to develop common property resource regimes which served to sustain the commons by limiting access and exploitation (Ostrom, 1990). If such self-organizing governance institutions could be made to work at the local level, then they might also provide a pattern for the institutionalization of effective commons governance at the international level. Thus, attention was directed towards the building of international regimes notably for stratospheric ozone and climate change (Vogler, 2000).

However, it soon became apparent that effective policy making cannot solely be a matter of governments negotiating with governments to produce new international legal instruments. First, there were regional bodies such as the EU, international organizations such as the World Bank and the agencies of the UN, as well as extensive networks of scientific expertise such as to be found within the OECD and the IPCC. In the case of the EU, but also of emergent regional bodies such as NAFTA, the line differentiating regional organizations from states has become much more blurred. In Europe, the EU may now lay claim to be a leading actor in global environmental politics in its own right. The Commission is present alongside the Member States when international environmental matters are discussed and negotiates on behalf of them when matters falling within Community competence (such as trade) are under consideration (Bretherton and Vogler, 1999).

Second, forms of activity outside the inter-governmental framework of environmental treaty-making were clearly of increasing significance as the NGO constituents of what was often termed 'global civil society' vied for influence alongside the representatives of transnational business and various industrial lobbies. In the case of the climate change regime, close scrutiny of the political dynamics of its development indicates that a purely inter-governmental account was seriously misleading (Newell, 2000). The most evident involvement of the many NGOs of varying political persuasions was as lobbyists, notably at international occasions such as the Conferences of the Parties to the climate convention. However their involvement in the governance process extended into other, perhaps more crucial, areas. Increasingly, NGOs have served to compensate for the lack of capability of nation state governments, especially, but by no means exclusively, in the poorer parts of the world. However, they also provide scientific expertise and above all political legitimacy. This type of involvement is, of course, not unique to the environmental field but represents a trend observable elsewhere. NGOs also operate as the field agents of the international community in administering aid, humanitarian relief and in managing projects promoting sustainable development at the local level. Equally they are often to be found within what are nominally national government delegations. Access at this level rests upon the provision of expertise for even the largest state delegations have found themselves to be inadequately staffed in the face of the ever-expanding volume of often highly technical diplomatic business and marketization. FIELD's connection with AOSIS provides a good case in point (see above). While the traditional image of the environmental NGO is one of green activism, it is worth recalling that other non-governmental interest groups may be equally heavily involved and may indeed wield more influence. The obvious examples are industrial groups such as the Global Climate Coalition.

The production of authoritative scientific knowledge is of primary importance to the development of global environmental governance. Theorists of epistemic communities (notably Haas, 1990) have suggested that the operation of such knowledge-based networks of scientists and policy makers provides a key explanatory variable for regime creation. But, in a significant counterpoint to the work on epistemic communities, it is also possible to portray parts of the transnational scientific community as a scarcely disinterested interest group. Extensive studies by Boehmer-Christiansen (1994; 1996) on the operation of the IPCC and GEF came to this very political conclusion, which complements other critical work investigating the construction and organization of global environmental science (Shackley and Wynne, 1995).

To summarize, research has highlighted the fact that governments were incapable of exercising fully effective sovereignty, that significant power rested with non-state actors, and that the whole process of making and implementing policy was much more plural, spanning different scales and institutional venues. With hindsight we can see more clearly that these insights resonated with a much broader trend in the political and policy sciences away from a preoccupation with state governments to one dominated by broader notions of governance.

We would argue, however, that this in turn raises even more complex problems than that of finding ways of involving a much wider network of actors in systems of international level policy making. Rather, the shift from government at the national level to a more diffuse system of governance spanning different administrative tiers or levels (that is supranational down through the sub-national to the local) raises awkward problems arising from the need to coordinate policy vertically between tiers of authority. These problems are not resolvable at the international level because they reach down into the heart of nation states and their systems of economic production, social consumption and governance. The term multi-level governance is now used to describe the increasingly dense set of interconnections between actors operating at different levels, sometimes channelled through states, but very often bypassing them (Jordan, 2001). According Gary Marks and his colleagues, multi-level governance in the EU has the following essential characteristics (Hooghe and Marks, 1996, pp. 23–4):

- The state no longer monopolizes policy making, but works alongside actors at different levels including supranational bodies such as the European Commission and the European Court, and private companies.
- Increasingly, collective decision-making among states involves a significant loss of control for individual states as they are forced to accept decisions adopted by the majority.
- Levels of governance are interconnected rather than nested: national and sub-national actors (both public and private) act directly at all levels, bypassing the normal channels of inter-state negotiation.

The advent of multi-level environmental governance brings with it new sources of politics and many new policy problems. For instance, with Jordan (1998b), Lowe and Ward (1998) undertook work on the Europeanization of British environmental policy, at a time when many still regarded the EU and British national politics as two essentially separate systems. They showed how the pressures arising from membership of the EU has altered the structures, styles and philosophies of British policy, creating new political opportunities for national pressure groups, which were previously marginalized from the locus of national policy making. In the same way, by showing that local land use planning in Britain is a powerful but greatly neglected tool for achieving sustainable development across multiple levels of governance, Susan Owens and co-workers (Owens and Cope, 1992; Owens and Cowell, 1994; Owens, 1994) have also done much to uncover the links between global, European and local policies.

TAKING THE ENVIRONMENT TO THE HEART OF THE POLITICAL SCIENCES?

In 1993 Steve Smith wrote that in both political and academic terms the environment was probably doomed to remain at the periphery. His comments were directed at the discipline of International Relations, but they could apply with equal force to the whole of the political and policy sciences. He asserted that there were compelling reasons why environmental issues lacked salience for national governments and publics, and that there were related and parallel tendencies that consigned academic specialists in environmental politics to a marginal role in their respective discipline(s). Such specialists, in International Relations at least, he agreed constituted 'a very closed group, nearly all of whom share the same theoretical assumptions' (Smith, 1993, p. 40). This group, he claimed, engaged in or contributed to few of the big theoretical discussions that absorbed the rest of the discipline, and was less self-conscious in its use of methods or theory (for a rejoinder, see Saurin, 1996).

In some respects, it is inevitable that environmental scholarship should find itself at the margins of political science. Environment has not been a mainstream political issue in Britain or the USA; environmental policy is weak relative to economic and social policy; and many of the core insights of green political thinking radically challenge the basic axioms of the modern economy, bureaucracies and politics and are therefore marginalized (see Dobson, 1998; Dobson, 1999; O'Riordan, 1999).

How far have things changed over the last decade? In some respects some of Smith's conclusions remain tenable, but in other respects, work on the politics of sustainability has been anything but peripheral or wedded to prevailing orthodoxies. The volume of scholarly writing on environmental social science and politics has undoubtedly increased, but relatively few articles appear in what are deemed the main policy and politics journals, and only a small number of senior professors of politics or international relations include the environment amongst their interests. For the most part, it appears that the study of environmental politics, environmental governance and (most of all) sustainability are still regarded as a separate sub-topic, with its own dedicated journals and specialized students. Research grants and fellowships may even encourage such compartmentalization by nurturing the existing environmental academic constituency, rather than making strenuous efforts to move beyond it by building links either with the natural sciences or other social science concerns.

In many ways researchers engaged in the study of the politics and international relations of the environment subscribed to a dominant orthodoxy. Instead of generating a distinctive theoretical approach, they have often relied heavily upon mainstream theoretical tools and assumptions. The debates on global sustainability were thus framed within existing theories developed in response to often quite different (that is, non-environmental) problematics. There are precious few examples in the political sciences of environmental social research exporting new ideas to the 'non' environmental cores of their respective sub-disciplines with a focus on problem solving as opposed to critical theory (Cox, 1981). It is easy to understand the pressure upon researchers to contribute to the solution of important policy-related questions through the use of existing theoretical approaches and tools, rather than to engage in the kind of critical reflection that might undermine their validity or create new frameworks.

The response was thus to incorporate the study of international environmental cooperation into an ongoing (and largely north American) debate about the formation of international regimes. This formulation includes international law and international organizations but goes well beyond them (Krasner, 1983). Regimes were seen as the basis of international order, providing a framework for the conduct of trade, monetary and even security relations. In this sense they reflected the defining assumptions of international relations concerning the achievement of order in an anarchic world of sovereign states. The debate pitted realists against liberal institutionalists and much of the ensuing discussion was reduced to microeconomic categories and the question of whether states could be assumed to pursue relative (realist) or absolute (liberal) gains. States were conceptualized as the primary, single and largely undifferentiated actors and scant regard was initially paid to the accumulating evidence of significant involvement in international institutions by a range of non-state actors, or to the more domestic aspects of international governance.

Although mainstream institutionalist research was very much a US activity (for example: Young, 1997; Haas et al., 1993; Victor et al., 1998), few were immune from this dominant state-centric regime approach to international cooperation, and a number of the studies, already mentioned, clearly operated within its confines. However, by the mid-1990s a number of dissenting voices and investigations had arisen.[1]

There are at least three respects in which the problem of global environmental change has stimulated responses that challenge Smith's (1993) description. First, drawing upon the revival of the application of political thought to the study of international relations, normative dimensions were taken seriously (Dyer, 1996). Second, a number of researchers engaged in the study of the environmental politics of global civil society generally (Willetts, 1995; 1996) or in relation to climate change (Newell, 2000) or in analysing how NGO influence on environmental policy links together activities at local, national and international scales (Thomas et al., 2000). This work could be seen as a contribution to a wider study of direct citizen and NGO involvement in world politics which challenges state-centric approaches (Princen and Finger, 1994; Wapner, 1995). Arguably it is green political thought that has taken the leading role in this development. At present it probably represents the most evident way in which the environmental problematic has influenced mainstream thinking. In recent years, the EU has emerged as a significant focus for cutting-edge work on the environment (for example, Weale et al., 2000) within comparative politics. However, very little of this work grapples with what might be termed the wider politics of sustainability triggered by geopolitical processes such as globalization, enlargement or the single market process (but see O'Riordan, 2001). Work on radical forms of environmental protest (e.g. direct action) is also mushrooming, but still remains very marginal to the mainstream concerns of the discipline such as elections, government reform, voting behaviour, economic and social policy development and so on. 'Where', Wolfgang Rüdig asks (1999):

> are the big studies of the comparative internal workings of environmental ministries and agencies...? Where are the empirically well-founded comparative studies of the systems of environmental policy advice; of parliamentary procedures in the environmental legislatory processes? Where are the comparative analyses of attempts to 'integrate' environmental policy with other policy concerns? (Rudig, 1999, p. xxix)

Without these insights, environmental social science cannot fully understand how environmental and sustainability policies are (or are not) being made in the most significant institutional domains of policy making.

In a longer perspective we may have to look elsewhere for a potentially more far-reaching change. At the moment approaches based upon radical political ecology (Saurin, 1996) and the analysis of the global political economy of international environmental politics (Kutting, 2000; Paterson, 1996; 2000) provide both a critique of more orthodox institutional analysis and a set of rather different questions as to the location and functions of governance. In this view international efforts at environmental management are embedded in and subordinate to dominant patterns of resource exploitation, consumption and corporate power. The development of such approaches to the point at which they would rank alongside the more orthodox study of governance would certainly provide one indication that environmental social science thinking had penetrated to the heart of the political and policy sciences.

As yet, the concept of sustainability simply has no common purchase or political profile in academia or in practical politics. In both day to day politics (at least, European) and textbooks, the environment (rather than sustainability) now receives a mention, but as one amongst a number of pressing issues and one which, in accordance with the low position of environment ministries within governmental hierarchies, rarely occupies pride of place.[2] In the final analysis a full engagement between the political sciences and an ecocentric worldview would involve a radical transformation of the former. It would involve a shift from an ontology dominated by the state and anthropocentric interests towards a more holistic conception of tightly interdependent natural and socio-political systems. It would also have deep epistemological implications subversive of the atomistic positivism that pervades the very idea of political science. At the moment, there are still too few willing to take up and actively respond to this challenge. Nonetheless, the crises in an agricultural system operating according to the demands of a global market, widespread consumer resistance to genetically modified food, and the reaction to the US renunciation of the Kyoto Protocol, against a backdrop of insistent evidence of climate change, may well lead to the conclusion that events may finally force the issue of governance for sustainability onto mainstream political and academic agendas. Yet it will have to contend with other international priorities, not least those arising from the events of 11 September 2001.

FUTURE CHALLENGES

What are the research questions raised by the shift towards multi-level environmental governance? Much depends on political agenda dynamics. A good deal of environmental international relations research has been apolitical in the sense that it has dealt with technical questions of institutional design and effectiveness. Enormous effort has been expended on the institutional construction of the climate change regime. Yet, since the renunciation of the Kyoto Protocol by the Bush administration, and its ratification by the EU and Japan, the political character of the challenges is now brutally apparent. Can the regime be preserved without US participation? Can it indeed exist in relative isolation from the WTO trade regime and the global monetary system? How can developed world consumers be persuaded to give political support to policies that limit their consumption? Underlying this is the vast politico-economic, but ultimately ethical, question of how the 'common but differentiated responsibilities' of North and South are to be apportioned in a future in which legitimate demands for development on top of profligate energy use by the already industrialized countries threaten ruinous levels of greenhouse gas emissions.

Then there is the festering dispute between Europe and the US over the development and marketing of new technologies such as GM food. This springs from cultural differences in the approach to handling risk, with the Europeans adopting a more precautionary line in the light of the potential environmental costs and the Americans emphasizing the trade and economic benefits (O'Riordan et al., 2001; see also Stirling, Chapter 2).

Finally, there is the whole question of how to ensure international and national decision making remains open and genuinely inclusive (see Munton, Chapter 4). In the past, international problem solving was a secretive affair, dominated by states and scientists. The collapse of the Multilateral Agreement in Investment (MAI) and the violent anti-WTO protests in Seattle in 2000 powerfully revealed the difficulty of governing in a more plural and globalizing world. These developments prompt the well known, but under-researched, question of the compatibility between the operation of democratic governance systems and sustainability. In its recent reports on energy policy and standard setting, the UK Royal Commission on Environmental Pollution made a powerful case for a more open and inclusive approach to reconciling conflicting values. International and large regional organizations such as the EU face particular difficulties in this respect, because they necessarily must act above the heads of states, several steps removed from the normal national democratic channels of representation.

There are a related set of issues surrounding the activities of NGOs and the various levels of governance that are now seen to be necessary components of a sustainable future. The significant role of global civil society has increasingly been recognized, but defining myriad organizations and loose associations and even business corporations as members does not in itself bestow legitimacy upon them. In a more globalized world, the state may be increasingly lacking in capability, but its potential partners, or even successors in a system of multi-level environmental governance, also need to acquire legitimacy. Nowhere is this more evident than in the contemporary politics of the EU, which has developed a highly successful environmental policy but is criticized for its persistent democratic deficit and widespread public suspicion about its activities. An even more worrying tendency is to be found in the trend towards the privatization of a number of functions that used to be performed by inter-state action but are now the responsibility of what Murphy (2000, p. 795) has called 'the global-level "private" authorities that regulate both states and much of transnational economic and social life'. A future research agenda will have not only to include questions of efficient environmental governance, but also the ancient political questions about political legitimacy, accountability, power and authority posed in a radically different setting (see Berkhout et al., Chapter 1).

Meanwhile, in many political jurisdictions new levels of governance are being added, making existing arrangements even more multi-level, or existing levels are becoming more powerful. A formal example is the continuing development of the EU. Another is the trend towards greater sub-national governance. In the UK devolution raises important research questions about the coordination of environment and sustainability policy. This may, for example, mean re-examining ongoing work on regime design, implementation and effectiveness. Also, international policy is reserved for the UK government, but much of the substance is devolved. So, for example, national climate change targets will continue to be negotiated by national government, but the implementation and enforcement will be undertaken by the devolved authorities which have their own political masters. Consequently, we may well witness the emergence of new inter- and intra-level conflicts, which will need to be addressed. Devolution also poses new challenges to those studying the Europeanization of national environmental policy, the implementation of international agreements and the difficulties of making policy more inclusive. Interestingly, it brings the governance characteristics of the UK closer to the continental mainstream, that is federal or quasi-federal, with all the attendant problems normally associated with multi-level systems (Scharpf, 1988).

The trend towards greater vertical differentiation also raises questions about the most effective level of action. The principle of subsidiarity requires decisions to be made at the lowest level commensurate with effective action (Jordan, 2000b). But upon what basis should responsibilities be allocated: economic, political or legal? Clearly, many environmental problems span political borders so there will have to be some role for international bodies. Yet, international bodies are several levels more remote from citizens than national governments, so careful trade-offs will be required. This could mean establishing, with much more analytical precision, the role of international cooperation and international agreements. At present, the academic argument is polarized between a mainstream assumption that regimes are self-evidently necessary and the radical ecological critique, which tends to dismiss them. In practice, the most effective path probably lies somewhere between these two extremes.

The transition to environmental governance is also associated with the deployment of many new environmental policy instruments such as eco-taxes, voluntary agreements, tradable permits and informational devices such as eco-labels (Golub, 1998). Nowhere is this more prominent than in relation to the climate convention, which has a whole arsenal of flexibility mechanisms to deploy against greenhouse gas emissions. The trend away from regulation raises many important questions related to the design, operation and effectiveness of new instruments. For example, what factors account for the uptake of these new instruments within and across different countries (Jordan and Wurzel, 2003)? Some countries are forging ahead in using certain instruments (for example, voluntary approaches in the Netherlands), whereas in others innovation is proceeding more slowly (for example, eco-taxation in the UK) (see Berkhout et al., Chapter 1). What are the institutional impediments to innovation and what scope is there for learning and transferring lessons across political borders? Finally, how effective are these instruments at addressing problems? Standard economic theory suggests that they are superior to regulation, but is this assumption borne out in reality?

Finally, research will need to respond to the challenge posed by EPI, that is the greening of other policy areas. This requires policy makers at all levels to tackle the underlying drivers of ecological damage by greening previously non-environmental policy sectors. Current examples of where EPI is proving especially challenging to implement include the EU (via the Cardiff process), the WTO and central government policy making (Lenschow, 2001). Social scientists have a lot to contribute when it comes to identifying the root causes of sectoral policy making (for example, Peters, 1998), and to identifying and transferring lessons from one level to another (for example, Jordan and Lenschow, 2000).

CONCLUSIONS

In this chapter we have sought to address four questions. First, we considered the academic and political challenges triggered by the transition from environmental to sustainability concerns. Here, there has been good progress with the scholars responding in novel and interesting ways to the more polycentric and diffuse challenge of implementing sustainable development.

Second, we looked at the transition from government to governance. Here, much work of international significance has helped to move the debate from an exclusive focus on international cooperation to a wider concern with environmental governance. An early assumption was that environmental problems would and indeed should be solved by state action within a framework of international cooperation. Research has increasingly revealed the significance of regional and sub-state levels of activity, as well as transnational companies, and the consequent requirement for multi-level governance.

Third, there has been a significant amount of progress in taking the environment to the heart of the political and social sciences, but important gaps remain. Sustainability demands a more concerted effort to link the environmental insights provided by environmental social science with the social and economic knowledge emerging from the mainstream. Of course, the most potent spur to greater integration would be another growth in the prominence of environmental issues in everyday politics. The 1990s witnessed an initial phase of integration following the pulse of concern in the late 1980s. But this now needs to be built upon, and much responsibility for doing so rests with environmental social science. In short, scholars of environmental policy and sustainability need to make a more concerted effort to sell their ideas and concepts to the mainstream by engaging in a common dialogue. This could mean adding an environmental dimension to mainstream debates on such issues as governance, policy transfer, policy learning, Europeanization, devolution and the identification and communication of risk. It could also mean a greater effort to adopt, test and refine theoretical tools and concepts used by the mainstream. Because, as long as environment is seen (as is the case in the more radical green theories) as somehow special and thus beyond compare, environmental science will remain cut off from the mainstream. This in turn will rob environmental social science of an opportunity to understand fully the factors that impede the uptake of environmental thinking in the nerve centres of modern governance.

There is certainly scope for much greater epistemological and methodological integration. Smith (1993) and also Murphy (2000) are probably right to assert that much of the study of global governance and environment is 'disciplined' and tends often to reject obviously relevant approaches like structuralist-Marxism while being determinedly positivistic. Is there, for example, room for more social constructivism and other, more reflective work in environmental social science? Post-positivism has been a significant influence particularly in European international relations, but it has not made much ground in mainstream political science. Green political theory – and the broader ecological critique – potentially have a lot to offer these discussions, and sensitivity to some of these alternative ways of perceiving the world and conducting research might pay dividends in the study of multi-level environmental governance and sustainability.

Finally, the shift from environment to sustainability and government to governance provides a conceptual problematic around which a new and ambitious research agenda can be identified. Sustainability is not the same as environment, yet social scientists have only just begun to integrate the fields of economic, social and environmental policy analysis. We fully expect the most critical, cutting edge research in the next decade to be undertaken at the intersection of these three domains, linking natural and social sciences in a joint endeavour.

NOTES

1. As with all such characterizations there are important exceptions. On the American side the critical work of Litfin (1994), Lipschutz (1996) and Wapner (1995) should be mentioned, although they would admit that they do not constitute the mainstream.
2. Four far from typical examples are: Burchill et al. (1996), White et al. (2001), Wallace and Wallace (2000), and Dunleavy et al. (2000).

REFERENCES

Adger, N. (2000), 'Institutional adaptation to environmental risk under the transition in Vietnam', *Annals of the Association of American Geographers*, 90 (4), 738–58.

Boehmer-Christiansen, S. (1994), 'Global climate protection policy', *Global Environmental Change*, 4 (2), 140–59.

Boehmer-Christiansen, S. (1996), 'The international research enterprise and global environmental change: climate change policy as a research process' in J. Vogler and M. Imber (eds), *The Environment and International Relations*, London: Routledge.

Bretherton, C. and J. Vogler (1999), *The European Union as a Global Actor*, London: Routledge.

Burchill, S., A. Linklater, R. Devetak, M. Paterson and J. True (1996), *Theories of International Relations*, Basingstoke: Macmillan.

Cameron, J., J. Werksman and P. Roderick (eds) (1995), *Improving Compliance with International Environmental Law*, London: Earthscan.

Churchill, R., G. Kutting and L. Warren (1995), 'The 1994 UN ECE Sulphur Protocol', *Journal of Environmental Law*, 7 (2), 169–97.

Cox, R. (1981), 'Social forces, states and world orders', *Millennium*, 10 (2), 126–53.

Dobson, A. (1998), *Justice and the Environment*, Oxford: Oxford University Press.

Dobson, A. (1999), *Fairness and Futurity: Essays on Environmental Sustainability and Social Justice*, Oxford: Oxford University Press.

Dunleavy, P., A. Gamble, I. Holiday and G. Peele (eds) (2000), *Developments in British Politics* 6, Basingstoke: Macmillan.

Dyer, H. (1996), 'Environmental security as a universal value: implications for international theory', in J. Vogler and M. Imber (eds), *The Environment and International Relations*, London: Routledge.

Golub, J. (ed.) (1998), *New Instruments for Environmental Policy in the EU*, London: Routledge.

Greene, O. (1996), 'Environmental regimes', in J. Vogler and M. Imber (eds) (1996), *The Environment and International Relations*, London: Routledge.

Greene, O. and J. Salt (1993), 'Verification issues in an effective climate change convention', *World Resources Review*, 5 (3), 271–85.

Haas, P.M. (1990), *Saving the Mediterranean: The Politics of International Environmental Cooperation*, New York: Columbia University Press.

Haas, P.M., R.O. Keohane and M. Levy (eds) (1993), *Institutions for the Earth: Sources of Effective Environmental Protection*, Cambridge, MA: MIT Press.

Hardin, G. (1968), 'The tragedy of the commons', *Science*, 162, 1243–8.

Hooghe, L. and G. Marks, (1996), 'Contending models of governance in the EU', in A. Cafruny and C. Lankowski (eds), *Europe's Ambiguous Unity,* Boulder, CO: Lynne Rienner.

Jordan, A.J. (1994), 'The international organisational machinery for sustainable development: Rio and the road beyond', *The Environmentalist*, 14 (1), 1–11.

Jordan, A.J. (1995), 'Designing new international organisations: a note on the structure and operation of the Global Environment Facility', *Public Administration*, 73 (2), 303–12.

Jordan, A.J. (1998a), 'The ozone endgame: the implementation of the Montreal Protocol in the UK', *Environmental Politics*, 7 (4), 23–52.

Jordan, A.J. (1998b), 'The impact on UK environmental administration', in P. Lowe and S. Ward (eds), *British Environmental Policy and Europe: Politics and Policy in Transition*, London: Routledge.

Jordan, A.J. (ed.) (1999), 'EU environmental policy at 25', *Environment and Planning C (Government and Policy)*, 17 (1), 1–112.

Jordan, A.J. (2000a), 'Environmental policy', in P. Dunleavy, A. Gamble, I. Holiday and G. Peele (eds) (2000), *Developments in British Politics* 6, Basingstoke: Macmillan.

Jordan, A.J. (2000b), 'The politics of multilevel environmental governance', *Environment and Planning A*, 32 (7), 1307–24.

Jordan, A.J. (2001), The European Union: An evolving system of multi-level governance ... or government? *Policy and Politics*, 29 (2), 197–212.

Jordan, A.J. and A. Lenschow (2000), '"Greening" the EU: what can be learned from the leaders of EU environmental policy?', *European Environment*, 10 (3), 109–20.

Jordan, A. and J. Werksman (1994), 'Additional funds, incremental costs and the global environment', *Review of European and International Environmental Law (RECIEL)*, 3 (2–3), 81–7.

Jordan, A. and J. Werksman (1995), 'Financing global environmental protection', in J. Cameron, J. Werksman and P. Roderick (eds) (1995), *Improving Compliance with International Environmental Law*, London: Earthscan.

Jordan, A. and R. Wurzel (2003), *New Instruments of Environmental Governance? National Experiences and Prospects*, London: Frank Cass.

Kooiman, T. (1993), 'Social and political governance', in: T. Kooiman (ed.), *Modern Governance*, London: Sage.

Krasner, S. (ed.) (1983), *International Regimes*, Ithaca, New York: Cornell University Press.

Kutting, G. (2000), *Environment, Society and International Relations: Towards More Effective International Environmental Agreements*, London: Routledge.

Lafferty, W. and J. Meadowcroft (eds) (2000), *Implementing Sustainable Development in High Consumption Societies*, Cambridge: Cambridge University Press.

Leggett, J. (2000), *The Carbon War: Global Warming at the End of the Oil Era*, Harmondsworth: Penguin.

Lenschow, A. (ed.) (2001), *Environmental Policy Integration: Greening Sectoral Policies in Europe*, London: Earthscan.

Lipschutz, R. (1996), *Global Civil Society and Global Environmental Governance*, New York: SUNY Press.

Litfin, K. (1994), *Ozone Discourses*, New York: Columbia University Press.

Lowe, P. and S. Ward (eds) (1998), *British Environmental Policy and Europe: Politics and Policy in Transition*, London: Routledge.

Murphy, C.N. (2000), 'Global governance: poorly done and poorly understood', *International Affairs*, 76 (4), 789–804.

Newell, P. (2000), *Climate for Change: Non-State Actors and the Global Politics of the Greenhouse*, Cambridge: Cambridge University Press.

O'Riordan, T. (ed.) (1999), *Environmental Science for Environmental Management*, 2nd edn, Harlow: Longman.

O'Riordan, T. (ed.) (2001), *Globalism, Localism and Identity*, London: Earthscan.

O'Riordan T., J. Cameron and A. Jordan (eds) (2001), *Reinterpreting the Precautionary Principle*, London: Cameron and May.

O'Riordan, T. and J. Jäger (eds) (1996), *Politics of Climate Change*, London: Routledge.

O'Riordan, T. and H. Voisey (eds) (1998), *The Transition to Sustainability: The Politics of Agenda 21 in Europe*, London: Earthscan.

Ostrom, E. (1990), *Governing the Commons*, Cambridge: Cambridge University Press.

Owens, S. (1994), 'Land, limits and sustainability', *Transactions of the Institute of British Geographers*, 19, 439-56.

Owens, S. and D. Cope (1992), *Land Use Planning and Climate Change*, London: DoE.

Owens, S. and R. Cowell, (1994), 'Lost land and limits to growth: conceptual problems for sustainable land use change', *Land Use Policy*, 11 (3), 168-80.

Paterson, M. (1996), *Global Warming and Global Politics*, London: Routledge.

Paterson, M. (2000), *Understanding Global Environmental Politics*, Basingstoke: Macmillan.

Peters, B.G. (1998), 'Managing horizontal government', *Public Administration*, 76 (2), 295-311.

Princen, T. and M. Finger (1994), *Environmental NGOs in World Politics: Linking the Global and the Local*, London: Routledge.

Purvis, M. et al. (1997), 'Fragmenting uncertainties: some British business responses to ozone depletion', *Global Environmental Change*, 7 (2), 93-111.

Rhodes, R. (1997), *Understanding Governance*, Milton Keynes: Open University Press.

Rosenau J.N. (1992), 'Citizenship in a changing global order', in J. Rosenau and E.O. Cziempel (eds) (1992), *Governance without Government: Order and Change in World Politics*, Cambridge: Cambridge University Press.

Rüdig, W. (ed.) (1999), *Environmental Policy, Volume I (National Environmental Policy)*, Cheltenham: Edward Elgar.

Saurin, J. (1996), 'International relations, social ecology and the globalisation of environmental change', in J. Vogler and M. Imber (eds) (1996), *The Environment and International Relations*, London: Routledge.

Scharpf, F. (1988), 'The joint decision trap', *Public Administration*, 66 (2), 239-78.

Selman, P. (1996), *Local Sustainability*, London: Paul Chapman Publishing.

Shackley, S. and B. Wynne (1995), 'Global climate change: the mutual construction of an emergent science-policy domain', *Science and Public Policy*, 22, 218-30.

Shove, E. (1995), 'Constructing regulation and regulating construction', in T. Gray (ed.), *British Environmental Policy in the 1990s*, Basingstoke: Macmillan.

Smith, S. (1993), 'Environment on the periphery of international relations: an explanation', *Environmental Politics*, 2 (4), 28-45.

Stoker, G. (1998), 'Governance as theory', *International Social Science Journal*, 155, 17-28.

Thomas, A., S. Carr and D. Humphreys (eds) (2000), *Environmental Politics and NGO Influence: Land Degradation and Sustainable Resource Management in Sub-Saharan Africa*, London: Routledge.

Victor, D.G., K. Raustiala and E. Skolnikoff (1998), *The Implementation and*

Effectiveness of International Environmental Commitments: Theory and Practice, Cambridge, MA: MIT Press.

Vogler, J. (2000), *The Global Commons: Environmental and Technological Governance*, Chichester: John Wiley.

Wallace, H. and W. Wallace (eds) (2000), *Policy Making in the European Union*, 4th edn, Oxford: Oxford University Press.

Wapner, P. (1995), 'The state and environmental challenges: a critical exploration of the alternatives to the state system', *Environmental Politics*, 4 (1), 44–69.

WCED (World Commission on Environment and Development) 'The Brundtland Report' (1987), *Our Common Future*, Oxford: Oxford University Press.

Weale, A. et al. (2000), *Environmental Governance in Europe*, Oxford: Oxford University Press.

White, B., R. Little and M. Smith (eds) (2001), *Issues in World Politics*, Basingstoke: Macmillan.

Willetts, P. (ed.) (1995), *We the Peoples: The Influence of Non-Governmental Organisations at the United Nations*, London: C. Hurst & Co.

Willetts, P. (1996), 'Who cares about the environment?', in J. Vogler and M. Imber (eds) (1996), *The Environment and International Relations*, London: Routledge.

Young, O. (ed.) (1997), *Global Governance: Drawing Insights from Environmental Experience*, Cambridge, MA: MIT Press.

Young, O. (1999a), 'Hitting the mark', *Environment*, 41 (8), 20–9.

Young, O. (1999b), *The Effectiveness of International Environmental Regimes*, Cambridge, MA: MIT Press.

Young, O. (2001), 'Inferences and indices; evaluating the effectiveness of international environmental regimes', *Global Environmental Politics*, 1, 1, 99–121.

Young, S. (2000), 'The UK response to sustainable development and Agenda 21: from containing the issue to cross-sectoral thinking', in W. Lafferty and J. Meadowcroft (eds), *Implementing Sustainable Development in High Consumption Societies*, Cambridge: Cambridge University Press.

6. After Seattle: what next for trade and the environment?

Paul Ekins

INTRODUCTION

The 1990s were dominated by three processes of global integration of historical importance. First, there were the reverberations from the collapse of the Soviet Union in 1989, and the gradual transition of central and eastern European countries, and those of the former Soviet Union itself, to market economies within the framework of global capitalism. Second, world trade expanded at rates substantially faster than the growth rate of the global economy. The process was reinforced by the conclusion of the Uruguay Round of trade negotiations and the setting up of the World Trade Organisation (WTO) in 1995 and was only one aspect of a more fundamental process of globalization which also included the growth and extended reach of transnational companies and greatly increased international interaction between and organization of civil society organizations. Third, there was the acceptance by the world community, at the United Nations Conference on Environment and Development (UNCED) in Rio de Janeiro in 1992, that the global environment was under unprecedented stress from human activities, and the conclusion of several agreements to begin to address some of the most serious perceived global problems (Vogler and Jordan, Chapter 5). This chapter is about the last two of these strands of globalization and, in particular, about the complex dialogue and relationships between them.

THE TRADE-ENVIRONMENT AGENDA

In retrospect it is surprising that it took until the 1990s for the perception that there was any relationship between trade and the environment to become generally established. The connections could have become clear many years before, for example:

- The concerns about economic growth and the environment which surfaced in the 1970s could have focused on trade as one of the engines of growth, but did not do so.

- The agreement on Technical Barriers to Trade (TBT), negotiated under the General Agreement on Tariffs and Trade (GATT) in 1979, could have led to worries about trade-induced constraints on environmental policy, but in fact these did not emerge until over a decade later.
- The inclusion of trade measures as possible sanctions in the Montreal Protocol on Ozone-Depleting Substances in 1988 could have prompted questions about their relationship to the GATT rules, but generally did not.

Yet the debate is still characterized by fundamental disagreement on some of the most basic issues, between those who consider that trade liberalization could, and should, be good for the environment, and those who fear that its effects will be negative, and could be disastrously so. The two points of view are set out in Box 6.1.

Trade-environment relationships are inextricably entwined both with social concerns (such as labour standards) and issues of north-south development co-operation. Indeed, it is likely that progress will only be made on trade-environment issues if these other issues are addressed as well. Undoubtedly this makes the situation much more complicated. But this is the particularly challenging nature of sustainable development: issues cannot be viewed in isolation and progress has to be made simultaneously in different areas or it is very difficult to make any progress at all.

ASSESSING TRADE-ENVIRONMENT EFFECTS

Very different views are held about the ways in which trade liberalization and the environment interact (Box 6.1). Despite their contradictory nature, none of these views can be totally dismissed, and for most of them a body of evidence can be cited in their favour. The uncertainty about the net environmental effect of trade liberalization is due to the difficulties involved both in quantifying the individual effects, and in determining what portion of the individual effects is due to trade liberalization rather than other causes. This section, and much of the rest of this chapter, considers the evidence for these different effects.

Trade, Growth and Environmental Quality

The first of the positive bullet points in Box 6.1 consists of two arguments: trade liberalization promotes economic growth; and economic growth engenders environmental protection. These arguments will be examined in turn.

BOX 6.1 DIFFERENT VIEWS OF THE EFFECT OF TRADE LIBERALIZATION ON THE ENVIRONMENT

Positive

- Trade liberalization promotes economic growth. As societies become richer, they acquire both the will and the resources to protect the environment.
- Trade liberalization promotes the efficient allocation of resources (including environmental resources), allowing the production of a given economic product with the least possible use of resources.
- Trade liberalization promotes the international transfer of environmentally-preferable technologies.
- Trade liberalization promotes the convergence of environmental standards for products and processes towards the higher levels of rich countries, and increases the markets for environmentally-preferable products.
- Trade liberalization promotes international co-operation in other areas, notably environmental protection.

Negative

- Trade liberalization amplifies environmental externalities through its promotion of economic growth.
- Trade often involves long-distance transport, which is one of the principal sources of environmental externalities.
- Because of competitiveness pressures, trade liberalization will result (at best) in political drag on environmental policy making by governments, and (at worst) in an environmental 'race to the bottom' through competitive deregulation.
- Trade rules arising from trade liberalization impede national governments in their attempts at environmental protection, either because of possible trade effects (e.g. through mandatory re-use of containers) or because of perceived discrimination (e.g. eco-labelling).
- Trade rules may inhibit the use of trade measures in multilateral environmental agreements.
- The production of some highly-traded goods (e.g. cotton, cigarettes, certain foods) is more environmentally-destructive than the production for domestic consumption which it replaces.
- Opportunities to use land for trade result in subsistence farmers being displaced onto environmentally-marginal land, where they may cause environmental damage.

There is a robust tradition of academic thought to the effect that trade liberalization both increases global income and allows all the parties to share in that growth. It is this perception of all-win possibilities from trade liberalization that enables trade agreements, in which countries give up cherished rights to the protection of some of their economic sectors in return for access to other sectors in other countries, to be concluded.

In his survey on the relationship between trade and growth in developing countries, Edwards (1993) was only able to come to tentative conclusions on this subject. There was no shortage of studies which showed a clear correlation between trade and growth, but this is not the same thing as trade–growth causality, and there are a number of reasons why high GDP growth might stimulate trade rather than the other way round. Many of the papers surveyed 'have been characterized by a lack of care in dealing with issues relating to endogeneity and measurement errors', resulting 'in many cases, in unconvincing results whose fragility has been exposed by subsequent work' (Edwards 1993, p. 1389). Recent advances in endogenous growth theory allow more convincing theoretical explanations of why trade liberalization may promote growth (greater opportunities for specialization, removal of bottle-necks, faster technological progress), but 'the new models of endogenous growth have made little progress in empirically analysing these issues' (Edwards 1993, p.1390).

More recently, Frankel and Romer's (1999) study has sought to address the causality problem by regressing national incomes against various geographical characteristics (population, area, proximity), which may have a significant effect on trade but not on income for the countries concerned. The actual methodology followed is complex, but the results lead the authors to some strong conclusions. They find no evidence that high incomes lead to more trade; and they find that the impact of trade on income is substantial. However, they also find that 'the null hypothesis that these variables [trade and size] have no effect is typically only marginally rejected at conventional levels. As a result, the estimates still leave considerable uncertainty about the magnitude of their effects' (Frankel and Romer 1999, p. 381).

Dollar and Kraay's paper, released to coincide with the publication of the World Bank's 2001 World Development Report, entitled 'Attacking Poverty' (World Bank, 2000), focuses on the impact of overall economic growth on the incomes of the poor. Their conclusion, emphasized in their paper's title, is that 'growth is good for the poor'. Because they also find that openness to trade raises overall incomes (perhaps reading rather more into Frankel and Romer's results in the process than those authors do themselves), they conclude that openness to trade is good for the poor.

Dollar and Kraay (2000) looked at the incomes of the lowest quintile in eighty countries. Fosu's (1996) focus is those countries which are especially dependent on non-fuel primary exports, which constitute the bulk of exports of many lower income countries. Fosu also distinguishes between the effect of exports on GDP as a whole (which, of course, has exports as a component) and their effect on non-export GDP. He finds that there is a beneficial effect of exports on non-export GDP (though, as would be expected, this is less than their effect on overall GDP). However, the growth of primary exports has an insignificant effect on non-export GDP growth. This raises questions as to whether trade benefits countries whose exports are principally of primary goods.

Despite these theoretical and empirical uncertainties, modelling of the income effects of trade liberalization routinely treats correlation as causality and finds that trade liberalization increases income substantially. Thus Goldin et al.'s (1993) work for the OECD and the World Bank finds that full trade liberalization would increase global GDP by $450 billion, while the liberalization then envisaged by the GATT's Uruguay Round was estimated to increase global GDP by $213 billion (Goldin et al., 1993, p. 13). It is these kinds of perceptions and calculations of the benefits of trade liberalization that provide the motivation for countries to dismantle their own trade barriers, as long as others do the same.

If the positive effects of trade on economic growth seem sufficiently likely both theoretically and empirically to be widely taken for granted, the same cannot be said for the effects of economic growth and trade on the environment. Van Beers and van den Bergh's (1996) review of methodological approaches in trade and environment research found that 'each method can only generate a limited and partial insight, because of restrictive assumptions and analytical complexities' (van Beers and van den Bergh 1996, p. 163). Similarly, Ulph's (1997) extensive review of the recent theoretical literature proved unable either to endorse the virtuous trade–growth–environment circle often invoked by advocates of trade liberalization, or the more pessimistic view espoused by its opponents (see Box 6.1 for typical statements of both views). Ulph concluded: 'Recent analysis is capable of providing starkly different predictions about environmental policy under liberalized trade regimes from those derived from traditional trade and environmental literature, but there is a severe problem of robustness of results' (Ulph, 1997, p. 238).

Most studies have not addressed these issues empirically. This is, however, far from sraightforward. Two problems are noted. First, the difficulty of linking physical and monetary dimensions, and, second, the challenge of defining and measuring unambiguous indicators of 'environmental effects, specific environmental measures, or strictness of environmental policy' (van Beers and van den Bergh, 1996, p. 162). One fairly obvious factor which will affect (and may determine) whether trade liberalization has a positive or negative environmental impact is the nature of the protection being dismantled. If more than averagely polluting sectors are being protected, then liberalization should reduce the relative importance of these sectors, and thereby yield environmental improvements. Jenkins (2001a) finds that this has proved so for Mexico. The hypothesis (in reverse) also fitted Argentina and Brazil, who were found, rather surprisingly, to have protected their relatively less polluting sectors, so that liberalization led to the growth of 'dirty' industries. Jenkins also finds that 'there are important inter-industry differences in the impact of producing for export on environmental performance', so that it is not possible to generalize about whether or not an increased orientation towards exports will be environmentally beneficial.

Studies specifically on the environmental impact of trade liberalization may be rare, but in one area there has been substantial empirical research. This is on the issue as to whether, where there are negative environmental externalities associated with production and/or consumption, economic growth will amplify these, or whether it will facilitate their abatement by intensifying preferences for environmental quality and providing the resources to give these preferences effect. This issue is broadly that addressed by the literature on the 'Environmental Kuznets Curve (EKC)' hypothesis, which in crude terms states that environmental quality tends to improve beyond a certain income threshold.

It is evident that this is true for some issues. For example, two of the greatest environmental problems in poorer countries are water pollution, due to lack of sanitation infrastructure, and indoor air pollution from indoor fires. It may be confidently expected that economic growth in the countries suffering from these problems would result in extra economic resources being allocated to address them. The same is likely to be true in due course for outdoor air pollution from the combustion of fossil fuels by households and in motor vehicles. However, a number of studies of the literature in this area (for example, Ekins, 1997; Cole et al., 1997; Bruyn et al., 1998) have concluded that, in general, the EKC hypothesis does not hold, and that, even for those measures which tend to exhibit the EKC income/environment relationship, there is nothing automatic about the relationship or the turning point income threshold. The role of environmental policy in achieving environmental improvement in a context of rising incomes is crucial: (1) policy to internalize environmental costs and to move towards market efficiency by making environmental damage subject to market pressures; (2) policy to stimulate technical and structural change to reduce the environmental intensity of the economy; (3) policy to give effect to increasing desires for environmental quality that cannot be privately bought; and (4) policy to bring about a distribution of environmental goods, both within and between generations, that is both fair and provides incentives for their sustainable use.

This leads directly to another issue of controversy in the trade–environment debate: the extent to which liberalization will reduce the political will to implement policies for effective environmental protection. There is little dispute in principle that the first-best means of addressing domestic environmental damage is likely to be through domestic policy that directly tackles the environmental problem, rather than through trade policy (for example GATT, 1992, p. 21; Anderson and Blackhurst, 1992, p. 20; Nordström and Vaughan 1999 p. 26). Similarly the first-best approach to global environmental problems is likely to be through international treaties involving all the relevant parties. However, there are a number of practical problems with the implementation of these approaches in a context of rules-based trade liberalization. The two issues will be explored in turn.

Trade Liberalization and Domestic Environmental Policy

Pressure on competitiveness
In all countries, environmental policy is enacted with reference to other policy objectives, of which economic policy objectives are among the most important. The most difficult environmental policies to implement are those which are perceived to have a negative impact on the economy. It is certainly true that world trading rules allow countries to protect their own environments. But they often do not allow countries to protect their domestic industry from competitors who do not protect their environment and thereby gain a competitive advantage. At the very least, as noted in Box 6.1, such a situation might be expected to put a drag on environmental policy making that is thought to have a negative effect on competitiveness. At worst, the result could be competitive environmental deregulation, whereby 'unrestricted trade imposes lower standards' (Daly, 1993, p. 27), or what has more dramatically been called 'the race to the bottom' (Esty and Geradin, 1997, p. 273; Esty and Gentry, 1999, p. 162; Mabey and McNally, 1999, p. 27).

The effects of trade liberalization on environmental policy making will depend strongly on the extent to which it is perceived environmental policy has, or may have, an impact on corporate competitiveness. Unfortunately, as with so many other issues in this area, opinions are divided on this as well.

The conventional economic view is that the realization of environmental benefits through environmental policy is likely to entail economic costs. The results of both Lucas et al. (1992) and Low and Yeats (1992) are consistent with the hypothesis that the costs associated with strict environmental regulation in OECD countries has led to the locational displacement of pollution-intensive industries to developing countries (the pollution haven hypothesis). Other studies, surveyed by Dean (1992, pp. 16–20), give conflicting results, but overall do not suggest that the forces for displacement are very great. In the same vein, Jenkins (2001b) has found that there is no relationship between pollution intensity and foreign ownership in the manufacturing sectors of Malaysia and Indonesia, suggesting that foreign direct investment in such developing countries is not disproportionately driven by the quest for pollution havens. Moreover, if it is true that environmentally intensive sectors are also capital-intensive, as suggested by Nordström and Vaughan (1999, p. 31), comparative advantage theory suggests that these industries would tend to be located in capital-abundant (that is, industrialized) countries. In fact, they present World Bank data which shows that high-income countries do indeed export more pollution-intensive goods than they import, while the reverse is true for upper-middle-income, lower-middle-income and low-income countries (Nordström and Vaughan, 1999, p. 32).

Any costs of environmental regulation to firms need to be set against a number of possible benefits, including cost reduction from reduced waste and waste management costs, first-mover advantages and stimulation to innovation, which may result in the development of new products or new business opportunities. Considerations of this sort have led Porter (1990, pp. 647-8) to hypothesize that environmental regulations may be good for economic competitiveness. This win–win hypothesis of the economic, as well as environmental, benefits of environmental regulation runs clearly counter to economists' normal assumptions of efficient, competitive markets. It has been attacked as being at best a marginal phenomenon with regard to the costs of environmental regulation as whole. Palmer et al. (1995, pp. 127-8) estimate that Porter's 'innovation offsets' amount to only a few percent of the total costs of conforming to environmental regulations, which in the US have been estimated by the EPA at $135 billion in 1992. They contend that the vast majority of these costs conform to the standard economic trade-off model, whereby environmental benefits are gained at the expense of growth and competitiveness.

Analysis by Jenkins gives marginal support to this view. He suggests that 'the evidence of a positive environmental effect in industries which do well competitively (the Porter hypothesis) is less strong than that for possible negative effects in industries which perform badly' (Jenkins, 1998, p. 37). Overall, however, Jenkins' review of the literature suggested that 'there was no strong universal relationship between environmental pressures and competitive performance, either at the firm level or the industry level' (Jenkins, 1998, p. 38).

It is not only competition for trade in goods and services which may affect environmental policy making. Just as potent a source of competitive pressure is the desire for foreign direct investment (FDI), which is important for all economies and is now the largest source of development finance for developing countries (Gentry, 1999, p. 25). As with competition for trade, there is the danger that a desire to attract FDI will cause a competitive lowering of environmental standards. Reviewing this issue, Zarsky (1999, pp. 47–8) concludes that there is no evidence that this desire is in general leading to 'pollution havens' or a 'race to the bottom'. However, there is also no shortage of case studies showing that FDI often causes great environmental damage, especially in developing countries, and in general environmental standards (and their enforcement) are not improving fast enough to offset the environmental degradation of the increased economic activity which FDI brings about. 'It is in this sense that the claim that foreign direct investment is bad for the environment has credibility.' (Zarsky, 1999, p. 49.)

Mabey and McNally (1999) review some of the case studies linking FDI to environmental degradation and discern evidence that FDI, especially in resource- and environment-intensive sectors, both seeks out weak environmental regimes and results in economic activity 'at a scale and pace which overwhelms host country regulatory capacity' (Mabey and McNally, 1999, p. 26).

Whatever the reality of the impact of environmental policy on competitiveness and flows of FDI, there is certainly a strong perception of its likely negative effects, both in business in respect of the former and in governments in respect of the latter. Ikwue and Skea (1996) have documented the strong anti-tax campaign that was mounted by business interests against the 1992 proposal by the European Commission to introduce a carbon-energy tax, even though the proposal exempted the six most energy-intensive economic sectors, and recommended that the tax be revenue-neutral. Zarsky (1997, pp. 31ff.) considers that the pressures of global economic competition have engendered in governments an unwillingness to effect unilateral measures for environmental protection, such that environmental policy has become 'stuck in the mud'. The result is generally low environmental performance that improves slowly or not at all. In a similar vein Esty (1994, p. 162) has noted: 'This political dimension of competitiveness is a reality in almost all environmental policy debates.' It would be surprising if it did not make environmental policy less stringent than it would otherwise be, and, arguably, can prevent it from being stringent enough to move economies decisively towards sustainable development.

Esty and Geradin (1997) have documented examples in both Europe and North America where environmental policy measures have been subjected to legal challenge on the grounds that they distort trade and where concerns about competitiveness have impacted on the process of environmental law making. With reference to the European Community (and like Zarsky in respect of FDI, as discussed above), they note that the 'risk of a regulatory race toward the bottom' has not so far been much of an issue. On the contrary, there is evidence that generally environmental regulations continue to tighten across a wide range of environmental concerns (for example, the signature in late 1999 of the multi-pollutant protocol of the countries of the United Nations Economic Commission for Europe (UNECE)).

However, they also consider that impacts of considerations of competitiveness on policy making 'illustrate the serious concerns of high-standard [EU] Member States about the cost differentials that arise from varying environmental process standards' (Esty and Geradin, 1997, p. 308), so that: 'The real effect is one of "political drag" or "regulatory chill", making it difficult for governments to move towards optimal environmental policies' (Esty and Geradin, 1997, p. 273). They speculate whether competitiveness concerns about low environmental standards may intensify with the accession to the European Community of central and eastern European countries, which have less developed systems of environmental regulation. They also note that the difference in such standards between the United States and Mexico has been an important factor in fuelling fears about a regulatory 'race toward the bottom' in the context of the North American Free Trade Agreement (NAFTA).

The extent to which this was recognised as an issue during the negotiations on NAFTA is shown by the fact that NAFTA's environmental 'side agreement' has a specific provision that all three NAFTA countries should fully implement their environmental legislation, and expresses their intention to achieve upward harmonization of this legislation over time, although Thomas and Weber (1999) do not give any indication that this intention has as yet been put into practice. The phenomenon of political drag and regulatory chill means that, in practice, there may be little governmental appetite for more stringent environmental standards. However, even where there is such appetite, it may be challenged not only by other governments, who perceive the standards to be an unacceptable constraint on trade, but also by private companies. The experience of such challenges is discussed in the next section.

Private challenges to environmental policies

The increased international interdependence of national economies, the increased flows of FDI between them, and the consequent increased presence of foreign investors in nearly all countries, have led to concerns that these investors should receive fair treatment from their host governments. One expression of this concern was the Agreement on Trade-Related Investment Measures (TRIMs, WTO, 1994, pp. 163ff.), which was one of the Uruguay Round agreements. Of far more relevance so far to the environment has been Chapter 11 of NAFTA (the North American Free Trade Agreement, concluded in 1992, see NAFTA, 1992).

NAFTA's Chapter 11 is intended to give foreign investors security in the country of their investment. It does this by setting out certain disciplines which must be respected by NAFTA governments, including non-discrimination between domestic and foreign investors, prohibitions on certain types of performance requirements on investment, and prohibitions on direct and indirect expropriations, or measures tantamount to expropriation. If an investor perceives that a host government has failed to observe a discipline, it can seek redress, and damages, in a special NAFTA dispute resolution process that may be kept completely secret to the parties concerned. Mann and von Moltke (1999, p. 3) consider that NAFTA's Chapter 11 'contains the most extensive set of rights and remedies ever provided to foreign investors in an international agreement'. They also consider that all the disciplines are potentially troubling from a sustainable development perspective (Mann and von Moltke, 1999, p. 4).

The discipline that has attracted most public concern is that concerned with the interpretation of expropriation. There is no space here to examine the legal issues involved in detail, but it is possible that this discipline 'establishes a potential right to compensation or damages for new environmental measures adopted by a NAFTA party', with 'taxpayers' money being required to pay for the right of a government to protect the environment' (Mann and von Moltke, 1999, p. 16), in total contravention of the polluter pays principle. This would turn the regulatory chill of the previous section into a regulatory freeze.

This situation is now more than a theoretical possibility. Mann and von Moltke (1999, p. 5) list eleven known cases that have been filed under Chapter 11, six of which are environmentally related (because of the secrecy surrounding disputes, their list may not be complete). They consider that these cases, and others which have been threatened, have changed investor–state provisions in Chapter 11 'from their traditional role as a defensive investor protection mechanism to a potent offensive strategic tool' (Mann and von Moltke, 1999, p. 15).

A number of the cases have now been adjudicated and add substance to this concern. In one case, Ethyl Corp. (US) sued Canada in 1996 over its import ban, on health grounds, on the fuel additive MMT. In 1998 Canada paid Ethyl Corp. $US13 million in an out-of-court settlement, withdrew the ban and denied that MMT had any health or environmental impacts (Mann and von Moltke, 1999, p. 66). In September 2000 Metalclad (US) won a $US16.7 million award against the Mexican Government when it was refused permission to operate a hazardous waste facility (BRIDGES 2000a). In a case still under adjudication (in June 2002), Methanex (Canada) has sued the State of California for $US970 million over its intention to ban the fuel additive MTBE on health grounds (BRIDGES 2000b).

Fears of such situations were a major factor in generating the opposition on environmental grounds to the Multilateral Agreement on Investment (MAI), negotiations on which were finally called off in 1998. They had started under the auspices of the Organisation for Economic Co-operation and Development (OECD) in 1995. They sought to extend to OECD countries as a whole (and, it is surmised, thence to the whole world through the WTO), the kind of investor protection afforded by NAFTA. As Huner (2000, p. 244) reveals, the negotiations were conducted in such secrecy that OECD government ministers in other policy areas often did not even know they were going on, they had no input from other policy areas, even though the OECD prides itself on being an interdisciplinary organization, and they did not consider the environment as an issue until environmental groups forced it onto their agenda in 1996. Even then the MAI Negotiating Group refused to meet with NGOs directly (although the business sector had been regularly consulted throughout the negotiations), and their papers remained confidential (Huner, 2000, pp. 246–7). Such procedures further undermined the perceived legitimacy of the negotiations, which were suspended in April 1998, and abandoned six months later.

The experience proved, if nothing else, that further liberalization of investment, and of trade, is going to require very different processes than those which the trade and investment communities have been accustomed to use.

Trade Liberalization and International Environmental Policy

At the international level the same problem of policy implementation arises as at the national level, albeit for different reasons. Multi-country environmental treaties are notoriously difficult to conclude. Unilateral actions involving trade policy can sometimes be an effective way of moving towards multi-lateral agreements or their implementation (see Charnovitz, 1992, p. 207, for examples). Moreover, trade policies may be among the only available instruments whereby countries that agree among themselves not to damage the global environment can prevent others from doing so. Currently about 20 out of 200 multilateral environmental agreements (MEAs), including some of the most important ones such as the Convention on International Trade in Endangered Species (CITES), the Montreal Protocol on ozone depleting substances, the Basel Convention on trade in waste, the Rotterdam Convention on trade in hazardous chemicals and the Biosafety Protocol to the Biodiversity Convention, provide for the use of trade policy to achieve their objectives. This may seek to restrict environmentally damaging trade per se, or may have the objective of encouraging compliance from signatories, or of encouraging participation in the MEA from, or imposing sanctions on, non-signatories to it. The OECD (1999a, p. 166) considers that trade measures in MEAs have been effective in both these and other ways. Yet it is not clear that such measures, especially in respect of non-signatories, are compatible with GATT/WTO rules.

This situation is undesirable for both environmental and trade reasons. Probably most importantly, it introduces uncertainty into the process of negotiating MEAs which cannot but inhibit the incorporation of trade measures, even when these would be both justified and necessary to the achievement of the MEA's environmental objectives. Moreover, in any actual conflict between the trade measures in an MEA and WTO rules, currently the only forum in which the conflict could be resolved is through the Disputes Settlement mechanism of the WTO. This effectively gives precedence to trade law over environmental considerations. Both these reasons will reinforce the perception that the multilateral trading system is inimical to effective environmental protection, on the one hand calling for international environmental problems to be resolved through multilateral agreements, but on the other perpetuating uncertainty over the validity of the principal class of measures that could make agreements effective. If environmental concerns become stronger, as seems likely, this perceived anti-environment bias to the trading system cannot but undermine the general acceptance of its legitimacy, and, at worst, could seriously affect its operation (by unilateral trade–environment measures becoming more common) or development (through further disruptions such as were witnessed at the Ministerial Meeting in Seattle in late 1999).

It is for such reasons that Brack (1999, pp. 294ff.) has proposed the negotiation of a new WTO Agreement on MEAs. This should cover such issues as the definition of an MEA, and of the trade measures which they might incorporate, the possible provision of resources to enable low-income countries to comply with MEAs and arrangements for dispute settlement. Brack considers that a failure specifically to address the linkage between the trading system and MEAs, and clarify existing uncertainties, can only lead to conflict between them in the future, similar to the kinds of trade-environment conflicts which have already emerged and which are the subject of the next section. It is presumably such considerations which led to this issue being included in the new round of WTO negotiations, which were launched in Doha in 2001.

CONFLICTS BETWEEN TRADE AND THE ENVIRONMENT

Of the three international economic institutions proposed following the Second World War, two – the International Bank for Reconstruction and Development (World Bank) and the International Monetary Fund – were formally established. The third, the International Trade Organisation (ITO), was only realized as a General Agreement on Tariffs and Trade (GATT). This came into force in 1948. By 1991 103 states were formal Contracting Parties (CPs) to GATT, including the 24 industrialized countries that then comprised the OECD and accounted for 75 per cent of world trade, and another 29 states were applying GATT on a de facto basis.

The GATT rules, expressed in articles, provide the essential framework conditions for most world trade and seek to embody for GATT's CPs 'reciprocal and mutually advantageous arrangements directed to the substantial reduction of tariffs and other barriers to trade and to the elimination of discriminatory treatment in international commerce.' (GATT, 1986, p. 1).

The GATT articles are amended, or their scope enlarged, by periodic 'rounds' of negotiations, of which the Uruguay Round, begun in 1986, was the eighth. The principal objectives of the Uruguay Round were to bring agriculture, textiles and services within the scope of GATT for the first time, and to formulate rules for trade-related investment and trade-related intellectual property. In 1991 the GATT Secretariat inserted a proposal in the Draft Final Act of the Uruguay Round to establish a World Trade Organisation (WTO), reminiscent of the original ITO proposal, to subsume GATT in future. The proposal was adopted as part of the Uruguay Round, and the WTO was established when the Uruguay Agreement came into force in January 1995.

The GATT articles are founded on the principle of non-discrimination in trade with regard to trading partners – any country that is a GATT signatory must accord all other GATT signatories the same trading conditions as it accords to its 'most favoured nation' – and national treatment – like products must be treated in the same way irrespective of their country of origin. Article XX permits limited exceptions to these most favoured nation and like product principles, including exceptions related to the protection of human health and the conservation of natural resources, but so far there has never been dispute over environmental resources under GATT in which an exception on these grounds has been upheld. September 2000 saw the first exception to be accepted on health grounds, in the Canada–France asbestos dispute, as discussed below.

In 1992 the GATT Secretariat spelt out what environmental protection is compatible with current trade rules:

> GATT rules ... place essentially no constraints on a country's right to protect its own environment against damage from either domestic production or the consumption of domestically produced or imported products. Generally speaking, a country can do anything to imports or exports that it does to its own products, and it can do anything it considers necessary to its production processes (GATT, 1992, p. 23).

Following the Uruguay Round agreement in 1994, this formulation somewhat overstates a country's discretion on policy towards the environment and human health. Most importantly, the Uruguay Round agreement contained an Agreement on the Application of Sanitary and Phytosanitary (SPS) Measures (WTO, 1994, pp. 69–84), based on the idea that 'food safety and related disputes should be settled by science-based rules' in order 'to prevent the use of unnecessary health measures that impede foreign exporters' (Charnovitz, 1999, p. 171). The tests to be satisfied under SPS are more stringent than those in the GATT articles and significantly reduce the scope for using human health protection as an argument under Article XX. The SPS agreement requires policies in these areas that affect importers to be based on scientific evidence if they are not to be open to challenge from another country which feels them to be too stringent. Given substantial scientific uncertainty in many issues related to the environment, there is likely to be a wide margin of interpretation of what constitutes scientific evidence (see Stirling, Chapter 2) in these cases.

Within the WTO, considerable influence on scientific issues related to food safety, and therefore power to adjudicate standards in this area, has been granted by the WTO to the Codex Alimentarius Commission. Although Codex is jointly financed by the UN Food and Agriculture Organisation (FAO) and World Health Organisation (WHO), concern has been expressed that it is unduly influenced by transnational corporations (Evans and Walsh, 1994, p. 23; Lang and Hines, 1993, pp. 100–103; NCC, 1998, pp. 96–7). It may therefore be more attuned to business and trade priorities than to safeguarding human health, and either discourage or disallow regulations stricter than Codex-agreed international standards, which some countries and interest groups perceive as being too lax.

Even leaving to one side the problem of what constitutes 'scientific evidence', or the procedures required in the SPS agreement to assess it, the GATT pronouncement quoted above about what a country can do to protect the environment throws into sharp relief what it cannot do under GATT rules.

- It may not use trade policy to protect its environment from foreign production. It could not impose trade sanctions, for example, on a neighbouring country which persistently exported air or water pollution, no matter how damaging its effects.
- It may not use trade policy to protect the environment outside its own jurisdiction, whether a global commons or the territory of another country. As noted above, it is unclear whether this is the case if a trade measure is applied under the terms of an MEA.
- It may not impose on imports charges or other restrictions related to their process and production methods (PPMs), even when it is imposing identical treatment on its own production (that is, its policy is non-discriminatory). As discussed above, this acts as a major

discouragement to apply strict environmental policy measures to production processes where it is perceived that such measures may have a negative effect on the competitiveness of domestic business.

● Some environmental regulations may be deemed inadmissible as technical (or non-tariff) barriers to trade. The GATT rules require such regulations to be the least GATT-inconsistent that are available. Esty (1994, p. 48) comments: 'This sets an almost impossibly high hurdle for environmental policy, because a policy approach that intrudes less on trade is almost always conceivable and therefore in some sense "available"'.

From an environmental point of view these GATT prohibitions impose considerable constraints on environmental policy. There have been a number of cases which illustrate how such provisions under GATT have either brought trade liberalization, trade rules and environmental policy into conflict, or might do so in the future. Ekins (2000, pp. 133ff.) reviews some of these cases, including the US/Mexico Tuna–Dolphin Dispute, the US/Venezuela Gasoline Reformulation Dispute, the Danish Bottles Case, and the European Commission's and the Finnish carbon taxes, of which space precludes further mention here. However, many of the relevant issues emerge from a discussion of some of other cases which follow.

The Shrimp–Turtle Dispute

This dispute arose when the United States banned imports of shrimps from countries which had not taken measures to its satisfaction to ensure that sea turtles (an endangered species) were not caught at the same time as the shrimp were harvested (see Ekins, 2000, pp. 136–7 for further background). In 1998 a WTO Panel found that the US import ban was in violation of Article XI, which prohibits the imposition of import restrictions on trade between members, and that the ban was not covered by the 'exceptions' article, Article XX (WTO 1998a). In fact, the panel ruling seemed to question whether the Article XX exceptions could ever be applied by a member, on the grounds that, if other members applied such exceptions, this 'would threaten the security and predictability of the multilateral trading system'.

On appeal, the WTO Appellate Body reversed the panel's decision on Article XX, finding that the US measure itself was legitimate under the terms of the article. However, it also found that the way the US had applied the measure involved 'unjustifiable and arbitrary discrimination', and therefore was not consistent with Article XX. This conclusion rested largely on the Appellate Body's view that 'it is not acceptable, in international trade relations, for one WTO Member to use an economic embargo to *require* other members to adopt essentially the same comprehensive regulatory program, to achieve a certain policy goal, as that in force within that member's territory, *without* taking into consideration different conditions which may occur in the territories of those other Members' (WTO, 1998b, para. 164).

The appellate body's conclusion also derived from the facts that the US had banned shrimp imported from uncertified countries even when they were caught under conditions which complied with US regulations; the US had failed to consult adequately before imposing its ban; and the US had not made adequate efforts to resolve the problem of the sea turtles through bilateral or multilateral negotiations, before imposing its unilateral ban.

Notwithstanding the fact that the US lost the case, Arden-Clarke from the World Wide Fund for Nature considers that the appellate body's ruling 'changed the face of the issue of process and production methods (PPMs) and trade' (Arden-Clarke, 2000 p. 183). The reason is because the ruling recognized for the first time that a trade measure related to PPMs and applied by a WTO member to conserve environmental resources outside the territory of that member could in principle be consistent with the relevant clause under Article XX and therefore not be inconsistent with GATT rules as a whole. It remains to be seen whether the appellate body fully intended this interpretation of its ruling and whether subsequent WTO rulings will build on, or seek to constrain, this interpretation.

The US was given until the end of 1999 to comply with the appellate body's ruling, which it intended to do by altering the requirements for the import of foreign shrimp, rather than lifting the import restrictions altogether. It is possible that Malaysia will institute a new WTO challenge on the grounds that the new requirements do not comply with the WTO ruling (ICTSD, 2000a, p. 7).

The Asbestos Dispute

In December 1996 France banned, on health grounds, the import of all varieties of asbestos, including chrysotile. Canada, which is a major exporter of chrysotile, challenged the ban as inconsistent with GATT rules, and asked the WTO to adjudicate. A WTO Panel was set up in November 1998 and reported in September 2000, upholding the French ban. Its reasoning marks a significant new development in WTO case law, in three main respects, and may prove of historic importance.

First, the panel acknowledged both that France had the right to set its health standards at any level it wished, and that asbestos constituted a generally accepted risk to human health. The forthright and explicit way in which the panel affirms that it is not its (or the WTO's) job 'to assess ... the level of protection of public health that France wishes to achieve' (WTO, 2000, para.

8.171, p. 434) might have been designed to allay concerns that the WTO represents an unjustifiable curtailment of national sovereignty in such matters as public health.

Second, the panel found that France had discriminated against asbestos in a way that was inconsistent with GATT rules, because it treated asbestos differently from other products, in particular domestic substitutes for asbestos, which in GATT terms should be classed as like products. It accepted Canada's assertion that, for WTO purposes: 'products may be considered like despite their differing impact on health ... The toxicity of a product is not recognised as a criterion for the evaluation of likeness' (WTO, 2000, para. 8.118, p. 423). The panel's reasoning for this counter-intuitive conclusion is that the evaluation of likeness under GATT should be in relation to market access for products (WTO, 2000, para. 8.122, p. 424). 'In the context of market access, it is not necessary for domestic products to posses all the properties of the imported product in order to be a like product. It suffices that, for a given utilisation, the properties are the same to the extent that one product can replace the other' (WTO, 2000, para. 8.124, p. 425). Otherwise products would have to be identical in all respects to be considered 'like', and this was clearly not intended to be the meaning of like products in the GATT rules. Not least, if differences in health impacts ruled out product likeness, then there would be no need for the exception clause for human health in Article XX. This must mean that the GATT articles did not intend likeness to be interpreted in this all-embracing way. Some environmentalists have been critical of this like products ruling on the grounds that claiming that a dangerously toxic substance is like a benign one 'defies common sense' (ICTSD, 2000b), and an environmental lawyer has claimed that 'the ruling defeats the spirit of the WTO Agreements and acts contrary to proper treaty interpretation by failing to consider the WTO Agreements as a whole' (Gray, 2000, p. 9).

The third, and perhaps most important, innovatory ruling of this panel was that, despite constituting a discrimination against an imported like product, the French ban was allowable under GATT, because it satisfied the criteria for exceptional treatment set out in Article XX, which allows discrimination in order to protect public health, provided it is both necessary and not implemented in an arbitrary and unjustifiable way. This is the first time that a GATT/WTO Panel has ruled that any particular act of discrimination is justifiable under Article XX. Previously Article XX had existed only as a theoretical possibility of giving the protection of human health precedence over free trade. This ruling has shown that the theoretical possibility can be realized in practice.

Canada appealed against the WTO panel's vindication of the French ban and the appellate body delivered its ruling on the appeal in March 2001. Not only did it find that France's ban on asbestos was consistent with GATT rules, it also overturned the panel's findings on like products, ruling that the comparative health risks of products could be an appropriate consideration in determining the likeness of products, and that in this case Canada had failed to establish such likeness. Canada therefore was only left to argue that asbestos did not constitute a health risk, which it failed to do against the weight of scientific evidence considered in this case. The ICTSD (2001, pp. 1-2) considers that the appellate body's rulings on this point are crucial, because they shift 'the burden of proof from the Member who restricts market access on health grounds to the Member who challenges that restriction'.

Other Important Disputes

A number of other trade disputes have been important in defining the current context and case law within which trade-environment issues are considered. The first of these illustrates the complexities that arise in trade disputes, and the consequent need for flexibility in interpretation of trade rules if environmental protection is to be achieved. The second and third show how the new SPS Agreement is starting to be interpreted.

The lobster dispute
Lobster stocks need conserving, to achieve which the US has rules prohibiting the sale of lobsters below a certain size. This led it to reject a proportion of the lobsters imported from Canada. Canada argued that this was discriminatory because its lobsters were mature, but smaller because of colder Canadian waters. The case was decided in the US's favour, on the grounds that its law was justified and exempting mature Canadian lobsters from it would involve unreasonable administrative expense (Lee, 1998, pp. 32ff.).

The beef hormones dispute
In 1989 the European Commission banned the importation of US beef on the grounds that it was produced with growth hormones that had been banned in the European Union (EU), because they might be carcinogenic. The US challenged the ban under the SPS Agreement. In 1998 the WTO appellate body ruled against the EU, on the grounds that it had not conducted a risk assessment to support its ban, as is required under the SPS Agreement. So far the EU has refused to revoke its ban and may become liable for damages or compensation.

The salmon dispute
Canada has used the SPS Agreement successfully to challenge an Australian

ban, introduced in 1975, on the importation of uncooked salmon. The ban is intended to protect Australian salmon fisheries against foreign salmon diseases. However, the appellate body in 1998 found that the ban was inconsistent with the SPS Agreement because it was not based on a proper scientific risk assessment. In addition, it fell foul of the SPS Agreement's requirement for national regulatory consistency. Charnovitz (1999, p. 180) considers that this is 'the most controversial SPS rule and the one most intrusive into national decision-making processes because it focuses on the "levels" of health protection'. It was seen above in the asbestos case that this was something which the WTO panel and subsequently the appellate body specifically eschewed. It seems inconsistent that levels of health protection in relation to food safety should be a WTO concern while other levels of health protection should not. Charnovitz (1999, pp. 189–90) recommends that this article of the SPS Agreement should be subject to further guidance before it is invoked again.

Finally, it is necessary to mention two other issues as core potential, if not yet actual, areas of WTO dispute: eco-labelling and the precautionary principle. The relationship of the former to the vexed issue of PPMs is obvious. Indeed, the purpose of eco-labels is often to give insights into aspects of PPMs (for example, 'dolphin-safe tuna' or 'sustainably harvested timber'). Appleton (1999, p. 196) considers that, unless countries negotiate a WTO agreement on eco-labels, 'it is only a matter of time before a WTO member launches an attack on an eco-labelling programme that it views as discriminatory'. Whatever the judgement in such a dispute, it would damage the WTO. Such a dispute was narrowly avoided in 1992, when the Austrian Parliament only withdrew a regulation requiring all tropical timber to be labelled on receipt of a threat of trade sanctions and a GATT challenge by Malaysia (Cairncross, 1995, pp. 230–31).

The precautionary principle 'says that the absence of full scientific certainty should not prevent action in cases of threats of serious or irreversible damage' (OECD, 1999a, p. 167). Cameron (1999, p. 247) notes: 'The precautionary principle has been included in virtually every recently adopted treaty and policy document related to the protection and preservation of the environment.' He goes on to argue that the principle has now become part of international customary law, but whether or not this is true it is certain that the principle will be increasingly invoked in trade contexts. Indeed, it is implicitly present in the SPS Agreement, and was explicitly referred to (but was not part of the final judgement) in the Beef Hormones case briefly discussed above. As with eco-labels, the WTO has the choice to clarify the relationship of the precautionary principle to WTO rules through negotiation, or for it to be clarified by successive rulings of the appellate body. Again, the latter seems the course most likely to cause disaffection with the WTO, whichever way the rulings go.

Three broad possibilities currently exist for ways in which the WTO could become more sensitive and responsive to environmental concerns. First, by changing the way in which the GATT rules (especially with regard to the Article XX exceptions) and WTO agreements are interpreted. Second, by developing new agreements as part of a new negotiating round, along the lines of the SPS or TRIPS (Trade-Related Aspects of Intellectual Property Rights) agreements, which were concluded as part of the Uruguay Round. Third, by changing the text of the GATT itself. For example, Cameron (2000, p. 204) considers that the desirable way to proceed in respect of MEAs would be to add a further exceptions clause to Article XX, with clarification also on the scope of the interpretation of its Preamble.

An important element in any moves towards even considering changes in this area is openness. IISD-UNEP (2000, pp. 67ff.) considers that this has two components in a WTO context: full access to information for affected parties, and participation in the decision-making process. The WTO is far more open than the GATT was in respect of the availability of information, and there are moves towards accepting third party submissions in disputes. Openness will be critical in winning broad agreement to any environmentally related changes in WTO rules which may be put forward. Another prerequisite for such agreement is that the WTO becomes an institution more reflective of developing country concerns and priorities. Far more work prior to WTO plenaries is required to establish common positions in which developing country concerns are fully taken into account, rather than powerful groups arriving at positions in closed negotiations at WTO meetings, which other countries are then simply expected to rubber-stamp.

PERCEPTIONS OF THE TRADE/ENVIRONMENT ISSUE FROM THE SOUTH

The kinds of trade and environment issues discussed above are approached by developing countries with deepening suspicion and concern. The reason is their belief that, if GATT rules are relaxed to permit greater discrimination in trade on environmental grounds, it will be impossible to prevent measures which, while oriented towards environmental protection, actually discriminate against the trade in goods from the south and further limit the access of developing countries to developed country markets. Developing countries have noted that, in each of the headline WTO trade-environment disputes (tuna–dolphin, gasoline reformulation, shrimp–turtle) the relevant environmental protection measure was applied in a way that was more discriminatory against southern producers than it needed to be. They suspect that any further accommodation to environmental issues in GATT rules would only multiply cases of this sort, and are deeply concerned that the ruling of the appellate body in the shrimp–turtle case opens the door to countries to 'pursue their own trade policy solutions unilaterally, in line with what they perceive today to be their environmental concerns', which 'would be a threat to the preservation of a multilateral trade system based on consensus and multilateral co-operation' (Shahin, 2000, p. 111).

Developing countries' fears in this regard have three dimensions. First, developed countries will be permitted under GATT to start discriminating against goods and services on the basis of their process and production methods (PPMs), rather than the nature of the products themselves. Second, developed countries will start to apply conditions, based on PPMs, for access to their markets for goods from abroad. The development of eco-labels, environmental management systems and benchmarking standards could provide a basis for such conditions. And third, developed countries will extend concerns and conditionalities related to environmental standards to other issues, such as labour standards, human rights observance, even wage rates.

In each of these areas developing countries feel that it would be their access to world markets that would be affected most. They cannot always afford PPMs with the least environmental impact, and their labour standards, working conditions and wage rates also inevitably reflect their level of development. Their small and medium enterprises (SMEs), in particular, are not well placed to compete environmentally with transnational corporations, most of which are based in the north. In effect they feel that, having been drawn into the world market with promises that this will be the way for them to overcome their poverty, and having opened up their markets to developed country goods and services on this basis, they will increasingly be denied access to developed country markets because they are still poor. The perceived asymmetry, injustice and Catch-22 quality of this situation explain the intensity of developing country engagement with these issues (see, for instance, Jha, 1998; Shahin, 1999, 2000).

Agenda 21, the major output from the United Nations Conference on Environment and Development (UNCED) in 1992, largely took a positive view of the trade–environment relationship, recommending: 'Trade liberalization should be pursued on a global basis across economic sectors, so as to contribute to sustainable development' and 'all countries should implement previous commitments to halt and reverse protectionism and further expand market access, particularly in areas of interest to developing countries'. Furthermore, countries should 'avoid unilateral actions to deal with environmental challenges outside the jurisdiction of the exporting country' (Quarrie, 1992, 92, pp. 50, 53).

Generally developing countries see little need to go beyond these kinds of statements in relation to trade and the environment. However, the Marrakesh Agreement which established the WTO in 1995 contained a commitment to sustainable development in its Preamble (WTO, 1994, p. 6), pressure largely from the European Union resulted also in a Decision on Trade and Environment, which led to the establishment of a Committee on Trade and the Environment (CTE) (WTO, 1994, p. 470).

The first report of the CTE to the WTO Ministerial Conference in Singapore in December 1996 concluded that some procedural modifications in terms of transparency and notification might be desirable, but made no recommendations about modifications to the GATT rules or the multilateral trading system themselves. Its principal conclusion was that it should continue its work on the basis of its 1994 terms of reference (WTO, 1996, p. 36). Cameron (1998, pp. 174, 178, 181) is highly critical of the results of the CTE's first two years' work: its 'extremely disappointing' contribution on MEAs and the WTO, the 'inadequacy' of its approach to WTO dispute settlement, and 'its failure to deal adequately with either PPMs or eco-labelling'. In conclusion, 'the overwhelming sense one has from assessing the CTE's work thus far is one of disappointment' (Cameron, 1998, p. 218).

This outcome will have surprised no one who followed the discussions of the CTE in 1995 and 1996 through its newsletter, when it was clear that many developing countries were determined that CTE should not become more than a talking shop and that it should not make recommendations for change in the substantive areas of trade–environment concerns, not least because there was no basis for consensus on such recommendations. Some from developing countries would clearly like the CTE to go on playing this role, to delay the time when proposals need to be formulated and recommendations put forward. Thus Shahin (1999, p. 40) writes: 'It is astonishing that, in spite of the general view that further work needs to be undertaken on all items of the agenda of the CTE, pre-determined positions are still taken … (such as) to press for amending the WTO rules to accommodate environment or … the legitimization of the processes and production methods approach in the GATT system'.

However, indefinite stalling on trade and environment issues is not a sustainable strategy for developing countries. The inclusion of the relationship between MEAs and the WTO rules in the Doha round of negotiations prefigures the spreading out of other trade–environment issues from the isolated confines of the CTE to the main fora of WTO discussions. Developing countries may now be best served by becoming proactive, rather than defensive, in respect of these issues, to ensure that they are ready with positive recommendations of their own, which further their trade interests as well as being environmentally beneficial, when the time comes.

Advocates of a proactive approach argue, first, for an emphasis on WTO's stated commitment to sustainable development. In the Preamble to its establishing Agreement, the WTO argues for an approach 'in a manner consistent with the countries' needs and concerns at different levels of development' (WTO, 1994, p. 6), which Shahin (2000, p. 103) interprets as giving priority to development over environmental concerns. Consistent with such an emphasis, Jha (1998, pp. 98–9) regards as particularly important for developing countries 'safeguarding existing market access conditions against the unwarranted trade effects of environmental policies ... improving market access conditions ... [and] removing trade restrictions and distortions, which may result in environmental benefits ...'. In other words, developing countries' trade and environment agendas will be an attempt to use environmental issues to promote their core trade objectives.

Jha and Vossenaar (1999, pp. 65ff.) develop some of the themes and positions which such a positive agenda could contain, although sceptics note that: 'the WTO itself does not provide an answer to environmental problems' (Shahin, 2000, p. 104). The positive agenda will be fashioned on the basis of a conviction that the trade–environment debate in the north has so far signally failed to give adequate attention to developing country concerns such as 'safeguarding and further improving market access, controlling the export of domestically prohibited goods and promoting technology transfer' (Jha and Vossenaar, 1999, p. 74), or to recognize the lack of capacity and resources in developing countries to address environmental issues, and the consequent need for 'supportive measures' to enable them to do this. The details of any proposals are beyond the scope of this chapter, but they have a common objective: to enable developing countries to engage with trade–environment issues in a way that is oriented to their basic development interests, rather than those of the north. It remains to be seen how this agenda fares in the Doha negotiation process which has just begun.

CONCLUSION

The evidence in the preceding sections allows a number of tentative conclusions to be drawn about trade–environment interactions:

- Neither of the positions at the ends of the spectrum of hypotheses about the trade–environment relationship can be sustained. In other words, trade liberalization has not led, and by itself will not lead, to general environmental improvement. Nor has trade liberalization led, or showed signs of leading, to extensive competitive environmental deregulation.
- Given continuing signs of serious environmental unsustainability, environmental policies and regulations continue to be introduced in

many countries. However, their stringency and pace of introduction are insufficient even to halt negative environmental trends in many areas, far less reverse them.

- At least part of the reason for this inadequate progress of environmental policy is that policy makers fear the impact of stringent environmental policy on competitiveness in the more competitive market conditions brought about by trade liberalization. In Zarsky's (1997) phrase, national environmental policy has got 'stuck in the mud'.
- Even where governments have the political will to introduce stringent environmental policies, there is a danger that these will be open to challenge as technical barriers to trade or found otherwise incompatible with trade rules, under the restrictive interpretations currently placed on the various sections in trade agreements.
- At the multilateral level the continuing uncertainty about the relationship between MEAs and trade rules is adding another obstacle to the already very difficult process of concluding effective global agreements for environmental protection.
- The regulatory chill, or political drag in respect of environmental policy making introduced by the above considerations is being heightened in the NAFTA area by the new phenomenon of investor–state disputes over environmental regulations. While the collapse of the MAI means that, at present, there is no immediate prospect of further multilateral extension of the NAFTA provisions, in a globalizing economy pressures for investor security will remain.

Thus it may be stated with confidence that trade is not the principal cause of environmental degradation. This is rather the result of economic activity in the absence of adequate policies for environmental protection. However, by expanding economic activity trade can amplify environmental damage. Given current environmental trends, it is unlikely that the potential environmental benefits of trade – such as more efficient resource allocation and technology transfer – are compensating for this negative amplifying impact. There is, in fact, something rather perverse about such statements from advocates of trade liberalization that 'trade would unambiguously raise welfare if proper environmental policies were in place' (Nordström and Vaughan, 1999, p. 2), when one of the most obvious characteristics of the world situation is that in every country, for some important environmental issues, proper environmental policies are not in place.

Such statements appear even more perverse, given the need for governments everywhere to implement environmental policies, in the light of the evidence presented above that trade liberalization and its attendant trade rules can and do make it more difficult to implement environmental policies, because of competitiveness effects (real or imagined), challenges that they are barriers to trade, and the uncertainty which surrounds trade measures in MEAs.

There are three possible ways in which the situation described above could develop. The first is continuing environmental degradation in a substantially unchanged multilateral trading system. This development would see environmental policy remaining 'stuck in the mud', with the social pressures for greater environmental conservation failing either to overcome governments' fear of adverse competitiveness impacts from more stringent environmental policy, or to effect reform of the trading system such that it becomes easier to protect the environment without contravening trade rules. Under this scenario environmental sustainability is the loser, with uncertain, but potentially very serious, implications for long-term human welfare.

The second possibility is that continuing environmental degradation will give environmental pressure groups the power to force (probably western) governments to introduce environmental policies in contravention of trade rules, which it proves impossible to change. This would put increasing strain on the multilateral trading system. In the extreme it could lead to its breakdown, as unilateral measures in this area spread to others and destroy the co-operative impulse that is necessary to sustain multilateral agreements. Some environmental activists and groups would welcome this outcome (see, for example, Lang and Hines, 1993). However, unless it was accompanied by fundamental changes in consumer aspirations, and social values generally (of which currently there is little sign), it is hard to see how such a development would encourage sustainable development in either the north or the south.

The third possibility is that the multilateral trading system will reform itself to ensure that, at least, it does not obstruct bona fide environmental policies and that it removes trade-related reasons for governments not to introduce them. Such a development would seek both to realize the environmental benefits of trade and to make it as easy as possible to avoid its environmental costs, and those of economic activity more generally. This would seem to offer the best prospect for maximizing the environmental performance of the current economic system and of therefore managing to achieve the complementarity between socio-economic development and environmental sustainability that is the core concept underlying sustainable development.

However, many uncertainties remain both about the trade–environment relationship itself, and about how each of these aspects of globalization may best make its contribution to increasing human welfare. Social science research has an important role in shedding further light on both these areas of uncertainty. In the following sections six key areas for future research in this field are identified.

The Environmental Impacts of Trade

There is now substantial analysis of the relationship between economic growth and the environment, and this is obviously relevant in general terms to trade liberalization. There is much less analysis of the environmental impacts specifically of trade growth. For example, what are the environmental impacts of the associated increase in transport? What is the evidence on the relative environmental impacts of traded products compared to the production for domestic use which they may replace? Does involvement in the global market place, compared to domestic production, have effects on domestic economic or social structures, and are these good or bad for the environment? For example, what is the effect of new trading opportunities on land ownership? (See Ekins et al., 1994; Ropke, 1994, and Steininger, 1994 for a preliminary discussion of such issues.)

Constructing a Trade Agenda for Environment and Development

As noted earlier, developing countries currently believe that a major component in the north's interest in trade–environment issues is its desire to use environmental policies to limit market access to southern goods and services. Even if this were not the case, the south considers it likely that it would be a loser if trade rules were to become more accommodating of environmental policies.

There was some suggestion before the Doha agreement that the next round of trade negotiations should be a 'development round' (Wang and Winters, 2000a; 2000b), with some elements especially favourable to the south, including giving credit for developing countries' past unilateral liberalization; re-inventing special and differential treatment to help developing countries implement liberalization programmes, legally binding promises of technical assistance, a firm commitment to liberalize textiles and clothing trade by 2005 and reform of WTO governance to give the south a greater voice. In recognition of southern sensitivities in this area, Wang and Winters also recommend that all environmental elements except MEAs should be kept off the agenda for such a development round. Policy-oriented research into how trade could improve southern environments as well as their living standards could provide the basis for a sustainable development round in due course. The Doha negotiations will touch on some of these issues, but there is still much basic work to be done to articulate the detail of how the global trading system can really promote development, and sustainable development, in the south.

Stimulating Environmentally Sustainable Trade

An example of trade responding to environment and development issues is the increasing desire of consumers in the north to factor social and environmental considerations into their purchase of products from abroad. For instance, IIED (1997) contains ten developing country case studies of export success and low environmental impact in manufacturing, tourism, agricultural commodities and forest products, although such initiatives still account for only a tiny proportion of world trade. Robins and Roberts' (2000, p. 112) assessment of this issue suggests that it now requires a 'strategic response' involving policy makers in the north and south, as well as market actors. However, there is as yet little understanding, or even scoping of the options, as to what such a strategic response might entail. Research into the realities of these infant markets might cast light on the kinds of responses that might help them to grow.

Introducing Elements of Harmonization

Full harmonization of environmental standards in very different situations, or at very different levels of development, is probably neither desirable nor possible. At the same time, sustainable development is certainly not a likely outcome if lax environmental standards remain or become something which governments regard as a source of competitive, or even comparative, advantage. Recognition of countries' different priorities and capacities (both environmental and regulatory) needs to be combined with an equally clear recognition of the need for all countries to increase their protection of the natural environment, and for standards everywhere to attain certain minimum levels in key areas. The latter already exists in respect of some MEAs (for example, the production of ozone-depleting substances in the Montreal Protocol, trade in endangered species in CITES). Esty and Geradin (1997, p. 282) consider that: 'Trade officials and economists too often dismiss "harmonization" as inefficient, treating total harmonization of standards as if it were the only available policy option.' In fact harmonization can include a wide variety of approaches, related to both products (to facilitate market access) and PPMs (to discourage too-lax standards). There is a rich research agenda here to document the processes of harmonization that have taken place (for example, in the European Union), to discuss different approaches to harmonization in a north–south context, and to model how such harmonization might proceed in the multilateral trade system.

Improving Assessment of the Environmental Effects of Trade Liberalization

One of the themes of this chapter has been the continuing uncertainty over the actual environmental impacts of trade liberalization. However, the work that has now been done in this area (see, for example, CEC, 1996, 1999; OECD, 1999b; IDPM, 2000; Canada, 2000) makes it unlikely that any further WTO negotiations will proceed without environ-mental or sustainability assessments, whether officially sanctioned by the WTO or not. This will form an important research area for the future, both in doing the assessments, and refining the methodologies in the light of experience.

Strengthening Global Environmental Governance

The previous suggestions would help to make the world's trading system more supportive of environment–development concerns, but it is illusory to suppose that any changes in trade rules or institutions would be sufficient by themselves to move the world economy systematically towards environmental sustainability. This would require far more fundamental and wide-reaching changes in global environmental governance. This is the subject of another chapter in this book (Vogler and Jordan, Chapter 5; see also Hyvarinen and Brack, 2000). As discussed by Vogler and Jordan (Chapter 5) research has an important role to help define the various tasks of global environmental governance, how they are (or are not) currently being carried out, and what kind of global institutional architecture, building on what already exists or starting afresh, might enable them to be carried out more effectively.

REFERENCES

Anderson, K. and R. Blackhurst (eds) (1992), *The Greening of World Trade Issues*, London: Harvester Wheatsheaf.

Appleton, A. (1999), 'Environmental labeling schemes: WTO law and developing country implications', in G. Sampson and W.B Chambers (eds) (1999), *Trade, Environment and the Millennium*, Tokyo: United Nations University Press, pp. 195–221.

Arden-Clarke, C. (2000), 'The impact of the shrimp/turtle dispute, in H. Ward and D. Brack (eds), *Trade, Investment and the Environment*, London: Earthscan/Royal Institute of International Affairs, pp. 183–6.

Brack, D. (2000), 'Environmental treaties and trade: multilateral environmental agreements and the multilateral trading system', in G. Sampson and W.B. Chambers (eds) (1999), *Trade, Environment and the Millennium*, Tokyo: United Nations University Press, pp. 271–98.

BRIDGES (2000a), 'Mexico loses NAFTA expropriation dispute on hazardous waste', *BRIDGES Weekly Trade News Digest* (bridges@iatp.org), September 5, Geneva: International Centre for Trade and Sustainable Development (ICTSD), http://www.ictsd.org.

BRIDGES (2000b) 'NAFTA methanex case could threaten public health laws', *BRIDGES Weekly Trade News Digest* (bridges@iatp.org), September 12, Geneva: International Centre for Trade and Sustainable Development (ICTSD), http://www.ictsd.org.

Bruyn, S.M. de, J. van den Bergh, and J.B Opschoor, (1998), 'Economic growth and emissions: reconsidering the empirical basis of environmental Kuznets Curves', *Ecological Economics*, 25, 161-75.

Cairncross, F. (1995), *Green, Inc.: A Guide to Business and the Environment*, London: Earthscan.

Cameron, J. (1998), 'The CTE: a renewed mandate for change or more dialogue?', in D. Brack (ed.), *Trade and Environment: Conflict or Compatibility?*, London: Earthscan/Royal Institute of International Affairs, pp. 168-86.

Cameron, J. (1999), 'The precautionary principle', in G. Sampson and W.B. Chambers (eds), *Trade, Environment and the Millennium*, Tokyo: United Nations University Press, pp. 239-69.

Cameron, J. (2000), 'The shrimp/turtle dispute and the future', in H. Ward and D. Brack (eds), *Trade, Investment and the Environment*, London: Earthscan/Royal Institute of International Affairs, pp. 203-8.

Canada (2000), *Canada's Draft Environmental Assessment Framework for Trade Negotiations*, Ottawa: Department of Foreign Affairs and International Trade, http://www.dfait-maeci.gc.ca/tna-nac/EAF-Sep2000-e.pdf.

CEC (Commission for Environmental Co-operation) (1996), *Building a Framework for Assessing NAFTA Environmental Effects*, Montreal: CEC Environment and Trade Series No. 4, CEC, http://www.cec.org/pubs_docs/publications/index.cfm?vanlax= english

CEC (Commission for Environmental Co-operation) (1999), *Assessing Environmental Effects of the North American Free Trade Agreement*, Montreal: CEC Environment and Trade Series No. 6, CEC, http://www.cec.org/pubs_docs/publications/ index.cfm?vanlax=english

Charnovitz, S. (1992), 'GATT and the environment: examining the issues', *International Environmental Affairs*, 4 (3), Summer, 203-33.

Charnovitz, S. (1999), 'Improving the agreement on sanitary and phytosanitary standards', in G. Sampson and W.B. Chambers (eds), *Trade, Environment and the Millennium*, Tokyo: United Nations University Press, pp. 171-94.

Cole, M., A. Rayner and J. Bates (1997), 'The environmental Kuznets Curve: an empirical analysis', *Environment and Development Economics*, 2, 401-16.

Daly, H. (1993), 'The perils of free trade', *Scientific American*, November, 24-9.

Dean, J. (1992), 'Trade and the environment: a survey of the literature', in P. Low (ed.), *International Trade and the Environment*, World Bank Discussion Paper No. 159, Washington DC: World Bank, pp. 15-28.

Dollar, D. and A. Kraay (2000), 'Growth is good for the poor', March, Washington, DC: World Bank, available on www.worldbank.org/research

Edwards, S. (1993), 'Openness, trade liberalization, and growth in developing countries', *Journal of Economic Literature*, 31, 1358-93.

Ekins (1997), 'The Kuznets Curve for the environment and economic growth: examining the evidence', *Environment and Planning A*, 29, 805-30.

Ekins (2000), 'The role of trade in sustainable consumption', in *Towards Sustainable Consumption – a European Perspective*, London: Royal Society, 129-41.

Ekins, C. Folke and R. Costanza (1994), 'Trade, environment and development: the issues in perspective', *Ecological Economics*, 9, 1-12 (special issue on trade and environment co-edited by the authors).

Esty, D. (1994), *Greening the GATT: Trade, the Environment and the Future*, Washington, DC: Institute for International Economics.

Esty, D. and D. Geradin (1997), 'Market access, competitiveness, and harmonization: environmental protection in regional trade agreements', *The Harvard Environmental Law Review*, 21 (2), 265–336.

Esty, D. and B. Gentry (1999), 'Foreign investment, globalisation and environment', in *Globalisation and Environment: Preliminary Perspectives*, Paris: OECD, pp. 141–72.

Evans and J. Walsh (1994), *The EIU Guide to the New GATT*, London: Economist Intelligence Unit (EIU).

Fosu, A. (1996), 'Primary exports and economic growth in developing countries', *The World Economy*, 19, 465–75.

Frankel, J. and D. Romer (1999), 'Does trade cause growth?', *American Economic Review*, 89 (3), 379–99.

GATT (General Agreement on Tariffs and Trade) (1986), *The Text of the General Agreement on Tariffs and Trade*, Geneva: GATT.

GATT (General Agreement on Tariffs and Trade) (1992), 'Trade and the environment', in *International Trade 1990–91*, Geneva: GATT, 19–48.

Gentry, B. (1999), 'Foreign direct investment and the environment: boon or bane?', OECD (Organisation for Economic Co-operation and Development), *Foreign Direct Investment and the Environment*, Paris: OECD, pp. 21–45.

Goldin, I., O. Knudsen and D. van der Mensbrugghe (1993), *Trade Liberalisation: Global Economic Implications*, Paris: OECD and Washington, DC: World Bank.

Gray, K. (2000), 'Asbestos ruling raises more questions than answers', *BRIDGES*, Year 4 No. 7, September, Geneva: ICTSD (International Centre for Trade and Sustainable Development), pp. 9–10.

Huner, J. (2000), 'Lessons from the multilateral agreement on investment: a view from the negotiating side', in H. Ward and D. Brack (eds), *Trade, Investment and the Environment*, London: Earthscan/Royal Institute of International Affairs, pp. 242–51.

Hyvarinen, J. and D. Brack (2000), *Global Environmental Institutions: Analysis and Options for Change*, a report prepared for the Department of the Environment, Transport and the Regions, London: Royal Institute of International Affairs.

ICTSD (International Centre for Trade and Sustainable Development) (2000a), 'The battle between environmental co-operation and trade embargoes flares up with possibility of tuna-dolphin III', *BRIDGES*, Year 4 No. 6, July–August, Geneva: ICTSD, pp. 1–2.

ICTSD (International Centre for Trade and Sustainable Development) (2000b), 'WTO rules in favour of french asbestos ban; NGOs remain sceptical' *BRIDGES* Weekly Trade News Digest (bridges@iatp.org), Vol. 4 No. 35, September 19, Geneva: ICTSD.

ICTSD (International Centre for Trade and Sustainable Development) (2001), 'Asbestos ruling breaks new ground in "like product" determination', *BRIDGES*, Year 5 No. 1–3, January–April, Geneva: ICTSD, pp. 1–2.

IDPM (Institute for Development Policy and Management) (2000), *Sustainable Impact Assessment of Proposed WTO New Round of Multilateral Trade Negotiations*, Manchester: IDPM, Manchester University, http://fs2.idpm.man.ac.uk/sia.

IIED (International Institute for Environment and Development) (1997), *Unlocking Trade Opportunities: Case Studies of Export Success from Developing Countries*, a Report for the UN Department of Policy Co-ordination and Sustainable Development (UNDPCSD), London: IIED/New York: UNDPCSD.

IISD-UNEP (International Institute for Sustainable Development – United Nations Environment Programme) (2000), 'Environment and trade: a handbook', Winnipeg, Canada: IISD/Geneva: UNEP, available on http://iisd.ca/trade/handbook and http://www.unep.ch/etu.

Ikwue, A. and J. Skea (1996), 'The energy sector response to european combustion emission regulations', in F. Lévêque, *Environmental Policy in Europe: Industry, Competition and the Policy Process*, Cheltenham, UK: Edward Elgar, pp. 75–111.

Jenkins, R. (1998), 'Environmental regulation and international competitiveness: a review of literature and some European evidence', *UNU/INTECH Discussion Paper #9801*, January, Maastricht: UNU/INTECH.

Jenkins, R. (2001a), 'Globalisation, trade liberalisation and industrial pollution in Latin America', in R. Jenkins (ed.), *Industry and Environment in Latin America*, London/New York: Routledge, pp. 13–42.

Jenkins, R. (2001b) 'Trade, investment and industrial pollution: lessons from South-East Asia', in N. Adger, N. and M. Kelly (eds), *Living with Environmental Change*, London/New York: Routledge, pp. 185–212.

Jha, V. (1998), 'Developing country perspectives', in D. Brack (ed.), *Trade and Environment: Conflict or Compatibility?*, London: Earthscan/Royal Institute of International Affairs, pp. 78–100.

Jha, V. and R. Vossenaar (1999), 'Breaking the deadlock: a positive agenda on trade, environment and development', in G. Sampson and W.B. Chambers (eds), *Trade, Environment and the Millennium*, Tokyo: United Nations University Press, pp. 65–95.

Lang, T. and C. Hines (1993), *The New Protectionism: Protecting the Future Against Free Trade*, London: Earthscan.

Lee, J. (1998), 'Trade-related environmental measures: how much is a dolphin worth?' in D. Brack (ed.), *Trade and Environment: Conflict or Compatibility?*, London: Earthscan/Royal Institute of International Affairs, pp. 27–48.

Low and A. Yeats (1992), 'Do "dirty" industries migrate?', in P. Low (ed.), *International Trade and the Environment*, World Bank Discussion Paper No. 159, Washington, DC: World Bank, pp. 89–103.

Lucas, R., D. Wheeler and H. Hettige (1992), 'Economic development, environmental regulation and the international migration of toxic industrial pollution: 1960–88', in P. Low (ed.) (1992), *International Trade and the Environment*, World Bank Discussion Paper 159, Washington, DC: World Bank, pp. 67–86.

Mabey, N. and R. McNally (1999), *Foreign Direct Investment and the Environment: From Pollution Havens to Sustainable Development*, October, Godalming, Surrey: WWF-UK.

Mann, H. and K. von Moltke (1999), 'NAFTA's Chapter 11 and the environment: addressing the impacts of the investor–state process on the environment', *Working Paper*, Winnipeg: International Institute for Sustainable Development (IISD), available on http://iisd.org.

NAFTA (North American Free Trade Agreement) (1992), *North American Free Trade Agreement*, full text available on http://nafta-sec-alena.org/english/index.htm

NCC (National Consumer Council) (1998), *Farm Policies and Our Food: The Need for Change*, London: NCC.

Nordström, H. and S. Vaughan (1999), 'Trade and environment', *Special Studies 4*, Geneva: World Trade Organisation (WTO).

OECD (Organisation for Economic Co-operation and Development) (1999a), *Trade Measures in Multilateral Environmental Agreements*, Paris: OECD.

OECD (Organisation for Economic Co-operation and Development) (1999b), *Methodologies for Environmental Assessment of Trade Liberalisation Agreements,* (COM/TD/ENV(99)92/FINAL), Paris: OECD, available on http://www.oecd.org/ ech/26-27oct/docs/report.pdf.

Palmer, K., W. Oates and P. Portney (1995), 'Tightening environmental standards: the benefit–cost or the no-cost paradigm?', *Journal of Economic Perspectives,* 9 (4), Fall, 97–118.

Porter, M. (1990), *The Competitive Advantage of Nations,* New York: Free Press.

Quarrie, J. (ed.) (1992), *Earth Summit 92,* London: The Regency Press Corporation, http://www.un.org/esa/sustdev/agenda21.htm

Robins, N. and S. Roberts (2000), *The Reality of Sustainable Trade,* London; International Institute for Environment and Development.

Ropke, I. (1994), 'Trade, development and sustainability: a critical assessment of the "free trade dogma"', *Ecological Economics,* 9, 13–22.

Shahin, M. (1999), 'Trade and environment: how real is the debate?', in G. Sampson and W.B. Chambers (eds), *Trade, Environment and the Millennium,* Tokyo: United Nations University Press, pp. 35–64.

Shahin, M. (2000), 'A view from the south', in H. Ward and D. Brack (eds), *Trade, Investment and the Environment,* London: Earthscan/Royal Institute of International Affairs, pp. 102–21.

Steininger, K. (1994), 'Reconciling trade and environment: towards a comparative advantage for long-term policy goals', *Ecological Economics,* 9, 23-42.

Thomas, C. and M. Weber (1999), 'New values and international organisation: balancing trade and environment in the North American Free Trade Agreement (NAFTA)', in A. Taylor and C. Thomas (eds), *Global Trade and Global Social Issues,* London/New York: Routledge.

Ulph, A. (1997), 'International trade and the environment: a survey of recent economic analysis', in H. Folmer and T. Tietenberg (eds), *The International Yearbook of Environmental and Resource Economics 1997/1998,* Cheltenham: Edward Elgar, pp. 204–42.

van Beers, C. and J. van den Bergh (1996), 'An overview of methodological approaches in the analysis of trade and environment', *Journal of World Trade,* 30 (1), pp.143-67.

Wang, Z.K. and L.A. Winters (2000a), *Putting Humpty Together Again: Including Developing Countries in a Consensus for the WTO,* CEPR Policy Paper No. 4, London: Centre for Economic Policy Research.

Wang, Z.K. and L.A. Winters (2000b), *Breaking the Seattle Deadlock,* London: The Royal Institute of International Affairs.

World Bank (2000), *World Development Report 2000/2001: Attacking Poverty,* Washington, DC: World Bank, available on http://www.worldbank.org.

WTO (World Trade Organisation) (1994), *The Results of the Uruguay Round of Multilateral Negotiations: The Legal Texts,* Geneva: WTO.

WTO (World Trade Organisation) (1996), *Report of the WTO Committee on Trade and Environment,* November 18, Geneva: WTO.

WTO (World Trade Organisation) (1998a), *United States – Import Prohibition of Certain Shrimp and Shrimp Products,* Report of the Panel, WT/DS58/R, May 15 1998, Geneva: WTO.

WTO (World Trade Organisation) (1998b), *United States – Import Prohibition of Certain Shrimp and Shrimp Products,* Report of the Appellate Body, WT/DS58/AB/R, October 12 1998, Geneva: WTO.

WTO (World Trade Organisation) (2000), *European Communities Measures Affecting Asbestos and Asbestos Containing Products*, Report of the Panel, WT/DS135/R, available on http://www.wto.org/english/tratop_e/dispu_e/ dispu_status_e.htm Zarsky 1994 (p. 28).

Zarsky, L. (1997), 'Stuck in the mud? Nation states, globalisation and environment', in OECD (Organisation for Economic Co-operation and Development), *Globalisation and Environment: Preliminary Perspectives*, Paris: OECD.

Zarsky, L. (1999), 'Havens, halos and spaghetti: untangling the evidence about foreign direct investment and the environment', in OECD (Organisation for Economic Co-operation and Development), *Foreign Direct Investment and the Environment*, Paris: OECD, pp. 47–73.

7. Governing natural resources: institutional adaptation and resilience

W. Neil Adger

GOVERNANCE IN AN UNCERTAIN WORLD

This chapter considers a key issue of environmental governance – how do institutional forms and the structure of societies constrain and enable the management of natural resources at different scales? The chapter details advances in the areas of property rights, the economics of growth and inequality, social resilience and their relationship with natural resource management. Resource management decisions at local scales influence global environmental change, though the whole notion of a global commons is being increasingly questioned. The chapter argues that economic and political globalization are not leading to a more equitable playing field, but are throwing up new institutions, new decisions and novel and unknown threats. The equity dimensions of poverty, empowerment and decision making in a global context therefore present an important interdisciplinary research challenge. The chapter outlines emerging ideas on institutional form, their resilience, and the implications for vulnerability and adaptation to global environmental change.

Governance is everything. The rules by which natural resources are managed have implications from the global to local. The chapter focuses on the evolution of the rules by which direct and indirect uses of the natural and physical assets of the world are socially sanctioned and constrained. It further examines the implications of sudden or unknown environmental change on these sets of rules. In conserving the global environment, it is often postulated that designing international level agreements will only succeed if they can be implemented at something called 'the local level' (Gibson et al., 2000). The chapter argues that the divisions between the global and local governance are indeed a major cause of continued global environmental change and are certainly a serious limitation on much of the rhetoric on solving global environmental problems that has been advocated over the past decade (Adger et al., 2001a; Goldman, 1998).

Given the perceived threats of global environmental change and the recognition of both opportunities and threats of an increasingly globalized world, there appear to be a number of key trends and policy debates on governance (see also Vogler and Jordan, Chapter 5). The first is recognition for urgent radical increases in resource efficiency, harnessing the benefits of novel technologies and innovative means of resource management. Second, there are social pressures and moral imperatives to utilize resources in a manner that alleviates poverty and insecurity at the global scale. Third, there are cogent arguments that inclusionary structures of governance are necessary to secure the widespread distribution of benefits in line with the need for security and resilience.

At the same time, however, the physical world is becoming more uncertain. The twenty-first century will see increased variability in the availability of resources and perhaps a more hazardous environment. Hazards can be conceived of as resources in the wrong place at the wrong time, with many aspects of natural hazards also conveying advantages to particular activities and hence social groups. Riverine flooding, for example, is an integral part of many farming systems in providing nutrients in fertile floodplain areas: it is abnormal flooding which causes damage and is the hazardous part of this partially natural phenomenon. In these cases a natural hazard is 'an occasionally disadvantageous aspect of a phenomenon which is beneficial to human activity over a different timescale' (Middleton, 1995, p. 265).

In general the mismatch between resource availability and resource demand could be exacerbated rather than alleviated through technological advance. The negative social and environmental aspects of Green Revolution technology in agriculture over the past decades (see Griffin, 1979; Conway, 1997), for example, could potentially be amplified by genetic modification technology as applied to food production. Technological intervention in environmental systems can, in other words, act to exacerbate risks – in food systems the entitlement to food along with the distribution of power interact with the diffusion of technologies to create vulnerability (Watts, 2000). Changes in risk profile as a result of environmental change have been shown to result in greater localized relative scarcity of some resources, such as fresh water and non-degraded urban land.

A distinctive set of environmental social science perspectives has emerged in response to these observed trends and policy debates. I review key issues of governance of natural resources in environmental social science highlighting developments primarily within economics, political science, anthropology and geography, arguing that fruitful and policy-relevant findings are most commonly revealed at the interface between these disciplines and in collaboration with the pertinent natural sciences. The following sections proceed by examining research on property rights and institutional form in the governance of natural resources, issues surrounding the role of resources and access to them in promoting economic well-being, and the issue of social and ecological resilience in resource use and governance. These themes capture the dynamic nature of change in socio-economic and ecological dimensions, the different contexts of natural resource use and management, and the different scales of interactions between society and resources. Theoretical research in these areas underpins policy interventions in natural resource management, with these issues highlighted both implicitly and explicitly within many international policy and research agendas.

PROPERTY RIGHTS AND THE INSTITUTIONAL ARCHITECTURE OF RESOURCE USE

Property relations facilitate and constrain environmental management and resource use. They span different scales of action, ranging from micro-level conflicts over particular resources, through to global and supra-national agreements creating new property rights and institutions for their management and regulation. The objectives of much of this research are to describe these complex interactions with a view to informing policy making in many aspects of the environment. This institutional architecture of resource use is central to policy making. At present most of the world's natural resources, from minerals to land and even marine resources, are controlled through the operation of imperfect markets or directly by the state. Some of the most innovative social science examines either the important exceptions to this situation – community or collective management – or the impact of ideological reliance on either markets or states as the exclusive means to manage natural resources. Collectively managed resources are often central to many resource users worldwide in providing the means for their livelihoods. Thus subsistence fishing communities, pastoralists in semi-arid regions, and forest dwellers often have sophisticated community-based rules for access to the scarce resources on which they depend. It is often argued that these community-based rules tend to break down when the state or external market forces intervene and disrupt these systems (reviewed in Baland and Platteau, 1996, for example).

Allocating property rights has not always led to successful management of common-pool resources. Other institutional arrangements such as co-management or collective action may lead to more supported management. Examples abound where private property rights have been allocated but management has not been supported because local stakeholders' interests have not been considered (see Baland and Platteau, 1996; Agrawal and Gibson, 1999; Clague, 1997). Many empirical studies note that the top-down allocation of property rights alone is not adequate to prevent resource degradation of common property resources.

I wish to highlight two emerging areas of research in this field. First there is increasing recognition of collective action problems across environmental and resource problems at different scales. Thus property rights research has begun to analyse global environmental problems, demonstrating how the community of resource users can potentially internalize significant global externalities associated with, for example, global climatic change, global scale loss of threatened habitats, or stratospheric ozone loss (Ostrom et al., 1999). Research by economists, political scientists and anthropologists indicates the complexity of these issues and characterizes property relations according to temporal, spatial, cultural, human and resource characteristics, recognizing the nestedness and overlapping aspects of property rights and the different actors and interests involved (Adger and Luttrell, 2000).

Other recent advances in this area have emphasized the ideas that so-called indigenous or traditional environmental knowledge should be recognized with realization that some traditional institutions act to regulate resource use and enhance the resilience of ecosystems through adaptive management (Berkes et al., 1998, 2000; Blaikie et al., 1997). Brown and Rosendo (2000) demonstrate, for example, that the institutional architecture of extractive reserves in Amazonia – designed to promote sustainable utilization of resources while maintaining high levels of ecological diversity – do not harmonize with traditional resource users' perceptions of property and hence may jeopardize their success. Early anthropological contributions to describing collective action in traditional resource systems provided an impetus for more generalized theories of collective action for natural resource management emerging in the 1980s and 1990s (reviewed in Baland and Platteau, 1996; Hanna et al., 1996; Bromley, 1999).

The second emerging area of research is, therefore, the recognition of complex and hybrid systems of property rights for natural resource management. Practice and theory are co-evolving phenomena in this area. The rolling back or hollowing out of the state in the 1980s and 1990s has resulted in a divergent set of property rights for natural resources. In some cases there has been a spontaneous re-assertion of traditional ways of managing resources, in fisheries management for example. In other cases there have been systematic experiments with planned co-management partnerships for common land or wildlife. But the most consistent set of property rights changes in the natural resource area has been towards private allocation of rights, sometimes backed up by market-based tradeable property rights.

In fisheries, for example, while some countries have implemented efficiency gaining private property rights, other areas have seen the necessary evolution of local management in the absence of the state. Ruddle (1998) and others have demonstrated the historical persistence of the *van chai* village fisheries system in Vietnam, whereby each local ancestral shrine in villages laid down the rules for fishing, including acceptable technologies, profit sharing and dispute conciliation. Ruddle (1998) also charts the re-emergence of the *van chai* system in the 1990s associated with a reduction in state planning. For other coastal resources, White (1994) demonstrates a range of co-management solutions to coral reef management – where the state has been ineffective in preventing overuse, the sharing of rights with local users can, in particular circumstances, lead to more sustainable management outcomes. In Chile, New Zealand and other countries, an individual transferable quota system has replaced state regulation of fisheries take (Hughey et al., 2000; Peña-Torres, 1997) to promote sustainable harvesting – evidence suggests that privatisation is not a panacea for over-fishing.

In agriculture, despite a predominance of private ownership or control, most land increasingly has multiple uses and users and complex hierarchies of property rights associated with these uses (Munton, 1995). The economic logic of the historic predominance of private landowning in agriculture continues to be debated – the eighteenth century enclosures in England may have been caused by the change in relative prices of grain in international markets (Clark, 1998; Dahlman, 1980). Perhaps this is an early example of the impacts of globalization on indigenous property rights regimes. But in the past fifty years in particular, agriculture and conservation policy in the UK has been based on the primacy of private property so that much policy rests on a system of incentives and compensation payments to private landowners. Hanley et al. (1998) for example, illustrate the concept of the 'provider gets principle' showing the implications of these implicit property rights for the supply of environmental goods by the agricultural sector. Thus the presumed policy entitlement (Bromley, 1991) of farmers to receive compensation for production of public goods is an aberration caused by historical policy objectives of food self-sufficiency, which are now argued to be untenable in the present need for sustainable rural development (Pretty, 1998; Winter, 1996). In Europe in particular proposals for the reform of the Common Agricultural Policy still cling to the efficiency notions of private and tradeable policy support (for example, Beard and Swinbank, 2001)

Given the tendency towards privatization of resources, from the enclosures onwards, there has been a renewed interest in why collective management of resources persists and under what conditions it is successful. Success has been hypothesized to be the result of a complex interaction of the resource, the technologies of enforcement, the relationships between resources and user groups, the features of the user group, and the relationship between users and the state and legal system. Under this formulation, the likelihood of successful management is affected by a number of factors (Wade, 1988; Ostrom, 1990 and others). First, the boundaries of the physical resource should be defined. The more clearly defined, the greater the chances of successful commons management. This is known in economic terms as universality. Second, if the users are resident in the location of the resource then this increases chances of success through reducing enforcement costs. Enforcement and other transaction costs are weighed against the benefits from the resource. Third, the greater the demand for the outputs and the reliance on the resource within a livelihood system, the greater the chance of successful common property management. Fourth, the better defined the user group, the greater chance of success. But conflicts can still occur between small groups of users. The congruence between appropriation and provision rules and local conditions is a critical prerequisite for successful management.

In addition to these 'design features', Taylor (1998) argues that 'community' is the most important ingredient for collective management. This tangible resource creates the environment for voluntary action to provide social order, resolve conflicts arising from externalities and to regulate common resources. If hybrid co-management between hierarchical government structures and communities is to succeed then they must mobilize and foster co-operative relations among the governed while 'the hierarchical relations between governors and governed must themselves be characterised by long-term repeated interactions, co-operation, reciprocity and trust' (Taylor, 1998, p. 252; and Taylor, 1996).

Neither co-management nor the emergence of collective action are ever simply spontaneous phenomena. Governments, agencies of governments, or private resource owners do not easily give up their vested interests and power bases. So why is co-management of resources – from wildlife in southern Africa to marine protected areas in Europe – so popular? For governments, the reason is often that of reducing the costs of governing – allocating rights and responsibilities to other stakeholders can reduce the transaction costs of management – rather than any notions of empowerment or reducing democratic deficits. Singleton (2000) has shown in the context of co-management of the Pacific Northwest salmon fishery in the US, however, that co-management, if successful, is equally resource intensive. Further, co-management does not guarantee either the elimination of conflicts between states and communities over resources or sustainable management. There is often uncritical acceptance that participation of all stakeholders is the key to sustainable management of natural resources (see Munton, Chapter 4). This tenet is presently being questioned from a variety of perspectives and disciplines which point out, for example, the heterogeneity of communities involved in resource management and the wider legislative and democratic framework within which such management occurs (for example Hayward, 1995).

The practice of resource management may appear, in effect, to be running ahead of theory. But as with the realization of multiple stakeholders and multiple use commons, careful consideration of this complexity along with uncertainty and scale issues are a further area of social science advance (see Mehta et al., 1999, 2001). A key distinction overlooked in much of the debate on collective action is whether it is outcome or process that defines success. As Steins and Edwards (1999) note, the definition of successful outcomes in common property management frequently varies among stakeholders for the same set of circumstances.

But how local does successful management have to be? Are there limits to participatory management in terms of complexity or of geographical area? The factors which determine whether participatory management can exist and flourish are scale-dependent (Tompkins et al., 2002). The density of networks and ability to combine information and resources outside the local sphere of institutions is one important means by which participatory processes are maintained.

Networks utilized by groups and organizations are scale-dependent. Cox (1998) and others argue that these networks – or sets of interactions between individuals and groups – are in fact distinguished by this scale characteristic. Social relations and interactions which cannot be undertaken other than locally and which are 'relied on for the realization of essential interests' can be defined as spaces of dependence (Cox, 1998). Institutions organize themselves to secure their existence and in doing so create networks at other levels – in the media, in other areas of political life, or even internationally. These networks can be defined as spaces of engagement. The importance of this classification of networks can be seen in participatory resource management. The greater the depth of networks of engagement, the greater the opportunities should be for social learning and the widespread adoption of new institutional forms. But spaces of dependence are equally important in defining the winners and losers in any resource allocation (see also Murdoch and Marsden, 1995; Edwards and Steins, 1999). Examples of the localized spaces of dependence and spaces of exchange for the institutions surrounding participatory natural resource management are outlined in Table 7.1. These show that operational arrangements generally exist at smaller spatial scales, while constitutional arrangements are often observed primarily at the national level. For all groups the spaces of exchange can expand the spatial scale sometimes up to international and global levels.

From the issues reviewed here it is clear first that property rights are institutionally determined and represent one important set of entitlements for individuals and groups to use and govern natural resources (see also Leach

*Table 7.1   Networks of resources and information of institutions of participa-
tory natural resource management*

	Spaces of dependence	Spaces of engagement
Constitutional arrangements	Often national level laws and socially sanctioned norms	Often international laws and pressures from international organizations
Institutional structures	Budgetary and other regulatory functions	Cross-department initiatives in government. Use of media and co-opting of associations and interest groups
Operational arrangements	Local organizations such as councils and local government as well as interest groups, associations and other outlets	Contacts to national and international media, campaigning groups and information

Source: Adapted from Tompkins et al. (2002).

et al., 1999). The distribution of income and wealth represents such a fundamental determinant of resilience and vulnerability. Emerging empirical research in economics is reassessing the impact of inequality on growth and social cohesion, while the evidence that inequality plays a role in exacerbated environmental degradation is compounded when wider conceptions of power and marginalization are included. Second, the changing nature of property rights both potentially undermine social resilience and create altered contexts in which people respond to social and political change through resistance and other strategies. Watts (2000) argues that the distribution of power and wealth needs to be seen in a broader context. It is the 'politics of redistribution and recognition' of entitlements that determines vulnerability and access to resources. In other words social resilience is enhanced or undermined both by the formal institutions of the state and the legal framework of *de jure* property rights on one hand, and on the other by the 'rough and tumble of actual democratic governance' (Watts, 2000, p. 210). If, however, these insights from social science remain unaware of emerging understanding of the dynamic nature of ecosystem change, they ultimately fail to provide enhanced normative prescriptions for sustainable utilization of natural resources.

RESILIENCE IN THE GOVERNANCE OF NATURAL RESOURCES

There has been a radical reconsideration of the objectives of resource management in the past decade because of the apparent failure of ecological models to redress unsustainable management of resources or to reduce the large-scale environmental consequences of resource use. This reconsideration involves recognizing the dynamics of systems and functions that ecosystems play in protecting and facilitating human society and in promoting the robustness or resilience of ecological systems. But, at the same time, there is recognition that flexibility and resilience are important characteristics of societies where environmental and societal risk permeate decision making. How societies adapt when there are external pressures on them leads to consideration of ecological resilience and fragility. Resilience in ecology is defined in one of two ways: the ability to withstand change, or the capacity to restore and replenish following some externally imposed shock. Social resilience is a measure of the enforced exposure to critical stress, or hazard, combined with the restricted capacity to cope (see discussions in Holling et al., 1995; Gunderson, 2000; Colding et al., 2002). Resilience is therefore a political and ethical issue, not a natural state. Global economic interests, property rights abuses and distorted information flows combine to create conditions where environments become critical, and people vulnerable.

Concepts of resilience and vulnerability are therefore evolving in parallel in the social and natural sciences. In the social sciences, research has focused on the vulnerability of individuals and social groups to stresses and shocks associated with food insecurity, famine, natural hazards, urbanization and other phenomena (see Bohle et al., 1994; Ribot et al., 1996; Pelling, 1998; Adger, 2000b; Adger et al. 2001b) – social vulnerability is distributed in spatial, social and economic dimensions. Resilience and vulnerability relate both to marginalization and the institutional arrangements for natural resource management discussed above. An alternative geographical perspective hypothesizes that regions and areas can be defined as critical based on the environmental and socio-economic pressures on them, stemming from the work of Kasperson et al. (1995). They argue that identifying criticality brings about opportunities to overcome adversity or stress through the focused application of technology and new institutional devices. The onset of criticality is a manifestation of ill-adapted institutional arrangements, acting without precaution.

As vulnerability is lowered and criticality reduced, so resilience increases. But in an ecological sense, resilience relates to the functioning of the system, rather than the stability of the component populations. Economists and other social scientists also argue that resilience is the key to sustainability in the wider sense. Resilience, in both its social and ecological manifestations, is an important criterion for the sustainability of development and resource use. Within the economics paradigm sustainable development requires that resources be allocated in such a way that they do not threaten the stability either of the system as a whole or of key components. Thus it is argued by ecological economists that ecological resilience is an important component of sustainable development, since all human welfare is ultimately dependent on the biosphere, and the resilience of ecosystems is an important characteristic in this sustainability equation. Arrow et al. (1995) argue that ecological resilience is important for human welfare for three related reasons. First, resilient systems are less prone to discontinuous change in ecosystem functions associated with loss of productivity – hence resilience provides necessary human life support. Second, loss of resilience may lead to irreversible change (for example, individual species loss) and hence loss of options for future use. Third, decreased resilience and change to unfamiliar states increases the uncertainty in impacts of other environmental change.

Certainly resilience is related to stability, but it is not clear whether these characteristics are always desirable. The resilience of social systems are themselves related in some way, though still undefined, to the resilience of the ecological systems on which they depend (see Adger, 2000b; Handmer and Dovers, 1996 for reviews). This is most clearly exhibited within social systems that are dependent on a single ecosystem or single resource. Taking the concept of resilience from the ecological sciences and applying it to social systems is controversial. One point of legitimate argument is that these are indeed essential differences in socialized institutions compared with ecosystem behaviour. Institutional resilience is based on trust, legitimacy and accountability. This is the basis of one definition of social fabric, namely the capability to observe and learn. The social fabric holds together in a pattern of norms and behaviours that knits the household to the community, and the community to the state. If these bonds are fragmented, social resilience breaks down and vulnerability is exacerbated.

The resilience of institutions can be found in the ability of communities to deal with the forces of globalization that impinge upon them. Social capital, ecological resilience and social resilience are all tested when upheaval and stress are placed on institutions: an example here is the management of traditional collective resources. Commonly managed resources are being degraded throughout the world through the breakdown of property rights or inappropriate privatization (Berkes and Folke, 1998). This is clear in the case of the management of coastal resources such as fisheries, coastal agriculture and other assets, which frequently involves incorporation of periodic risk of disturbance as a result, for example, of extreme climatic phenomena (see Pethick and Crooks, 2000). Similarly, vulnerability within global and national level agriculture to food availability and hunger results from, not only the exposure to agricultural production, but more fundamentally to uneven distribution of entitlements and access to resources (Watts, 2000). Interdisciplinary research from both ecological and social science has begun to address institutional resilience and resource governance.

Olsson and Folke (2001) examine the local knowledge of ecosystem processes for a coastal crayfish fishery in Sweden and argue that the collective management of this resource involves institutions at diverse scales. They find that local-level institutions for direct management (harvesting strategies and seasonal patterns, for example) have been self-organizing, have created spaces for evolutionary re-organization, and give precedence to knowledgeable individuals. These institutional characteristics, they argue, provide evidence both of the importance of local knowledge at the ecosystems scale (see also Berkes et al., 1998), and that evolution of institutions takes place through strategies of adaptive management as they move to higher and deeper levels of knowledge (see also Muchagata and Brown, 2000).

Adger (2000a) examines the relationship between social resilience, changing property rights and institutional evolution in an example from coastal Vietnam. Coastal districts in Vietnam are impacted seasonally by landfall typhoons and coastal storms. Although fishing, farming and other activities have evolved to cope with this risk over the millennia, the radical redirection of the economy during the 1990s towards individual responsibility and private property and away from central planning has disturbed the risk profile. Collective action for coastal protection was decimated in the 1990s such that the resilience of coastal residents is presently diminished. The direct cause is the action of the institutions of local government that subvert collective action and redirect resources towards the growth of unsustainable aquaculture. Thus vulnerability of particular marginalized groups is created and collective resilience is undermined in Vietnam.

The relationship between economic globalization and resilience is not always straightforward. While globalization of food production and trade is often undermining for local food security and employment, increased mobility can be beneficial to resilience. Migration often represents a resilience-enhancing strategy for resource-dependent communities in the developing world (Locke et al., 2000; Connell and Conway, 2000; Adger et al., 2002). Similarly, the diversification of farm incomes into niche markets in the UK is seen as an important component of the new sustainable development of regions in a fragmented rural economy and society (Midmore, 1996). An example of the positive role of migration in enhancing resilience is found in small island economies where remittance income is expanded at times of stress. So, although the agricultural economy of Western Samoa, for example, is dependent on cash crops, such as pineapple and coconuts, recovery from the impacts of natural hazards such as hurricane damage is often facilitated through remittance income. In the early 1990s Paulson (1993) demonstrated that non-monetary informal arrangements for social security persist in Western Samoa and helped, along with remittances, to sustain and enable recovery of the resilient human population following a devastating hurricane.

Social resilience is thus not simply determined by adverse events or risk, but by the inability of individuals or groups to adjust and adapt to changing social and environmental circumstances, or only to do so at high cost. Given uncertainty about the nature, causes and extent of some environmental change processes, it is particularly important to recognize that policy changes associated with land use are as significant as the environmental changes brought about by both global and local processes. In general, the wider political economy of decentralization and the rolling back of the state, discussed in the section above, is often less associated with increased freedom than with opening societies to the vagaries of global economic forces and environmental risks (Adger et al., 2001b; O'Brien and Leichenko, 2000; Slater, 1995).

Ultimately insights by social scientists into social resilience demonstrate the co-evolutionary nature of social and natural systems – resilient ecosystems and resilient societies can better cope with external physical as well as social stresses. An emerging research agenda within ecological economics, environmental and economic history link these topics in social and natural systems (see Scoones, 1999; Norgaard, 1994; Sneddon, 2000 for reviews). The policy implications of resilience are less clear. Institutional diversity and autonomy to promote resilience are, for example, often in conflict with larger scale planning that is often believed to be necessary to manage the global or trans-boundary nature of resource use issues.

CONCLUSIONS

Appropriate institutions for governance of natural resources are essential for the realization of sustainability. Advances in the social sciences have recognized that there is no blueprint for such institutions. The scale of diverse environmental impacts of resource use, as well as the diversity of multiple use resources and common goods, translates into a demand for a diverse institutional architecture. But decentralizing and divesting responsibility to local resource users on its own is not necessarily compatible with sustainable development, as the wider political economy of globalization limits the ability of lower-scale solutions to environmental problems. The playing field is not even and the distribution of entitlements to natural resources and power act as a constraint on environmental management. Certainly economic growth cannot be relied upon to trickle down environmental awareness, empowerment or the means to implement sustainability. The robustness and diversity of governance structures therefore need to be seen as part of the wider landscape of social and natural systems, co-evolving towards an interdisciplinary understanding of society–environment relationships.

REFERENCES

Adger, W.N. (2000a), 'Institutional adaptation to environmental risk under the transition in Vietnam', *Annals of the Association of American Geographers*, 90, 738-58.

Adger, W.N. (2000b), 'Social and ecological resilience: are they related?' *Progress in Human Geography*, 24, 347-64.

Adger, W.N. and C. Luttrell (2000), 'Property rights and the utilisation of wetlands', *Ecological Economics*, 35, 75-89.

Adger, W.N., T.A. Benjaminsen, K. Brown and H. Svarstad (2001a), 'Advancing a political ecology of global environmental discourses', *Development and Change*, 32 (4), 687-715.

Adger, W.N., P.M. Kelly and N.H. Ninh (eds) (2001b), *Living with Environmental Change: Social Resilience, Adaptation and Vulnerability in Vietnam*, London: Routledge.

Adger, W.N., M. Kelly, C. Locke, A. Winkels and Huy Luong Quang (2002), 'Migration, remittances, livelihood trajectories and social resilience', *Ambio*, 31 (4), 358-66.

Agrawal, A. and C.C. Gibson (1999), 'Enchantment and disenchantment: the role of community in natural resource conservation', *World Development*, 27, 629-49.

Arrow, K., B. Bolin, R. Costanza, P. Dasgupta, C. Folke, C.S. Holling, B.O. Jansson, S. Levin, K.G. Mäler, C. Perrings and D. Pimentel (1995), 'Economic growth, carrying capacity and the environment', *Science*, 268, 520-21.

Baland, J.M. and J.P. Platteau (1996), *Halting Degradation of Natural Resources: Is there a Role for Rural Communities?* Oxford: Clarendon.

Beard, N. and A. Swinbank (2001), 'Decoupled payments to facilitate CAP reform', *Agricultural Systems*, 65, 113-36.

Berkes, F. and Folke, C. (eds) (1998), *Linking Social and Ecological Systems*, Cambridge: Cambridge University Press.

Berkes, F., J. Colding and C. Folke (2000), 'Rediscovery of traditional ecological knowledge as adaptive management', *Ecological Applications,* 10, 1251-62.

Berkes, F., M. Kislalioglu, C. Folke and M. Gadgil (1998), 'Exploring the basic ecological unit: ecosystem-like concepts in traditional societies', *Ecosystems*, 1, 409-15.

Blaikie, P., K. Brown, P. Dixon, P. Sillitoe, M. Stocking and L. Tang (1997), 'Knowledge in action: local knowledge as a development resource and barriers to its incorporation in natural resource research and development', *Agricultural Systems*, 55, 217-37.

Bohle, H.G., T.E. Downing, and M.J. Watts (1994), 'Climate change and social vulnerability: toward a sociology and geography of food insecurity', *Global Environmental Change*, 4, 37-48.

Bromley, D.W. (1991), *Environment and Economy: Property Rights and Public Policy*, Oxford: Blackwell.

Bromley, D.W. (1999), *Sustaining Development: Environmental Resources in Developing Countries*, Cheltenham: Edward Elgar.

Brown, K. and S. Rosendo (2000), 'The institutional architecture of extractive reserves in Brazil', *Geographical Journal*, 166, 35–48.

Clague, C. (1997), 'The new institutional economics and economic development', in Clague, C. (ed.), *Institutions and Economic Development: Growth and Governance in Less Developed and Post-Socialist Countries*, Baltimore, MD: Johns Hopkins University Press, pp. 13–36.

Clark, G. (1998), 'Common sense: common property rights, efficiency and institutional change', *Journal of Economic History*, 58, 73–102.

Colding, J., T. Elmqvist and P. Olsson (2002), 'Living with disturbance: building resilience in social–ecological systems', in F. Berkes and C. Folke (eds), *Social-Ecological Systems: Building Resilience for Complexity and Change*, Cambridge: Cambridge University Press.

Connell, J. and D. Conway (2000), 'Migration and remittances in island micro-states: a comparative perspective on the South Pacific and the Caribbean', *International Journal of Urban and Regional Research*, 24, 52–78.

Conway, G.R. (1997), *The Doubly Green Revolution: Food for All in the 21st Century*, London: Penguin.

Cox, K.R. (1998), 'Spaces of dependence, spaces of engagement and the politics of scale, or: looking for local politics', *Political Geography*, 17, 1–23.

Dahlman, C.J. (1980), *The Open Field System and Beyond*, Cambridge: Cambridge University Press.

Edwards, V.M. and N.A. Steins (1999), 'A framework for analysing contextual factors in common pool resource research', *Journal of Environmental Policy and Planning*, 1, 205–21.

Gibson, C.C., E. Ostrom and T.K. Ahn (2000), 'The concept of scale and the human dimensions of global change: a survey', *Ecological Economics*, 32, 217–39.

Goldman, M. (ed.) (1998), *Privatising Nature: Political Struggles for the Global Commons*, New Brunswick, NJ: Rutgers University Press.

Griffin, K. (1979), *The Political Economy of Agrarian Change: An Essay on the Green Revolution*, 2nd edn, London: Macmillan.

Gunderson, L.H. (2000), 'Ecological resilience: in theory and application', *Annual Review of Ecology and Systematics*, 31, 425–39.

Handmer, J.W. and S.R. Dovers (1996), 'A typology of resilience: rethinking institutions for sustainable development', *Industrial and Environmental Crisis Quarterly*, 9, 482–511.

Hanley, N., H. Kirkpatrick, I. Simpson and D. Oglethorpe (1998), 'Principles for the provision of public goods from agriculture: modelling moorland conservation in Scotland', *Land Economics*, 74, 102–13.

Hanna, S.S., C. Folke and K.G. Mäler (eds) (1996), *Rights to Nature: Ecological, Economic, Cultural and Political Principles of Institutions for the Environment*, Washington, DC: Island Press.

Hayward, B.M. (1995), 'The greening of participatory democracy: reconsideration of theory', *Environmental Politics*, 4, 215–36.

Holling, C.S., D.W. Schindler, B.W. Walker and J. Roughgarden (1995), 'Biodiversity in the functioning of ecosystems: an ecological synthesis', in C. Perrings, K.G. Mäler, C. Folke, C.S. Holling and B.O. Jansson (eds), *Biodiversity Loss:*

Economic and Ecological Issues, Cambridge: Cambridge University Press, pp. 44–83.

Hughey, K.F.D., R. Cullen, and G.N. Kerr (2000), 'Stakeholder groups in fisheries management', *Marine Policy*, 24, 119–27.

Kasperson, J.X., R.E. Kasperson and B.L. Turner (eds) (1995), *Regions at Risk: Comparisons of Threatened Environments*, Tokyo: United Nations University Press.

Leach, M., R. Mearns and I. Scoones (1999), 'Environmental entitlements: dynamics and institutions in community-based natural resource management', *World Development*, 27, 225–47.

Locke, C., W.N. Adger and P.M. Kelly (2000), 'Changing places: migration's social and environmental consequences', *Environment*, 42 (7), 24–35.

Mehta, L., M. Leach, P. Newell, I. Scoones, K. Sivaramakrishnan and S.-A. Way (1999), 'Exploring understandings of institutions and uncertainty: new directions in natural resource management', IDS Discussion Paper, 372, Brighton: IDS.

Mehta, L., M. Leach and I. Scoones (eds) (2001), 'Environmental governance in an uncertain world', IDS Bulletin, 32 (4), Brighton: IDS.

Middleton, N. (1995), *The Global Casino*, London: Arnold.

Midmore, P. (1996), 'Towards a postmodern agricultural economics', *Journal of Agricultural Economics*, 47, 1–17.

Muchagata, M. and K. Brown (2000), 'Colonist farmers' perceptions of fertility and the frontier environment in eastern Amazonia', *Agriculture and Human Values*, 17, 371–84.

Munton, R. (1995), 'Regulating rural change: property rights, economy and environment: a case study from Cumbria, UK', *Journal of Rural Studies*, 11, 269–84.

Murdoch, J. and T. Marsden (1995), 'The spatialisation of politics: local and national actor spaces in environmental conflict', *Transactions of the Institute of British Geographers*, 20, 368–80.

Norgaard, R.B. (1994), *Development Betrayed: The End of Progress and a Coevolutionary Revisioning of the Future*, London: Routledge.

O'Brien, K.L. and R.M. Leichenko (2000), 'Double exposure: assessing the impacts of climate change within the context of economic globalisation', *Global Environmental Change*, 10, 221–32.

Olsson, P. and C. Folke (2001), 'Local ecological knowledge and institutional dynamics for ecosystem management: a study of crayfish management in the Lake Racken watershed, Sweden', *Ecosystems*, 4, 85–104.

Ostrom, E. (1990), *Governing the Commons: The Evolution of Institutions for Collective Action*, Cambridge: Cambridge University Press.

Ostrom, E., J. Burger, C.B. Field, R.B. Norgaard and D. Policansky (1999), 'Revisiting the commons: local lessons, global challenges', *Science*, 284, 278–82.

Paulson, D.D. (1993), 'Hurricane hazard in Western Samoa', *Geographical Review*, 83, 43–53.

Pelling, M. (1998), 'Participation, social capital and vulnerability to urban flooding in Guyana', *Journal of International Development*, 10, 469–86.

Peña-Torres, J. (1997), 'The political economy of fishing regulation: the case of Chile', *Marine Resource Economics*, 12, 239–48.

Pethick, J.S. and S. Crooks (2000), 'Development of a coastal vulnerability index: a geomorphological perspective', *Environmental Conservation*, 27, 359–67.

Pretty, J. (1998), *The Living Land*, London: Earthscan.

Ribot, J.C., A.R. Magalhães and S.S. Panagides (eds) (1996), *Climate Variability, Climate Change and Social Vulnerability in the semi-arid Tropics*, Cambridge: Cambridge University Press.

Ruddle, K. (1998), 'Traditional community-based coastal marine fisheries management in Vietnam', *Ocean and Coastal Management*, 40, 1–22.

Scoones, I. (1999), 'New ecology and the social sciences: what prospects for fruitful engagement?', *Annual Review of Anthropology*, 28, 479–507.

Singleton, S. (2000), 'Co-operation or capture? The paradox of co-management and community participation in natural resource management and environmental policy-making', *Environmental Politics*, 9 (2), 1–21.

Slater, D. (1995), 'Trajectories of development theory: capitalism, socialism and beyond', in R.J. Johnston, P.J. Taylor and M.J. Watts (eds), *Geographies of Global Change*, Oxford: Blackwell, pp. 63–76.

Sneddon, C.S. (2000), 'Sustainability in ecological economics, ecology and livelihoods: a review', *Progress in Human Geography*, 24, 521–49.

Steins, N.A and V.M. Edwards (1999), 'Collective action in common-pool resource management: the contribution of a social constructivist perspective to existing theory', *Society and Natural Resources*, 12, 539–57.

Taylor, M. (1996), 'Good government: on hierarchy, social capital, and the limitations of rational choice theory', *Journal of Political Philosophy*, 4, 1–28.

Taylor, M. (1998), 'Governing natural resources', *Society and Natural Resources*, 11, 251–8.

Tompkins, E., W.N. Adger and K. Brown (2002), 'Institutional networks for inclusive coastal management in Trinidad and Tobago', *Environment and Planning A*, 34, 1095–1111.

Wade, R. (1988), *Village Republics: Economic Conditions for Collective Action in South India*, Cambridge: Cambridge University Press.

Watts, M.J. (2000), 'The great tablecloth: bread and butter politics, and the political economy of food and poverty', in G.L Clark, M.S. Gertler and M.P. Feldman (eds), *Oxford Handbook of Economic Geography*, Oxford: Oxford University Press, pp. 195–212.

White, A.T. (ed.) (1994), *Collaborative and Community-based Management of Coral Reefs*, West Hartford, CT: Kumarian Press.

Winter, M. (1996), *Rural Politics: Policies for Agriculture, Forestry and the Environment*, London: Routledge.

8. Sustainable business organizations?

Anja Schaefer, Andrea Coulson, Ken Green, Steve New and Jim Skea

INTRODUCTION

Sustainable business organizations would be an important part of sustainable societies. As Gladwin et al. (1995) point out, sustainability is not merely an ecological (biophysical) concept. It is equally important as a socio-economic and moral concept. In this chapter, we look mostly at the socio-economic and, to a lesser extent, the moral aspects of sustainability in the context of business organizations.

In order to understand where business organizations currently stand in terms of environmental impact and the chances for an eventual state of sustainability, it is paramount to understand not only their environmental impacts in technical terms but also the way in which they understand environmental issues and frame their role in contributing to sustainability. The environment should not be understood as a given, unproblematic concept but – as far as human involvement in it is concerned – as a socially constructed one.

In this chapter, we will assess the evidence from about ten years of research into business and the environment in order to understand how the business–environment problem has been framed by the literature; we will survey the current state of empirical knowledge about the way in which managers think about environmental problems and the organizational change processes involved in corporate greening, as well as the various barriers towards greater ecological soundness of business. In line with the above discussion, we are taking a broadly social-constructionist view of the business–environment problem. However, it should be noted that this approach has been applied to business and the environment research only relatively recently and that much of the existing literature takes more of a pressure–response or functional stance. This will be reflected in our discussion.

CONSTRUCTING THE POSITION OF BUSINESS IN THE ENVIRONMENT

What is the place and role of business in relation to the environment? This is not only an important philosophical and ethical question; it also has implications for practical management. The question has been discussed from a conceptual point of view in a number of seminal publications, including Schmidheiny (1992), Gladwin et al. (1995), Shrivastava (1995), Starik and Rands (1995) and Stead and Stead (1996). This literature, whose main purpose has been to raise awareness of the business–environment issue and establish the subject as a legitimate pursuit of academic endeavour, is by now quite well known and a detailed discussion of the different conceptualizations espoused is beyond the scope of the present chapter. We will therefore limit ourselves to introducing just one of these conceptualizations of the relationship between business and the environment and what might constitute an appropriate world-view to guide the environmental efforts of business organizations.

Different authors differ significantly in terms of the breadth of their treatment of the business and the environment subject. Gladwin et al. (1995) take a very broad view, reviewing techno-centric and eco-centric notions of humanity. The techno-centric (also called, confusingly, anthropocentric) view holds that humans and all their activities, including economic ones – are separate from nature and that the single-minded pursuit of human goals without much regard for ecological concerns is justified. Eco-centrism holds that nature is superior to humankind and that all human activity should be guided first and foremost by ecological principles. The same authors suggest that neither position is very helpful in practice and propose a third philosophy, which they term 'sustain-centrism'. This recognizes the legitimacy of human concerns over safety and property, but argues that these concerns need to be pursued with proper regard for the carrying capacity of the Earth. Starik and Rands (1995) also take a broad view, suggesting that business organizations should not only look at environmental issues from a narrow, technical perspective, but understand business's place within wider bio-physical and social systems in order to make progress towards sustainability. On the other hand, Lamming et al. (1999) prefer a narrower view of the field, suggesting that 'sustainable development', which includes important social aspects as well as economic and ecological ones, is not an appropriate goal for business. Instead, they argue, business organizations should focus on 'environmental soundness', which includes only the ecological and economic elements. However, it is unclear whether business as a whole has moved towards even this somewhat less ambitious goal, or whether significant progress in that direction is likely in the near future.

Looking at the means of achieving such aims, Shrivastava (1995) introduces four ways in which organizations might contribute to sustainability: (1) total quality environmental management (looking at the processes employed to manufacture physical goods or deliver services); (2) ecologically sustainable competitive strategies (developing more environmentally benign products and services); (3) technology transfer (for instance, offering more environmentally benign technology to developing countries in return for market access or raw materials); and (4) population impact control (referring to ways in which companies could use their distribution and promotion networks to promote voluntary family planning and/or distribute means of birth control).

There is also a huge literature which deals more specifically with practical recommendations for managers who want to improve their companies' environmental performance. Most of these recommendations for environmental management acknowledge a primacy of economic goals, at least implicitly, and sell corporate greening mostly on the basis that there need be no conflict between environmental, social and business goals (the so-called triple bottom line – see Elkington, 1994). Greater corporate environmental efforts are promoted on the basis that, in the medium to long term, better environmental performance will mean better business performance. This is mostly justified with reference to greater environmental concern in (western) society and hence more customer demand for environmentally sensitive products and production processes, tighter environmental legislation, better access to finance and insurance for environmentally conscious enterprises and, possibly, the ultimate loss of companies' licence to operate if they show persistently poor environmental performance (see Hunt and Auster, 1990; Roome, 1992; Greeno, 1991, among others).

The notion that ecological and social sustainability might not be compatible with a free market economy and that radical changes to the economic system and to modes of production and consumption might be necessary may be advocated by environmentalists, but it has not found its way into the environmental management literature. Sustainability is rarely discussed as a viable short- to medium-term business goal. Fineman (2000) argues that modern business organizations are not well placed to take up the sustainability agenda. The relative modesty of the greening advocated in management and practitioner literatures should not surprise us, as much of it is concerned with changing management practices, and is only likely to persuade managers of the need and feasibility of change if it does not question the basic premises by which their enterprises operate.

Relatively little empirical research has been done on how managers frame the relationship between business and the environment but what has been done suggests that much of the environmental management discourse in companies tends to be economic and technical, emphasizing the business case for corporate greening as well as its feasibility, rather than taking up long-term sustainability or moral considerations. Fineman (1996) and Crane (2000) show that practising managers tend to construct environmental issues mostly in business centred, economic terms, not in moral ones, what Crane (2000) calls the 'amoralization' of corporate greening. The term sustainability may be used in corporate environmental reports, which are destined for public consumption, but rarely in company internal discourses. Environment is therefore often constructed in externally mediated terms. This matters, because organizational discourse, the way in which organizational realities are rationalized and given meaning, has significant implications for organizational action.

DEFINING ENVIRONMENTAL ISSUES

What are the environmental issues that businesses need to concern themselves with? The way in which managers, explicitly or implicitly, answer this question has repercussions for practical environmental management, in terms of analysing environmental impacts, collecting environmental data and allocating financial and managerial resources to improve environmental performance. What is – and what is not – considered to be an environmentally important issue to be addressed within a company is often externally mediated, through regulation, market forces and, to some extent, other stakeholders' actions.

Environmental legislation and regulation remains one of the most significant frames of reference for the definition of environmental issues in companies. Environmental legislation differs from country to country and from industry to industry. Hunt and Raman (2000) show how managers in different industries defined their environmental responsibilities mostly in terms of what environmental issues were legislated for in their particular industry. While managers were aware, as private citizens, of global environmental issues, such as ozone depletion and climate change, they found it difficult to relate these issues to their work contexts unless industry-specific legislation relating to these issues existed. Similarly, Schaefer and Harvey (2000a) found that companies tended to focus their environmental management systems on those environmental effects where industry-specific legislation applied. Indeed, one of the chief purposes of environmental management systems was often seen as their capacity to reduce or eliminate incidents which might lead to prosecution by the environmental regulator. Because of the perceived costs associated with environmental legislation, companies also try to use voluntary environmental strategies and industry codes to influence government either to block legislation or to water down impending laws. (Lyon and Maxwell, 1999.)

The impact of the legislative and regulatory framework is even felt in the area of non-governmental initiatives, such as ISO 14000, the international environmental management standard, or Responsible Care, the voluntary environmental code of the US and UK chemical industries. Prakash (1999) found that regulators are important in shaping perceptions of benefits and costs associated with introducing such voluntary schemes into a company and that they should be seen as operating under the influence of governments.

Yet, legislation is not a static, given force. The way environmental legislation is enacted in day-to-day encounters between business managers and regulators is often flexible and subject to the contingencies of circumstance. Fineman (1998) and Fineman and Sturdy (1999) found that the attitudes displayed by managers during such encounters, the compliance history of the company and the company's ability to meet legal environmental standards economically, all had significant influence on the outcome of the regulatory encounter. This was partly due to long-standing regulatory relations between inspectors and companies, which meant that the players knew each other well; so each new regulatory encounter unfolded in the light of previous experiences with each other. In a similar vein, Howard et al. (1999) found that companies adopting a voluntary environmental code, such as Responsible Care, varied considerably in the way in which they implemented the codes and how organizational members interpreted their importance. Like regulation, the adoption of voluntary codes does not appear to guarantee that companies follow a uniform set of practices or comply fully with desired norms.

A further issue regarding the relationship between business and environmental regulation concerns the question of whether stringent environmental legislation might improve the competitive situation of companies exposed to it. Porter and van der Linde (1995) argue that stringent legislation induces companies to invest in innovation into better processes and products and would thus lead to a competitive advantage. However, Wubben (1999) found this not to be so straightforward, in so far as environmental legislation seemed to lead to a short-term increase in cost, whilst long-term increases in competitiveness mostly accrued to larger firms – at the cost of smaller ones – and only where legislation was properly enforced.

FINANCIAL INSTITUTIONS AND CUSTOMERS

In this way, companies' approaches to environmental issues, including what managers consider to be environmental problems within their responsibility and the priority which they accord different issues, is significantly mediated by their perception of what the law, regulators and other stakeholders demand of them. However, while clearly important, legislation and regulation are obviously not the only external frame of reference for the classification of environmental issues. The power of market forces in promoting corporate environmental change has been discussed in the literature for some time (for example, Greeno, 1991; Winsemius and Guntram, 1992). The two market actors of most importance in this respect are financial institutions and customers.

Financial institutions are thought to influence corporate environmental performance in two significant respects, namely the availability and price of finance and insurance. A number of financial institutions, such as the Co-op Bank in the UK, have established market positions based on ethical and environmental concerns and state that they will not invest in nor lend to companies that pollute the environment or act unethically. Business managers realize that they can only expect finance from such institutions if they fulfil certain environmental and social criteria. In return, businesses can often take advantage of financial incentives such as interest rate discounts on loans that come as part of ethical financial packages. Nonetheless, the environmental and ethical financial sector still represents only a small proportion of the financial industry as a whole.

Mainstream banks and insurers are also increasingly seen to put green pressure on companies. Lenders fear that they may suffer financial loss if held liable for environmental damage caused by their corporate borrowers, or that their reputation could be tarnished through association with a polluter (BBA, 1993; Barrett, 1994; Jewell and Waite, 1997). For example, a lender may inherit clean-up liabilities attached to land taken as security on a debt, or alternatively if borrowers incur penalties or lose market position for non-compliance with environmental legislation, this creates risk to financial return for the lender (Coulson and Monks, 1999). As a result, most high street lenders have begun to integrate environmental considerations into their credit risk assessment processes, focusing attention on three integral categories; land contamination, industrial processing and business management (Coulson, 2001). The same considerations are seen to apply to the insurance sector. A number of highly publicized cases of huge insurance payments becoming due following major environmental incidents, such as the Exxon Valdez disaster in 1989, have promoted the impression that insurers stand to lose significant amounts of money if an insured company causes major environmental damage. They are thus reluctant to insure environmental liabilities of companies without good environmental management systems and performance (Raphael, 1994). Companies would therefore try to avoid falling into the category of organizations that lenders are unwilling to lend to or insurers unwilling to insure due to perceived environmental risks. Conversely, fund managers and banks with socially responsible investment (SRI) products argue that these represent more reliable value over the longer term.

The other major market actor seen to influence the framing of environmental issues by companies is customers. End consumers are sometimes thought to hold the key to achieving sustainable development. With increasing environmental awareness, in market economies it should be possible for consumers to take their green convictions to the market place and demand ecologically responsible products and services. This will include concern for the way a product is made, the raw materials that go into it, its environmental impact during use, and the environmental cost of disposing of it after its useful life. Consumers' environmental concerns may also stretch to other company activities, including related issues like animal welfare, treatment of employees and relations with the local community, particularly across global supply systems. It has been assumed that this demand for more sustainable products will grow to become a substantial segment of the market, thereby making it worthwhile for companies to improve the environmental performance of their products and manufacturing processes. (See Ottman (1993) for a practically oriented discussion of the logic of green consumerism and the attendant implications for business practice.) A great variety of green marketing tools and initiatives have appeared in the wake of this presumed consumer demand. Companies are likely to perceive environmental issues as significant and under their control if they think consumer concern will stimulate active demand for green product alternatives.

The same can be said for industrial purchasing. By a considerable margin, most buying and selling in industrial economies goes on between organizations, with public sector buying playing a significant role. For manufacturing firms, the percentage of total revenue spent on purchasing things is often greater than 60 per cent, and can be higher (see Dobler and Burt, 1996). The perceived priorities and demands of industrial customers could play a significant role in framing environmental issues. Put crudely, if there is a perception that customers (industrial or end consumers) attach importance to environmental issues, companies are likely to take this seriously and concentrate their environmental efforts in such areas. Thus Wycherley (1999) found that suppliers to the Body Shop International felt that the company communicated a clear commitment to environmental goals. There remained a number of barriers for them to take greening further, including potentially higher costs and the indifference of other customers. Other than the Body Shop, few customers were really interested in green supplies.

What does this mean for the construction of environmental issues? On the positive side it may mean environmental issues taken up by legislation and through market forces are likely to figure relatively highly in managers' concerns. They are the issues they may consider important in their organizational role and this means that they are likely to invest resources into addressing them. On the other hand, not all major environmental concerns have found their way into environmental legislation and the environmental concerns of investors and customers may be highly selective.

Investors and insurers, particularly mainstream as opposed to niche players, may be mostly interested in reducing financial risks rather than promoting genuine environmental concerns for their own sake. It would seem that certain environmental risks, such as large scale pollution incidents, are likely to carry a far greater financial risk in terms of liabilities, than other, more diffuse risks, such as energy use and contribution to ozone depletion. Consumer opinion and demand may be swayed by issues that have a high media profile, and this may be similar for industrial purchasing (see below for a more detailed discussion on green purchasing). Add to this the fact that, so far, only the minority of customers are using environmental criteria in buying decisions in a consistent and predictable way. So, market forces would seem to be only a skewed frame of reference for the definition of environmental issues.

The same is true of other environmental stakeholders. Pressure groups cannot take up every environmental concern with every company, their campaigns tend to be highly selective and many companies do not feel that green pressure groups have any influence on them.

If managers define environmental issues mostly in terms of what regulations, investors, customers and other influential stakeholders expect of them, then this is likely to lead to a partial picture of the environmental issues that could concern the company. It is likely to favour the local over the global, given that local environmental effects are often more visible and better understood, and are thus more frequently addressed by legislation, more liable to financial risk and more likely to be of immediate concern to customers. It is also likely that environmental effects that can be addressed through technological solutions, often mandated by regulation (such as best available technology regulations) are more likely to lead to viable product and process alternatives that satisfy campaigners and green customers, than issues for which technological solutions may be less easy. In addition, many small enterprises which are not exposed to significant environmental legislation or environmental demands from investors or customers and which are considered too small to warrant the attention of green pressure groups, have few of these external frames of reference by which to construct environmental engagement. Many of these smaller firms may not engage with environmental issues in any significant way (Petts et al., 1999) or find that models of organizational greening that have been developed for larger organizations are inappropriate. This leaves managers of small firms with difficulties in translating ideals, values and aspirations into green action (Tilley, 1999).

CONSTRUCTING GREEN ORGANIZATIONS?

The ways in which business organizations make sense of their place in the environment are inextricably linked to the way in which they organize themselves for environmental management. The construction of green organizations implies organizational change. This much is obvious from much of the literature, perhaps most notably those publications which suggest a 'stage model' of organizational transformation towards greater environmental sensitivity and, possibly, ultimate sustainability (for example, Hunt and Auster, 1990; Roome, 1992). These models argue that companies improve their environmental management by moving through a series of discrete stages, from being unaware and uninvolved with environmental issues, to a final stage of fully tuned environmentally sensitive corporate culture and pro-active management towards sustainability objectives. While the stage models are problematic, both theoretically and empirically (Räsänen et al., 1995; Hass, 1996; Schaefer and Harvey, 1998; Vickers, 2000) the notion of organizational transformation pervades the business and environmental literature as well as the discourse of practising managers.

What then, is the likely nature of pro-environmental organizational change? The underlying assumptions of both stage models and much of the business and environment literature appears to be one of gradual, incremental change. King (2000) is one of the few authors to carry out an explicit empirical study to test this assumption of incremental change against the competing major organizational change theory of the 'punctuated equilibrium' (see Tushman and Romanelli, 1985, and Gersick, 1991, for a discussion of the punctuated equilibrium). He found that, in a number of companies exposed to new environmental legislation, some predictions of the punctuated equilibrium theory held, in so far as managers tried to build buffers in the form of specialist environmental staff and end-of-pipe technological solutions in order to protect the rest of the organization from deeper change. However, in some companies these new members of staff and technologies then initiated a process of incremental change reaching deeper into the organization. More research is needed before any confident assertions about the nature of pro-environmental organizational change can be made.

In what follows we will first look at two sub-concepts of pro-environmental organizational change, namely organizational learning and the role of individual change agents or environmental champions. We will then take a closer look at two more specific aspects of such change: green purchasing and green innovation and technologies.

Organizational Learning

Managing environmental issues in companies is characterized by uncertainty, increased complexity, and ambiguity, all of which constitute 'occasions for sense-making', according to Weick (1995). Weick's concept of sense-making stems from his overall model of organizations as entities with no fixed structure or meaning but which are 'enacted' through the interactions and interpretations of their members. This enactment of organizational reality depends on the ability of organizational members to make sense of what they perceive to be their surroundings and their interests. Under circumstances of complexity and ambiguity, existing interpretations may no longer be seen as adequate and therefore new sense-making (or learning if following a more mainstream terminology) must take place. In terms of business and the environment and from a manager's point of view, uncertainty is increased by a mounting but not particularly consistent public concern about green issues and by a rapidly growing body of environmental legislation. Complexity is increased by environmental management because it is one more aspect of the business to manage and because many environmental issues are in themselves very complex. Learning is therefore an important aspect of corporate greening. Learning may be needed in many different respects. When starting to introduce environmental management, organizations often have no clear idea what the environmental effects of their business are, how they should be measured or what should be done about them. Members of the business have to agree among themselves, and consult their external stakeholders, about their environmental effects and their significance. Often they have little data on critical waste streams, energy uses or other environmentally relevant processes; ways of measuring them need to be developed. Appropriate monitoring, analytical and reporting structures are needed for this purpose. Even when a company has a clear picture of the nature and magnitude of its environmental impacts, there may be a range of responses available from which to choose.

Despite the considerable literature on organizational learning in general (see Easterby-Smith, 1997, for an overview) and its obvious relevance for the study of organizational greening, organizational learning has only recently begun to attract the attention and interest of business and the environment scholars. Clearly, some form of learning must be going on in companies trying to implement some form of environmental management. However, the extent of such learning, even in companies adopting an explicit environmental strategy, is not clear. In a study of environmental management in small and medium sized enterprizes in the UK, Petts (2000) found that the majority of the companies studied had some characteristics of learning organizations. Most of the employees held positive attitudes towards environmental issues and the companies tended to possess flat hierarchies without functional divisions, which should aid the capacity for reflection. On the other hand, both employees and managers often found it difficult to relate environmental issues to their workplace and most of the companies had yet to develop an organizational context and prevailing social norms to support learning about environmental issues.

Schaefer and Harvey (2000b) also found some evidence for organizational learning when they looked at how companies acquire information about environmental issues and how such information is disseminated throughout the company. But they found such learning to be limited in so far as companies seemed to strive for early closure of the questions in strictly circumscribed limits within the organizations and displayed a tendency to limit the dissemination of environmental information within the company to certain key individuals, usually those with an official environmental brief. Most companies employed information acquisition strategies that relied heavily on outside experts, such as environmental management consultants with knowledge of what was considered as best practice within an industry. Taken together these trends were likely to reduce environmental debate and redundancy of information (similar or identical knowledge held by several individuals within the organization), considered crucial for successful organizational learning (see Nonaka, 1994). Organizing for green organizational learning therefore has to be seen as an important task, although the best organizational structure to facilitate this is not certain. Llerena (1999) suggests that while a decentralized structure will facilitate diversity and relevance of learning in local contexts, an element of centralization is necessary to ensure that learning is coherent across the firm. Coulson's (2000) work with the banking sector adds support for Llerena's proposal by illustrating how in one bank environmental learning among lenders took place through a focus on policy interpretation across the organization and its role in the development of mental models of environmental assessment. In the study, some bank lenders learn how to identify and assess environment credit risk according to bank policy by working together on borrower cases or sharing experiences of loan process through story telling.

Vickers (2000), in a study of a domestic appliances firm, also found that some environmental learning took place, but not as widely as might be considered desirable from an environmental point of view. He suggests that there are often formidable structural and cultural barriers to far-reaching green organizational learning, which should be understood in terms of the relative power of individuals and groups within the organization to define and activate learning agendas and in terms of the emphasis that the company gives to cost, skill and trust as a means of improving competitive standing. Such a limited extent of green organizational learning may have significant negative consequences for the overall greening of companies. For instance, Kirkland and Thompson (1999) found that some of the barriers to successful implementation of environmental management systems were avoidance of the unknown, resistance to complexity, lack of skills, knowledge and expertise and inappropriate environmental solutions, all clear signs of poor organizational learning.

Negotiating environmental change

Environmental Champions

Often, the only people in an organization who genuinely try to acquire environmental knowledge and skills may be those charged with specific environmental responsibility or those who have a personal interest in environmental issues. These environmental champions, tend to play a significant role in many accounts of organizational pro-environmental change or greening. The extent to which individuals really can change the organization, or that part of the organization that they work in, is not entirely clear but these stories seem to exist in all companies that have embarked on a successful – from members' points of view – greening process. Likewise, the normative literature frequently extols the need for environmental champions, who take it upon themselves to persuade others around them of the need for change and to start developing ways of changing organizational processes to improve environmental performance.

Environmental champions may be found at any level of a company's hierarchy. The most obvious environmental champions are environmental managers and staff with environment in the job title. The importance of a good environmental manager is stressed by Hunt and Auster (1990), who see this person as the main internal driver of practical pro-environmental change. Environmental managers are charged with acquiring and disseminating environmental information, collating and reporting on environmental performance data from the company, and liaising with outside bodies, such as regulators, pressure groups, local communities, industry bodies, and the public at large. They are also required to co-ordinate environmental management efforts throughout the company. Their most important activity lies in motivating, nudging, and cajoling other members of the organization into greater environmental management efforts and increasing the general environmental awareness within the organization. Officially appointed environmental champions at lower levels in the organization hierarchy do pretty much the same thing for the smaller part of the organization in which they operate (see Schaefer and Harvey, 2000a; Petts, 2000; for a fuller discussion).

So far, there is only a tentative picture emerging regarding the actual effectiveness of environmental champions. If, as some of the findings on pro-environmental organizational learning suggest, environmental championship, and hence environmental expertise, is confined to relatively few people in an organization and if the number and variety of environmental issues that champions feel they can successfully introduce within their sphere of influence are fairly restricted, then we would expect a relatively limited influence of champions. Indeed, they may act as a buffer by which the organization protects itself from what it considers to be external environmental demands and threats. On a more optimistic note, King's (2000) findings suggest that, over time and given favourable circumstances, environmental champions may succeed in changing deeper reaching processes and attitudes.

We will conclude with a closer look at two domains of environmental management which are often considered to be the most promising avenues for far-reaching pro-environmental change, namely green purchasing and green technological innovation. Clearly these two topics do not exhaust the applications of green management in organizations – total quality environmental management, green marketing, and so on are also of importance.

Green Purchasing

It is often thought that one way in which organizations can make a significant change to their environmental impact is by incorporating environmental criteria into purchasing decisions, particularly where significant volumes of goods are being purchased. The complexity of modern production systems and industrial structures is such that any significant corporate response to environmental issues is likely to imply some connection with procurement and supplier relations. This context is vastly different to the relative simplicity of individual consumer purchasing, and is a long way from the atomistic, impersonal and discrete market exchanges imagined by some economists (see Green et al., 2000).

Incorporating the environmental agenda into corporate procurement has been promoted from a number of quarters for several years (see Lamming and Hampson, 1996; Russel, 1998). Two main lessons have become apparent: first, there exists a huge range of options and tactics for organizations to pursue; second, very few organizations have begun to exploit the options and tactics that are available. The range of possibilities implied by greening supply is linked to the variability of purchasing organizations and the wide range of products and services secured. The simplest situation is procurement based on the choice of a greener product compared to a browner alternative. This may be a straightforward choice. As an example, one might consider the selection of an environmentally friendly cleaning fluid over a conventional one. In this case, the relationship between the buyer and seller may be at some distance, and there may be no interaction other than the transaction itself – the market in its purest form. The next possibility is that of purchasing not on the basis of a green product, but on a green process by which the product is manufactured. Third, environmental considerations may be brought to bear even if they do not play a role in the purchasing decision itself. For example, environmental considerations may be used to pre-qualify those from whom the purchaser will select; again, this can relate to product and process. Even without formal processes of pre-qualification, this softer approach to green supply allows the buyer to communicate priorities to the vendor.

The scope for green issues affecting the purchasing relationship, then, is considerable. There are many ways in which an organization's own environmental agenda can be expressed in procurement. Indeed, one might expect to see purchasing as the main focus of environmental activity in firms. Curiously, this is not the case. Although many organizations have made some effort, and the idea of environment and procurement being linked is reflected in the official publications and training syllabuses of professional institutions (CIPS/BIE, 1993), green procurement has been slow to get off the ground.

Some of the reasons for this can be illustrated by a study conducted by New, Morton and Green (1999) on green supply issues relating to one particular kind of product – medical equipment, especially relating to intravenous therapies (IV) – made from plastic polyvinyl chloride (PVC). This is considered by some to be a hazardous product, in particular because of its association with chlorine and oestrogen-mimicing chemicals. On the other hand, PVC is almost the perfect material for many applications especially in health care. It is light, flexible, transparent, unbreakable, easy to sterilize and cheap enough to dispose of after a single use. Yet, all the major manufacturers are actively seeking to develop replacement materials; this is in response to those markets, notably Scandinavia and Germany, where the use of PVC has been constrained by both legislation and procurement practice. Despite the controversy, the health service in the UK has continued to purchase PVC equipment. The controversy was not well understood in the UK National Health Service (NHS) purchasing authorities and there was negligible pressure from purchasers on the dominant suppliers. The health care industry typically purchases through consortia in which the supply chain for goods between manufacturer and users is mediated by purchasing organizations that exist to achieve economies due to their purchasing power and reduced administration costs. With these pressures to deliver very low prices, the purchasing organizations have few incentives to purchase on the basis of non-price criteria like lower environmental impact.

In these situations, the complexity of the procurement process, and the introduction of an extra tier of authority, meant that it was difficult for some kinds of information to flow between users and manufacturers. Even though there exists considerable, if vaguely expressed, interest in environmental improvement within the NHS, users find it difficult to translate this into substantial changes to the specification of their requirements, specifications which are then passed to the consortia with the mandate to buy as cheaply as possible. This is particularly the case where more environmental purchasing would require significant extra spending, or where the benefits might not accrue to the budget holding unit responsible for the purchase.

Despite its being hailed as a major chance to effect pro-environmental change not only in individual organizations but throughout entire supply chains, it seems that there remain significant obstacles to widespread green purchasing. These lie chiefly in, first, conflicting economic and ecological goals that purchasing managers see themselves exposed to; and, second, in the complexity of supply chain management, which may leave purchasing managers with a sense of impotence to effect real changes, particularly in the light of rigid supply chain structures. This leaves green purchasing in the somewhat paradoxical situation where, in some cases, there may be a temptation for firms to overestimate the degree of influence that their green purchasing can have, while in other situations the opportunities to harness suppliers' environmentally innovative capabilities have yet to be realized. The existing literature thus suggests that the potential for pro-environmental change through supply chain management remains strong but in practice this potential is far from being realized in most purchasing organizations.

Green Innovation and Technology

The introduction to this chapter pointed out how the use of natural resources to provide goods and services has led many to identify the business sector as the cause of environmental problems. Current patterns of production and consumption are the result of decades of accumulated technological innovation. Therefore technology can be seen as the cause of environmental degradation (Braun, 1995).

More recently, however, technological change has come to be seen as a solution, not just a contributor, to environmental problems. Recent writers have emphasized the capacity of suitably directed technology to break the link between environmental damage and levels of consumption (von Weizsäcker et al., 1997). The capacity to reduce the amount of energy and materials required to deliver any given level of service to consumers has been thoroughly documented. The idea that technology can deliver both environmental and economic benefits has been embraced at the highest political level in the UK (Blair, 2000).

'Clean technology' has been adopted as an umbrella term to describe the wide range of possible technological responses to the environmental challenge. Use of the related term 'clean production' signals the fact that the management of technology is just as important as the hardware itself. Some writers have used the term 'cleaner' production rather than 'clean' production (Christie et al., 1995). This acknowledges the fact that no technology can ever avoid having some environmental impact. More recently, the term 'sustainable technology' has been used to highlight the wider contribution that technology can make to sustainable development (DTI, 2000). Various taxonomies of clean technology have been proposed (ACOST, 1992; Christie et al., 1995; Clayton et al., 1999; Howes et al, 1997; Skea, 2000). Although these differ in minor respects, each has the same basic elements. Clean-up technologies are used to remediate environmental problems, such as contaminated land, caused by past activities. End-of-pipe technologies, such as flue gas desulphurization at power stations or effluent treatment at paper mills, are used to reduce discharges from existing production processes, though they often succeed in simply transferring pollution from one medium to another (from the air to disposal of sludge to land in the case of flue gas desulphurization). Recycling reduces environmental impacts through the re-use of materials recovered from waste streams. Waste minimization refers to the modification of production processes so that waste streams are reduced in the first place. Finally, clean technology refers to production processes that, by their nature, give rise to low levels of environmental impact without recourse to end-of-pipe controls or recycling.

The mainstream literature on technological innovation distinguishes between: (1) incremental process change; (2) radical change; and (3) shifts to new technological paradigms where there are significant changes in entire technological–economic systems. This echoes the general debate of incremental versus punctuated change in organizational greening (see above; King, 2000). Several researchers have focused on the way that firms approach the adoption of clean technology (Irwin and Vergragt, 1989; Groenewegen and Vergragt, 1991; Irwin and Hooper, 1992; Green et al., 1994). This work emphasizes the social and organizational context within which innovation takes place, identifying the networks of actors, both internal and external to the firm, that are involved in the negotiation of technology development and adoption. In that sense, organizational learning is also clearly an important aspect of technological change.

Like other aspects of pro-environmental organizational change, green technological innovation in companies is – at least partly – framed through styles of regulation. More traditional approaches to regulation involving technological prescription or rigid standard-setting generally lead firms to adopt end-of-pipe technologies that meet the specific requirements of the regulator. Allenby (2000) suggests that cleaner technology, as commonly employed in a majority of firms, focuses on end-of-pipe technology and embeds within it the mental model of environmental issues as peripheral to general economic and policy activities. Novel policy instruments such as emissions trading and negotiated agreements, on the other hand, are often seen as more likely to reduce the cost of achieving environmental goals and at the same time to encourage companies to adopt solutions other than end-of-pipe technology (Burtraw, 1999). A similar point can be made about the role of markets for green technology. Clearly, companies up-stream in the supply chain are only going to develop technologies if they perceive that there is a market for such products. The environmental goods and services market is often said to be growing, particularly in countries with strong environmental legislation, such as Germany and the Netherlands. It is, however, also fragmented and remains focused on end-of-pipe solutions rather than technology that radically changes production processes. In addition, general problems with greening the supply chain, discussed above, are likely to hamper the large scale development of cleaner technology. The overall picture regarding green technological change is, again, one where much potential for pro-environmental change seems to exist but where this potential is far from being realized.

DISCUSSION AND CONCLUSION

Is business on its way to sustainability? The answer is a qualified 'no', although many, particularly larger business organizations in western countries may be on their way to institutionalizing some form of environmental management. As we have seen, this environmental engagement is framed primarily in terms of legislative and market drivers; internal changes often follow this external frame of reference in terms of environmental issues recognized, environmental management systems installed, organizational learning achieved and technological changes made. In this sense, business takes a techno-centric approach to external drivers (regulation, consumers, and so on) which have a more eco-centric motivation. This is often portrayed as sustainable corporate behaviour but it is doubtful whether it really amounts to this.

By framing environmental problems in terms of legislation and market drivers, companies take on board some of the more salient environmental concerns of society, namely those that have already been codified in law or have found their way into the decision making of financial institutions and purchases from consumers, other businesses, and governmental and institutional buyers. Additionally, some of the main concerns of powerful pressure groups may be taken into consideration as well. However, a number of potentially very significant environmental issues may remain outside the company's definition of its environmental concerns. In particular, this includes those issues of global concern, which have only recently become the subject of official concern and have found their way into legislation only very incompletely. They may also not form part of market-driven environmental concerns, particularly considering that most organizations only apply environmental criteria to a minority of purchasing decisions, if at all.

The fact that some environmental learning seems to be taking place in organizations is encouraging but an early institutionalization of what is considered to be accepted knowledge about environmental issues and best practice may also be a concern. The goals of sustainability, as briefly outlined in the introduction, require more than mere adjustments to the present system. Yet, an early closure of the environmental debate within business organizations will leave environmental management firmly within current business practice and embedded in the current economic system, considered unsustainable by many.

The same may be said of other aspects of companies' internalization of environmental issues. As we have shown, the greening of purchasing does not appear to be happening to anywhere near the extent that its advocates expected and hoped for. Often, purchasing managers only feel able to incorporate environmental criteria into purchasing decisions in a limited way, as they are subject to other constraints, including legislative requirements, long-standing business network relationships, and the stricture to keep down costs. Additionally, the actual managing of supply chains for environmental goals (or perhaps any other goals, for that matter) is considered difficult. Environmental purchasing practices, so far, seem to lead only to minor adaptations within the existing business system, rather than the far-reaching changes that sustainability might require. This also hampers the development of cleaner technologies, thought to be vital for achieving more sustainable business. A concentration on end-of-pipe technologies may meet current environmental regulation but is unlikely to take business towards sustainability.

The conclusions to be drawn from the last decade of academic research on business and the environment are therefore sombre. Despite numerous business initiatives promoting environmental change and the services offered by an increasing number of environmental management consultants, not to mention practice-oriented and academic publications on the subject, we seem to be little closer to sustainable business than we were ten or twenty years ago.

From the point of view of the academic researchers it is perhaps important to note that business and the environment research does not appear to have significantly reduced the gap between environmental awareness and genuine progress towards more sustainable business practices (Stubbs, 2000). Clearly, the research done over the last decade has contributed to our understanding of the responses of individual businesses to external pressures, of organizational learning, green purchasing, green technology development and environmental management systems, among others. Yet, in some important ways business and the environment research has perhaps not really addressed the problems of business systems under the current stage of global capitalism. A substantive research agenda remains in understanding global business networks and connections and their implications for sustainability. Some recent publications have called for more research from a network perspective (Roome, 2001;

Steward and Conway, 1998) and for more critical research (Welford, 1998), focusing on the nature of free market economic systems and how they interact with the environmental performance of individual businesses. Whether such a research agenda will help business to become more sustainable will remain to be seen.

REFERENCES

Advisory Council on Science and Technology (ACOST) (1992), *Cleaner Technology*, London: HMSO.

Allenby, B.R. (2000), 'The fallacy of "green technology"', *American Behavioural Scientist*, 44 (2), 213–28.

Barrett, J. (1994), 'Weighing up the risks', *Certified Accountant*, October, pp. 42–44.

BBA (1993), *Position Statement: Banks and the Environment*, September, London: British Bankers' Association.

Blair, A. (2000), *Richer and Greener*, Speech to the Green Alliance–CBI Conference on the Environment, London, October 24.

Braun, E. (1995), *Futile Progress, Technology's Empty Promise*, London: Earthscan.

Burtraw, D. (1999), 'Cost savings, market performance and economic benefits of the US Acid Rain program', in S. Sorrell and J. Skea (eds), *Pollution for Sale: Emissions Trading and Joint Implementation*, Cheltenham, UK and Northampton, MA: Edward Elgar.

Chartered Institute of Purchasing and Supply/Business in the Environment (CIPS/BIE) (1993), *Buying into the Environment*, Stamford: CIPS.

Christie, I. and H. Rolfe, with R. Legard (1995), *Cleaner Production in Industry*, London: Policy Studies Institute.

Clayton, A., G. Spinardi and R. Williams (1999), *Policies for Cleaner Technology: A New Agenda for Government and Industry*, London: Earthscan.

Coulson, A.B. (2000), 'Banking on the environment: risk and rationality', Part 1, Chapter 5, in S. Fineman (ed.), *The Business of Greening*, London: Routledge Global Environmental Change Series.

Coulson, A.B. (2001), 'Corporate environmental assessment by a bank lender – the reality?', Part 4, Chapter 23, in Jan Jaap Bouma, Marcel Jeucken and Leon Klinkers (eds), *Sustainable Banking: The Greening of Finance*, published in association with Deloitte & Touche, Sheffield: Greenleaf Publishing.

Coulson, A.B. and V. Monks (1999), 'Corporate environmental performance considerations within bank lending decisions', *Eco-management and Auditing*, 6, 1–10.

Crane, A. (2000), 'Corporate greening an amoralization', *Organization Studies*, 21 (4), 673–96.

Department of Trade and Industry (DTI) (2000), *Sustainable Technologies Initiative*, http://www.dti.gov.uk/sti/index.htm.

Dobler, D.W. and D.N. Burt (1996), *Purchasing and Supply Management: Texts and Cases*, New York: McGraw-Hill.

Easterby-Smith, M. (1997), 'Disciplines of organizational learning: contributions and critique', *Human Relations*, 50 (9), 1085–113.

Elkington, J. (1994), 'Towards the sustainable corporation: win-win-win business strategies for sustainable development', *California Management Review*, Winter, 90–100.

Fineman, S. (1996), 'Emotional subtexts in corporate greening', *Organization Studies*, 17 (3), 479–500.

Fineman, S. (1998), 'Street level bureaucrats and the social construction of environmental control', *Organization Studies*, 19 (6), 953–74.

Fineman, S. (2000), 'The business of greening: an introduction', in S. Fineman (ed.), *The Business of Greening*, London: Routledge.

Fineman, S. and A. Sturdy (1999), 'The emotions of control: a qualitative exploration of environmental regulation', *Human Relations*, 52 (5), 631–63.

Gersick, C.J.G. (1991), 'Revolutionary change theories: a multilevel exploration of the punctuated equilibrium paradigm', *Academy of Management Review*, 16 (1), 10–36.

Gladwin, T., J.J. Kennelly and T.-S. Krause (1995), 'Shifting paradigms for sustainable development: implications for management theory and research', *Academy of Management Review*, 20 (4), 874–907.

Green K, A. McMeekin and A. Irwin (1994), 'Technological trajectories and R&D for environmental innovation in UK firms', *Futures*, 26 (10), 1047–59.

Green, K., B. Morton and S. New (2000), 'Greening organizations: purchasing, consumption, and innovation', *Organization and Environment*, 13 (2), 206–25.

Greeno, J.L. (1991), 'Environmental excellence: meeting the challenge', in A.D. Little (ed.), *Prism*, Third Quarter, 13–31.

Groenewegen, P. and P. Vergragt (1991), 'Environmental issues as threats and opportunities for technological innovation', *Technology Analysis and Strategic Management*, 3 (1).

Hass, J.L. (1996), 'Environmental ("green") management typologies: an evaluation, operationalization and empirical development', *Business Strategy and the Environment*, 5 (2), 59–68.

Howard, J., J. Nash and J. Ehrenfeld (1999), 'Industry codes as agents of change: responsible care adoption by US chemical companies', *Business Strategy and the Environment*, 8 (5), 281–95.

Howes, R., J. Skea and R. Whelan (1997), *Clean and Competitive: Motivating Environmental Performance in Industry*, London: Earthscan.

Hunt, C.B. and E.R. Auster (1990), 'Proactive environmental management: avoiding the toxic trap', *Sloan Management Review*, 31 (2), 7–18.

Hunt, J. and S. Raman (2000), 'Regulation matters: global environmental discourse and business response', in S. Fineman (ed.), *The Business of Greening*, London: Routledge.

Irwin, A. and P. Hooper (1992), 'Clean technology, successful innovation and the greening of industry: a case-study analysis', *Business Strategy and the Environment*, 1 (2), 1–12.

Irwin A. and P. Vergragt (1989), 'Re-thinking the relationship between environmental regulation and industrial innovation: the social negotiation of technical change', *Technology Analysis and Strategic Management*, 1 (1).

Jewell, T. and A. Waite (1997), *Environmental Law in Property Transactions*, London: Butterworths.

King, A. (2000), 'Organizational response to environmental regulation: punctuated change or autogenesis?', *Business Strategy and the Environment*, 9 (4), 224–38.

Kirkland, L.-H. and D. Thompson (1999), 'Challenges in designing, implementing and operating an environmental management system', *Business Strategy and the Environment*, 8 (2), 128–43.

Lamming, R., A. Faruk and P. Cousins (1999), 'Environmental soundness: a pragmatic alternative to expectations of sustainable development in business strategy', *Business Strategy and the Environment*, 8 (3), 177-99.

Lamming, R. and J. Hampson (1996), 'The environment as a supply chain issue', *British Journal of Management*, 7, S45-S62.

Llerena, D. (1999), 'Integration of environmental issues in the firm: learning processes and coordination', *International Journal of Sustainable Development*, 2 (2), 263-82.

Lyon, T.P. and J.W. Maxwell (1999), 'Corporate environmental strategies as tools to influence regulation', *Business Strategy and the Environment*, 8 (3), 189-96.

New, S., Morton, B. and K. Green (1999), 'Deconstructing green supply and demand: PVC, healthcare products and the environment', *Risk Decision and Policy*, 4 (1), 221-54.

Nonaka, I. (1994), 'A dynamic theory of organizational knowledge creation', *Organization Science*, 5 (1), 15-35.

Ottman, J. (1993), *Green Marketing: Challenges and Opportunities for the New Marketing Age*, Lincolnwood, Il: NTO Business Books.

Petts, J. (2000), 'Smaller enterprises and the environment: organisational learning potential?', in S. Fineman (ed.), *The Business of Greening*, London: Routledge.

Petts, J., A. Herd, S. Gerrard and C. Horne (1999), 'The climate and culture of environmental compliance within SMEs', *Business Strategy and the Environment*, 8 (1), 14-30.

Porter, M. and C. van der Linde (1995), 'Toward a new conception of the environment-competitiveness relationship', *Journal of Economic Perspectives*, 9, 97-118.

Prakash, A. (1999), 'A new-institutional perspective on ISO 14000 and responsible care', *Business Strategy and the Environment*, 8 (6), 322-35.

Raphael, A. (1994), *Ultimate Risk*, London: Bantham Press.

Räsänen, K., S. Meriläinen and R. Lovio (1995), 'Pioneering descriptions of corporate greening: notes and doubts on the emerging discussion', *Business Strategy and the Environment*, 3 (4), 9-16.

Roome, N. (1992), 'Developing environmental management strategies', *Business Strategy and the Environment*, 1 (1), 11-24.

Roome, N. (2001), 'Editorial - conceptualizing and studying the contribution of networks in environmental management and sustainable development', *Business Strategy and the Environment*, 10 (2), 69-76.

Russel, T. (ed.) (1998), *Greener Purchasing*, Sheffield: Greenleaf Publishing.

Schaefer, A. and B. Harvey (1998), 'Stage models of corporate greening: a critical evaluation', *Business Strategy and the Environment*, 7 (2), 109-23.

Schaefer, A. and B. Harvey (2000a), 'Agents of change in corporate greening: case studies in water and electricity utilities', in S. Fineman (ed.), *The Business of Greening*, London: Routledge.

Schaefer, A. and B. Harvey (2000b), 'Environmental knowledge and the adoption of ready-made environmental management solutions', *Eco-Management and Auditing*, 7 (2), 74-81.

Schmidheiny, S. (1992), *Changing Course: A Global Business Perspective on Development and the Environment*, Cambridge, MA: MIT Press.

Shrivastava, P. (1995), 'The role of corporations in achieving ecological sustainability', *Academy of Management Review*, 20 (4), 936-60.

Skea, J. (2000), 'Environmental technology', in H. Folmer and H.L. Gabel (eds), *Principles of Environmental and Resource Economics*, 2nd edn, Cheltenham: Edward Elgar, pp. 338-62.

Starik, M. and G.P. Rands (1995), 'Weaving an integrated web: multilevel and multisystem perspectives of ecologically sustainable organisations', *Academy of Management Review*, 20 (4): 908-35.

Stead, W.E. and J.G. Stead (1996), *Management for a Small Planet*, 2nd edn, Thousand Oaks, CA: Sage.

Steward, F. and S. Conway (1998), 'Situating discourse in environmental innovation networks', *Organization*, 5 (4), 479-502.

Stubbs, M. (2000), 'Action, knowledge and business-environment research: a case for grounded constitutive process theories and a sense of audience', *Business Strategy and the Environment*, 9 (1), 24-35.

Tilley, F. (1999), 'The gap between the environmental attitudes and the environmental behaviours of small firms', *Business Strategy and the Environment*, 8 (4), 238-48.

Tushman, M.L. and E. Romanelli (1985), 'Organizational evolution: a metamorphosis model of convergence and reorientation', in B.M. Staw and L.L. Cummings (eds), *Research in Organizational Behaviour*, Vol. 7, pp. 171-222, Greenwich, CT: JAI Press.

Vickers, I. (2000), 'Cleaner production: organizational learning or business as usual? An example from the domestic appliances industry', *Business Strategy and the Environment*, 9 (4), 255-68.

von Weizsäcker, E., A.B. Lovins and L.H. Lovins (1997), *Factor Four: Doubling Wealth, Halving Resource Use*, London: Earthscan.

Weick, K.E. (1995), *Sense-making in Organisations*, Thousand Oaks, CA: Sage.

Welford, R. (1998), 'Corporate environmental management, technology and sustainable development: post-modern perspectives and the need for a critical research agenda', *Business Strategy and the Environment*, 7 (1), 1-12.

Winsemius, P. and U. Guntram (1992), 'Responding to the environmental challenge', *Business Horizons*, March-April, 12-20.

Wubben, E. (1999), 'What's in it for us? or: the impact of environmental legislation on competitiveness', *Business Strategy and the Environment*, 8 (2), 95-107.

Wycherley, I. (1999), 'Green supply chains: the case of the Body Shop International', *Business Strategy and the Environment*, 8 (2), 120-27.

9. Inducing, shaping, modulating: perspectives on technology and environmental policy

Frans Berkhout and Andy Gouldson

INTRODUCTION

Technology is widely seen as having an ambiguous role in relation to the natural environment. For many environmentalists and other critics, technology is regarded as an instrument of control and exploitation, enabling deeper intrusions into natural systems and ever-greater appropriation of natural resources. Through technology, natural processes are seen to be increasingly dominated and harnessed to human interests. For these critics, technologies are symbols of an apparent imbalance between man and nature. As a result, many major technological systems (nuclear power and genetically modified organisms) have become the focus for intense social debates and conflicts about protecting the environment and, more generally, about societies' relationship to the environment.

But technology is also held to be a tool of liberation, freeing human societies from the constraints (for example, the availability of food and water) and vulnerabilities (disease and natural disasters) that are imposed by the natural environment. Many of the conditions for modern development have been brought about by new knowledge, tools and machines, and by the conventions, habits and institutions within which they become embedded. More instrumentally, many environmental changes that arise from human development have stimulated technological responses, mitigating through 'technical fixes' problems that may originally have resulted from the use of technologies. Over the longer term, a more dramatic liberation – termed 'liberation of the environment' (Ausubel, 1996) – may also be possible in which human development is increasingly based on renewable and reusable resources, loosening the links between the use of natural resources and economic and social development, so reducing the extent of the human imprint on natural systems.

Reflecting these apparent ambiguities, this chapter aims to review recent debates about the role of technology in mediating between economic and social development, and natural environments. In these debates we are faced with both analytical and normative ambitions. The question is not just: how is technology and technological change acting on the environment? but also: how can technological change be influenced (induced, shaped, modulated) to achieve normative goals such as reduced greenhouse gas emissions? Keeping these two questions separate can be difficult because many uses of technology are already infused with normative assumptions. But in the discussion that follows we will presume that they are distinct problems.

Two theoretical traditions dominate the field. Analysis in the neo-classical tradition has been concerned primarily with the question of how changes can be induced in technology to achieve given environmental ends. Research, which we may define as being in an alternative 'institutionalist' tradition, is concerned with understanding processes of socio-technical change which it sees as being complex and taking place under conditions of uncertainty and ambiguity. This tradition focuses not so much on the technologies per se but on the institutional processes that both shape and are shaped by the processes of technological change. In this sense, the frames of reference of the two traditions are somewhat different, perhaps explaining the lack of dialogue there has been between them. In discussing the contributions of the two traditions, four roles for technology in mediating between societies and their natural environments are highlighted: (1) the role of technology in revealing and measuring environmental states and change and in diffusing environmental information (information effects); (2) the role of technology in motivating growth and economic change (structural effects); (3) the role of technology in influencing the exploitation of natural resources (efficiency effects); and (4) technology's role in mitigating environmental impacts of human activities and natural processes as they impact on human activities (mitigation effects).

TWO TRADITIONS IN TECHNOLOGY-ENVIRONMENT STUDIES

By technology we mean everything involved in 'transforming inputs into outputs' (Fransman, 1983) or more abstractly a configuration that works (Rip and Kemp, 1998). Technology is embodied in stabilized networks of hardware, software, and human and organizational capabilities to achieve some instrumental end (Pavitt, 1987). Technology is the outcome of institutional and social processes, and should not be regarded as autonomous – that is, determined by a separate and distinct set of factors and rules. The social or environmental impacts of technologies and of technical change are also not inevitable or predetermined. The process of creating new technologies (invention and innovation) and the ways in which new knowledge and techniques become widely used in the economy (adoption and diffusion) are economically and socially shaped. During processes of innovation and diffusion of many technologies, potential social and environmental impacts are typically appraised and modified, either voluntarily by the innovating or adopting agents themselves, or as the result of some pressure or norm exerted by competitors, policy, consumers or other stakeholders. Processes of technological change, accumulation and use are therefore bound up in institutional routines in which environmental and social impacts are being continually adapted and modified.

The observation that technology needs to be seen as being embedded within institutional settings raises the difficult question of whether technology and technical change *per se* is the right object of analysis, or whether the institutions (markets, policies, incentives, norms, behaviours) that give rise to technologies and to their adaptation should be the focus of inquiry instead. A constructivist critique of technology–environment problems would see the pattern of technology as being the outcome of specific contests between socially-organized networks of actors and institutions. From this perspective the critical questions concern the ways in which social interest groups are configured around contests over the shaping of technology to achieve certain environmental and social objectives (Yearley, 1991). Debates about technology and the environment can often appear to represent deeper social contests – about the role of science and experts, the responsibility of business, or assumptions about modes of consumption.

In contrast, in this chapter we are interested in how the process of purposive shaping of technology takes place once a social contest has been configured. Given that there is an institutional process that has the expressed aim of modifying technology to achieve normative objectives, how does this influence the development, accumulation and use of technology. We see this debate about technology and the environment as mirroring the long-standing debate about the role of technology in economic growth and change.

Technical change is widely accepted as being a factor crucial to economic growth (Schumpeter, 1942; Abramowitz, 1956; Solow, 1957; Romer, 1986; Lucas, 1988). Growth theories have increasingly come to incorporate assumptions about the conditions and incentives for technical change, primarily by seeking to account for investments in research and development (R&D) by firms and governments. Neo-Schumpeterian growth theories take as a starting point an analysis of the processes by which firms generate technical and organizational innovations that are then diffused into markets (Nelson and Winter, 1982). From this perspective, knowledge, technology and learning are central to the economic analysis of industrial change and growth. Likewise, the analysis of knowledge and technology has been regarded as critical to environmental social studies, both because of the multiple roles they play in mediating between social processes and environmental processes, and because responses to environmental problems frequently involve some attempt to modify technologies through the application of scientific knowledge. Technology plays a part in enabling the use of environmental services, in recognizing and understanding environmental problems, and in channelling the social adaptations that take place as a result. An account of how technology plays these multiple roles, in whose interests, and with what outcomes is therefore critical to an understanding of the relationship between societies and their environments. Indeed, it is arguable that as with economic theories of growth, technology and technical change are becoming more central to debates about environmental analysis and policy.

The multiple roles that technologies play in generating and framing environmental disputes, policy problems, and ways of resolving them, has made them an obvious target of environmental policy. Environmental policy makers are frequently concerned with intervening in the process of innovation and diffusion of technology. From a policy perspective, the efficiency and effectiveness of these interventions is vital, leading to a strong interest in tracing the links between policy-driven inducements to innovate or adopt new techniques, and changes in investment, producer and consumer behaviour that reduce their environmental burdens.

Having argued for a focus on processes of technological change, we are confronted with serious theoretical differences about how to analyse technical change – with consequences for research agendas and for policy prescriptions. Simplifying a set of often overlapping debates, we can distinguish between two traditions in the treatment of technical change that mirror, to a large extent, competing traditions in economic growth theories outlined above. Broadly, the neo-classical school treats investments in research and development, and decisions about innovation and adoption as a problem of decision-making by rational and profit-maximizing economic agents with perfect information about the costs and benefits of their actions. Given these assumptions about the ability of rational and responsive actors to search for optimality, the process of technological change is often seen to be less important than the 'inducing' pressure for such change (Ruttan, 2000). Neo-classical economics assumes therefore that where the appropriate drivers – typically price signals – are in place a socially desirable suite of technological changes will indeed happen. Making a physical analogy, once a force has been applied a predictable deformation or motion will result.

In contrast, the neo-Schumpeterian school views investments in technical and organizational innovation as being the outcome of satisficing behaviour under conditions of uncertainty by economic agents with bounded rationality who are embedded in historically-assembled social structures (Simon, 1947; Dosi, 1988). Producers and consumers make decisions on the basis of habit and past experience, and are influenced by what they learn through institutionally-situated processes in a search for solutions to problems that have been recognized as important. They are unable to judge all of the consequences of their actions because private costs and social benefits are not fully known, because end points are highly uncertain, or because there may be a diversity of views about what the outcomes could be (compare Anderson et al. 2001). Uncertainty is an inherent feature of innovation processes.

This analysis calls into question two key assumptions of the neo-classical position. The first is that it is possible to anticipate the outcomes of efforts to shape or modify technological systems (in the sense suggested by the term 'induce'). Under conditions of uncertainty about technological outcomes there is less confidence about the outcomes of efforts to influence technological change, and correspondingly greater attention is paid to the intervening factors (knowledge, technological capability, role of key individuals) that can explain the way in which firms and other economic actors actually behave. The second is that economic agents seek to make optimal decisions in judging how to make trade-offs between the benefits and costs of acting to change their environmental or social impact. If optimality is no longer the yardstick by which the decisions and strategies of firms can be judged, then it is possible to envisage processes of learning (learning by doing, learning by using) and problem-solving that identify solutions that not only enhance profitability, but also environmental and social performance (the so-called 'win-win', Jaffe et al., 2000). Neo-classical economists have tended to remain sceptical about these 'free lunches' (Jaffe et al., 1995).

A related tradition of work argues that the accumulation of technology may be shaped by self-reinforcing ideas, structures and behaviours so that dominant technological regimes emerge. Several explanations for these processes of technological channelling, path dependence, 'lock in' and 'lock out' have been proposed. Dosi (1988), using the term 'technological paradigm', argued that technological regimes were defined as 'a pattern for solution of selected techno-economic problems based on highly selected principles...' (p. 1127). In this analysis the choice of technical problems is defined by prevailing knowledge and problem-solving heuristics that 'restrict the actual combinations in a notional characteristics space to a certain number of prototypical bundles.' Arthur (1989) argued that learning effects and increasing returns to economic scale would lead to a process of technological 'lock in' that would systematically exclude competing and possibly superior (in some dimensions) technologies. David (1985) in his famous, though controversial, example of the QWERTY keyboard argued for three factors leading to path dependency in technological change: technical interrelatedness; economies of scale; and quasi-irreversibility. The first and the last of these relate to the 'switching costs' involved in moving from one technological regime to another. Finally, Walker (2000) in analysing the persistence of nuclear reprocessing technology in the UK stressed the importance of institutional, political and economic commitments to a particular technological regime identified with a long-term economic or social need. He argued that this process of institutional 'entrapment' is ubiquitous in large technical systems. In sum, the literature on technological systems places emphasis on persistence of change along well-defined pathways either because the generation of novelty is bounded by working assumptions and procedures inherent in that regime, or because there are a range of institutional and technical barriers to switching from one regime to another.

Although neo-classical economists have paid more attention to issues relating to technological change in recent years, there are still significant differences in perspective between the neo-classical and the neo-Schumpeterian schools.[1] These different perspectives are reflected in how analysts from each tradition engage in policy debates. Analysts in the neo-classical tradition are interested in shaping incentives to invest in R&D, in the role of relative prices of factors of production and in the economic valuation of the environment. The key environmental policy question is to define the point at which the marginal cost of abatement (borne by the polluter) and the social marginal benefit of pollution control are equivalent, and to set an optimal tax or quantity target to achieve this level of abatement.

By contrast, analysts operating in the neo-Schumpeterian tradition are more concerned with how organizations learn and make decisions under uncertainty, how to reduce uncertainties that affect environmental innovation, and how to relax the 'boundedness' of decision-makers' rationality. The key environmental policy questions here concern the creation of policy frameworks including a variety of regulatory, fiscal and information measures that encourage a path towards more efficient, lower impact economies (Anderson and Cavendish, 1999). Unsurprisingly, the two traditions also have quite different research agendas. Neo-classical analysts have been principally concerned with prices (of inputs and externalities) and their impacts on inducing innovation and adoption of less polluting technologies. From their perspective, neo-Schumpeterian analysts are more interested in understanding the institutional factors that determine innovation and technological accumulation, tending to stress stimuli for collective action (such as regulation and stakeholder norms) rather than private action (such as prices) in explaining processes of change.

TECHNICAL CHANGE AND THE ENVIRONMENT

As already implied, technology has a multiplicity of influences on social interpretations of and interactions with the environment. It can be argued that one of the characteristics of industrial and economic development is that technology comes to play progressively deeper and more diverse roles in mediating between society and the environment, and in influencing both. Broadly speaking, we suggest that technical change can be characterized as having four main environmental effects: (1) sensing and providing information about the state of the environment (information effects); (2) stimulating growth and structural change in the economy (growth and structural effects); (3) improving the efficiency with which resources are harvested and transformed into outputs (efficiency effects); and (4) providing means for mitigating and remediating environmental impacts caused by economic activities (mitigation effects). In the following section, we review a range of debates linked to each of these different roles.

Information Effects

Sensors, monitors and other instruments collect information about the distribution of resources (seismic surveys for oil and gas), the environmental impacts of economic activities (emissions concentrations at production sites) and the state of the environment (census of fish stocks) at all levels from the planetary and global, to the local and microscopic. There has been a vast increase in environmental monitoring and surveillance by business, governments and international organizations over the past fifty years, but the role of these technologies has not been much appreciated or studied.

There appear to be two reasons why sensing technologies need to be considered more carefully. First, the understanding of environmental problems is increasingly mediated by scientific instruments and interpretation (Irwin and Wynne, 1996). The capacity to understand non-tangible environmental changes and risks, and those taking place at broader spatial and temporal scales (stratospheric ozone depletion, climate change), depends on sensing technologies that measure the state of the environment. Perceptions of the environment are becoming increasingly instrumentalized and separated from direct experience. The processes by which sensing technologies and the scientific theories and practices they are embedded in develop are therefore crucial to determining the shape of public contests about managing the environment.

One model of this process views the development of instruments and science as being closely linked to each other, driven primarily by the curiosity of scientists. The development of new instruments and analytical capabilities makes new environmental phenomena and processes 'visible' to science, while the development of scientific theory spurs the development of scientific instruments to confirm or falsify predictions. In this interpretation, science and instruments constitute a more or less autonomous system each supporting and reinforcing the other. An alternative 'mutual construction' model of this process (Shackley and Wynne, 1995) sees the development of scientific agendas (and by extension also the development of instruments) as interacting with the interests and assumptions of policy communities and broader coalitions of interest. Decisions on investments in environmental detection (remote sensing from space, for instance) are linked to the pursuit of other interests that may not be scientific. Likewise, the search for evidence of environmental change (the population ecology of signature animal species, for example) may not be conditioned by curiosity alone, but by its value for broader policy objectives. Finally, detection and sensing (monitoring of acidity in lakes or radioactivity in marine environments, for example) is often functional to the implementation of environmental and resources policies.

A second reason for treating environmental information technologies more seriously is the role they are coming to play in modulating the behaviour of all economic and social actors, not just policy makers. With miniaturization and cost reductions, complex environmental information is becoming much more widely available. For instance, the use of sonar radar and global positioning systems (GPS) is enabling the more intensive and destructive exploitation of fisheries. Likewise, nutrient mapping and GPS are being used to increase the efficiency of fertiliser application in farming. The integration of environmental detection and information and communication technologies also opens up opportunities to establish more clearly the environmental burdens associated with specific social and economic activities (the journey to work, for instance). These burdens could then be accounted for and, in principle, property rights and costs could be allocated more efficiently. One example is the idea of household carbon budgets proposed by Fleming (1997). This kind of innovation could provide the basis for informational and economic incentives to induce changes in behaviour of producers and consumers (Esty, 2001).

Structural Effects

Technical change is an important driver of structural change in economies, with significant consequences for the environmental burden they exert. New technologies, especially 'general purpose technologies' (GPTs) like the microprocessor, can lead to growth of new sectors of the economy and may precipitate change in other sectors. More generally, processes of economic development are characterized by the adoption and use of more complex technologies, and with a shift from economies dominated by agriculture, through manufacturing, and towards more service- and knowledge-intensive industries. In general, there is an assumption that this trajectory of structural change will lead to a less materials intensive or 'dematerialized' economy in which fewer resources are used in generating each unit of GDP.

It has long been commonplace to argue that structural change in economies, technological progress and materials and energy substitutions will tend to compensate for a depletion of natural resources (Tilton, 1986). The 'intensity of use' hypothesis which suggests that a de-linking between resource intensity and growth in higher income economies emerged in the 1970s and was supported by a number of empirical studies (Malenbaum, 1978; Jänicke et al., 1989; Bernardini and Galli, 1993). In the early and mid-1990s there was a flowering of econometric research which purported to show that there was an 'inverted U' relationship (an Environmental Kuznets Curve, EKC) between levels of per capita income and a wide range of indicators of environmental quality and performance (Grossman and Kreuger, 1995; Seldon and Song, 1994; Shafik, 1994; Holtz-Eakin and Seldon, 1995). According to this hypothesis, economies passed through a phase of high resource intensity and environmental damage before further growth became decoupled from resource use and damage to the environment. At the same time, much effort was devoted to mapping the physical scale and throughput of national, regional and local economies (compare Baccini and Brunner, 1991; Wernick and Ausubel, 1995; Adriaanse et al., 1997). All of these studies appear to confirm that for a variety of environmental and resource use indicators, a process of relative decoupling (fewer natural resources are used in the creation of each unit of wealth) does occur at higher incomes. However, while some relative decoupling has certainly occurred, in absolute terms many industrialized economies are still 'materializing' because rates of decoupling are overwhelmed by rates of growth. There is also evidence that more resource-intensive activities have been displaced to less developed economies, so increasing the 'rucksack' of more developed economies (Matthews, 2000).

The EKC/declining intensity of use hypothesis has been criticized on a number of grounds. First, there has been controversy over its empirical validity (Stern and Common, 2001) and universality. There are also striking examples of indicators that appear to remain linked to growth (waste and carbon dioxide emissions, for instance). It is clear that while there may be a link between income and environmental quality, the specification of the threshold or the levels of income at which decoupling starts to occur varies greatly between studies (Moomaw and Unruh, 1997). The predictive value of the EKC hypothesis is therefore questionable. There is also evidence that the overall intensity of resource use in highly developed economies - their 'throughput intensity' – may go through periods of growth as well as decline (de Bruyn, 1998): that is, there may be re-linking between economic growth and resource use. In addition, there is evidence that changing trade patterns have allowed developed economies to switch to value and service intensive modes of production whilst importing many of their manufactured goods. This criticism is closely linked to the concepts of 'ecological footprints' (Wackernagel and Rees, 1996) and 'environmental space' (McLaren et al., 1998). Finally, the EKC hypothesis has been criticized for its treatment of technical change (Pearson, 1994; Ekins, 1997). By taking income as the primary factor explaining the environmental performance of economies, no explicit allowance is made for technical change or for the impacts of environmental and other policies.

Efficiency and Mitigation Effects

Technology plays an important role in enabling the transformation of resource inputs into outputs, and in modifying the environmental impacts of production and consumption. For many analysts interested in technology and the environment, the key question is how invention, innovation and diffusion can be induced through the imposition of environmental requirements either directly (for example, through technology-based standards) or indirectly (for example, through the imposition of environmental taxes or subsidies).[2] This requires an understanding of technological changes relevant to the environment, and knowledge of how these changes may be influenced by external shaping factors. In fact this definition of the problem may be too constraining since many technical changes with apparently beneficial environmental effects are not the outcome of environmentally-motivated actions, but are the unintended result of changes in technology that have occurred for other reasons. For instance, better environmental performance may be the unintended outcome of cost- or labour-saving changes in production. Berkhout et al. (2000) found that in the European pulp and paper and PVC sectors, across many dimensions of environmental performance, the primary drivers of environmental performance improvement over time were incremental technical changes that occurred as a result of interactions between innovations in abatement techniques, processes and products generated as a result of normal problem-solving activity within firms and by a mixture of market and regulatory pressures.

Nevertheless, most analysis has been concerned broadly with how specifically 'environmental pressures' influence technical changes. In seeking to examine the factors that shape such changes, we separate our discussion into a consideration first of invention and innovation (the generation and commercialization of new knowledge and techniques) of cleaner technologies, and second of their diffusion (the adoption of available techniques in the market).[3]

Innovation

The economics debate about innovation and the environment has centred around arguments about whether relative price changes of pollution or resource inputs can induce innovation, and about how technical change can be made endogenous (rather than being made available spontaneously as an exogenous factor) in environment–technology models (Grubler et al., 1999). These models seek to portray the development and diffusion of new technologies, their costs, and their environmental and employment effects. On the first question, the empirical evidence for environmentally-induced innovation is rather sketchy. Lanjouw and Mody (1996) found that there was a strong association between expenditures on pollution abatement as a result of stronger regulatory pressure and the rate of patenting in related technology fields. However, this type of analysis is hampered by definitional problems (for instance, what is an environmental expenditure? Is price or a technology standard a better signal to innovating firms?), and by the problem of understanding causality (is an environmental expenditure a response to 'pressure', or is it the outcome of a competitive strategy of the firm?). Perhaps more seriously, the framing of the problem of innovation merely as a response to changes in relative costs of factors of production (the costs of resources and pollution prevention among them) appears to ignore many important aspects of innovation processes. In particular, this approach does not deal with the essential conditions of uncertainty, and boundedness and path dependency that are a feature of technological accumulation.

Central to research on technology–environment modelling over the past ten years have been the related questions of how to represent learning effects and uncertainty in research and development (Grubb, 1996b). The debate has important implications for environmental policy since these models can be used to make predictions about the likely future costs and benefits of investing in more environmentally-resource-efficient technologies. In climate policy an important debate developed about whether to invest early or late in new low-carbon energy technologies that are not yet commercially competitive (wind power, photovoltaics, hydrogen fuel cells and biomass, for instance). Models treating technical change as exogenous tend to suggest that abatement policies should be delayed because the benefits are realized in the long term. Models treating technical change as endogenous come to the opposite conclusion. Historical evidence shows clearly that R&D and practical experience in the early phases of commercialization lead to learning, lowering costs and improving performance of new technologies. Through learning, technologies become more competitive in the market, opening the way to their broader diffusion. A simple expression of this process is the 'learning rate' – the rate at which prices for a technology fall with a doubling of installed capacity. Historically, energy technologies have displayed learning rates of 10–20 per cent (see Figure 9.1).

But even though learning clearly does occur in documented cases of successful technologies, there are also many examples of promising technologies that have failed to be widely adopted. Uncertainty about the future – about the learning rate, about the final performance of a technology, about the final costs, about the (economic and environmental) costs and benefits of competing technologies, and about social expectations for a clean environment – are endemic, unavoidable and serious. Major new technologies take time to develop (25 years in the case of flue gas desulphurization, Balzheiser and Yaeger, 1987), and once they become commercially available the rate at which they can substitute for existing capital stock may be slow. For instance, paper-making machines may have operating lives of 30 years or more, with major re-builds every 10–15 years. Anderson et al. (2001) argue that these problems of uncertain costs, environmental benefits and outcomes

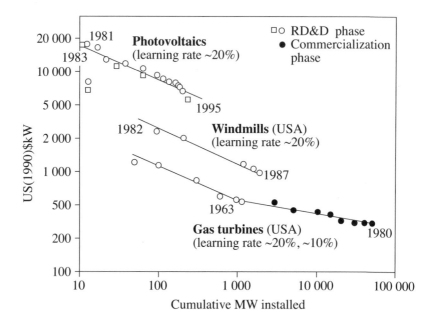

Source: Grubler, Nakicenovic and Victor (1999), p. 254.

Figure 9.1   Learning curves for three electricity generation technologies

of technical change suggest that what matters is the path of policy and market inducements that shape processes of technological accumulation and adjustment. Static assessments of costs and benefits that assume a knowledge of the long-term 'end point' of innovation processes, underestimate the economic and wider social value of investments in environmental innovation, and overlook opportunities to deal with environmental problems sooner.

The deepening recognition of uncertainty and the gradualness of technological accumulation has produced a further insight. Under conditions of uncertainty, firms and societies more generally hedge risks by investing in portfolios of new technologies that may be potentially useful (Mansfield et al., 1977). The greater the uncertainty, the more diverse the range of technological options that should, in principle, be supported. This broad portfolio of alternatives may include the improvement of already available technologies, as well as investments in completely new techniques and systems. Even if there is no prior knowledge of the long-term usefulness of a specific new technology, each new option that is made available has a value (an option value) because it expands the universe of approaches that are available to adapt to market opportunities and environmental problems as they arise. Maintaining a diverse range of options and limiting commercial and policy commitments to any single technology is therefore rational under conditions of greater uncertainty. Finding the balance between a perceived level of uncertainty and maintenance of a requisite variety of options is far from straightforward (for a review: see Stirling, 1998). Differing views will exist about the degree of economic, social and environmental uncertainty of competing technological and institutional systems.

Besides these debates about short- and long-term innovative responses to environmental pressures, there have also been debates informed more by science and engineering about the nature of the technical changes that are necessary to mitigate the environmental burdens of economic activity. This literature has emphasized the need for a more 'systems' view of production and consumption and its links to the biophysical world, arguing that technological systems as a whole can be reconfigured and adapted to be more environmentally sustainable (for an early articulation of these arguments, see Ayres and Kneese, 1969). Much of the work in this tradition has drawn inspiration from examples of resource use in nature,[4] developing notions of 'industrial metabolism' (Frosch and Gallapoulos, 1992) and 'industrial ecology' (Socolow et al., 1994; Ayres and Ayres, 1996) in which industrial systems are conceptualized as consuming and discarding energy and material resources extracted from natural environments. By ordering industrial systems with the objective of high overall environmental efficiency, not just according to contingent criteria imposed by the needs of short-term economic efficiency, general welfare could be reconciled with the sustainability of key environmental services, such as biodiversity, the global climate, global nutrient cycles, and so on. Underlying this perspective is a forward-looking, instrumental and 'preventionist' approach to the management of environmental burdens. It argues that, through better design and organization of industrial processes, waste can be eliminated and greater final economic and social value generated from a given resource use. 'End of pipe' abatement of pollution and the treatment of wastes are regarded as signs of inefficiency which can be overcome only through innovation of industrial processes (Jackson, 1993; Freeman et al., 1992), products and entire technological regimes – the notion of 'systems innovations'.

One of the main conclusions to be drawn from this analysis is that innovation management in firms will tend, under conditions of environmental pressure, to become oriented towards novel processes and products, moving away from incremental improvements and innovations in abatement techniques and waste management (Howes et al., 1997). The logic of this 'micro' technological transition is that by promoting process innovation technological systems can be reconfigured, bringing resource productivity and competitiveness gains, while also improving environmental efficiency more sharply. This emphasis on prevention has been influential in policy debates during the 1990s (for instance in framing the 1995 European integrated pollution prevention and control (IPPC) directive). However, evidence of this induced generic shift of technological effort in companies towards process innovation is hard to find. Nor is it clear that the most rapid or effective approach to improving the environmental profile of an industry will always be through novel process or product innovations (Berkhout, 2002). Radical innovations are, by definition, further removed from current practice, market demand and institutional routines. They tend to be less well-defined and potentially more disruptive, and may fall outside those options that are considered feasible or desirable, partly because of the multiple and systemic impacts of their adoption.

The notion of environmentally-driven technological transitions has been extended by Kemp and Rotmans (2001) to include broader-scale shifts that can be induced in linked market niches, technological regimes and socio-technical landscapes creating, over periods of decades, more sustainable industrial systems. This more institutionalist approach starts from the observation that technologies are embedded within and co-evolve with markets and governance systems. Changing individual sub-components of a technological system is likely to be both difficult and perhaps fruitless if the larger system is left unaddressed. The scale of analysis (and of policy intervention) therefore needs to change from the specific to the general, focusing primarily on the conditions that permit more sustainable assemblages of technologies and institutions to emerge.

In these overlapping and still unresolved debates about the accumulation of technological knowledge there remain a number of important open questions. First, how long and under what conditions does support for a technology need to be sustained to enable learning to take place? Second, is it possible through policy interventions to accelerate the learning rate, so bringing forward the time of commercialization of more sustainable technologies? Third, what are the conditions under which a new technology can overcome the inherent economic and institutional advantages that a dominant, already embedded, technology possesses? While there is much empirical evidence of technological transitions, such as a 'primary fuels succession' from wood, to coal, to oil and gas, and, for a period, to nuclear (Grubler and Nakicenovic, 1991), the conditions under which one technology achieves dominance over another are often shaped by political and institutional factors, as much as by economic factors, and cannot be assumed to follow predictable and stable patterns in future.

Diffusion

Much literature on technology change concerns the uptake and diffusion of knowledge, techniques and management approaches (for a review: Lissoni and Metcalfe, 1994). And much of this is dominated by the 'paradox' that proven and cost-effective technical solutions are not more widely and rapidly adopted. That is, much analysis is devoted to trying to understand obstacles or barriers that stand in the way of the substitution of incumbent technologies with newer technologies that are perceived as being economically and environmentally superior. A range of possible explanations has been developed for this gap between innovation and diffusion. Although the failure of apparently effective and economic technologies is a feature of many markets, greater analytical focus is given to this problem in the case of sustainable technologies because of the greater normative expectations associated with this class of technologies. Non-market constituencies promote sustainable technologies and may continue to promote them even when they fail to be taken up and applied. Sorrell et al. (2000) offer a useful typology of this literature, identifying three disciplinary perspectives: the economic; the behavioural; and the organizational (see Table 9.1).

Among neo-classical economic perspectives, a key distinction found in the literature is between market barriers and market failures. Market barriers are factors that explain why an apparently cost-effective option is not adopted. Market failures are that subset of barriers that justify public policy intervention to encourage more economically efficient diffusion of technologies. Market barriers are therefore obstacles that may be the result of rationale behaviour (for instance, because the new technology imposes hidden costs on the adopter), the removal of which through policy intervention would not

Table 9.1 Perspectives on barriers to diffusion of more efficient and cleaner technologies

Perspective	Examples	Actors	Theory
Economic	Imperfect information, asymmetric information, hidden costs, risk	Individuals and organizations conceived of as rational and utility maximising	Neo-classical economics
Behavioural	Inability to process information, form of information, trust, inertia	Individuals have bounded rationality with non-financial motives and a variety of social influences	Transaction cost economics, psychology, decision theory
Organizational	Energy manager lacks power and influence; organizational culture lead to neglect of energy/ environmental issues	Organizations conceived of as social systems influenced by goals, routines, culture, power structures	Organizational theory

Source: Sorrell et al. (2000).

generate wider social benefits. Flowing from this distinction is the argument that policy intervention is justified only in cases identified as market failures, when resources are inefficiently allocated despite the existence of well functioning markets with fully rational actors. Classic market failures include: incomplete markets (such as when external environmental costs are not represented in the prices of goods, so that there are no clear benefits to adoption of cleaner technologies among users); imperfect competition (such as when dominant firms misuse their market power); and imperfect and asymmetric information (cases in which one party, such as the customer or the regulator, is prevented from seeing the whole picture).

Many obstacles to the diffusion of environmentally-superior technologies can be understood using these ideas. The market may transmit insufficient information about the environmental or energy performance of different technologies (for instance, because these are features that are not immediately tangible to the consumer), or the costs of acquiring this information for the customer may be higher than for other aspects of a product's performance (more tangible aspects of a product's functionality). Environmental perform-ance is rarely of immediate utility to the consumer, and in many cases 'green claims' about the superior environmental performance of a product will not be directly experienced or validated by the consumer. The exception is where savings accrue to the consumer, such as in energy-saving devices. Many sources of 'friction' therefore stand in the way of markets selecting apparently more sustainable technologies.

But the assumption that actors are rational has also been criticized as a poor representation of actual behaviour. Alternative 'behavioural' perspectives on barriers emphasize bounded rationality, arguing that actors are subject to constraints on attention, habits, resources and the capacity to make use of information that may be available to them (Cyert and March, 1963). For the most part, individuals and organizations will be concerned with their core activities and engage in a familiar set of routines to solve problems that may arise. Organizations do not evaluate each decision taking all possible factors into account. This is because information about benefits, risks and costs is not available, because large uncertainties about outcomes cloud technology choice decisions and because actors employ 'rules of thumb' to deal quickly with complex choices. The economic rationality assumed in neo-classical analysis does not, according to this perspective, match the behavioural rationality of institutionally-situated actors. The third, and least well-defined perspective, is rooted in organizational theory (for review see: Morgan, 1986). This perspective stresses power and the extent to which power relationships within organizations affect the ability of individuals to influence decisions, the extent to which values, principles and norms of behaviour encourage or discourage investments in more sustainable technologies.

Beyond interpretations focused on the motivations and knowledge of actors making technology choice decisions, the notions of technology 'lock in' and path dependency are also important in understanding the diffusion of more environmentally-efficient technologies. Lock-in implies that once a technique or approach has been widely adopted, technical, economic, institutional and other barriers will significantly raise the costs of switching to an alternative technology (Hirsch and Gillespie, 2001). From this perspective, the barriers literature can be seen as analysing the landscape of economic, behavioural and organizational costs of switching between technologies. As with all structural explanations, however, the problem for this approach is that it is poor at explaining how switching costs may be lowered so that opportunities to breach or overcome barriers emerge. Even subtle changes in incentive structures and attitudes to new technologies can quite suddenly change adoption behaviour, revealing in the process the highly contingent and constructed nature of barriers and switching costs. In other words, barriers and switching costs should not be seen as fixed and immutable facts, but as mobile phenomena and the outcome of specific institutional interests and practices.

All major technological systems acquire inertia as they become embedded and matched to prevailing economic and institutional settings. To be diffused successfully, new technologies need to be able to subvert or redirect the inertia of incumbent technologies and become imprinted on prevailing socio-technical landscapes. Technological regimes, once established, can be very persistent. To give a few examples: the Fourdrinier process for paper making was developed in the 1840s; the internal combustion engine was developed in the 1890s; while catalytic cracking of hydrocarbon molecules was industrialized in the 1940s. Over time all of these processes have been refined and altered leading to changes in their environmental performance. Transitions towards more sustainable socio-technical regimes may involve the gradual, emergent replacement of one regime for another, or they may involve more abrupt and serial substitutions (as in computing and telecommunications).

THE ROLE OF POLICY: INDUCING AND MODULATING

Our discussion about the role of policy returns to the distinction drawn above between two competing traditions in technology–environment studies. On the one hand, the neo-classical approach suggests that by changing incentives and disincentives to correct for market failures, markets can drive desirable forms of technical change. This view emphasizes the responsiveness of economic activity and the opportunities for policy to induce 'optimal' levels and forms of technical change. The best signal from this perspective is price. The role for policy is therefore to ensure that the price of resources and the use of environmental services properly reflect the economic value of externalities (the prices are right). The price signal will induce an innovatory response amongst firms and consumers.

On the other hand, the neo-Schumpeterian approach, stressing uncertainty and the importance of routine behaviours in the innovation and adoption process, argues that policy signals rarely have clear and predictable impacts, partly because these signals are the outcome of institutionally-situated negotiations and expectations. They resemble less a message transmitted between a speaker and a listener, and seem more like commonly-held ideas that emerge in a debate involving many voices, and moreover a debate that is unfolding more or less continuously. As with all debates, there are conventions to be upheld and differing interpretations about the significance of competing claims. In this characterization, innovation is seen as a distributed process with inputs of knowledge and resources distributed among many participants linked to each other in networks of relationships (Soete and Arundel, 1995). In these complex institutional settings, the role of regulation is seen as one of modulating the process of technological change and accumulation (Kemp et al., 2000). From this perspective, policy needs to adopt a broader approach, focusing not so much on the technologies themselves but on the social processes and institutional factors that give rise to and shape technologies. This view suggests that economic activity is less susceptible to the influence of traditional forms of policy and that decision making commonly takes place under conditions of considerable uncertainty for both regulator and regulated. Alternative policy approaches are therefore called for, particularly for those long-term, more systemic environmental problems that traditional policy instruments do not properly address.

Traditional Approaches, Contemporary Developments

Although historically governments have tended to favour the application of command and control regulations, it is now widely accepted that there is a need to explore the potential of other forms of policy intervention that will encourage, enable and enforce change (Majone, 1976; Weale, 1992). In part this interest in the potential of other forms of intervention reflects aspects of the neo-classical view that command and control regulations are an inefficient way of realizing environmental objectives. Other than in those instances where efficiency is seen to be less important than efficacy, as is often the case when 'guaranteed' minimum standards have to be introduced, neo-classical analysts generally argue that it is better to introduce instruments that establish dynamic incentives for innovation and to create the market conditions that will allow rational actors to respond to these incentives.

However, evolution in policy and changes in the broader mode of governance also reflect the view that governments are often unwilling or unable to impose their will from above. As Hanf and O'Toole (1992) suggest:

> Not so long ago, the standard image was that of the 'can-do', nearly omnipotent state. More recently, the picture has altered to one of an overloaded and perhaps chronically weakened system of governance, one which [has] but a limited ability to direct the course of the broad-scale action needed to address policy difficulties. (Hanf and O'Toole, 1992.)

Whether by default (because of the lack of government capacity) or by design (following a reshaping of governance – the 'facilitative state'), many governments have started to move beyond their traditional reliance on the direct application of command and control regulations. However, in most instances new policy instruments have been adopted to complement rather than replace command and control regulations. Alongside the wider adoption of 'classical' instruments there has been a significant increase in the implementation of voluntary or negotiated agreements, in information-based instruments and in the development of new 'hybrid' approaches that seek to combine the better attributes of the different instruments. Thus, in most settings changes in environmental policy have been more along the lines of 're-regulation' than 'de-regulation' (Majone, 1990).

The absence of a capacity for control and the desire to introduce forms of intervention that work *with* rather than *against* the grain of the market has also led to the emergence of more co-operative relations between the public and the private sectors and between the regulators and the regulated. Some suggest that under some circumstances such co-operation can lead to regulatory capture (Ayres and Braithwaite, 1992) as only those issues that can be addressed in economically acceptable ways will be the source of public and private attention. However, others argue that more co-operative approaches to policy can offer the public sector new opportunities to mobilize the resources of the private sector in order to realize environmental policy goals (Ostrom, 1990; Glasbergen, 1998; Lahusen, 2000).

Despite the changing context for environmental governance and the significance of policy innovations it is still relatively unusual for governments to adopt a mix of different policy instruments as part of a concerted effort to stimulate technological change. This lack of co-ordination within environmental policy is a significant failing as it is apparent that when various complementary conditions and signals are in place a 'regulatory space' (Hancher and Moran, 1989) can emerge where technological change can more readily take place. Indeed, through the co-ordinated or 'integrated' application of a range of different policy instruments, the influence of individual instruments can be reinforced. In essence, synergies can emerge in the interplay between the different instruments that mean that the influence of the policy framework as a whole can be greater than that of the sum of its parts (Smith and Sorrell, 2001).

Although most attention has been placed on policy design, it is now widely accepted that the influence of environmental policy depends not only on its design but also on its implementation. Consequently, governments have explored new approaches to policy implementation. While there has been considerable debate about the need to deliver more innovation-friendly regulations (see Porter and van der Linde, 1995; Wallace, 1995; Klemmer, 1999; Hemmelskamp et al., 2000; Anderson et al., 2001), it can be difficult to balance the need to establish strong imperatives through hierarchical control with the desire to build the capacities for compliance through co-operation in the implementation process (see Gouldson and Murphy, 1998; Murphy and Gouldson, 2000). The 'responsive regulation' concept proposed by Ayres and

Braithwaite (1992) suggests that different strategies can be adopted in the implementation process to take account of variations in the capacity and commitment of regulated actors (see also Gunningham and Grabosky, 1999). By tailoring the implementation process so that regulations distinguish between leaders and laggards, environmental regulations have the potential to exert a much greater influence on innovation and technological change. Of course this potential is likely to be significantly enhanced if regulations are applied in combination with other, complementary policy instruments.

While it is important to acknowledge that national policy styles can be deeply embedded, resistant to change and limiting the capacity of regulators to be responsive, considerable potential for policy learning often exists (Granovetter, 1985). One of the institutional consequences of processes of policy learning is that they can create or extend 'regulatory spaces' by creating new networks of actors and new incentive structures. This broadening base of actors and instruments is generally seen as functional to more effective innovation–environment policy. However, as part of this debate, different conceptualizations of the environment–economy inter-relationship have emerged in recent years that describe and analyse contemporary policy developments and to prescribe different policy responses.

Two related but different conceptualizations are relevant here, namely those relating to the free-market oriented concept of eco-efficiency (see DeSimone and Popoff, 1997; OECD, 1998) and those relating to the more interventionist concept of ecological modernization (see Gouldson and Murphy, 1997 or for a broader debate see Young, 2000 or Mol and Sonnenfeld, 2000). Although interpretations of these concepts naturally differ, both emphasize the potential for markets and/or governments to stimulate environmentally beneficial forms of technological change. In other words they argue that regulatory spaces exist where there is a coincidence of (or at least the lack of conflict between) environmental and economic interests within the market (eco-efficiency) and that they can be created or extended with the aid of enabling forms of government intervention.

While some environmentalists have welcomed the possibilities that are associated with these conceptions, they also recognize that these policy discourses can serve to split the green lobby (Gouldson and Murphy, 1997; Jacobs, 1999). As the pragmatists in the environmental movement play for what they can get in the 'realpolitik' of the short to medium term, the radical green movement can be seen to have been marginalized from many policy debates because of its scepticism about the longer term value of concepts such as eco-efficiency or ecological modernization (McLaren, 1998). This scepticism stems from a variety of significant misgivings relating to the world view that is associated with these concepts.

At the most basic level, many environmentalists object because by focusing on discrete issues and particular technologies little is done to challenge broader institutional commitments and structures. Indeed, it can be argued that these perspectives serve to legitimize and reinforce the growth logic of industrial capitalism by suggesting that economic growth can be reconciled with environmental protection. Critically, many environmentalists argue that technical and associated organizational change offers only a partial and temporary resolution to underlying problems: partial because they offer only to protect those aspects of the environment that can be addressed without challenging social and economic structures; and temporary because easy options (low hanging fruit) that exist will diminish as structural conflicts between environment and economy re-emerge. Thus, in some senses the environmental movement continues to be reluctant to be co-opted into the mainstream policy debate as long as it confines itself to offering technological solutions to what it sees as fundamental problems of over-consumption and the abuse of environmental values. This said, it is worth noting that rather than seeing themselves as pragmatic insiders or radical outsiders, many environmental groups have sought to be both and to engage pragmatically in the short term whilst maintaining longer-term or more radical objectives.

CONCLUSION: REFRAMING ENVIRONMENTAL PROBLEMS AND THE ROLE OF TECHNOLOGY

We have argued that debates about technology, policy and the environment are characterized by two distinct theoretical traditions, each with specific conse-quences for the framing of research questions and for the policy conclusions that may be drawn. Debates within each tradition and between them have been influenced by a growing awareness that the social framing of environmental problems themselves has changed. As environmental problems have been reconceived, so the role attributed to technology in causing and adapting to environmental change has been transformed. We argue therefore that notions of environment, technology and policy are intimately linked to each other, changes in one influencing changes in the others.

Traditionally, environmental problems were conceived of as tangible and local (smogs and fish kills). The causes of environmental and health damage could be identified and typically these were point sources at industrial production sites. The technological response was also well established and tended to focus on the dual strategy of abatement and dispersal. Environmental systems were thought of as being resilient below given thresholds of harm, so the problem for environmental policy and management was to calibrate damage thresholds and to modify industrial processes to ensure they were not being overstepped. Most policy systems responded to this expression of the technology–environment problematique by imposing uniform technology-based emissions limits for industrial processes, which often became the subject of case-by-case re-negotiation, taking into account the specific economic circumstances of industrial operators ('not entailing excessive cost…'). Welfare economics has gradually come to play a growing role in informing the formulation of policy problems and choices within this framework, leading to a growing role for cost-benefit analysis and the consensus that market-based instruments provide the most efficient means of inducing technical change.

This technology–environment–policy programme has been disrupted in a number of ways over the past decade or more, particularly in the industrialized world. Many environmental problems are no longer conceived of as being predominantly tangible and local. As the scale and scope of anthropogenic intrusion in environmental processes is seen to have deepened, so the analysis of causes has also changed. No longer is it possible to identify specific sources of harm because harm appears to emerge from many sources that are widely distributed. Critically, for the set of environmental problems termed 'regional' and 'global', sources of harm appear to interact so that no clear link between the sources of harm and specific evidence of environmental damage can sometimes be established. The link between cause and harm may be uncertain because environmental processes are incompletely understood or because they are inherently variable. Systems approaches to modelling environmental change that stress complexity, non-linearity and threshold effects reflect this. For many of the most serious environmental problems, the new science of the environment rarely provides the clarity and confidence about causes and effects available for 'old' environmental problems that are tangible and local.

Uncertainties also exist about the technological causes of environmental change, and these affect ideas about the governability of technologies and technological systems for environmental ends. The problem of governability emerges because of the changing nature of states and due to an apparent mismatch in the political and temporal scope of 'new' environmental problems and the political and temporal scope of traditional structures of governance. The problem of political scope has been incompletely addressed through the internationalization of environmental policy. For instance, the governance of technologies has played an important role in international environmental agreements (access to CFC substitutes was critical to broad participation in the Montreal Protocol, and the Clean Development Mechanism under the Kyoto Protocol). The problem of temporal scope is more difficult to address and goes to the heart of the problem of technology policy. Responses to larger, more complex and more uncertain environmental problems are likely to include larger and more deep-seated changes. In general, this has been taken to mean the innovation and adoption of radically new technologies and the associated systems-level changes which they precipitate. For instance, the widespread diffusion of renewable energy sources is likely to require major restructuring of energy systems and infrastructures. These kinds of changes are complex, operate across multiple scales, occur over longer periods of time and will have unknown and unexpected outcomes.

Under these conditions of uncertainty about causes and effects, and given the mismatch between environmental problems and their governability, the terms and instruments of policy are altered. If the preferred technological choice or pathway is no longer clear, or if the economic costs and benefits (and their distribution) of alternatives cannot be calculated with any certainty, then the perspectives and instruments of policy also need to change. Governance of technology through policy now becomes more tentative and adaptive. Greater emphasis is placed on policy learning (from experiments by others, from past successes and failures). Learning implies a much stronger role for monitoring and evaluation of the impacts of technology and of the impacts of policy on technology. Rather than positing a final objective, more importance comes to be placed on general features of a technological pathway (reversibility, flexibility, robustness) and the general principles that are applied in the purposive social shaping of technology (including precaution). The institutional context of the technology also comes more sharply into view, partly because learning takes place in institutions and partly because the broader the scope of the anticipated technical changes, the greater the importance of institutional settings in inducing, shaping and modulating change.

NOTES

1. This characterization does not have a clear place for researchers in the neo-classical tradition who are seeking to include learning effects and uncertainty into the analysis of the diffusion of cleaner technologies (for example: Grubb, 1996; Gritsevskyi and Nakicenovic, 2000; Grubler, Nakicenovic and Victor, 1999).
2. In using the term 'induced' we mean something wider than is implied in the induced innovation hypothesis stated by Hicks (1932) to the effect that 'a change in the relative prices of factors of production is itself a spur to invention ... directed to economising the use of a factor which has become relatively expensive.' For us, 'induced' implies all forms of external pressures on economic agents, whether through prices or other sources, that are intended to change their environmental performance.
3. Skea (1995) suggests a useful taxonomy of cleaner technologies: pollution control; waste management; recycling; waste minimization; clean technology; measurement and monitoring; and cleaner products.
4. Albeit often rather idealized ones, see Chadwick (1998).

REFERENCES

Abramowitz, M. (1956), 'Resource and output trends in the U.S. since 1870', *American Economic Review Papers and Procs*, 46, 5–23.

Adriaanse, A., S. Bringezu, A. Hammond, Y. Moriguchi, E. Rodenburg, D. Rogich and H. Schütz (1997), *Resource Flows: The Material Basis of Industrial Economies*, Washington, DC: World Resource Institute.

Anderson, D. and W. Cavendish (1999), *Dynamic Simulation and Environmental Policy Analysis: Beyond Comparative Statics and the Environmental Kuznets Curve*, London: T.H. Huxley School, Imperial College.

Anderson, D., C. Clark, T. Foxon, R. Gross and M. Jacobs (2001), *Innovation and the Environment: Challenges and Policy Options for the UK*, London: Imperial College/Fabian Society/ESRC.

Arthur, W.B. (1989), 'Competing technologies, increasing returns and lock-in by historical events', *The Economic Journal*, 99, 116–31.

Ausubel, J. (1996), 'The liberation of the environment', in J. Ausubel and H.D. Langford (eds), *Technological Trajectories and the Human Environment*, Washington, DC: National Academy Press, 1–13.

Ayres, R.U. and L.W. Ayres (1996), *Industrial Ecology: Towards Closing the Materials Cycle*, Cheltenham, UK and Northampton, MA: Edward Elgar.

Ayres, R. and J. Braithwaite (1992), *Responsive Regulation: Transcending the De-regulation Debate*, Oxford: Oxford University Press.

Ayres, R.U. and A.V. Kneese (1969), 'Production, consumption and externalities', *American Economic Review*, 59 (3), 282–97.

Baccini, P. and P.H. Brunner (1991), *The Metabolism of the Anthroposphere*, Berlin: Springer.

Balzheiser, R.E. and K.E. Yeager (1987), 'Coal-fired power plants of the future', *Scientific American*, 257 (3), 100–107.

Berkhout, F. (2002), 'Technological regimes, path dependency and the environment', *Global Environmental Change*, 12: 1–4.

Berkhout, F., M. Almemark, L. Lindfors, K. Holm-Mueller, I. Hanhoff-Stemping, A. Smith and H. Stripple (2000), *Sustainability, Competitiveness and Technical Change (SCOTCH): Final Report to the European Commission*, Brighton: SPRU-Science and Technology Policy Research, 2 vols.

Bernadini, O. and R. Galli (1993), 'Dematerialisation: long term trends in the intensity of use of materials and energy', *Futures*, May, 431–48.

Chadwick, M. (1998), 'Substance flows through environment and society', in P. Vellinga, F. Berkhout and J. Gupta (eds), *Managing a Material World: Perspectives in Industrial Ecology*, Dordrecht: Kluwer Academic Publishers.

Cyert, R.M. and J.G. March (1963), *A Behavioral Theory of the Firm*, Englewood Cliffs, NJ: Prentice-Hall.

David, P.A. (1985), 'Clio and the Economics of QWERTY', *American Economic Review*, 76, 332–7.

de Bruyn, S. (1998), 'Dematerialisation and rematerialisation', in P. Vellinga, F. Berkhout and J. Gupta (eds), *Managing a Material World: Perspectives in Industrial Ecology*, Dordrecht: Kluwer Academic Publishers, 147–64.

DeSimone, L. and F. Popoff (1997), *Eco-efficiency: The Business Link to Sustainable Development*, Cambridge, MA: MIT Press.

Dosi, G. (1988), 'The nature of the innovative process', in G. Dosi, C. Freeman,

R, Nelson, G. Silverberg and L. Soete (eds), *Technical Change and Economic Theory*, London: Pinter, pp. 221–38.

Ekins, P. (1997), 'The Kuznets Curve for the environment and economic growth: examining the evidence', *Environment and Planning, A*, 29, 805–30.

Esty, D.C. (2001), 'Information age environmental protection', *OECD Observer*, 226/227, 68–70.

Fleming, D. (1997), 'Tradable quotas: using information technology to cap national carbon emissions', *European Environment*, 7, 139–48.

Fransman, M. (1983), 'Explaining technical change – a case-study in the philosophy of science', *Nature*, 305 (5936), 745–6.

Freeman, H., T. Harten, J. Springer, P. Randall, A. Curran and K. Stone (1992), 'Industrial pollution prevention', *Journal of Air and Waste Management Association*, 42 (5), 618–56.

Frosch, R.A. and N.E. Gallapoulos (1992), 'Strategies for manufacturing', *Scientific American*, 261 (3), 144–52.

Glasbergen, P. (ed.) (1998), *Cooperative Environmental Governance*, Dordrecht: Kluwer.

Gouldson, A. and J. Murphy (1997), 'Ecological modernization: restructuring industrial economies', in M. Jacobs (ed.), *Greening the Millenium? The New Politics of the Environment*, Oxford: Blackwell.

Gouldson, A. and J. Murphy (1998), *Regulatory Realities: The Implementation and Impact of Industrial Environmental Regulation*, London: Earthscan.

Granovetter, M. (1985), 'Economic action and social structure: the problem of embeddedness', *American Journal of Sociology*, pp. 481–510.

Gritsevskyi, A. and N. Nakicenovic (2000), 'Modelling uncertainty of induced technological change', *Energy Policy*, 28, 907–21.

Grossman, G.M. and A.B. Kreuger (1995), 'Economic growth and the environment', *Quarterly Journal of Economics*, 110, 353–78.

Grubb, M. (1996a), 'Technologies, energy systems and the timing of CO_2 emissions abatement: an overview of the economic issues', in N. Nakicenovic, W.D. Nordhaus, R. Richels and F.L. Toth (eds), *Climate Change: Integrating Science, Economics and Policy,* Laxenburg: International Institute for Applied Systems Analysis, pp. 249–70.

Grubb, M. (1996b), 'The economics of changing course', *Energy Policy*, 23, 1–14.

Grubler, A. and N. Nakicenovic (1991), 'Long waves, technological diffusion and substitution', *Review*, 14 (2), 313–42.

Grubler, A., N. Nakicenovic and D.G. Victor (1999), 'Dynamics of energy technologies and global change', *Energy Policy*, 27, 247–80.

Gunningham, N. and P. Grabosky (1999), *Smart Regulation: Designing Environmental Policy*, Oxford: Clarendon Press.

Hemmelskamp, J., K. Rennings, and F. Leone (eds) (2000), *Innovation-oriented Environmental Regulations: Theoretical Approaches and Empirical Analysis*, Heidelberg: Physica-Verlag.

Hancher, L. and M. Moran (1989), *Capitalism, Culture and Economic Regulation*, Oxford: Clarendon Press.

Hanf, K. and L. O'Toole (1992), 'Revisiting old friends: networks, implementation structures and the management of inter-organisational relations', *European Journal of Political Research*, 21, 163–80.

Hicks, J. (1932), *The Theory of Wages*, London: Macmillan.

Hirsch, P.M. and J.J. Gillespie (2001), 'Unpacking path dependence: differential valuations accorded history across disciplines', in R. Garud and P. Karnoe, *Path Dependence and Creation*, Mahwah, NJ: Lawrence Erlbaum Associates, pp. 69–90.

Holtz-Eakin, D. and T. Seldon (1995), 'Stoking the fires? CO_2 emissions and economic growth', *Journal of Public Economics*, 57, 85–101.

Howes, R., J. Skea and B. Whelan (1997), *Clean and Competitive? Motivating Environmental Performance in Industry*, London: Earthscan.

Irwin, A. and B. Wynne (1996), *Misunderstanding Science? The Public Reconstruction of Science and Technology*, Cambridge/New York: Cambridge University Press.

Jackson, T. (ed.) (1993), *Clean Production Strategies: Developing Preventive Environmental Management in the Industrial Economy*, Boca Raton: CRC Press.

Jacobs, M. (1999), *Environmental Modernisation*, London: The Fabian Society.

Jaffe, A., S. Peterson and R. Stavins (1995), 'Environmental regulation and the competitiveness of U.S. manufacturing: what does the evidence tell us?', *Journal of Economic Literature*, 33, 132–63.

Jaffe, A.B., R.G. Newell and R.N. Stavins (2000), *Technological Change and the Environment*, Cambridge: National Bureau of Economic Research, Working Paper 7970.

Jänicke, M., H. Mönch, T. Ranneberg and U.E. Simonis (1989), 'Structural change and environmental impact. Empirical evidence on thirty-one countries in east and west', *Environmental Monitoring and Assessment*, 12 (2), 99–114.

Kemp, R. and J. Rotmans (2001), *The Management of the Co-evolution of Technical, Environmental and Social Systems*, Towards Environmental Innovation Systems Conference, Garmisch-Partenkirchen.

Kemp, R., K. Smith and G. Becher (2000), 'How should we study the relationship between environmental regulation and innovation?', in J. Hemmelskamp, K. Rennings and F. Leone (eds), *Innovation-Oriented Environmental Regulation*, Heidelberg: Springer-Verlag, pp. 43–66.

Klemmer, P. (ed.) (1999), *Innovation and Environment: Case Studies on Adaptive Behaviour in Society and the Economy*, Berlin: Analytica.

Lahusen, C. (2000), 'The good government: cooperative environmental regulation in a comparative perspective', *European Environment*, 10, 6, 253–64.

Lanjouw, J. and A. Mody (1996), 'Innovation and the international diffusion of environmentally responsive technology', *Research Policy*, 25: 549–71.

Lissoni, F. and J.S. Metcalfe (1994), 'Diffusion of innovation ancient and modern: a review of the main themes', in M. Dodgson and R. Rothwell (eds), *The Handbook of Industrial Innovation*, Cheltenham: Edward Elgar.

Lucas, R. (1988), 'On the mechanics of economic development', *Journal of Monetary Economics*, 22, 3–42.

Majone, G. (1976), 'Choice among policy instruments for pollution control', *Policy Analysis*, 2, 589–613.

Majone, G. (ed.) (1990), *Deregulation or Re-regulation? Regulatory Reform in Europe and the United States*, London: Pinter.

Malenbaum, W. (1978), *World Demand for Raw Materials in 1985 and 2000*, New York: McGraw-Hill.

Mansfield, E., J. Rapoport, A. Romeo, E. Villani, S. Wagner and F. Husic (1977), *The Production and Application of New Industrial Technology*, New York: W.W. Norton.

Matthews, E. (2000), *The Weight of Nations: Material Outflows from Industrial Economies*, Washington, DC: World Resources Institute, p. 126.

McLaren, D. (1998), *Tomorrow's World: Britain's Share in a Sustainable Future*, London: Friends of the Earth.

McLaren, D., S. Bullock and N. Yousuf (1998), *Tomorrow's World: Britain's Share in a Sustainable Future*, London: Earthscan.

Mol, A. and D. Sonnenfeld (eds) (2000), *Ecological Modernisation Around the World: Perspectives and Critical Debates*, London: Frank Cass.

Moomaw, W.R. and G.C. Unruh (1997), 'Are environmental Kuznets Curves misleading us? The case of CO_2 emissions', *Environmental and Development Economics*, 2, 451-63.

Morgan, G. (1986), *Images of Organization*, Beverly Hills/Newbury Park: Sage Publications.

Murphy, J. and A. Gouldson (2000), 'Integrating environment and economy through ecological modernisation? An assessment of the impact of environmental policy on industrial innovation', *Geoforum*, 31, 33-44.

Nelson, R. and S. Winter (1982), *An Evolutionary Theory of Economic Change*, Cambridge, MA and London: Belknap Press of Harvard University Press.

OECD (1998), *Eco-efficiency*, Paris: OECD.

Ostrom, E. (1990), *Governing the Commons: The Evolution of Institutions for Collective Action*, Cambridge: Cambridge University Press.

Pavitt, K. (1987), 'The objectives of technology policy', *Science and Public Policy*, 14 (4), 182-8.

Pearson, P.J.G. (1994), 'Energy, externalities and environmental quality: will development cure the ills it creates?', *Energy Studies Review*, 6 (3), 199-216.

Porter, M. (1991), 'America's green strategy', *Scientific American*, April.

Porter, M. and C. van der Linde (1995), 'Green and competitive: ending the stalemate', *Harvard Business Review*, 73, 5, September-October.

Rip, A. and R. Kemp (1998), 'Technological change', in S. Rayner and E.L. Malone, *Human Choices and Climate Change: Resources and Technology*, Columbus, Ohio: Battelle, 2.

Romer, P.M. (1986), 'Increasing returns and long run growth', *Journal of Political Economy*, 94, 1002-37.

Ruttan, V.W. (2000), *Technology, Growth and Environment: An Induced Innovation Perspective*, St Paul, MN: University of Minnesota Press.

Schumpeter, J. (1942), *Capitalism, Socialism and Democracy*, New York: Harper.

Seldon, T.M. and D. Song (1994), 'Environmental quality and development: is there a Kuznets Curve for air pollution emissions?', *Journal of Environmental Economics and Management*, 27 (2), 147-62.

Shackley, S. and B. Wynne (1995), 'Global Climate Change: The Mutual Construction of an Emergent Science-Policy Domain', *Science and Public Policy*, 22 (4), 218-30.

Shafik, N. (1994), 'Economic development and environmental quality: an econometric analysis', *Oxford Economic Papers*, 46, 757-73.

Simon, H.A. (1947), *Administrative Behaviour: A Study of Decision-making Processes in Administrative Organisation*, New York: Macmillan.

Skea, J. (1995), 'Environmental technology', in H. Folmer, H.L. Gabel and H. Opschoor, *Principles of Environmental and Resource Economics*, Aldershot: Edward Elgar.

Smith, A. and S. Sorrell (2001), 'Interaction between environmental policy instruments: carbon emissions trading and integrated pollution prevention and control', *International Journal of Environment and Pollution*, 15 (1), 22–41.

Socolow, R., C. Andrews, F. Berkhout and V. Thomas (eds) (1994), *Industrial Ecology and Global Change*, Cambridge: Cambridge University Press.

Soete, L. and A. Arundel (1995), 'European innovation policy for environmentally sustainable development: application of a systems model of technical change', *Journal of Public Policy*, 2, 2.

Solow, R.M. (1957), 'Technical change and the aggregate production function', *Review of Economics and Statistics*, 39, 312–20.

Sorrell, S., J. Schleich, S. Scott, E. O'Malley, F. Trace, U. Boede, K. Ostertag and P. Radgen (2000), *Barriers to Energy Efficiency in Public and Private Organisations*, Brighton: SPRU-Science and Technology Policy Research.

Stern, D.I. and M.S. Common (2001), 'Is there an environmental Kuznets Curve for sulfur?', *Journal of Environmental Economics and Management*, 41, 162–78.

Stirling, A. (1998), *On the Economics and Analysis of Diversity*, SPRU Electronic Working Paper Series 28, Brighton: SPRU-Science and Technology Policy Research.

Tilton, J.E. (1986), 'Beyond Intensity of Use', *Materials and Society*, 10, 245–50.

Wackernagel, M. and W. Rees (1996), *Our Ecological Footprint-Reducing Human Impact on Earth*, Vancouver: New Society.

Walker W. (2000), 'Entrapment in large technology systems: institutional commitment and power relations', *Research Policy*, 29 (7–8), 833–46.

Wallace, D. (1995), *Environmental Policy and Industrial Innovation*, London: Earthscan.

Weale, A. (1992), *The New Politics of Pollution*, Manchester/New York: Manchester University Press.

Wernick, I. and J. Ausubel (1995), 'National materials flows and the environment', *Annual Review of Energy and Environment*, 20, 463–92.

Yearley, S. (1991), *The Green Case: A Sociology of Environmental Issues, Arguments and Politics*, London/New York: Harper Collins Academic.

Young, S. (ed.) (2000), *The Emergence of Ecological Modernisation: Integrating the Environment and the Economy?*, Routledge: London.

10. (Un)sustainable consumption

Jacquelin Burgess, Tracey Bedford, Kersty Hobson, Gail Davies and Carolyn Harrison

In historical terms, the causal connections between economic growth, increases in personal consumption and increasing environmental damage have remained steady in industrial economies for the last two centuries ... What awaits on the horizon are limits and constraints never before encountered, from a dizzying height of economic prosperity never before attained (Goldblatt, 1996, pp. 39–40; p. 43).

We will be working with our allies to reduce greenhouse gases, but I will not accept a plan that will harm our economy and hurt American workers (President George W. Bush, commenting on his administration's decision to withdraw American support from the Kyoto climate change agreement, 30 March 2001).

INTRODUCTION

Over the last two hundred years, the potent combination of capitalism and industrialization has resulted in unprecedented pressure on the physical, chemical and biological systems that support life on earth. Dramatic changes are occurring in the numbers and geographical ranges of animal and plant species; the climate system is becoming more unstable; increasing numbers of toxins permeate air, soil and water systems. Scientific evidence suggests that environmental limits are being reached – and breached – with uncertain outcomes for the future well-being of people and nature.

Questions of whether and how to ameliorate the impact of human activities on nature have surfaced periodically over the last 150 years (Thomas, 1955; Worster, 1994). Current debate was stimulated by the first UN Environment conference in Stockholm, in 1972. The context was one in which the depletion of natural resources seemed to be setting limits to the continued growth of industrial economies (Meadows et al., 1972). In the 20 years between Stockholm and Rio in 1992, debate shifted to focus on the inability of environmental systems to cope with present (and predicted) levels of economic activity. The 1992 Earth Summit addressed global human impacts on climate and habitats, and how to achieve more equitable but sustainable growth within bio-physical limits. Given hardening evidence of anthropogenic climatic change, Johannesburg in 2002 was dominated by debate about how best to manage the accelerating impacts of human activities on destabilizing and degrading environmental systems.

The pressures, at a global scale, increased dramatically in the second half of the twentieth century:

> Between 1950 and 1990, the world's human population more than doubled (from 2.6 billion to 5.3 billion) ... water use nearly tripled, fish consumption grew 4.4-fold, and energy use quintupled ... The use of chemical fertilisers increased roughly tenfold; world production of organic chemicals, major sources of air and water pollution, rose 20-fold; and global air travel, which causes significant atmospheric pollution, soared nearly 70-fold. On average, resource use per person nearly tripled between 1950 and 1990. This growth ... resulted in roughly a six-fold increase in human impact on the global environment during the four decades.'
> (Corson, 1994, pp. 206-7)

The economic–technological systems which made these levels of consumption possible has also improved methodologies for measuring and modelling environmental change. One significant consequence is that scientists can now demonstrate the impacts of human activity on air, soil, water and climate at finer levels of resolution than ever before and at different spatial scales. More sophisticated monitoring networks provided the evidence needed to convince the majority of the world's governments of the reality of climate change. However, the scientific challenges of demonstrating the impacts of economic activities on biophysical systems are complex because they act together 'often in non additive and non-linear ways' (Stern et al., 1997, p. 131). These problems are further complicated by context – geographical and historical variability across space and through time.

In responding to the growing scientific evidence of human impacts on environmental systems, most social scientific research and policy development has focused on production issues such as the role of new technologies in widening the range and usefulness of material resources; the significance of capital formation and structural changes in economies in stimulating demand; and the impact of deregulation in a globalized economy (Berkhout and Gouldson, Chapter 9; Jacobs, 1994). However, a major shift in emphasis was flagged in the Brundtland Report (United Nations, 1987) where the wealthy countries of the north were identified as bearing most responsibility for the depletion and degradation of environmental resources.

Global summaries such as Corson's obscure the highly uneven geographical distribution of economic activities. The majority of productive resources have come from the poorer countries of the south, whilst their consumption is concentrated in the rich industrialized nations of the north. It is also clear that the huge investment in the science of global environmental change has deflected political (and scientific) attention away from local environmental problems – such as soil erosion/loss of fertility/destruction of habitat – which leads to further impoverishment of poor people in many parts of the world (Agnew and Warren, 1996).

The social practices and environmental consequences of contemporary consumerism were placed on the policy agenda following the Brundtland Report. Accordingly, the 1992 Earth Summit called for 'national policies and strategies to encourage changes in consumption patterns' among the OECD states, in particular (UNCED 1993, p. 64). One of the first book-length arguments about the social and environmental injustices embodied in consumption practices was published in the same year (Durning, 1992). Durning began by classifying the world's population into one of three 'ecological classes' (see Table 10.1), using average annual income and lifestyle/livelihood as proxy measures for uneven development. Although crude, the classification is a useful heuristic for bringing home the scale of differences in lifestyles and livelihoods of people living in different parts of the world.

The glaring inequalities represented in statistics such as these fuelled the determination of many parties at the Rio summit to reach a workable definition of sustainability which encompassed social issues of equity. Non-governmental organizations (NGOs) began to work in partnership with national governments in the north to promote the concept of 'environmentally friendly lifestyles': first, to address production issues in poorer countries through the promotion of fairly traded goods, and latterly to reduce the impacts of consumption practices on environmental systems.

This chapter will concentrate on issues of (un)sustainable consumption in the affluent north. Readers are referred to work by Peet and Watts (1996) for a critical appraisal of environment and development issues in the south. The chapter is divided into three sections. The first provides a brief historical overview of the economic, social and cultural significance of consumption in modernity before clarifying some important differences in disciplinary framings of sustainable consumption. This is followed by two sections which discuss a range of social scientific research addressing sustainable consumption and lifestyles which takes further the enquiry begun by Harrison and Davies (Harrison and Davies, 1998). The second section concentrates on research by psychologists, economists and social scientists which focuses on the individual, with a particular emphasis on the importance of cognitive processes in consumption choices and other environmentally-relevant behaviours. The third section discusses a range of new research that is drawing sociology, cultural geography, anthropology, and science and technology studies to understand consumption discourses and practices. An emerging research agenda is identified, based around the ecological–socio-technological networks that bind producers and consumers, plants and animals, natural and physical systems into relationships across space and through time.

Table 10.1   World consumption classes

Category of consumption	Consumers (1.1 billion)	Middle (3.3 billion)	Poor (1.1 billion)
Diet	Meat, packaged food, soft drinks	Grain, clean water	Insufficient grain, unsafe water
Housing	Buildings with high technological specifications	Buildings, with basic services, including electricity	Huts, shanty dwellings
Transport	Private cars, aeroplanes	Bicycles, buses, trains	Walking
Materials	Throwaways: high redundancy built into electrical, clothing and other consumer goods	Durables: such as radios, TV; washing machines, fridges	Local biomass, providing fuel, clothing, domestic utensils
Average annual income per family member	Above $7500	$7000–$7500	Less than $700
% of world's income earned	64%	33%	2%
Geographical distribution	North America, Western Europe, Japan, Australia, Hong Kong and Singapore; plus the elites in other parts of the world	Mainly Latin America, Middle East, China, East Asia; lower income families in former USSR, and western industrial countries	Africa, India, South Asia

Source: Adapted from Durning (1992) (pp. 26–8), based on Worldwatch Institute data.

'(UN)SUSTAINABLE CONSUMPTION': MAPPING DIFFERENT DISCIPLINARY APPROACHES

One of the attractions of 'consumption' as a central concept for environmental research and policy-making is that it seems to unite the natural and social sciences in common endeavour. But there are dangers in promoting a word which is freighted with different meanings and interpretations. Clarion calls to reduce consumption could easily backfire and lead to the kind of semantic wars that have dogged the development of a workable concept of sustainability (Princen, 1999). Different meanings are attributed to consumption as a process in the natural and in the social sciences. Furthermore, normative (moral) values pervade contemporary discourse about consumption levels and practices, especially in the context of equity issues between rich and poor, and these can sit uneasily alongside scientific discourses which seek to maintain a value-neutral position.

It is also important to bear in mind that at other times in different places, consumption practices have had very different meanings and values. Although the rapid growth of consumerism, the stimulation of economic production and the distribution of an expanding range of goods and services for purchase is a distinctive phenomenon of the twentieth century, its historical roots are deep. Historians such as Jardine and Brotton (2000), for example, show how the growth of mercantile capitalism in the late medieval and early modern period was fuelled by the demands of the nobility for luxuries with which to parade their wealth and aesthetic discernment. The valorization of consumption has been central to modernity. At the heart of the eighteenth century 'English Enlightenment' (Porter, 2000), philosophers such as Locke, Hume, Smith and Bentham argued that the goal of human beings was to achieve happiness in this life rather than defer gratification for the afterlife. Happiness was to be achieved through the satisfaction of individual needs and desires, within a social context where the selfishness of individuals was 'polished' through interaction with others to ensure collective, as well as individual benefit. Not surprisingly, such a revolution in ethics, morals and practice was underpinned by a new understanding of nature as providing an inexhaustible source of resources, power and pleasure – often expressed in terms of nature's 'plenitude' (Glacken, 1967).

A distinctive feature of the twentieth century has been the rapid expansion of consumption from relatively wealthy elites to mass populations, and the emergence of the home as an important locus for consumption activity. This process began in the United States in the 1920s and 1930s, driven by large industrial corporations such as General Electric and Ford. Mass advertising helped create popular demand for domestic technologies, cars and an ever-expanding range of goods and services (Nye, 1992; Schwartz Cowan, 1983), resonating with aspirations, especially among women as principal home-makers, for higher standards of comfort and healthfulness. 'The dream of light, air and privacy and the continuous process of home-making contribute considerably to consumption growth' as Inge Ropke (1999, p. 413) puts it. These socio-economic and cultural transformations spread rapidly from

America to Europe, Japan and other industrialized nations post-second world war.

Dramatic changes in ways of living are highlighted in economic data such as those reported in Jackson and Marks (1999). In the UK, for example, figures from the National Accounts for the period 1954–94 (Table 10.2) reveal long term trends in the market take-up of technological innovations (video recorders, personal computers, mobile phones and so on); and changing socio-cultural activities (eating out, taking foreign holidays, watching television rather than reading newspapers and so on) in the decades identified as most significant in exacerbating human impacts on rates of environmental degradation. The figures reveal that per capita consumption has more than doubled over the period, with considerable variations in growth across different sectors (see Noorman and Uiterkamp, 1998 for comparable Dutch statistics).

Table 10.2   Changes in per capita consumer expenditure in the UK, 1954–1994

Expenditure category	% inc.	Expenditure category	% inc.
Recreation and entertainment	398	Housing	78
Household appliances	385	Catering	75
Communication	341	Fuel	55
Travel	293	Tobacco and alcohol	33
Maintenance	140	Food	29
		Books, newspapers and education	14
		Other	78

Source: Jackson and Marks, 1999, p. 432.

Different academic disciplines will approach numbers like these with rather different questions and understandings of the significance of consumption. For example, within economics, consumption completes the circuit of commodity and service production and distribution through the purchase of goods and services. Many different actors are engaged in consumption, ranging from individual consumers managing their household accounts through to the purchasing decisions of governments and their agencies, and commercial organizations. In making purchasing decisions, consumers exercise rational choice based on product information and individual preferences to maximize utility. Within sociology and cultural studies, consumption encapsulates the discourses and practices associated with the purchase and/or use of material and symbolic commodities which are used to construct a lifestyle and, thereby, a self identity. Baumann (1992) goes further, arguing that: 'in present society, consumer conduct (consumer freedom geared to the consumer market) moves steadily into the position of simultaneously representing the cognitive and moral focus of life, the integrative bond of the society... In other words, it moves into the self-same position which, in the past during the "modernist" phase of capitalist society was occupied by work' (p. 49).

Within the environmental and natural sciences, 'consumption' describes physical processes that transform matter and energy. Under the First Law of Thermodynamics, consumption – in the sense of energy and matter being 'used up' – is impossible. Rather, matter/energy are transformed in use. Often this transformation will take the form of degradation of the resource, and/or pollution of another part of the system. Stern summarizes the problem of environmentally unsustainable consumption:

> Consumption consists of human and human-induced transformations of materials and energy. Consumption is environmentally important to the extent that it makes materials or energy less available for future use, moves a biophysical system towards a different state or, through its effects on those systems, threatens human health, welfare, or other things people value. (Stern, 1997, p. 20)

When considered as matter–energy transformations, then critical questions must address the impacts of the full circuit of economic activity – that is, consumption of resources and production of waste products in the production of goods and services for purchase and use.

As suggested earlier, consumption issues represent a new focus for research and policy-making. Stern et al. (1997) report on one of the first discussions about environmentally sustainable consumption organized in 1994. The outcome is an analysis of environmentally sustainable consumption framed tightly by science. The proposed research agenda follows a 'state–pressure–response' model of environmental change (see Burgess et al., 1999). The focus for scientific enquiry is to determine (1) the environmentally significant impacts of transformations of energy and materials on specific biophysical systems; (2) the proximate causes of these environmental effects; and (3) the driving forces behind the proximate causes. In the case of climate change, for example, the proximate causes of changes in the concentrations of atmospheric gases are widely agreed to include the burning of fossil fuels which releases CO_2 and methane into the atmosphere. The key driving forces are identified as 'human population growth; levels of economic activity; technologies used in actions that affect the environment; political and economic institutions affecting action; and individual's attitudes and beliefs' (Stern et al., 1997, p. 131). It is striking that there is no explicit recognition of social and cultural life in this list. Larger political and institutional issues arise in how best to modify the driving forces. The workshop contributors favoured an 'evidence-based' environmental policy agenda to encompass new regulations, novel policy instruments and appeals for individuals and organizations to change aspects of their everyday consumption practices.

The Stern et al. (1997) volume is, without doubt, a major contribution to the developing agenda of research on environmentally sustainable consumption. But it is also a text which refuses to engage with normative issues, preferring to leave such debates to others who might be engaged in what the editors describe as 'environmental high politics', and insisting that 'the drastically different quantities and qualities of consumption around the world are a matter for empirical investigation rather than polemic' (Stern et al., 1997, p. 22)

From a social and cultural perspective, it is not sensible to frame such a significant area of human activity so narrowly. Consumption practices are fundamentally political. Large organizations, public authorities, the military, and commercial companies, are largely responsible for the bulk of human-environment transactions which lead to damage to bio-physical systems, as Stern et al. acknowledge (1997). But the focus of attention in terms of achieving changing consumption practices has remained firmly fixed on individual consumers and their domestic consumption. One reason why this should be so is the role played by the environmental movement. Whilst science is helping to make environmental change 'visible' in terms of capturing physical, chemical and biological changes to natural systems, the environmental movement has played the fundamental role in giving these environmental changes social meaning. Crucially, the movement has been extremely successful in framing the impacts of economic activity on nature, and (to a lesser extent) on the poor as a moral issue.

Over the last 20 years, the NGOs have brought the consequences of consumption-production practices into public consciousness through highly effective media campaigns. Friends of the Earth began in 1979 by dumping non-returnable bottles on the doorstep of Schweppes (Greenberg, 1985); Greenpeace campaigned against the slaughter of cetaceans in the fishing nets of factory trawlers; Oxfam led consumer campaigns for fair trade and ethical investment. Consumption choices (and the production processes behind them) have become an ethical issue; a question of 'obligations of duty to others, both near and far' (Crocker and Linden, 1998, p. 9). With their emphasis on consumption and consumer power, the NGOs have politicized questions of environmental responsibility. Accepting responsibility for one's actions puts pressure on individuals to make changes in their everyday lives and spaces, and to endorse political campaigns for increased regulations, standards and controls (see McCormick, 1995; Eden, 1993).

To argue that all consumption practices are wrong or damaging to the environment is absurd. The challenge is to identify those consumption practices which philosophers Crocker and Linden (1998) label 'inappropriate'. Inappropriate consumption is consumption which has negative consequences for consumers themselves; for others who may be close or distant in terms of time and/or space; which may directly or indirectly damage important values and/or institutions; and have damaging impacts on the environment. Normative issues are fundamental to the discussion: 'before *assessing* consumption practices, we must *understand* their causes, meanings and consequences' (Crocker and Linden, 1998, p. 4; italics in the original). In the following two sections, we explore the different theoretical and methodological strategies that are helping researchers understand contemporary consumption practices as they have a bearing on the environment. Two themes are important – although neither has yet received sufficient research attention. First, as suggested above and reflecting a tradition of environmental attitude–behaviour research, the primary focus has been the individual consumer, but this is an individual disassociated from their everyday lives. The challenge is to re-contextualize individuals in their specific places and social spaces of home, work, and leisure. Second, much of what is consumed (notably matter/energy) in everyday life is not visible or tangible in any obvious sense. For example, the buildings that people live in and work in embody specific histories of technological, economic and social changes, all of which make demands on material resources and bio-physical systems (Lutzenhiser, 1994; Hinchliffe, 1996a). The localities people live in are bound together through flows of material, energy and information into complex networks at many different spatial scales (Massey, 1994; Castells, 1997). A thorough-going theoretical and methodological engagement with the networks that bind nature and culture is beginning to gather speed (see Goodman, 1999; Whatmore, 2001).

COGNITIVE PERSPECTIVES: CONSUMPTION FRAMED BY A FOCUS ON THE INDIVIDUAL

A substantial body of work from a variety of social scientific disciplines has focused at a 'micro-level' on the individual consumer and, in particular, the cognitive and motivational bases of their behaviour as it relates to environmental concerns (Neuman, 1986; Oskamp et al. 1991; de Young, 1993). To what extent are individuals changing aspects of their behaviour 'for the sake of the environment?' perhaps by buying organic products or refusing extra packaging; modifying household regimes by turning down the central heating or only using the washing machines with a full load; choosing not to use the car to travel to work.

Cognitive perspectives construe the problem as one of individual (and social) learning – that is, how, over time, understanding of the necessity for behavioural change is achieved and then, critically, implemented. Developmental theories underpin micro studies of individuals' environmental attitudes and behaviour, as Finger's (1994) concise summary of the 'dominant' environmental attitude and behaviour framework shows (Figure 10.1). Developmental psychology tracks the development of mental constructs and schemas through which complex information is assimilated into workable cognitive frameworks; social psychology is able to explain how individuals' value systems reflect bundles of more or less consistent sets of attitudes and beliefs, including important social norms; while environmental educationalists engage in pedagogic practices to ensure that children acquire the information and knowledge necessary to engender environmental concern and commitment.

The model assumes that as the individual acquires new information and knowledge about the impacts of human activity on bio-physical systems, whether through formal education at school, targeted information from government departments or informal channels such as mass media, environmental awareness will rise, and existing environmental values and attitudes will change. In this 'virtuous circle', more information will enhance the individual's willingness to reduce the environmental impacts of their activities through behavioural changes.

The dominant methodological approach measuring environmental attitudes and behaviour is the questionnaire survey. A substantial body of data exists which charts rises and falls in public awareness of environmental problems, changes in environmental attitudes and reported behavioural changes (see Dunlap and Scarce, 1991; Ungar 1994; Worcester, 1993; Dunlap, 1998 for

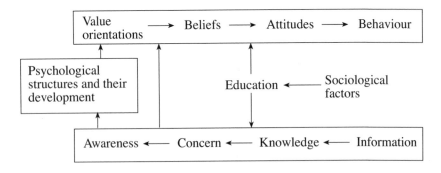

Source: Finger, 1994.

Figure 10.1   The dominant framework in environmental education

examples). A key finding from studies in many different parts of the industrialized world is paradoxical. The remarkably rapid increase in public awareness of environmental issues and embracing of pro-environmental attitudes is coupled with virtually no substantive changes in behaviours at all.

The failure to demonstrate any convincing correlation between environmental awareness, attitudes and behaviour is, to say the least, unfortunate. For policy, through reliance on cognitive models of behaviour, research and related policy responses, places great emphasis of the role of information as a motivational factor in achieving more pro-environmental behaviours by individual consumers (Harrison and Davies, 1998). The strategy for engendering more sustainable lifestyles is seen as a matter of providing more and better information, with the expectation that this will raise environmental awareness and concern; lead to more informed consumer choices; and change purchase decisions and/or routine, everyday behaviours. Pro-environmental behaviour is thus construed as the outcome of a linear and ultimately rational process.

Policy responses consistent with this framework include mass media campaigns exhorting the public to adopt more sustainable practices such as the 1992–4 UK campaign Helping the Earth Begins at Home (Hinchliffe, 1996b); risk communication strategies informed by science and experts (Wiegman and Gutteling, 1995); and practical initiatives such as kerb-side waste collection, park-and-ride schemes and recycling facilities to help create an environment which should support individuals' intentions to behave rationally. Although there is evidence to suggest that fear and anxiety are powerful motivators in sensitizing individuals to the risks associated with environmental changes, recent empirical studies show that such communications are failing to persuade individuals of the necessity of changing their behaviours (Harrison et al., 1996; Myers and Macnaghten, 1998; Blake, 1999).

The problem may partly be a methodological one. Many questionnaire surveys measure broad categories of environmental concern rather than the knowledge and attitudes individuals hold about specific environmental issues (Ungar, 1994). Surprisingly few studies have tested the psychological model empirically against actual behaviour (Rutherford, 1998). Rather, studies rely on measuring reported environmental behaviours which are subject to social desirability effects, as well as failures to recall accurately routine behaviours. New research is focusing on specific consumption practices, on the assumption that different domains of environmentally significant consumption may well engender different attitudinal and behavioural responses. One recent example is a major study by two economic psychologists (Brandon and Lewis, 1999) who conducted a field study with 120 households in Bath, UK. Households were placed in one of six 'feedback groups' to assess the effectiveness of information delivered in different ways in reducing domestic energy consumption, over a nine-month period. The study had a hybrid methodology. A questionnaire was used to measure respondents' general environmental attitudes and their knowledge and attitudes with regard to energy conservation. This was complemented by a structural survey of each dwelling, and focus group discussions at the end of the study period. The evidence suggested that 'financial considerations are of equal or even greater importance' in decisions to reduce energy consumption than environmental attitudes (Brandon and Lewis, 1999, p. 83). Overall, the results indicated that feedback was significant in reducing energy consumption over the period, but that the complexity of controlling for different kinds of dwellings, demographics, socio-economic characteristics and information feedback mechanisms made it difficult to draw firm, statistically-sound conclusions from the data.

Given the apparent failure of information to deliver changes in environmental practices, a number of economists and psychologists interested in consumption practices are reconsidering the attitude–behaviour model (see Ropke, 1999; Princen, 1999). The focus is shifting to analysis of the biological, psychological, social and economic drivers behind consumption practices. In this new work, the 'needs hierarchy' of Abram Maslow is being pressed into service once more. In Maslow's (1968) original formulation, a set of objective human needs exists within every human being: needs for food, shelter, love, security and so on. Arguing that the satisfaction of biological needs was more fundamental than other kinds of need, Maslow formulated a hierarchy within which emotional and spiritual needs are met only when more basic physical and material needs have been satisfied. Crudely, saving the whale will not be a need unless one has a full stomach, warm house and discretionary income. Readers will recognize this as the basic proposition underpinning the new Environmental Paradigm of the late 1970s and, especially, Ingelhart's (1990) 'post materialism' thesis of environmentalism which argued that environmental concern was a 'luxury' which arose among the new service class in the affluent decades of the 1960s and 1970s.

New work on human needs as drivers of consumption practices by Max-Neef and colleagues (1992) is conceptually more sophisticated (see Jackson and Marks, 1999 for an excellent account). Needs range from basic requirements of subsistence and protection through to affection, understanding, participation, leisure, creation, identity and freedom. These motivational needs are expressed in a matrix form with different categories of experiential encounters – being, having, doing and interacting – recognized as being equally important in satisfying them. The formulation recognises that 'needs' are experienced either as a deprivation – a lack; or as a potential – a want which is satisfied through different modes of encounter. Jackson and Marks

(1999) endeavour, through their analysis of patterns of expenditure (cited above) to explicate the relationship between the consumption of economic goods and needs satisfaction. Their analysis addresses the distinction in the Max-Neef matrix between 'material needs' - which require, in some sense, resource use; and 'non-material' needs which are, in effect, outcomes of processes of human interaction. Jackson and Marks conclude: 'the pattern of consumption in the UK appears increasingly to implicate material artefacts in the attempted satisfaction of non-material needs' (p. 437).

Some of the most detailed experimental work endeavouring to link human needs with consumption behaviours has been undertaken in the Netherlands by researchers engaged in the HOMES project (Household Metabolism Effectively Sustained) (Noorman and Uiterkamp, 1998). Working within a cognitive tradition which emphasizes the rationality of human action, Gatersleben and Vlek (1998) put forward a Needs–Opportunity–Ability model of consumer behaviour (Figure 10.2).

The model acknowledges that any hypothesized causal link between attitudes and behaviour is mediated by (1) internal cognitive processes, including beliefs and values; and (2) situational variables such as social norms (or in the case of the NOA model by contextual factors such as 'technology' and 'culture'). It builds on the work of Fishbein and Ajzen (1975), in acknowledging that consumer behaviour will be more likely to take place if there is an intention to act. Consumer motivation is expressed through a

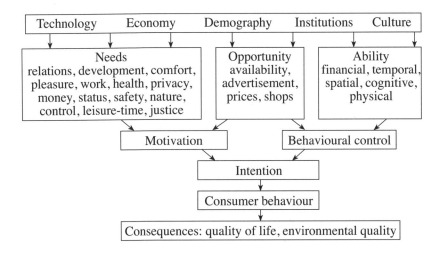

Source: From Gatersleben and Vlek, 1998, p. 146.

Figure 10.2   The needs-opportunity-ability model of consumer behaviour

categorization of needs (increased to 15 'indicators of well-being') and opportunities represented by the economic and technological availability of goods to satisfy needs. 'Behavioural control' – that is consumption practices, represents the ability of the individual or household to exercise their options to acquire the goods and services.

The NOA model has been empirically tested in a study of the consumption behaviours of 496 Dutch households. In a face-to-face, questionnaire-based interview, respondents were asked about their consumption behaviours in relation to 39 household goods and their consumer needs as expressed in the 15 quality of life indices. Ownership and usage of household goods was most strongly differentiated by income groups, household types, and age. Gender does not seem to have been explored in the analysis. The survey shows that in responses to questions ranking the environmental impacts of many different kinds of household activity (from bathing and cooking to taking a holiday), 'respondents evaluated all of their behaviours as moderately damaging to the environment, except for the use of the computer' (Gatersleben and Vlek, 1998, p. 173). Larger households thought they had greater impacts than smaller households did. Similarly, higher income groups thought they had greater environmental impacts than lower income groups did. Very little variance in the evaluations could be explained by the possession and use of particular products. Respondents thought it was necessary to recycle, and reduce their use of the car, and energy use, and expressed willingness to change certain behaviours but only where there was little inconvenience to them. Of particular note, household goods which satisfy a number of quality of life attributes simultaneously will be used more often, will be considered a necessity, and will not be given up without a struggle. The car is the archetypal consumer good of this kind. In other words, material and non-material needs are inextricably linked in specific consumption practices. Furthermore, while human needs may be relatively few and consistent across cultures, the extent to which those needs might be satisfied by different economic goods is enormously variable, complex and culturally specific.

Cognitive approaches construct individual consumers as rational decision-makers whose behaviour is governed by economic efficiency rather than for example, equity or ethics. Appropriate policy responses guided by these approaches involve a variety of fiscal measures, including financial incentives and penalties, in order to engineer a market that takes account of environmental costs and benefit (Hanley and Atkinson, Chapter 3). Economic measures such as increased taxes or environmental levies such as congestion charging may be a more effective way, in practice, of changing discretionary consumption behaviours which have environmentally damaging consequences. When UK government sustainability indicators show that the real costs of motoring have remained static since 1974 against substantial increases in the cost of public transport over the same period (DOE, 1996), then individual consumers are behaving rationally when they prefer to use the car rather than travel by bus or train. But the use of economic instruments also raises significant political issues, including their differential impacts on the poorer sections of society. Voluntary measures must also be taken, but how are consumers to be persuaded to accept more responsibility for their 'inappropriate consumption'?

CONTEXTUALIST APPROACHES: EMBEDDING LIFESTYLES IN COLLECTIVE SOCIO-MATERIAL NETWORKS

Over the last decade, cognitive approaches represented by the environmental attitude–behaviour tradition have been criticized on both theoretical and methodological grounds (see Macnaghten and Urry, 1998). Spaargaren and van Vliet (2000), for example, assert that 'the search for determinants of environmentally (un) friendly behaviours - grounded in models from social psychology - came close to deception. The environmental impacts of what consumers actually do turned out to be very complex' (p. 51). A closely reasoned critique of environmental attitude–behaviour research leads Ungar to conclude:

> with the accretion of impacts, environment and environmental concern have become extensive constructs, reflecting an extraordinary population of behaviours by individuals and large actors. Such all-embracing macro-categories lead to problems of incommensurability, and hence may be better understood as political tools rather than as scientific concepts. (Ungar, 1994, p. 292)

A new interdisciplinary field of environmental social science is emerging which draws on a range of theoretical perspectives and methodological strategies to try to better understand the contextual, relational, structural elements of sustainability. Much of this new thinking has been presented in the foregoing chapters of this book and the earlier collection edited by Benton and Redclift (1995). Important theoretical developments address questions of the interplay of human agents and institutional structures in shaping social practices (Giddens, 1984, 1991): (1) the role of discourses and reflexivity in shaping knowledge, understanding and action, including constructions of environmental risk (Beck, 1992; Harvey 1996; Lash et al., 1996); (2) the relations between science, technology and society, notably in the life histories of particular technologies which have, in Schwartz Cowan's (1983) term 'industrialised the home' (Guy and Shove, 2000); and (3) the importance of specific time–space routines and informational networks embodied in the domestic spaces and local places which ground daily life (Glennie and Thrift, 1996; Castells, 1997).

In consumption terms, these theoretical debates are centred on concepts of lifestyle and self-identity. Lifestyles are relatively consistent sets of practices that make sense in particular places, spaces and times. Giddens (1991, p. 81) defines lifestyle as: 'a more or less integrated set of practices which an individual embraces not only because such practices fulfil utilitarian needs, but because they give material form to a particular narrative or self-identity'. Although different sets of practices may cohere to create a 'work identity' which is different, in part, to a 'home identity', there must be sufficient consistency and integration for the individual to maintain a sense of coherence. The critical insight from Giddens' work is that the negotiation and achievement of a lifestyle is not entirely voluntaristic. All human actors are embedded in social systems made up of different kinds of institutions, the agreed rules or codes of conduct which are considered appropriate and/or necessary for the conduct of social life. Individuals make choices but always within specific social, cultural and geographical contexts, according to the agreed rules of particular social practices which, of course, will change as actors' experiences, interests and capabilities change. Work on sustainable livelihoods in the south takes a similar institutional approach (see Johnson, 1997; Scoones, 1998).

Bundles of social practices which contribute to a recognizable lifestyle segment thus also always embody a 'life-story' (Spaargaren and van Vliet, 2000; see also Finger, 1994) in the sense that they represent the outcome of experiences in accommodating oneself to the social constraints of everyday life both inside and outside the home. Lifestyles map onto conventional social categories of class, income, age, gender and ethnicity, but also transcend them. Often expressed through what is consumed and through leisure practices, lifestyles embrace material, aesthetic and symbolic dimensions (Chaney, 1996; Corrigan, 1997). Critically, lifestyles reflect identity choices: about how individuals wish to be and be seen by others, culturally and historically contextualized. In a society often regarded as highly fragmented and individualized, lifestyle can also be a new means of negotiating space between the private and the public, demonstrating the active and engaged processes through which people construct their identities in relation to their lived experiences.

Progress is being made in understanding the social, cultural and political dimensions of consumption practices. Material objects which can be classed as 'consumer durables' such as fridges, vacuum cleaners, washing machines and cars have a recognizable role in lifestyle research. But a new theoretical approach is needed to understand how technological innovation meshes with social processes in consumption studies, especially in the production and management of the physical settings of daily life. For example, as Lutzenhiser comments: 'the built environment is a physical accretion of the products of socio-technological change – embodying historical social arrangements (for example, family size and class structure) in built form – forms to which present occupants must behaviourally adapt' (1997, p. 97). Recent empirical work on domestic energy consumption provides interesting examples of socio-technological systems (Guy and Shove, 2000; Hinchliffe, 1997).

Given this complex theoretical terrain, Spaargaren and van Vliet (2000) have produced a very useful conceptual model drawing particularly on the work of Giddens to link actors, lifestyle practices, institutional structures and the material systems which are essential for the progress of daily life (see Figure 10.3).

Constraining actors' practices are the rules and resources which structure the institutions of social life (the right-hand side of the figure). These rules and resources are embodied in the concept of 'systems of provision' which Spaargaren and van Vliet take from Fine and Leopold (1993). 'Different commodities or groups of commodities ... [will be] distinctly structured by the chain or system of provision that unites a particular pattern of production with a particular pattern of consumption' (quoted in Spaargaren and van Vliet, 2000, p. 59). In other words, the rules and regulations which structure different resource networks such as food, transport and housing can be clarified. Through the application of actor network theory, major advances are being made in understanding of the agro-food system, for example (see Goodman, 1999).

One fundamental aspect of the relationship between human actors and systems of provision concerns the 'invisibility' of bio-technological systems,

Actors . . . Human action . . . Social practices . . . Structures

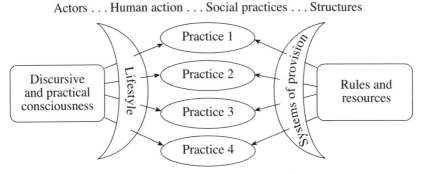

Source: Spaargaren and van Vliet, 2000.

Figure 10.3   A conceptual model for studying consumption practices

especially those distant in space and time, and the ways in which they support routinized behaviours. On the left-hand side of Figure 10.3, and again drawing from Giddens, a distinction is made between 'discursive' and 'practical' consciousness. Many different kinds of social practices and behaviours are learned in childhood and subsequently enacted without any kind of conscious thought or reasoning. New technologies such as mobile phones are rapidly enfolded into the practical experience of getting on in the world. Technological systems, notably water, energy and transportation are fundamental in this regard, not least because the execution of modern life is dependent on these 'collective, socio-material systems' (Spaargaren and van Vleit, 2000). Ruth Schwarz Cowan's wonderful book explores the paradox that ever increasingly sophisticated technologies have not resulted in freeing women from the burdens of housework but have, rather, increased it. She emphasizes the linkages between domestic 'labour-saving devices', economic entrepreneurship and technological infrastructure. 'The Jones's washing machine would not have done them a bit of good if the town fathers had not decided to create a municipal water system several years earlier, and if the local gas and electric company had not gotten around to running wires and pipes into the neighbourhood.' (Schwartz Cowan, 1983, pp. 13–14).

There is a small but growing number of studies, some like Schwartz Cowan and Otnes (1988) using historical methods of research, others deploying qualitative research methods in empirical research with contemporary consumers, to explore the connections between lifestyles, identity issues and technological systems (Guy and Shove, 2000). Other empirical work concentrates more on exploring, discursively, the ways in which human subjects understand their own and others' social practices in relation to environmental issues, and calls for them to become more environmentally responsible (see Macnaghten and Jacobs, 1997; Macnaghten and Myers, 1998). The work of Billig (1996) in particular has suggested that the expression of personal attitudes is not so much an expression of an underlying belief, but rather a position whose meanings are only realized when located within wider societal beliefs.

BARRIERS TO ACHIEVING MORE SUSTAINABLE LIFESTYLES: A CROSS-CULTURAL ANALYSIS

Three case studies suggest a more complex, contingent and conflicting construction of identity and its relation to lifestyle choice. The first study works with informants who have no demonstrable commitment to environmentally responsible behaviours; the second with individuals who chose to participate in a six-month programme designed to support small scale changes in domestic consumption practices; and the third with women who identify as 'ethical' consumers; that is, whose lifestyles and consumption practices most demonstrably seek to embody a commitment to environmental and social responsibility.

Working in the mid 1990s, this research set out to explore the discursive reasoning through which men and women decided whether to accept greater responsibility for the environmental impacts of their everyday behaviours (Harrison et al., 1996; Burgess et al., 1998). The research was based in two cities: Nottingham in the UK, and Eindhoven in the Netherlands in 1993-4. A hybrid methodological strategy combined representative quota samples of residents who answered the same questionnaire in the two cities with qualitative research based on in-depth discussion groups drawn from respondents to the surveys; and workshops with representatives of local stakeholders and policymakers. The questionnaire survey provided comparative data on environmental awareness, attitudes, reported pro-environmental behaviours, and depth of understanding of specific global and local environmental issues in the two samples. The researchers were particularly interested in potential differences between women's and men's understanding of, and identification with, environmentally sustainable consumption practices. So, the four in-depth discussion groups were single gender. Over five sessions each lasting 90 minutes, people were encouraged to arrive at practical judgements about their everyday practices. In these wide-ranging and intense discussions, it is striking that gender was often a stronger bond than nationality in certain issues. So, for example, the Dutch and UK women were in full accord about the unacceptability of risks associated with certain agricultural technologies, whereas the men were much more sanguine.

Normative questions were pervasive. The transcripts are full of discussions of what people felt they (and others) ought to be doing, not only for the sake of the environment, but also to meet their social obligations, especially at the local level. For some individuals – both women and men – such ethical commitment reflected deep, personal conviction and was expressed with considerable emotional force. For others, there was a much weaker emotional commitment, but a desire to engage altruistically in contributing to the collective good. Joining the in-depth groups and engaging with others in debate about environmental issues represented a practical demonstration of this commitment. The UK women's group, in particular, felt modern consumerism as an essentially immoral force: 'people now are just so greedy and selfish. You know, we don't seem to have a moral conscience any more'.

Supporting discussion in the literature (Douglas and Isherwood, 1978; Ropke, 1999) resource constraints, especially shortages of money and time, were significant in household consumption practices. These constraints were discussed far more extensively by the women's groups than by the men, reflecting different responsibilities for managing the household. For example, both the UK and Dutch women believed that organically-produced foodstuffs were better for their children, but most could not afford to pay the premium to buy such products. Their inability to be 'a good mother' in these circumstances left many feeling angry, frustrated and guilty, especially when risks associated with 'unwholesome foods' were the subject of media reports. (In 1993-4, BSE was a significant issue, while applications of genetic modification were just beginning to be discussed in Dutch and UK media.) Similarly with issues of air pollution and use of the car. There was anxiety about the possible health impacts of car emissions, especially on children. But many of the women's schedules, especially those with 'dual careers' in paid work and housework, lacked flexibility to change their routines, especially given the inflexibility of public transport systems.

Discussions turned repeatedly on the expert systems driving environmental concerns. A major theme in this, as in similar research (Eden, 1993; Macnaghten and Jacobs, 1997) concerns the efficacy of changing everyday practices for environmental goals. Efficacy was addressed in the context of three institutional regimes - economic, political and scientific. The first was economic: how, in current systems of production and consumption, could businesses make money from more sustainable consumption practices? Was there a market for recycled waste products? Was the extra cost for organic foods actually justified or were supermarkets simply increasing their profit margins? Why did companies not develop, promote and implement greener technologies? These questions were both substantive - individuals genuinely wanted more information on such issues; and rhetorical, in the sense that the groups already had answers based on their understanding of political processes. There were notable differences between the UK and Dutch groups in this regard. The UK groups were deeply cynical about government-sponsored messages appealing for changes in behaviour. These were dismissed as meaningless because government itself was making no commitment to changing its own practices.[1] The Dutch groups expressed scepticism about the scale of changes apparently needed to save the environment. Of the government's climate change campaign which depicted an image of a burning candle/globe, with a message exhorting people to act locally, think globally, one of the Dutch men observed 'one person cannot blow out the candle to save the world - it's much more complex than that'. But a much stronger social contract in local and national government institutions meant there was more trust in government's assertions about the need for change (see Burgess et al., 1998).

Efficacy was judged on the basis of people's encounters with the institutions of science and technology, especially in relation to questions of expertise. How much reliance could be placed on scientific explanations of the rate and scale of environmental degradation? How would changes in everyday behaviour actually contribute to easing the environmental crisis? Were not environmental problems actually the result of scientific and technological innovations and so, why could science not resolve them? How much uncertainty was there about different strategies? The men's groups were more suspicious of scientific expertise than the women, and also more frustrated at not being able to engage effectively in debate because they lacked sufficient knowledge and information. The contingent nature of environmental 'truths' was a powerful theme in all the groups and the workshops where one UK local authority officer posed an unanswerable question: 'how can you tell people the truth when you don't know how long the truth is to be for?'. Questions of public understanding of, and relations to the institutions of science have come to dominate academic discussion in the last few years and need no further comment here (see Irwin and Wynne, 1996).

ENGAGING WITH A BEHAVIOUR CHANGE PROGRAMME

Research by Hobson (2000) has focused more closely on how participants in a sustainable consumption behaviour change programme go about reconsidering their everyday behaviours and routines. The work was carried out in collaboration with the environmental charity Global Action Plan (UK), on their programme *Action at Home* (AaH). *Action at Home* is a six month voluntary scheme which aims to encourage individuals to make small changes to their domestic consumption practices though the provision of monthly information packs (see also Georg, 1999).[2]

Using in-depth interviews (one-to-one and focus groups), Hobson examined what happened to participants living in different parts of England as they worked through the programme either in their homes or in the workplace. Although just under half the participants made changes to one or more no-cost or low-cost behaviours, most practices remained unchanged. The information in the AaH packs was subject to intense debate and questioning by the participants. As with the Anglo-Dutch study, questions were raised about whose information, science and authority was represented by the information; who was responsible for making the consumption changes needed; how, and why, society is not geared towards sustainable living; vested interests; and issues of trust and responsibility. The contingent and contested nature of environmental information *per se* meant that taking part in AaH was primarily a discursive process.

To expand on this point, the AaH volunteers were not being driven by a desire to shift to 'green' lifestyle practices. Participants were not filling a personal 'information deficit' which was then rationalized into behaviour changes. Instead, it was the process of taking AaH that motivated and/or engaged those taking part. Its purpose was to allow a form of self-evaluation, enabling individuals to better understand their own lifestyles, as part of a larger project of reflexive awareness. Many interviewees said they had become aware that environmental issues were being discussed more widely. They volunteered for AaH out of curiosity and a desire to view their own lifestyles from a perspective of the 'other' – which AaH comes to represent. Thus, there is no coherent 'value' starting point for interviewees and also no clear intention, for most participants, to alter their practices (compare Karp, 1996).

This process of self-evaluation is also part of a broader moral project. As well as permitting individuals to take a closer look at themselves, the AaH process addresses concerns about institutional issues of equity, justice and power. In asking questions about themselves and their ways of living, the participants were actively moving into social debates about rights and responsibilities in modern society. They were not just concerned with their own lifestyles, but also how these lifestyles are part of and contribute to issues of 'quality of life', encapsulated in debates about lack of community, interaction and mutual respect. With this in mind, it is clearer why so much behaviour does not change when exposed to new environmental information. Individuals get involved in AaH because they want to be made to think. They become involved in inter- and intra-personal debates about why they can and cannot change their practices. Knowledges are mobilized and in the process there is an active construction of the meanings and boundaries of each individual's lifestyle.

The research suggests that taking part in AaH creates a newly-focused narrative of individual and social identity, enabling individuals to position themselves in relation to environmental discourse, in this case represented in the information packs. Starting with no clear expectations appears to be part of this process. Interviewees had to bring their routinized behaviours from practical into discursive consciousness. This is caught in comments such as: 'ah, this is why I do this and why I should not do that!". But gaining this clearer perspective of the self, behaviours and their impacts does not necessarily entail making changes to practices. In fact, a retrenchment of lifestyle practices in the face of these discursive processes is partially necessary. As they work through *Action at Home* participants become more aware of the wider social implications of their practices. They find themselves positioned within spaces of 'joint action' and it becomes apparent that the debates surrounding AaH are not just about practices per se, but are also about the nature of the rules and distribution of resources that exist within modern western society. The research calls into question the epistemological foundation of environmental communications that seek to bring about lifestyle changes to the public at large, for they have cast the human subject as one learning and then acting, rather than curious and then debating, as this case study suggests.

ETHICAL CONSUMERS AND THE CHALLENGE OF DOING DIFFERENTLY

Finally, we turn to a qualitative study of the most actively committed, ethical consumers (Bedford, 1999). Studies of ethical consumers complicate the ideal of 'ascetic' consumption often demanded by environmentalists (Irvine, 1989), and challenge an over-reliance on fiscal measures for changing behaviour by positioning consumption as a vital component of identity formation and social bonds. The circulation of contemporary consumerism does entail rapidly changing demands for different products, services and places. It builds in redundancy which has detrimental consequences for the environment. However, it is also the development of forms of reflexive consumption of places, environments, goods and services which has generated the environmental critique (see, for example, Urry, 1995). Trends in 'ethical' consumption reveal these tensions in the shift from minimizing consumption to asserting consumer autonomy and power through seeking ethical products, supporting consumer boycotts and demanding the right of the citizen as a consumer – for example the right to a non-polluted environment (Lowe et al., 1997). The broadening of consumption also recognizes that all consumption is 'ethical', whilst exploring different ethical systems of care for self, family and environment. One often cited example is the work by the anthropologist, Danny Miller, who argues that rather than being self-indulgent, consumption comes to be seen as an act of selflessness, where the consumer's primary concern is their relationship to significant others: 'what the shopper desires above all is for others to want and appreciate what she brings' (Miller, 1998, p. 149).

Bedford's (1999) research with 15 women who purchased fair trade and animal welfare products as well as environmentally friendly goods, reveals the importance of ethical and environmental products having meaning for the self. Previous research has suggested that reducing consumption for the sake of environment left consumers unable to participate within the social and cultural realm of conspicuous consumption (Sadalla and Krull, 1995). If the dominant philosophy of contemporary consumer society is hedonistic pleasure, environmentally conscious consumption connotes self-denial and appears as a new moral discourse of renunciation (Schulze, 1997, p. 39). Indeed, Bedford's informants commented that friends and family saw them as denying themselves pleasure and sitting outside of 'normal' society which judges people on their purchasing patterns. Moreover, choosing to adopt a more environmentally conscious lifestyle had left the ethical consumers with some uncomfortable social images of their character: gullible, weird, idealistic and embarrassing were among the negative connotations mentioned during the interviews. Whilst the consumers themselves may simply have been choosing more environmentally friendly products, the signal this gives to other people is more than just one of ethical concern. Any consumption choice is mediated through a variety of factors such as the efficacy of the product, price and aesthetics. But it is also a conveyor of information for social use (see Warde, 1994, p. 881).

The outcome of these negative identity connotations is to prevent the consumer from acting in accordance with their environmental concerns, unless there is a deeper meaning for the action. The ethical consumers interviewed tended to have friends or family who were ethical consumers, or jobs which were environmentally related: thus lessening the impact of social barriers to green consumption. When the specifically environmental ethics and actions undertaken by the interviewees were compared to their animal welfare and fair trade ethics and actions, it became clear that the environment was consistently the most difficult area to negotiate. It requires a greater level of information to allow action, is subject to considerable uncertainty, and action is rarely deemed as efficacious unless collectively undertaken. Even the most positive of the ethical consumers found environmentally related consumption challenging. As one said: 'sometimes I think anything we do won't make any difference and I start getting really depressed. And then I phone someone and say, you know "I can't make any difference"'. It is not surprising that the campaigning issues cited by retailers as those most likely to stimulate a consumer response are associated with health and animal welfare – issues where there is a more knowable outcome from changing consumption practices.

Equally significant, the research shows that even where the consumer has overcome social stigma and knowledge deficiencies, it is still remarkably difficult to be a green consumer with any consistency. Whilst some forms of environmentally friendly practices are now fairly well-established and workable – recycling, greener transport options, buying organic – to attempt to live a green lifestyle across different spaces and social contexts is almost an impossibility. In effect, green consumerism is something that people do at home. Outside the home, the world is a 'captured market' (Wrigley and Lowe, 1996, p. 26) for the green consumer, that is, one where there is no real choice. The vegetarians in the study, for example, would never eat meat. But the same pattern of consistent behaviour was not demonstrated for environmental products. None of the interviewees would ever ask a hostess to cook them an organic meal, or refuse to eat in a restaurant where the napkins were not made from recycled material. This limits environmentally sensitive consumption dramatically, as people have to negotiate different values and social identities in different spaces. The majority of participants in the study were surprised, when they came to analyse their consumption habits, at just how little they did, despite the enormous effort that sustaining their lifestyles involved. What is clear from the research is that an individual cannot be expected to take responsibility for uncertain environmental risks in a captured market. It is asking too much of the consumer to adopt a green lifestyle unless there is a social context which gives green consumption greater meaning, or better processes to allow the green consumer freedom of choice wherever they are.

CONCLUSIONS

The theory of Ecological Modernisation (Spaargaren and Mol, 1992) is playing an important role in explaining the growing salience of the environment in decision-making at local, national and international scales. The claim is being made that ecological considerations now operate as independent criteria, alongside traditional economic, social and political concerns. Spaargaren and van Vleit (2000) are hopeful that individual 'citizen-consumers' will search for better information about the environmental impacts of their bundles of lifestyle choices and, through a budgeting process, will choose to reduce or change aspects of their everyday behaviours accordingly. In 2001, Global Action Plan (UK) launched a carbon calculator on the internet which allows households to compute the amount of CO_2 they produce through their different activities (www.carboncalculator.org), it offers suggestions for reducing the amount of emissions, and proposes a trade-off (planting trees with the Woodland Trust) for the irreducible amount. It all helps but, as the evidence in the paper suggests, human actors are not often or exclusively rational in deciding what kind of lifestyle they will lead. The cultural and social dimensions of consumption practices, including important values such as comfort, care and cleanliness (Shove and Southerton, 2000) conflict strongly with the sustainability mantra to reduce, re-use and recycle. More research is needed to find answers to the question posed by Crocker and Linden (1998, p. 15): 'How to understand and weigh the sometimes competing claims/duties to ourselves, our institutions, others and the environment?'

Capitalism and industrialization lie at the heart of increasing consumption although, as the evidence has shown, consumption meanings and practices are both context-specific and dynamic. There are also geographical differences in terms of the cultural and political interpretations of these practices. What may be defined as acceptable in one place and time may not be so in another. As

Crocker and Linden (1998) ask: who is to define what is 'appropriate' or 'inappropriate' consumption? What should be done about inappropriate consumption and who should do it? What institutions, if any, have obligations to reinforce or alter consumption practices, or promote better practices? Although there is as yet very little empirical work to demonstrate the ways in which different countries and cultures approach questions of consumer responsibilities, there do appear to be interesting differences between, for example, the consumer culture of the USA and those of the social democratic countries of northern Europe.

Finally, as the chapter has emphasized, identity and lifestyles are constructed through consumption practices structured by systems of provision, but it is important to distinguish between different kinds of practices. 'Conspicuous consumption' describes lifestyle and identity choices between largely tradable goods and services – a fur coat rather than a duffle coat; an Audi Quattro rather than a bicycle; a holiday in the Seychelles rather than Skegness. Expenditure on conspicuous consumption accounts is discretionary income and may or may not have detrimental effects on natural systems. Choices are possible, even allowing for the difficulties environmental scientists face in demonstrating that specific consumption practices cause significant environmental degradation at different spatial and temporal scales. Then there is the 'inconspicuous consumption' which arises from the technological and economic infrastructures that support modern lifestyles: the energy used by fridge and freezer, the air conditioning plant, the central heating, the water required to flush the toilet and run the washing machine. In the way that the world of commodities is a captured market, so are citizens captured by the collective socio-material systems that bind social life into the physical and built environment. The research challenge is to develop theoretical understanding, supported by detailed empirical research, of how human and non-human actors are enrolled in the systems of provision which support contemporary consumer lifestyles. From such insights, it might then be possible to develop a convincing suite of new, evidence-based policies for managing the impacts of inappropriate consumption practices on people and nature.

NOTES

1. The local context was significant here, too. Government imposition of VAT on domestic fuel had raised the costs of domestic heating and the Nottinghamshire coal mines were being closed at this time.
2. To date, AaH has had over 25,000 participants across the UK. It provides participants with one information pack per month on the topics of waste, water, energy, transport, shopping and the 'next steps'. These packs contain tips of small changes that can be made and step-by-step actions to take.

REFERENCES

Agnew, C. and A. Warren (1996), 'A framework for tackling drought and land degradation', *Journal of Arid Environments*, 33, 309-20.

Baumann, Z. (1992), *Intimations of Post Modernity*, London: Routledge.

Beck, U. (1992), *Risk Society: Towards a New Modernity*, London: Sage.

Bedford, T. (1999), 'Ethical consumerism: everyday negotiations in the construction of an ethical self', unpublished PhD thesis, University of London: University College London.

Benton, T. and M. Redclift (eds) (1995), *Social Theory and the Global Environment*, London: Routledge.

Billig, M. (1996), *Arguing and Thinking: A Rhetorical Approach to Social Psychology*, Cambridge: Cambridge University Press.

Blake, J. (1999), 'Overcoming the "value-action" gap in environmental policy: tensions between national policy and local experience', *Local Environment*, 4, 257-78.

Brandon, G. and A. Lewis (1999), 'Reducing household energy consumption: a qualitative and quantitative field study', *Journal of Environmental Psychology*, 19, 75-85.

Burgess, J., C. Harrison and P. Filius (1998), 'Environmental communication and the cultural politics of environmental citizenship', *Environment and Planning A*, 30, 1445-60.

Burgess, J., K. Collins, C.M. Harrison, R. Munton and J. Murlis (1999), 'An analytical and descriptive model of sustainable development for the Environment Agency', *R&D Paper* No. 32, The Environment Agency, Rio House, Bristol, UK.

Castells, M. (1997), *The Information Age: Economy, Society and Culture*, Oxford: Blackwell.

Chaney, D. (1996), *Lifestyles*, London: Routledge.

Corrigan, P. (1997), *The Sociology of Consumption: An Introduction*, London: Sage.

Corson, W.H. (1994), 'Changing course: an outline of strategies for a sustainable future', *Futures: The Journal of Forecasting and Planning*, 26 (2), 206-23.

Crocker, D.A. and T. Linden (eds) (1998), *Ethics of Consumption: the Good Life, Justice and Global Stewardship*, New York: Rowman and Littlefield.

de Young, R. (1993), 'Changing behavior and making it stick: the conceptualisation and management of conservation behaviour', *Environment and Behavior*, 25, 485-505.

Department of the Environment (DOE) (1996), *Indicators of Sustainable Development for the United Kingdom*, London: HMSO.

Douglas, M. and B. Isherwood (1978), *The World of Goods: Towards an Anthropology of Consumption*, London: Allen Lane.

Dunlap, R.E. (1998), 'Lay perceptions of global risk – public views of global warming in cross national context', *International Sociology*, 13, 473-98.

Dunlap, R. and R. Scarce (1991), 'The polls–poll trends: environmental problems and protection', *Public Opinion Quarterly*, 55, 651-72.

Durning, A. (1992), *How Much is Enough? The Consumer Society and the Future of the Earth*, London: Earthscan.

Eden, S. (1993), 'Individual environmental responsibility and its role in public environmentalism', *Environment and Planning A*, 25, 1743-58.

Fine, B. and E. Leopold (1993), *The World of Consumption*, London: Routledge.

Finger, M. (1994), 'From knowledge to action? Exploring the relationships between environmental experiences, learning and behavior', *Journal of Social Issues*, 50, 141-60.

Fishbein, M. and I. Ajzen (1975), *Belief, Attitude, Intention and Behavior: An Introduction to Theory and Research*, Reading, MA: Addison-Wesley.

Gatersleben, B. and C. Vlek (1998), 'Household consumption, quality of life and environmental impacts: a psychological perspective and empirical study', in K.J. Noorman and T.S. Uiterkamp (eds) (1998), *Green Households? Domestic Consumers, Environment and Sustainability*, London: Earthscan, pp. 143-83.

Georg, S. (1999), 'The social shaping of consumption'. *Ecological Economics*, 28, 455-66.

Giddens, A. (1984), *The Constitution of Society: An Outline of the Theory of Structuration*, Cambridge: Polity Press.

Giddens, A. (1991), *Modernity and Self Identity: Self and Society in the Late Modern Age*, Cambridge: Polity Press.

Glacken, C. (1967), *Traces on the Rhodian Shore*, Berkeley, CA: University of California Press.

Glennie, P. and N. Thrift (1996), 'Reworking E.P. Thompson's "Time, Work-discipline and industrial capitalism"', *Time and Society*, 5, 275-99.

Goldblatt, D. (1996), *Social Theory and the Environment*, Cambridge: Polity Press

Goodman, D. (1999), 'Agro-food studies in the "Age of Ecology": nature, corporeality, bio-politics', *Sociologia Ruralis*, 39, 17-38.

Greenberg, D.W. (1985), 'Staging media events to achieve legitimacy: a case study of Britain's Friends of the Earth', *Political Communication and Persuasion*, 2, 347-62.

Guy, S. and E. Shove (2000), *A Sociology of Energy, Buildings and the Environment: Constructing Knowledge, Designing Practice*, London: Routledge, Global Environmental Change research series.

Harrison, C.M. and D. Davies (1998), 'Lifestyles and the environment', A desk study for the ESRC's Environment and Sustainability Programme.

Harrison, C.M., J. Burgess and P. Filius (1996), 'Rationalising environmental responsibilities: a comparison of lay publics in the UK and the Netherlands', *Global Environmental Change*, 6 (3), 215-34.

Harvey, D. (1996), *Justice, Nature and the Geography of Difference*, Oxford: Blackwell.

Hinchliffe, S. (1996a), 'Technology, power and space – the means and ends of geographies of technology', *Environment and Planning D: Society and Space*, 14, 659-82.

Hinchliffe, S. (1996b), 'Helping the earth begins at home: the social construction of socio-environmental responsibilities', *Global Environmental Change*, 6, 53-62.

Hinchliffe, S. (1997), 'Locating risk: the "ideal" home and the non-ideal world', *Transactions*, Institute of British Geographers, 22, 197-209.

Hobson, K. (2000), 'Talking habits into action: an investigation into Global Action Plan's "Action at Home" Programme', unpublished PhD thesis, University of London: University College London.

Inglehart, R. (1990), *Culture Shift in Advanced Industrial Society*, Princeton, NJ: Princeton University Press.

Irvine, S. (1989), 'Consuming fashions? The limits of green consumerism', *The Ecologist*, 19 (3), 88-93.

Irwin, A. and B. Wynne (eds) (1996), *Misunderstanding Science? The Public Reconstruction of Science and Technology*, Cambridge: Cambridge University Press.

Jackson, T. and N. Marks (1999), 'Consumption, sustainable welfare and human needs – with reference to UK expenditure patterns between 1954 and 1994', *Ecological Economics*, 28, 421–41.

Jacobs, M. (1994), 'The limits to neoclassicism: towards an institutional environmental economics', in M. Redclift and T. Benton (eds), *Social Theory and the Global Environment*, London: Routledge, pp. 67–91.

Jardine, L. and J. Brotton (2000), *Global Interest: The Material Culture of Early Modern Europe*, Ithaca, NY: Cornell University Press.

Johnson, C.A. (1997), 'Rules, norms and the pursuit of sustainable livelihoods', *IDS Working Paper* 52, Sussex: University of Sussex.

Karp, D. (1996), 'Values and their effect on pro-environmental behaviour', *Environment and Behaviour*, 28 (1), 111–33.

Lash, S.B., B. Szerszynski and B. Wynne (eds) (1996), *Risk, Environment and Modernity: Towards a New Ecology*, London: Sage.

Lowe, P., J. Clark, S. Seymour and N. Ward (1997), *Moralising the Environment: Countryside Change, Farming and Pollution*, London: UCL Press.

Lutzenhiser, L. (1994), 'Sociology, energy and interdisciplinary environmental science', *The American Sociologist*, 25, 57–78.

Lutzenhiser, L. (1997), 'Social structure, culture and technology: modelling the driving forces of household energy consumption', in P.C. Stern, T. Dietz, V.W. Ruttan, R.H. Socolow and J.L. Sweeney (eds), *Environmentally Significant Consumption: Research Directions*, Washington, DC: National Academy Press, pp. 77–91.

Macnaghten, P. and M. Jacobs (1997), 'Public identification with sustainable development: investigating cultural barriers to participation', *Global Environmental Change*, 7, 5–24.

Macnaghten, P. and G. Myers (1998), 'Rhetorics of environmental sustainability: commonplaces and places', *Environment and Planning A*, 30, 333–53.

Macnaghten, P. and J. Urry (1998), *Contested Natures*, London: Routledge.

Maslow, A. (1968), *Towards a Psychology of Being*, New York: van Nostrand Reinhold.

Massey, D. (1994), *Space, Place and Gender*, Cambridge: Polity.

Max-Neef, M. (1992), *Human Scale Development: Conceptions, Applications and Further Reflections*, London: Zed Books.

McCormick, J. (1995), *The Global Environmental Movement*, Chichester: Wiley (2nd edn).

Meadows, D.H., D.L. Meadows, J. Randers and W. Behrens (1972), *Limits to Growth*, London: Earth Island Press.

Miller, D. (1998), *A Theory of Shopping*, Cambridge: Polity Press.

Myers, G. and P. Macnaghten (1998), 'Rhetorics of environmental sustainability: commonplaces and places', *Environment and Planning A*, 30, 333–53.

Neuman, K. (1986), 'Personal values and commitment to energy conservation', *Environment and Behavior*, 18, 53–74.

Noorman, K.J. and T.S. Uiterkamp (eds) (1998), *Green Households? Domestic Consumers, Environment and Sustainability*, London: Earthscan.

Nye, D.E. (1992), *Electrifying America: Social Meanings of a New Technology, 1880–1940*, Cambridge, MA: MIT Press.

Oskamp, S., M. Harrington, T.C. Edwards, D.L. Sherwood, S.M. Okuda and D.C. Swanson (1991), 'Factors influencing household recycling behaviour', *Environment and Behavior*, 23, 494–519.

Otnes, P. (ed.) (1988), *The Sociology of Consumption: An Anthology*, Oslo: Solum Forlag and Humanities Press International.

Peet, R. and M. Watts (eds) (1996), *Liberation Ecologies: Environment, Development, Social Movements*, London: Routledge.

Porter, R. (2000), *Enlightenment: Britain and the Creation of the Modern World*, Harmondsworth: Penguin Books.

Princen, T. (1999), 'Consumption and environment: some conceptual issues', *Ecological Economics*, 31, 347–63.

Ropke, I. (1999), 'The dynamics of willingness to consume', *Ecological Economics*, 28, 399–420.

Rutherford, C. (1998), 'Individual participation in environmental actions and schemes', Research Report for Centre for Interdisciplinary Environmental Studies, University of Cambridge.

Sadalla, E. and J. Krull (1995), 'Self-presentational barriers to resource conservation', *Environment and Behaviour*, 27 (3), 328–53.

Schulze, G. (1997), 'From situations to subjects: moral discourse in transition', in P. Sulkumen, J. Holmwood, H. Radner and G. Schulze, *Constructing the New Consumer Society*, Basingstoke: Macmillan Press.

Schwartz Cowan, R. (1983), *More Work for Mother: the Ironies of Household Technology from the Open Hearth to the Microwave*, New York: Basic Books.

Scoones, I. (1998), 'Sustainable rural livelihoods: a framework for analysis', *IDS Working Paper 72*, University of Sussex.

Shove, E. and D. Southerton (2000), 'Defrosting the freezer: from novelty to convenience – a narrative of normalization', *Journal of Material Culture*, 5, 301–19.

Spaargaren, G. and A.P.J. Mol (1992), 'Sociology, environment and modernity: ecological modernisation as a theory of social change', *Society and Natural Resources*, 8, 578–81.

Spaargaren, G. and B. van Vliet (2000), 'Lifestyles, consumption and the environment: the ecological modernisation of domestic consumption', *Environmental Politics*, 9, 50–76.

Stern, P.C. (1997), 'Towards a working definition of consumption for environmental research and policy', in P.C. Stern, T. Dietz, V.W. Ruttan, R.H. Socolow and J.L. Sweeney (eds) (1997), *Environmentally Significant Consumption: Research Directions*, Washington, DC: National Academy Press, pp. 12–15.

Stern, P.C., T. Dietz, V.W. Ruttan, R.H. Socolow and J.L. Sweeney (eds) (1997), *Environmentally Significant Consumption: Research Directions*, Washington, DC: National Academy Press.

Thomas, Balogh (1955), *The Economics of Poverty*, London: Weidenfeld and Nicolson.

Ungar, S. (1994), 'Apples and oranges: probing the attitude–behaviour relationship for the environment', *Canadian Review of Sociology and Anthropology*, 31, 288–304.

United Nations (1987), *Our Common Future: The Brundtland Report*, Oxford: Oxford University Press.

United Nations Conference on Environment and Development (UNCED) (1993), *Agenda 21: Programme of Action for Sustainable Development*, New York, NY: UN Department of Public Information.

Urry, J. (1995), *Consuming Places*, London: Routledge.

Warde, A. (1994), 'Consumption, identity-formation and uncertainty', *Sociology*, 28 (4), 877–98.

Wiegman, O. and J.M. Gutteling (1995), 'Risk appraisal and risk communication: some empirical data from the Netherlands', *Basic and Applied Psychology*, 16, 227–49.

Whatmore, S. (2001), *Hybris Geographies*, London: Sage.

Worcester, R.M. (1993), 'Public and elite attitudes to environmental issues', *International Journal of Public Opinion Research*, 5, 315–34.

Worster, D. (1994), *Nature's Economy: A History of Ecological Ideas*, Cambridge: Cambridge University Press (2nd edn).

Wrigley, N. and M. Lowe (1996), *Retailing, Consumption and Capital: Towards the New Retail Geography*, Harlow: Longman.

Index